D1255914

SPECTACLES & PREDICAMENTS

ERNEST GELLNER

Spectacles & Predicaments

ESSAYS IN SOCIAL THEORY

CAMBRIDGE UNIVERSITY PRESS

CAMBRIDGE

LONDON   NEW YORK   NEW ROCHELLE

MELBOURNE   SYDNEY

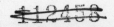

Published by the Press Syndicate of the University of Cambridge
The Pitt Building, Trumpington Street, Cambridge CB2 1RP
32 East 57th Street, New York, NY 10022, USA
296 Beaconsfield Parade, Middle Park, Melbourne 3206, Australia

First published 1979

Printed in Great Britain by
Western Printing Services Ltd, Bristol

Library of Congress Cataloguing in Publication Data

Gellner, Ernest.
Spectacles and predicaments.

Bibliography: p.
Includes indexes.
1. Philosophy – Addresses, essays, lectures. 2. Social sciences – Addresses,
essays, lectures. 3. Political science – Addresses, essays, lectures.
I. Title.
B63.G44   120   78–67304

ISBN 0 521 22486 1

Editorial Preface

In the five years that have elapsed since we sent to press the third volume of Gellner's selected papers – *The Devil in Modern Philosophy* – his rate of scholarly output has, if anything, increased. Most notable is the rate at which he has produced long and substantial papers. In editing Gellner's work our original aim was to bring it to greater public attention. Our effort has been fortunate in achieving this goal. If, in addition, we have in any way encouraged the author and helped raise his output, then we are highly gratified.

The papers to be found in the present collection have been selected and edited with an eye to their coherence and unity. The three parts of this collection contain papers all of which show the same concerns, approached only under different headings. Part I is primarily, but only primarily, about philosophers and their philosophy, Part II is more about the cognitive implications of philosophy and Part III more about the political applications of philosophy. As ever, Gellner begins as a critic, expounds alternative views of his own, and applies them to current concerns.

The most characteristic quality of Gellner's output in general, and in this volume in particular, is the fusion of philosophy and the social sciences. There are philosophers who frown at such fusions – at any fusion – and there are those who tolerate them for pedagogical purposes. In Gellner's work the fusion persists because the problems on which he reflects lead over old boundaries, the problems lead us to consider whether there is here a fusion at all, or rather an approach that starts from a very different kind of separation. The test of this should be, of course, how does his philosophy treat the old borders. This leads to a simple problem, from Gellner's vantage point, and, indeed, he meets the problem repeatedly and with an infectious and unfailing fascination: what do professional philosophers have to say about everyday life, about society? He animadverts on this, and he offers his own views, both about philosophers' views of society, and about society as he sees and examines it in detail, studying its diverse forms, i.e. the industrialised world, capitalist and socialist. He develops a political and social philosophy meant to be suitable for our time, to answer the theoretical and practical problems it poses to us all, philosophers as well as common men who feel responsible enough to want to think them out. Or, perhaps we should say he does only some of the preliminary work in that direction; perhaps one can only credit him with an attempt to discuss what is on the agenda, what are the more significant and urgent questions at issue. For example, he has long poured scorn on academic philosophers who advocated moral or cognitive relativism. In this volume he makes quite explicit his view that not only is relativism a recipe for disaster, but that the endorsement of and the preoccupation with modern empirical science is itself based on a moral imperative. Discussing the problems of Britain or of Czechoslovakia he continues to be exploratory and tentative. Czechoslovakia does not show that liberalisation is impossible, Britain does not show that liberal societies can never harm themselves. As ever, Gellner is concerned with major decisions regarding social science and social policy. Most political thinkers are, he claims, trying to decide what will happen and arguing about what should happen. This is, he remarks, mostly like reading the entrails. Rather, he urges, the question is whether proceduralism or substantivism will prevail; his guess is that both will co-exist for some time.

None of this should suggest that we endorse Gellner's political views, or even that we share his outlook in detail. It is simply that we find his work valuable enough, thought-provoking enough, to deserve greater accessibility than it has scattered through the back runs of diverse serials. Collection highlights its unity and coherence, and hence is a treat for the public.

Toronto I. C. Jarvie
Boston and Tel Aviv J. Agassi

Contents

Contents

Contents

Introduction

The present collection of essays falls into three parts. There are those which deal with the basic images in terms of which we see humanity, those which deal with knowledge, and those concerned with socio-political questions. The underlying themes are however the same. These fields have intimate and inescapable connections.

Modern thought faces two problems above all (though they are not always recognised under these names): the issue of Validation, and that of Enchantment. We want an entry permit to our world; and we also want it to be in a good state of decorative repair. This is all the more essential nowadays, since we can no longer trust a top management to keep an eye on it. The problem of right of entry to a world or its validation arises in many diverse fields – the various branches of science, politics, personal morality, aesthetics – and has a very simple basic form: why or on what grounds do we do things *this* way rather than *that*? For instance: with what justi-fication does science favour causal rather than purpose-stressing explanations, or open generalisations rather than idiosyncrasy-stressing accounts? Why do we, or should we, favour pluralistic polities, or permissive morals? These questions could only be pseudo-questions if we had no options, or if the choices amongst them were obvious, if we were already inside one unique world, rather than facing the possibility or threat of migration. In fact we do have options. The choices are seldom obvious, and they are sometimes acutely painful.

Men meet the problem of validation (which has many other names as well) under terms of reference which make it extremely difficult to handle – some might say, impossible. (The view that philosophical questions are not quite genuine is actually encouraged by this, by means of two *highly* questionable arguments. One consists of assuming that nature, or whatever or whoever is responsible for our predicament, does not set us problems which are too hard for us – so this cannot be *our* problem; and the second one suggests that if we cannot find good reasons for an answer, why then *any* answer will do.) The terms of reference are these: a conclusive, so to speak *terminal* validation is required. This may be supported by reasons: but then of course it is no longer terminal. Then it is those reasons which are then really terminal. Or it is not supported by reasons. In that case it is arbitrary. Either way, the enterprise fails.

This problem can be called the problem of the Regress (of reasons). Of late, certain to my mind facile and inadequate solutions have been proposed. One consists of the contention that the problem only arises because we mistakenly seek too general a base for our activities, whether cognitive or other. No such bases exist, on this view. We must be content with more specific justifications, which are part and parcel of the activity in question. Nothing more general is either possible or necessary, on this view. Another solution consists of attempting to replace the pursuit of justifications by the more modest activity of eliminating erroneous views, without for all that definitively justifying any residual truth – and declaring such justification to be unnecessary. Each of these strategies would only work *if* we had no options in the choice of the general, over-all world which we choose to inhabit; and such alternative worlds also include the criteria we employ in various spheres of life. In fact, we are not option-less in that way.

The problem of the regress is not the only factor contributing to the acuteness of the validation issue. A part of our background is an earlier social order, within which the official and enforced doctrine proclaimed that the problem of validation was already solved, finally and conclusively. This heritage has left behind a certain after-taste and a certain expectation, whilst at the same time the conditions for satisfying this expectation have been withdrawn. At the very moment when the rug is being pulled away from under his feet, the thinker is expected to carry an even bigger load than he had done before. The raised expectation has a double source: past dogmatism is one of them, and the phenomenal success of the cognitive enterprise in some limited spheres – notably natural science – is another. Technology has justified that particular faith by works. Both the confidence lost, and the demonstration effect in successful adjoining areas, act as spurs to endeavour.

One response was to attempt to read Nature or History, in the hope of eliciting from them pronouncements as clear and firm as those which the deity was previously said to provide. An alternative and sophisticated answer consists of trying to turn the tables, and finding a solution not in firm knowledge, but in doubt or ignorance. Instead of saying – things are such and such, and therefore our life should follow a certain mould – one can say – we do *not* know how things stand, and *therefore* a certain style of life would appear to commend itself. *This* set of institutions is the best bet in conditions of certainty-deprivation. Thus the cognitively liberal *Weltanschauung* endeavours to use a vacuum rather than a plenum for its foundation. Its critics on the left tend to suspect that the supposedly neutral and impartial void is surreptitiously loaded against them, and that it is not nearly as empty and agnostic as it is painted.

The importance and pervasiveness of the problem of validation has led to the centrality of the theory of knowledge in modern thought. The theory of knowledge however has not as yet attained a full awareness of its own proper role and status. Often, it appears to itself as a positive, descriptive or explanatory account of the actual processes of cognition. As such, its merits are limited. Its real significance lies in its normative function of codifying, and in some measure justifying, *a* style of cognition amongst others – in being an *ethic of cognition*. Its founder/hero is Descartes/Crusoe, the cognitive self-made-man, who builds up his own wealth with his own self-made tools. As ownership was validated by mixing one's labour with things, so was belief. Being thus beholden to no-one, Robinson need not fear that some cognitive creditor will one day turn up and deprive him of what he has built up.

The Crusoe tradition in the theory of knowledge is a myth which, like others, highlights some aspects of the situation and obscures others. Crusoe's most obvious feature is his solitude, and it is easy to say that he symbolises the solitary intellectual entrepreneur, and speaks for a kind of cognitive possessive individualism. But the solitude has another aspect which is more important. Being alone and shipwrecked, he had to start *anew*. This is hard: as Spinoza observes in his discussion of the problem of validation and truth, it takes hammers to make hammers, so how can you ever make the first one? Crusoe starts with nothing but *himself* as his first tool. This means he has to start afresh without taking over a cultural stock of tools, and with it, whatever bias may be built into them.

Thus, under the individualism, there is also a recognition of radical discontinuity, a break, a *coupure*, between the new style of thought which we are trying to codify and establish, and the one which preceded it. There is a major dividing line in the theory of knowledge between those who believe this chasm to be real and those who do not. Those who (to my mind mistakenly) hold the *coupure* to be illusory and who believe continuity to be the rule, do not necessarily also oppose the 'modern', secular, experimental, sceptical vision. On the contrary, they are as often men who take that vision for granted, all too much so, and have no sharp sense of how very unique and eccentric it is in human history, and who also believe it to have been ever-present, ever since the stone age or since the amoeba. (For some reason, this modern and cognitively effective vision just wasn't fully effective, operational and manifest during various Dark Ages, which were just regrettable periods of temporary stagnation to which they pay scant attention.) Those born after enlightenment sometimes mistakenly suppose it to be a human birthright, ever with us. This is an error. Were it so, there would indeed be no problem – other than, perhaps, explaining why some have eyes but see not. In fact, far from being a birthright, it is a miraculous and precarious privilege which needs to be understood if it is to be safeguarded.

In as far as the seemingly individualistic Crusoe story conveys the sense of a fresh start and radical discontinuity, it is valid and illuminating. It was quite natural, but mistaken, to deny discontinuity, and to seek instead a new foundation, a new safe basis, in the General (and hence perpetual) Trend of Things, as was done by so many nineteenth-century philosophies, from Hegelians to pragmatists. That was how things looked then. But our time no longer encourages this illusion.

In other words, the story is misleading. The trouble with Robinson Crusoe (or his philosophic parallel René Descartes) is that he is such a solid, sturdy, *balanced* character. Nothing very neurotic about him. Good officer material, you might say, but the epistemological tradition is not only about Crusoe. It is also about Hamlet, Don Quixote, or Dostoevsky of the *Notes from Underground*. It is about the difficulty of living without confidence in the reality of one's perception of one's world, or alternatively, living with a despairing and unjustified conviction, springing from an intolerable divergence between the world as one would like to think it and as it is. One can laugh at Don Quixote because he is seen from the outside, which means that one knows the truth about what reality is really like.

The windmill is but a windmill. But from the inside, the matter is never certain. One may sin on the side of excessive prosaic realism as well as on the side of romantic illusion, and the correct midpoint is never unambiguously and clearly indicated. What is more, most people are bound to have different 'correct' midpoints at different times of the day and in different contexts. Such opportunism is neither comfortable nor honourable.

The point about the break, the re-valuation of ideas, is that it makes a tool and a virtue of *doubt*. Cognitively, so it is. But is it a virtue in conduct? Does it not erode character or will-power? Crusoe only re-created the material culture of his own society by his own scarcely aided efforts, in some small measure – but he did not tinker with his own self. That came with the deal. Descartes saw the danger and coped with it by segregating morals from cognition, proscribing the method of doubt in the sphere of action. But the separation was difficult to sustain, and the hero of *Notes from Underground* was only echoing many other intellectuals when he commiserates with his own inability to rush into action like an enraged bull – such feebleness being the price of sophistication: 'the real moral man. . .is stupid. . .[but] the antithesis of the normal man. . .the man of acute consciousness. . .is sometimes so nonplussed. . .that with all his ex-aggerated consciousness he genuinely thinks of himself as a mouse and not a man'. Admittedly, Aschenbach in *Death in Venice*, 'taught a whole grateful generation that a man can still be capable of moral resolution even after he has plumbed the depths of knowledge'. But then, he did come to a bad end.

So our cognitive predicament is really rather more complex than the Crusoe/Descartes story suggests. There are a number of complications. First of all, ideas, whether clear and distinct or not, come not singly but in large package deals. Important choices are often between such package deals rather than between isolated and insulated alternatives. Don Quixote, who tries to act in terms of one culture, past or fictitious, whilst living in another, is in some ways a far better paradigm of an epistemological problem than Crusoe. How do you know which world is the real one? From the outside, we *know* the answer, in his case. The Age of Chivalry was past or had never existed. But life is lived from the inside, and then the question is open. Frequently, the question – which world am I in? – does *not* have an obvious answer, and the bull-like gentlemen, who have no doubts, normally prevail and impose their worlds.

These large package deals, world-options, as recent thinkers have reminded us, are generally not commensurate with each other, they are not articulated in a shared idiom, and hence it is difficult to judge them 'from the outside'. They not only have their own idioms, but also their own morality which is part and parcel of each of them, and so the Cartesian separation of morals and cognition fails to work. Doubt, which is a virtue of cognition (perhaps the cardinal one), is an impediment in conduct, and this is Hamlet's problem. The virtues of thought and of behaviour are not the same ones. There is one morality for theoretical reason and another for practical reason. Those ideological package deals often demand assent with menaces – those who refuse to accept their morality or code of thought, thereby damn themselves, or so they say. They generally have their allies within the human breast, and find their support and anchorage in one mood or humour or another. How can one mood judge another, or ensure its own stability, or validate itself? One man's inner validation is another man's weakness. There are striking parallels between the logic of inner conflict and of genuine philosophic thought. It can only be resolved by doing violence to itself. A victory is always also a pre-judgement. Self-conquest is betrayal. Moral fibre is intellectual ossification. Begging the question is the only form of answering it. The requirements of life and thought are incompatible.

But there is worse to come. The conceptual package deals do not merely have their own idioms and moralities, they also generally operate what may be called the Pirandello effect. It was Luigi Pirandello who popularised the theatrical device of deliberately and systematically subverting the clear and distinct separation of audience, actors and characters, of subject and object in effect, by making the characters speak to their author, the actors pretend to be part of the audience and interact with it, and so forth. He tried to ensure that the play was not a spectacle but a predicament. The re-tooling of tools by Crusoe, the re-conceptualising of concepts by the Cartesian tradition, had all been done in a highly conventional theatre, where you could be sure that the actors would not invade your privacy, and your identity was not in question. You brought your own identity to the stalls and took it home again at the end.

Once the Pirandello effect is achieved – and in modern thought it invariably *is* achieved – the aseptic separation of observer and drama is ended. We cannot sit back and assess rival worlds and make our choice, because we do not possess any single, independent, pre-existent *we* (or *I*) to do the job. It appears that we chose (or are chosen) jointly with a world, by bulk purchase, and then, inside it, go through the process of ratifying that world. . .a somewhat circular procedure. (One particular world, namely our own, had developed an idiosyncratic tendency to self-doubt. Some of us feel that just this makes it a better one than its rivals. Is this reasonable or is it the ultimate in narcissism?) Some philosophies specialise in camouflaging or justifying the circularity.

I do not believe that all this shows that the evaluative, validation-seeking and doubting activity was pointless. It only shows that it is far more difficult and problematic than may at first appear. There is no diamond-hard cognitive ego, no Pure Visitor to this world, who could submit a definitive and impartial intelligence report on its general condition. Still less can we seek a base-line in an alleged common sense or its linguistic shadow. But though all this may seem to show that the task is impossible, it *must* nevertheless be attempted. Though not feasible, it is mandatory.

This impasse of the cognitive endeavour, however, does relate to the other problem, that of Enchantment. The codification of knowledge and its procedures, when it seemed to be going well, appeared to extract a certain bitter price. The necessity of orderly explanation seemed to subject the world, including humanity itself, to the laws of causation, thus depriving us of freedom and spon-taneity. (The replacement of causal laws by statisical ones, where it occurs, does not humanise the picture much.) The generality and impersonality of explanation seemed to deprive us of our individu-ality and idiosyncrasy. Generally speaking, knowledge consists of showing that the thing known is really something else, where the something else is but a specimen of a substrate which is very general and impersonal. This is known in the trade as the 'covering law' theory of explanation. Also, the account of knowledge as constructed from 'data', which in turn are seen atomistically, leaves us with a highly disenchanted vision of the world. The atoms are cold and inhuman.

This cold vision is not merely the product of philosophies. If it were, it might not matter so much. It is equally or more conspicuous in the *content* of science. Philosophy only adds the insight, which has still escaped the attention of some, that the disenchantment is not a contingent consequence of this or that specific discovery, but inheres in the very method and procedure of rational inquiry, of impartial subsumption under symmetrical generalisations, of treating all data as equal. Reductionism is not an aberration, it is inherent in the very method of science. If we 'scientifically' established the reality of some 'human' and seemingly reduction-resisting element in the world, we would ipso facto thereby also 'reduce' it, in some new way.

The demonstrative vindication of a value is but its demolition by other means. Sociologists rather than philosophers noted the pervasiveness of this phenomenon, and it was Max Weber who christened it 'disenchantment'. The orderliness and symmetry of procedure, corroding identity and idiosyncrasy, operates in social organisation as well as in knowledge, and in a parallel manner, and it then tends to be called 'bureaucratisation' or 'rational production'.

At almost the same time that thought faced the problem of revalidation – or at any rate, not long after – it also faced the problem of Enchantment, the requirement that the world be shown to be not *too* cold and inhuman, too impersonally icy. Ironically, success in handling one problem hampered the solution of the other. Kant was the most heroic of philosophers, trying to do both things at the same time: to establish the regularity of nature and causation in order to validate science, and yet also to exempt us from it, so as to validate morality and (minimally) to re-enchant the world, by allowing us at least freedom, responsibility, and valid thought. Many philosophers have tended to be on one side or the other. Roughly speaking, the romantics specialised in enchantment, the positivists in validation and hence also the exclusion of that which did not meet the criteria of validation. The Enchantment also presented itself as a validation, whereas the positivist validation made out that we did not really need the old enchantment, and that the scientistic vision constituted a purer, better variant, one which we could learn to live with or even love. But in any given concrete philosophy, there tend to be different proportions of each element, presented in diverse ways and with differing measures of consistency.

The political problems of our time are inevitably viewed against the backcloth of these two problems and their putative solutions. It is these formulations or would-be solutions which provide the idiom, and set the limits to the legitimations of social and political systems. Our intellectual and political options emerge from the same background and from the same problem situation; the cognitive and political predicaments are intertwined. The Social Contract theory was of course the political accompaniment of Crusoe epistemology: a social order was to be made anew, or at any rate re-validated, without relying on the old legitimation-equipment which had gone down with the ship. The new contract, unlike the old covenant, had only human signatories. That was a step forward. But in fact, these human signatories are as hard to come by as the divine one. Fully formed people only come into being after the Contract – in a specific culture – and thus cannot easily, without circularity, validate the compact by their endorsement. The lack of a hard, *given* ego is a problem for both epistemology and politics. Since then, liberal legitimations-by-doubt and romantic re-enchantment myths, and many other systems, have competed for our loyalties. These are the underlying links.

Part 1
Understanding humanity

1

The Absolute in braces

There is an old Oxford chestnut about the don who gave a lecture on Hegel, Schlegel, and Begel. At the end of it, he advised the undergraduates to disregard what he had said about Begel, because Begel did not exist. But that was a pedantic point. It makes very little difference whether or not Begel existed: he obviously belonged to a generation which had changed the idiom in which men speak and think about human affairs. As Charles Taylor observes,

> Hegel along with many contemporaries believed that his age was the axial period. 'It is surely not difficult to see that our time is a time of birth and transition to a new period' (Hegel's *Phenomenology of Spirit*). And Hegel goes on to speak in this passage of a 'qualitative leap' [p. 76].

Precisely who belonged to this generation and who said what is less well known; and in so far as what is at issue is a vision and style of thought rather than a set of precise propositions, it does not matter too much. (Just how many Schlegels were there?) The way in which this generation spoke would have been unintelligible some decades earlier. Many would claim that it was just as unintelligible at the time when they did speak, and indeed ever since. But whether or not what they said makes sense, much of what men have *done* since they spoke cannot be understood without referring to what this generation said.

Sir Karl Popper, the most influential modern critic of Hegel, does sometimes give the impression of being spread-eagled between the view that Hegel's doctrines are devoid of meaning, and that they are nevertheless very false and wicked. The critic is in a certain dilemma; he has to interpret men's actions in terms of their beliefs which at the same time he holds beyond the reach of rational interpretation.

When modern man speaks nonsense, the chances are more than even that he borrows his idiom either from Hegel or from Freud. Each had invented a language, a set of concepts which are fairly easy to learn, which sometimes *click*, which seem profound and confer depth and status on the speaker (and make him feel good), which are difficult to falsify or check, and which exercise both fascination and revulsion. In the case of Hegel, this was achieved without Hegel himself becoming a household word: the real diffusion of his notions was done by his followers and successors, and one of them in particular.

There are few philosophers who provoke, as Hegel does, quite such an extreme span of reactions, ranging from the utmost admiration to the most total contempt. The admiration, when it is given, is of a different kind from that which is accorded to most other thinkers. There is often a total and religious quality about it. It is not so much that Hegel is seen as a champion performer in a game at which other people do a bit less well (at thinking up true statements about the universe, for instance); it is rather that he is seen as being in a different league altogether, offering some kind of liberation, revelation, completion – or, in Marx's view, as offering the next best thing to the real fulfilment. He is not an informant about the universe: he is its mouthpiece. Marx's remarks about philosophy and reality are liable to be misunderstood by English-speaking readers as some kind of positivist denigration of philosophy. What Marx really meant was that Hegel went as far as it is possible to go in philosophy, in thought – all that now remained was to do something similar in real life, to complement fulfilment in mere concepts by fulfilment in life itself. Kierkegaard, Hegel's second most important disciple, had a similar reaction, though he envisaged the contrasted reality in a different manner.

The capacity to generate such extremities of reaction seems to be of the very essence of his thought. The Hegelian doctrine about opposites generating or interpenetrating each other, or whatever it is that they do with or to each other, certainly applies in at least one case, namely to his own thought-system. Nothing could be more pointless than some kind of sober, moderate interpretation and assessment of Hegel. Some dullish commentators have indeed attempted it, and come out with a subject-by-subject school-report on Hegel,

G. W. F.: very interesting ideas in history, perceptive on politics, unsound in natural science, will plough in maths, and is promising though cloudy in divinity...This will not do. Not for nothing is his system known as Absolute Idealism. He is everything, or he is nothing, or, as he said, both at once.

Does this mean that Hegel really succeeded, like Pascal's God, in placing each of us before a total wager, with no bet-hedging allowed? Are we compelled to say Yea or Nay to this conceptual bulk-purchase, and either join the Hegel-spurners like Schopenhauer, Hobhouse, or Popper, or those who see Hegel like Marx, Kierkegaard, or Bradley? Dr J. O. Wisdom (of York University, Toronto) once observed to me that he knew people who thought there was no philosophy after Hegel, and others who thought there was none before Wittgenstein; and he saw no reason for excluding the possibility that both were right.

But no such *salto mortale* of faith, for or against Hegel, any longer imposes itself on us. An obligation which does however impose itself on any expositor of Hegel is to explain why Hegel did once secure such a total response. What was it about his ideas and their context which gave them this awe-inspiring power, which compelled men to embrace them or to repudiate them with such completeness? It is here that Professor Charles Taylor succeeds brilliantly.[1] He does explain how this came to be. Accounts of Hegelianism from the inside, in the terminology and within the assumptions of the system – and such exegeses are available – are not much use; and refutations totally from the outside are no better. For instance, there is Popper's erstwhile and useless refutation of the dialectic by invoking the weird principle of modern logic, that a contradiction entails any other proposition whatever, and hence a contradiction-recognising logic is unselective and thus unusable. What is required, here as so often, is real understanding which nevertheless does not forgive everything. *Taylor comprend tout, et il pardonne beaucoup; il en pardonne même trop.* Which is quite in order, because he does not forgive all and he does not oblige his readers to follow him on the path of forgiveness. An inward understanding which does not become hopelessly intoxicated, which re-emerges, sane and whole, at the end, to report on the journey – this is Taylor's achievement, and it is an impressive one.

It is interesting to note that there is a marked convergence between

[1] *Hegel*. By Charles Taylor. Cambridge University Press, 1975.

Taylor's and Popper's views of Hegel. This may seem paradoxical, but it only appears so because Taylor likes what he sees, and Popper detests it; but what they actually see is very similar. Popper's diagnosis of the appeal of both Plato and Hegel is that their adherents are lured by the appeal of belonging, of togetherness, of the 'closed society'. Taylor sternly tells us that we owe our identities to our culture, that we should not fear this social holism, that 'only an exaggerated atomism could make the condition of alienated man seem the inescapable human norm'; and he sees Hegel's central merit in the fact that he forcefully reminded us of all this. The diagnosis of the appeal is thus quite identical; only the evaluation and idioms differ. It is perhaps a pity that Taylor tells us relatively little of the other transformations of Hegelianism in other climes; of the way in which, for instance, T. H. Green used it to teach the nonconformist conscience to speak through secular metaphysics and lay the bases of the Welfare State (a story well told by Melvin Richter in *The Politics of Conscience*); or of the way in which, in Cambridge, Michael Oakeshott developed a water-colour variant of Hegelianism designed mainly for the preservation of the amenities and privileges of rural England. But let us be grateful for the account of the use of Hegel by the romantic Left.

The opening passages of the book, in which Taylor makes his basic approach to Hegel, are among its most interesting parts. Taylor rightly approaches Hegel through the overall problem to which Hegel responded: and the question is at least as important as the answer. His starting point is that there is a certain widely-held view of the contrast between us modern men, and our superstitious or anthropomorphically-minded predecessors:

> Understanding the world in categories of meaning, as
> existing to embody or express an order of Ideas or arche-
> types, as manifesting the rhythm of divine life, of the
> foundational acts of the gods, or the will of God; seeing the
> world as a text, or the universe as a book. . .this kind of
> interpretive vision of things which in one form or another
> played such an important role in many pre-modern societies
> may appear to us the paradigm of anthropomorphic pro-
> jection on to the world, suitable to an age in which man was
> not fully adult [p. 5].

Taylor does not altogether repudiate this view of the contrast between *us* and immature humanity, but he clearly holds it to be less than the full story. To swallow it whole is for Taylor a grave impediment not merely to the understanding of Hegel and of his generation, but equally and above all to a proper understanding of our contemporary collective and individual predicaments. This gap between the old and the new visions is the keynote of the whole book. It is not merely a clue to Taylor's interpretations of Hegel, but equally to his substantive comments on the modern world. It is of course also the explanation of why Hegel attracts him. Taylor chides us for the incompleteness, complacency, or narrowness of our vision.

> This way of seeing things is not uncommon, but it very much misses the point of [the] reactions [of Goethe, Schelling, Hegel and their generation], as well as obscuring the way in which the issues then remain central today.
>
> The modern notion of the self, which is the locus of this struggle between indulgence and austerity, really only comes...in the seventeenth century...
>
> The essential difference can perhaps be put this way; the modern subject is self-defining, where on previous views the subject is defined in relation to a cosmic order.
>
> The situation is now reversed: full self-possession now requires that we free ourselves from the projection of meanings onto things, that we be able to draw back from the world, and concentrate purely on our own processes of observation and thought about things. The old model now looks like a dream of self-dispersal; self-presence is now to be aware of what we are doing in abstraction from the world we observe and judge.
>
> ...a transformation in philosophical outlook, which as such could only touch a minority in seventeenth-century Europe. But the modern notion of the subject has left no one untouched and unchanged in European society, or indeed the world [pp. 5–9].

This is the plot of the drama in terms of which Taylor interprets Hegel, and assesses his present relevance. Two notions of the self confront each other: the old cosmically pervasive one, and the modern Neutral Visitor, so to speak. (These are my terms rather than Taylor's.) The latter vision is the one which is favoured by contemporary society and by its organisation, but that is not a decisive point in its favour, or perhaps not a point in its favour at all.

On the contrary, those who have deep misgivings about the modern world, as Taylor has, will also have their misgivings about the associated conception of the self, at the very least. They will look to the rival view with a great deal of sympathy. And in it they will seek a clue to what has gone wrong with us, our world and its remedies, and the articulation of norms in terms of which the present could be judged. Hence this book is not merely an interpretation of Hegel but also a substantive contribution to social thought – though the two themes are inseparably intertwined.

Taylor sees Hegel as a very major event in this debate, and no doubt this is the correct way to see him. Hegelianism was an important move in the re-humanisation of the world. It opposed its disenchantment, in Max Weber's phrase; and it represented that anti-Copernican counter-revolution, to use Bertrand Russell's expression, which tries to put man back at the centre of things. Taylor's very way of putting the issue is, of course, just a little question-begging and perhaps too kind to Hegel. He presents the situation as follows. Conceptions of the universe and of the self go hand in hand. But there are two rival views of the self – so may we not fix ourselves up with a universe such as will, quite literally, suit our *selves*? This rather underplays one very major possible consideration on the other side, namely, that the universe is what it is, quite irrespective of our selves and of our concepts, and of our concepts of our selves; and if one particular vision of the self demands a certain corresponding universe, well then so much the worse for that vision of the self. The universe is not here to pander to our self-image – or is it? Taylor's presentation makes it all sound just a little too optional. But let it pass; it is a small price to pay for such an excellent exposition.

What exactly did Hegel achieve, and by what means? He rehumanised the world, and as if this weren't quite a big enough job on its own, he did a few further things on the side. He also and at the same time re-divinised the world. He made the world safe for the *Geisteswissenschaften*, and those who practise them, by attributing a certain role to ideas, and a further one to intellectual commentary. He welded the notions of political legitimacy and social change, in a manner relevant to modern Europe; he helped to start the debasement of intellectual currency known as modernist Christianity, with a God who can switch from merely being his own creation to being the old independently existing deity; he made Europeans more aware of cultural and historical diversity, and the fact that it is located inside us as much as or more than in externals; and no doubt a few further things into the bargain.

Despite this variety of achievements, the manner of attaining them was not eclectic; Hegel's philosophy is no hotchpotch. There is a unity, or at any rate a coherence, about its grandeur. The strands which go into it fuse and blend. But what are these individual strands?

First, there is the idea of progress. Taylor admittedly concentrates on the contrast between two rival visions of world and self: roughly, the world-as-meaningful and the world-as-external. But this opposition cuts across another one, which is at least as important: the world as static, and the world as developing, as growing. The old religious worlds were generally static: radical events occurred mainly at the beginning and the end, with possibly some crucial divine interventions along the way. The vision of perpetual progress as the key, as the central plot of history, is new. The historical perspective of the late eighteenth century encouraged such a view, and the then contemporary experience of radical political, social, and intellectual change made it seem natural.

The idea of progress contains some further important elements: change is not merely perpetual and directed, it is also self-generating and self-sufficient. It has an inner logic, and does not require external intervention or manipulation.

It could be put like this: about the same time as Europeans were losing their faith in God, they also discovered progress. What better solution to this predicament than to say: but God is progress, or progress is God?

Hegel found a portentous, and suitably obscure, idiom for saying just this. In an interesting survey of recent Hegel literature,[2] Mr Anthony Quinton complains that it is not clear whether Hegel's Absolute Spirit is or is not to be identified with the old-fashioned straightforward transcendent God. It is not fully clear whether the naïvety of the question is deliberate or genuine. The highly successful marketing of Hegelianism depended, of course, precisely on no one ever knowing the answer to this question. Hegel lets you have your old God back if that is what you want, and by a method which seemed, at least at the time, modern and invulnerable. (It was the

[2] 'Spreading Hegel's Wings', *The New York Review of Books*, 29 May and 12 June 1975.

very facility of the procedure which offended Kierkegaard.) But he also gives you a new kind of God, inseparable from his creation or its development, if you find the old one no longer acceptable. Moreover, you can switch between the two interpretations according to whether you are young or old, under critical pressure or not (and from which angle), according to mood, and so on. The language in which the position is articulated certainly will not impede any such metamorphoses.

On the point which continues to puzzle Quinton, Taylor is rather kind and tolerant of Hegel:

> it is clear that Hegel is neither a theist in the ordinary sense, nor an atheist. Whatever the sincerity of his claims to be an orthodox Lutheran, it is clear that Hegel only accepted a Christianity which had been systematically reinterpreted to be a vehicle of his own philosophy. . .some of his followers could reinterpret him in the direction of orthodox theism. Hegel's position was in a sense on a narrow crest between theism and some form of naturalism or pantheism. The atmosphere was so rarefied on top that it was easy to fall off, and remains so [p. 102].

Quite. But this doesn't really tell us just what the position is, up there on the *arrête*. It looks to me like one of those Alpine ridges which has to be climbed on one side or the other, according to which way the wind is blowing.

Taylor does tell us that

> what distinguished Hegel's position from pantheism in his own mind was the rational necessity which, it is true, could not exist without the world as the ensemble of finite things, but which was in this sense superior to the world, that it determined its structure [p. 102].

This was pantheism, it seems, with a differential density of the divine. All things are divine but some less so than others. Apart from its convenient knife-edge ambiguity between theism, atheism, and pantheism, the doctrine also has the important merit of offering a truly splendid theodicy, a justification of the ways of god/universe/history to man.

> Hegel. . .speaks of his philosophy of history as a 'theodicy'. . .more than for the death of men, Hegel in his

philosophy of history accounts for the death of civilisations.
What seems senseless. . .the destruction and decay. . .is
shown to be a necessary stage on the road to realisation of
Geist in the law-state and reason. That is, not only death
itself, but the particular incidence of fate in history is shown
to be part of the meaningful plan, with which man as
reason can be fully reconciled.

One may stop well short of conviction before Hegel's
theodicy [p. 121].

One may indeed. But in an evolving universe, tribulations can indeed
plausibly be justified as the price and the spur of development. The
Hegelo-Marxist tradition of course provides an easy do-it-yourself
legitimation of either the *status quo* or of revolution; it only depends
on which edition of the *Geist*'s edicts you care to read, today's or
tomorrow's (assuming that you credit yourself with access to the
future version).

Hegel appealed to a bourgeois age. Middle-class life is, above all, a
career: we strive and suffer, and it is all well worth it if the career is
successfully accomplished. And so it is with things-at-large and the
grand totality. Hegel told us that the universe does it too. The *Geist*
is the driving and guiding spirit of a careerist cosmos. . .

There is also an old joke about the Edwardian lieutenant, asked at
his military examination – what is the role of cavalry in modern
warfare? He replied: Sir, it is, I suppose, to add a touch of class to
what would otherwise be a mere vulgar brawl. Similarly, Hegelianism confers metaphysical depths on European history which might
otherwise be a mere sordid scramble for power. It thereby, incidentally, makes intellectual depth-commentary (*ex post* only, in the
interests of safety) indispensable; and hence the intellectuals, who
purvey it, acquire great self-importance.

Note that, though the *Geist* used most mundane instruments –
passion and violence – for the accomplishment of Its aims, It
remained Itself rational, cerebral, abstract, and decent. The ends
which men unwittingly served were still edifying ones. One might
say that as the nineteenth century moved on from Hegel to Freud, it
advanced from the Cunning of Reason to the Cunning of Unreason.
So Hegel's romanticism is in a way rather limited. The *Geist* uses
violence and passion in its manipulation of men for its own higher
ends, but those higher ends seem impeccably cerebral and orderly.

It is a most *bürgerlich* spirit. The *Geist* seems almost to be a Prussian civil servant concerned with the proper management of universal historical development.

The Cunning of Reason was Hegel's term for what contemporary sociologists call Latent Function: the unwitting satisfaction of ends of which the agent suspects little. Hegel was of course a great functionalist, much given to seeing society and the world as unwittingly interlocking and purposive. The *Sein/Sollen* rapprochement which preoccupies Taylor is an early version of Functionalism. But Hegel was also *the* philosopher of historical change, of social transformations. There is a certain irony about this conjunction. The commonest criticism heard of functionalism nowadays is that 'it cannot account for change'. Hegel found no such difficulty.

The second strand is the logician's way to the sense of Unity of all things. This is an old theme in philosophy, both in the West and in India. In the West it dates back at least to Parmenides, but was powerfully revived by Spinoza, to whom Hegel owed so much. Spinoza taught

> I have explained the nature and properties of God: that he necessarily exists: that he is one alone: that he exists and acts merely from the necessity of his nature: that he is the free cause of all things...that all things are in God, and so depend upon him that without him they could neither exist nor be conceived...that all things were predetermined by God, not through his free or good will, but through his absolute nature or infinite power.

What mattered about Spinoza's pantheism was not merely its content, but above all the manner of its exposition or putative demonstration. He claimed it was 'proved in geometric order'. In effect, the demonstration consisted of extracting the alleged implications of some basic concepts we use, or did use, when speaking of the world (in the case of the Cartesian Spinoza: substance, attribute, mode, and so forth). It is then held that the conclusions somehow constrain, must apply to, reality. The reality established by Spinoza was monistic, and the complex plurality of the real world was somehow its emanation.

Hegel took over this logician's way to reality. His world was, like Spinoza's, monistic. But it was also very much a world *on the move*. He was a philosopher of change and progress. But his views on the development of the world and his logician's way of establishing the world's unity complemented each other. The world knew tension; so do concepts. In concepts as in historical situations, the *status quo* provokes its own opposition. In the world and amongst concepts, harmony is sometimes re-established. Thus the Hegelian-style 'dialectic' arrived in Western thought.

Thirdly, there is the 'overcoming' of the Kantian heritage.

Kant is perhaps the greatest and shrewdest commentator of that cold, disenchanted vision which, as Taylor stresses so much, provided Hegel with his problem. The self as conceived by Kant is totally alienated from the natural world (though Kant does not use this terminology). Kant believed himself to be describing not modern man, but man as such. Kantian man owes nothing, but nothing, to nature or the cosmos: his morality, his key conceptions, even his belief in God emanate in the end from the structure of his own mind. Kant made a virtue of this necessity. If our morals, our concepts, were not 'autonomous' in this way, if they were indebted to something outside which gave them authority, then they would be worthless. Their glory lay in the fact that we and we alone made them: we were alone and self-sufficient, Robinson Crusoes in a world which we never made and in which we forged our own cognitive and ethical tools.

Kant's philosophy was a kind of individualistic protestantism driven to an extreme of self-sufficiency. Hence that sharp dualism between man the cognising and moral subject and the external world (which, as Taylor stresses, constitutes Hegel's problem situation). The dualisms appear so sharply in Kant that generally it is most difficult to see, how, on Kant's own terms, the two separated partners can ever meet.

Hegelianism solves this problem, at least to its own satisfaction. (Whether the solution is more than verbal is another matter.) The iron curtain between the real and the rational, between subject and object, is suspended, eroded, dissolved, overcome. In the Hegelian world, a blissful *détente* reigns. The barriers go down, or are only allowed a temporary role, as functional spurs to competition which in the end is beneficial to all.

Each of the previous themes contributes to this solution. The unity of everything, derived by means borrowed from the Parmenidean-Spinozistic tradition, melds with the idea of growth or progress. This is now a totality which is growing; or conversely, growth is of the very essence of the totality, not just an attribute of some part of it, or of some segment of its history.

As Taylor puts it,

> The aim of Kant was to cut loose altogether from. . . reliance on nature, and to draw the content of obligation purely from the will [p. 368].
>
> . . .Kantian morality remains one of division. . .The Kantian self is ultimately identified with the faculty which gives laws to ourselves, reason: man is thus free even against inclination. But Hegel holds fundamentally to the expressivist views of man: the self is the inner single source which expresses itself in the unfolding of reason and inclination alike [p. 60].

So we are being offered a re-unification, a re-enchantment of the world, but (as Taylor stresses) on quite a new basis.

Hegel's expressivism is the attainment of global togetherness by other means. If we are no longer part of cosmos, as religion taught, then cosmos is at least part of us, because it is pervaded by and suffused with our concepts. It is a kind of neo-Ptolemaic global togetherness, placing man (or rather his culture) at the very centre of things.

Fourth, there is a sense of culture. Men have always known that customs, clothes, buildings, etc., are liable to differ from community to community. But it is fair to suspect that, until the late eighteenth century, they had on the whole tended to underrate the extent to which the differences also existed *inside* them, pervaded their very ideas and concepts, and the extent to which, in turn, their ideas suffused the world they inhabited. This idea intoxicated Hegel and some of his generation. Taylor, following Jean Hippolyte, and probably Isaiah Berlin, makes this central to his interpretation of Hegel.

Note how this idea dovetails with the other themes enumerated. Culture is unitary, and it pervades the individuals and parts who compose it: this latches on to the theme of unity inherited from Spinoza. Culture is conceptual; it resides in the living, active ideas of its carriers. This somehow perpetuates the conceptualist method in philosophy, the approach to reality through a contemplation of the crucial notions we employ for characterising it. But culture develops and grows; this melds with the theme of progress. Culture is cosy and concrete; its moral demands emerge from the identity which it confers on the individual, and it promises the reward of blissful identification with a larger totality, and thus overcomes the cold Kantian morality which spurns rewards or extraneous identities. The problem of knowledge also has a pleasing solution: truth is neither transcendent, hidden and distant, nor private and capricious. The collective *Geist* – being *us* – guarantees that we are not excluded from it; but being conveniently more-than-us, and certainly more-than-any-single-one-of-us, it firmly scotches individual deviations. When Naphta in *The Magic Mountain* observes that Hegelianism is the philosophy of the objective, he is not saying something paradoxical. It may not be a philosophy of the transcendent, but its centre of gravity is in institutions or practices which, from the individual's viewpoint, are hard, external, and objective. All is well.

Many of the themes of Taylor's book also reappear in an interesting but difficult book, difficult perhaps because it is somewhat literary/ declamatory, and because, unlike the admirably correct Taylor, its author rather snobbishly refrains from spelling out the rules of the game within which she is arguing. Instead, she dares the reader either to catch on to the game or to confess himself unsophisticated. The book is Judith Shklar's *Freedom and Independence*.[3]

She stresses the historic importance of successive ideas of the self, only in a different phraseology:

> This history of the experiences of human self-consciousness
> is of necessity the history of ethics [p. 57].

In other words, our values are the shadows of our self-images. The nostalgia for a world in which 'expressivist' yearnings were more fully satisfied also appears: 'The beautiful ethical polity is now only a memory...' So does the 'cultural' interpretation of Hegel's metaphysics:

> A people is not a random assemblage of human beings.
> It is composed of individuals whose lives are shaped by the
> same beliefs and rules of conduct and linked by language
> and work. They share an ethos, or to use Hegel's word, a
> spirit [p. 142].

[3] *Freedom and Independence: A Study in the Political Ideas of Hegel's 'Phenomenology of Mind'*. By Judith Shklar. Cambridge University Press.

And as far as I can see, the 'over-coming' of Kantianism, of an ethic of individual self-sufficiency, is endorsed by her almost with venom:

> The age of the 'moral point of view' is not a glorious one.
> It is the expression both of more and less than Kant's moral philosophy...This autonomous self which is its own master, or practical reason imposing itself on the world, is not 'character', only knowledge. We are again reminded how far we are from Antigone. Indeed, if this outlook creates any recognisable human type, it is the hypocrite. And it expresses itself not only in a hypocritical personality but in a veritable culture of hypocrisy [p. 181].

These words are harsh as well as occasionally obscure. But one does get her message: Kantian individualism out; and instead, we are to look towards the Hegelian spirit (culture) and at the very least to respect the idea that it can reach a final culmination, a totalisation, a summary:

> While it is clear that Hegel's notion of 'spirit'...does subject moral and political values to the logic of development, to becoming; there is for Hegel an ultimate aim; the knowledge that comes at the end of the ages.

This, then, is the heady brew which intoxicated a generation, which is still potent, and inadvisable for those who cannot hold their ideological liquor. It indisputably altered the idiom of European thought and life. For instance, in a book[4] published as late as 1964, we find the author, Eugène Fleischman, complaining, '*la pensée de Hegel ne fut jamais acceptée par une civilisation occidentale à laquelle, plus qu'à aucune autre peut-être, elle donne tout sons sens*'. Taylor's account of this sense-giving vision is rewarding, in particular in the early and the final passages of the book: the opening ones specify the conditions in which Hegelianism was born and seemed plausible, the final ones relate it to our contemporary problems. But in between these two high points, there is a deep valley which also needs and deserves to be traversed. As Taylor trudges across it, he seems slowly to become possessed and taken over by Hegel. We set off into this low-lying jungle with an amiable and lucid guide, who speaks our language and tells us, in our own terms, about the oddities of the terrain. We listen entranced, but as we pass through the

---

[4] Eugène Fleischman, *La Philosophie Politique de Hegel* (Plon, 1964).

steaming swamps near the centre of the lowlands, we look up and are
seized by anxiety: our guide is a native, he is Hegel! We control our
fear, so as not to encourage an ambush. . .and we are duly rewarded
for our *sangfroid*. As we begin to climb up into the highlands on the
other side, the natives no longer seem restless, our guide is gradually
retransformed once again and comes to speak, if not quite ordinary
philosopher's English, at least nothing more exotic than the romantic
idiom of the 1960s. Hegel's features gradually leave his visage, and
he becomes, once again, dear familiar Chuck Taylor, as we wipe the
sweat of fear and exhaustion from our brows.

In other words, in the long central chapters, Taylor does not
altogether escape one of the dangers which has befallen so many
other expositors: that of being absorbed by the system and its
language, and ending up by expounding it from the inside.

Taylor is, to my mind, too kind to his subject (though this is a
judgement which no doubt reflects disagreement with Taylor's own
position, of which more later). The excessive indulgence to Hegel,
treated on its own, has various aspects: kindness to his general
character, and to various specific doctrines. Let me take these in turn.

Hegel is clearly the most megalomaniac of all philosophers, claiming as he does to reveal and to embody the cosmic plot. Like
Mohammed, he does not claim divinity, but evidently the god-
head speaks through him. Taylor, with entirely appropriate patience,
makes plain why these pretensions were not wholly absurd: the condition of Europe was such that a message of this very kind was to be
expected, and Hegel merely put it together and articulated it. I for
one would find it hard to deny that had Hegel not existed, it would
have been necessary to invent him. Taylor conveys, with some tact
and sympathy, both the megalomania (without calling it such) and
its plausibility.

But apart from the megalomania there was also something plain
and downright *spiessbürgerlich* about Hegel; he is not altogether
unlike something between Kumpf and Schleppfuss in Thomas
Mann's *Dr Faustus*. Taylor's sympathy for his subject, while succeeding in making the megalomania understandable and perhaps for-
givable, somehow misses out on this aspect of Hegel. (Perhaps the
coexistence of the Grand Vision and the Everyday was entirely
consistent: Hegelianism requires not merely that the grand design
be rational and necessary, but also insists on a place for the humdrum
and contingent.) I rather miss this vulgar-professorial Hegel in

Taylor; Hegel may perhaps be the Absolute, but he is also the *Absolute in braces, eating sauerkraut.* This aspect ought not to be wholly neglected. For full local flavour, try humming the italicised phrase to the tune of *Lilli Marlene.*

What of the frequently made charge that Hegel is an illiberal, authoritarian worshipper of the State and/or of the March of History? Here Taylor springs to Hegel's defence and endeavours to exonerate him. I find the defence unconvincing and off the point. Taylor does not deny that Hegel: 'thought that Prussia was on the right track, and...that he believed that the state was somehow divine and deserving of the individual's highest earthly allegiance' (p. 457). But, Taylor insists, if we look at the small print, we find that Hegel had a whole host of reservations about Prussia as it then was (although it *was* on the right track). It all depends on what you stress. Another distinguished Hegel commentator, Professor Shlomo Avineri, is also quite aware of the small print:

> Hegel admits that there is still 'work to be done': but, this...belongs to the 'empirical side'. The absolutisation of the present period of history is thus very strongly emphasised.

And, more strongly,

> It is in the modern, post-1815 world of Western Europe that Hegel sees the apex of historical development. It is here that 'the empire of thought is established actually and and concretely...Freedom has found the means of realizing its Ideal – its true actuality.'[5]

Or, again, take Herbert Marcuse, who is otherwise inclined, like Taylor, to be kind to Hegel, and who has also read the small print:

> Hegel's exaltation of the state's political power has, however, some clearly critical traits...Nevertheless, these critical qualities are dwarfed by the oppressive traits inherent in all authoritarianism, which manifest their full force in Hegel's doctrine of external sovereignty.[6]

With philosophers, the small print seldom matters. If a philosopher tells us that the Real is the Rational, it is no use telling us in small print that some bits of the real are less rational than others. One

[5] Shlomo Avineri, *Hegel's Theory of the Modern State* (1972), p. 235.
[6] Herbert Marcuse, *Reason and Revolution* (1954), pp. 220–1.

always knew that. That is precisely why one is interested in having some independent criteria of the rational, which are not in the pay of the real. That is the old and ordinary way of doing philosophy. Taylor seems to advise and sympathise with Hegel's 'overcoming' of a morality of a mere *sollen*, of an 'ought' which claims independence of what is real in the world. But when later a bit of the real diverges from what Hegel wishes, the merits of *sollen* seem to be surreptitiously rediscovered...and above all, the fact that this is done is invoked as a refutation of the State- or History-worshipping charge. No, it only shows that the system is not consistent. As far as I am concerned, Hegel can worship that state, or not worship it. It's a free country. What he cannot do is both do so and not do so, according to which criticism he is facing. We are back on that ridge which is climbed on either side, according to the prevailing direction of the wind.

But Taylor's book must not be judged simply as an exegesis of Hegel. It also intends to be a contribution to social thought in its own right, and an important one. The intimate connection between its two themes – the current concerns which led the author to Hegel, and the inspiration he derives from Hegel for the present – is what gives the book its distinctive character.

For the author is not merely Professor Charles Taylor of McGill University (and about to take up a chair at Oxford), but also Chuck Taylor, a key figure in the early heroic age of the New Left, founding father of the *New Left Review*, a man who helped temporarily to convert the annual conference of the Labour Party to CND, and altogether an important influence of that movement which helped lay the foundation of the intellectual dissidence of the 1960s. Chuck was one of the Young Hegelians of 1956. What is more important, Chuck and the Professor are one and the same person in a far more than superficial sense. In his *Hegel*, he gives us by far the best formulations of the kind of social criticism which was characteristic of the 1960s. As is right and proper in an Hegelian context, which requires that the Owl of Minerva only takes flight at dusk, he gives us the benefit of the wisdom only after the event, but better late than never, and whether or not one agrees with it, it is well worth hearing.

The key notion in Taylor's critique of the modern world, *and* of his exegesis both of Hegel and of Marx, is *expressivism*. Though Taylor gives a very thorough and exhaustive account of all aspects of

Hegelianism, it is the culture-romanticism – which he calls expressivism – which really turns him on, and which receives a disproportionately large share of his attention when he actually interprets Hegel. This notion overlaps closely with what I would call a sense of culture: an awareness that our concepts pervade nature through the classifications we impose on it (so that a man–nature continuum is re-established, this time from inside outwards, so to speak), and that our life is lived, our identity articulated, in a conceptually-saturated world which forms a system, and which is carried by a collectivity. The negative aspect of this is the denial of atomistic, mechanistic, and what might be called separationist philosophies. All this seems to me very close to Taylor's expressivism, but perhaps it might be best to quote his own words (p. 539).

> The conception of human life which I call 'expressivist'. . . is in part a reaction to [associationist psychology, utilitarian ethics, atomistic politics of social engineering, and ultimately a mechanistic science of man]. It is a rejection of the view of human life as a mere external association of elements without intrinsic connection. . .Expressivism returns to the sense of the intrinsic value of certain actions or modes of life. . .and these actions or modes of life are seen as wholes, as either true expressions, or distortions of what we authentically are.

Taylor warns us not to underestimate this critique.

> We might be tempted to think that this current touches only a minority of intellectuals and artists, leaving the majority of 'ordinary' men unaffected. But the wide resonance of this kind of critique has been shown if nothing else in periodic outbursts of unrest which have troubled industrial civilisation. Deep expressivist dissatisfaction contributed to the success of Fascism, and underlies the revolt of many young people against the 'system' in many Western countries.

Thus, a century after Stirling published a book with that title, *The Secret of Hegel* (according to Taylor) stands revealed at last: Hegel is the philosopher of the 'expressivist' critique of modern society. Thus Taylor's Hegel stands contrasted, for instance, to Avineri's:

> in Germany. . .the political debate about Hegel. . .appears as just another phase in the battle between rationalists

and the romantics...For the romantics, Hegel stood for
1789 and universalism, against historical nationalism and
the *völkisch* virtues.[7]

Taylor's Hegel is apparently far closer to the romantics.

Hegel's philosophy can be seen as an attempt to realise a
synthesis that the Romantic generation was groping
towards: to combine the rational, self-legislating freedom
of the Kantian subject with the expressive unity within
man and with nature for which the age longed [p. 539].

And this is not merely the secret of Hegel, it is also the secret of Marx

Many...would object to an interpretation of Marxism
which places it within what I have called the expressivist
tradition. Of course, Marxism is more than this. But I do
not think we can understand it...if we try to abstract
from this...Certainly few would want to deny that the
young Marx is the heir, through Hegel, of the expressivist
aspiration...Marx takes up [the] radical critique of in-
humanity. But the principal justifying myth which he
denounces as the alibi for exploitation...is not the old
religion but the new atomistic, utilitarian Enlightenment
philosophy itself...the tremendous power of Marx's theory
comes from joining [the] thrust of the radical Enlightenment to the expressivist tradition [pp. 547–8].

Nor are Hegel and Marx alone:

many...are moved by a profound sense of the inadequacy
of modern society which has its roots in the Romantic
protest. Since the end of the eighteenth century there has
been a continuing stream of complaint against modern
civilization...In different ways these critics castigate
modern society as expressively dead, as stifling expressive
fulfilment [p. 544].

I should like, first, to record a grave worry about this elusive
'expressivism'. It is used as a stick with which to beat atomistic or
mechanistic accounts of man or society. These accounts must be
wrong (it is claimed) because they misrepresent the real, i.e. expressivist, state of affairs. Well then, what the devil is the complaint?

[7] 'Hegel Revisited', *Journal of Contemporary History*, vol. III, no. 2
(April 1968), p. 146.

If this is how things (generally) are, it can hardly be used as a discriminating principle of how they *should* be! Taylor himself gets into trouble in his account of what expressivism is:

> modes of life are seen as wholes. . .either true expressions or distortions of what we authentically are.

All human activities are expressive, but some are more so than others; it seems some of them 'distort'. But if expressivism is to be a moral norm rather than a universal description, we should need, if not a justification, at least a more precise specification of what does and does not satisfy – and not one which, in Hegelian fashion, only passes judgement in retrospect!

Taylor's own critique of Hegelianism is quite different and much milder, in fact it is hardly a criticism at all: Hegelianism is not so much wrong as obsolete.

> Modern civilisation has. . .seen the proliferation of Romantic views in private life and fulfilment, along with growing rationalisation of collective structures, and a frankly exploitative stance towards nature. Modern society, we might say, is Romantic in its private and imaginative life and utilitarian or instrumentalist in its public, effective side [p. 541].

Hence, says Taylor, we are no longer tempted to project expressivism to our collectivities, and for a number of good reasons: it has lost all plausibility, and we are only allowed to indulge this taste in the privacy of our homes. Revisionist Marxists used to argue that the revolution is no longer necessary, thanks to parliamentary reform and the welfare state. Taylor seems to say (regretfully, perhaps) that total Hegelian expressivism is no longer compelling, because so many of us can now have hi-fi at home.

But Taylor, like Hegel, must be stood on his head. He considers Hegel dated in his specific social observations, but valuable in his great central insights. The opposite seems to me true. Hegel's specific observations on the need to avoid either unrestrained *laissez-faire* or virulent political turbulence from below ring truer now than ever, and are in any case immeasurably superior to Marx's anticipations. But it is the central idea of Hegel's which simply will not do.

There seem to be two central ploys by which Hegelianism evades all testing and danger of falsification. Ordinary theories point to (*a*) structures beyond the phenomena they describe, and (*b*) predictions which follow from these for the future. The Owl of Minerva exempts this mythology from any tests by subsequent events; and the non-transcendence of the Hegelian *Geist*, so much stressed by Taylor – this *Geist*, unlike his predecessor the God of Abraham, cannot exist without the world – exempts it from the former requirement. The explanatory concept turns out to be no more than the phenomenon it covers. So, in the end, or at least when under critical scrutiny, Hegelianism covertly retrenches and ceases to be any kind of *theory* at all. It shrinks into being just a certain kind of mystifying description of the pattern of events *so far*, with nothing said about any *beyond* or any *henceforth*. Real knowledge does not disavow its own applicability to the *beyond* or the *later*. Hegel is a punter who can explain the rational necessity of all football-pool results, but only after the matches have been played.

The regretful-obsolescence criticism which Taylor allows himself does not move me much. I am far more worried by some other strictures which Taylor fails to press home; he touches on them in an all too gingerly manner.

First of all – and this is perhaps fundamental philosophically – it is not enough to say that Hegel was a somewhat inaccurate sociological forecaster (while hedging his bets by saying that he was not a forecaster at all), who did not see just where modern society was going and hence did not make up exactly the right recipe for restoring our sense of belonging. (On the contrary, I find him as a proto-sociologist still quite illuminating and more convincing than Marx.) His error is far deeper than that. The stuff simply is not true. Of course, all that mumbo-jumbo about the Absolute Spirit can indeed be taken as just a fanciful way of saying that our life is lived in terms of concepts which we individually did not invent, which are parts of a much larger cultural tradition which evolves, and to which we contribute. If that is all it is, we may also choose other idioms for saying it: there have always been a lot of them available. But if it is more, then what on earth would be the independent evidence for that alleged *Geist*? Ah, replies the Hegelian fellow-traveller, that is the wrong question. For the Hegelian God is not one 'who could exist quite independently of men, even if men did not exist, as the God of Abraham, Isaac and Jacob before the creation'. So we must just not ask for *more*. . .and if we compound this with that little saying about the Owl of Minerva, that overrated piece of poultry which precludes us from testing the system by checking on its sociological predictions, we are entirely covered. Thus the tautological vacuity of it all becomes evident.

Should we be so indulgent? I would prefer to echo Moses Hess when he asked 'if it is within the possibilities of reason to comprehend the essence of God, freedom and immortality, why should the essence of the future be excluded from it?'[8] This coy Hegelian reticence about the future, the reluctance to do anything more than comment on and ratify the past, may have something to do with hedging one's bets. Happily, Hegel does not always remember these prudent and cautious principles, and the absent-minded owl has occasionally been known to flutter at dawn. Thus, in the Appendix to the *Lectures on the Philosophy of World History*[9] (entitled 'The Natural Context or the Geographical Basis of World History') he predicts a monarchy for the United States of America:

> The example of the USA is frequently cited as an objection to the proposition that it is impossible in our times for a large state to have a liberal constitution. . .But this argument is inadmissible; North America cannot yet be regarded as a developed and mature state. . .it has not yet progressed far enough to feel the need for a monarchy [p. 169].

Are the United States of America fully developed now, one wonders? Here I can only recall what Isaac Deutscher once said about Lev Trotsky: his predictions were *so* far ahead of his time that some of them are *still* not fulfilled.

Taylor himself comes close to making the really basic criticism in the only passage where he allows himself a joke at Hegel's expense:

> There is something in Hegel's philosophy which is irresistibly reminiscent of Baron Münchhausen. The baron. . . after falling from his horse in a swamp, extricated himself by seizing his own hair and heaving himself back on his horse. Hegel's God is a Münchhausen God [p. 101].

8 Quoted in Shlomo Avineri, *Hegel's Theory of the Modern State.*
9 *Lectures on The Philosophy of World History. Introduction: Reason in History.* By George Wilhelm Friedrich Hegel. Translated by H. B. Nisbet, with an Introduction by Duncan Forbes. Cambridge University Press.

But that's just it! The Hegelian version of the 'ontological proof' works exactly in this way. The grand, meaningful, and active totality is 'proved' by the argument that the part presupposes the whole – if indeed we know that the part, which we indisputably are, is a part of that particular whole. . .The whole exercise is endowed with some plausibility – though not cogency – by the consideration that it would seem hard to deny to the totality, at least potentially, certain traits found in large parts of it (e.g. consciousness, purpose). It also gains plausibility by that crucial ambiguity, located in the fact that it is far from clear whether the totality is being credited with these traits in any sense over and above, and other than, that parts of it (indisputably) sometimes do attain both purposiveness and consciousness.

So much for the no doubt naive question concerning whether the whole system is true, or whether it really tells us anything. But let us leave pure philosophy and look at this entire intellectual tradition – from Hegel and Marx to Taylor – for its social comments and suggestiveness. Leaving aside the question whether Marx properly belongs in the 'expressivist' camp, and granting Taylor for the sake of argument that he does, it seems to me that *within* this tradition, Hegel is greatly superior to Marx. Hegel deified political institutions whereas Marx would, in the end, abolish them altogether.

Taylor notes that Marxism has no answer, and can have none, to the question of how post-exploitation society is to be organised.

> Not only does classical Marxism have no answer to this, it
> implies that the answer is 'none'; that our only situation
> will be that of generic man, harmoniously united, in contest
> with nature. But this predicament is not only unbelievable,
> but arguably unlivable. It would be an utterly empty
> freedom [p. 558].

Of the two errors, I prefer the Hegelian, which at least recognises that we need institutions, even if it grossly exaggerates their status.

Taylor is fully aware of this weakness in Marxism and he alludes to it openly:

> this was not a blind spot particular to Marx. It affects
> the whole communist movement. Just a few months
> before October 1917, in his *State and Revolution*, Lenin
> still expressed an incredibly simple view about the

> administration of communist society. The Bolshevik Party
> was thrown into the real history of state power with this
> simple image of human freedom as the unproblematic
> administration of things. And Soviet communist society
> has remained somehow fixated on it; so that it continues
> to resist the adequate conception of itself as a social form
> [p. 555].

One may resent the *somehow* in the above sentence, which seems to imply that it is 'somehow' a mystery why the Soviets cannot give an accurate account of their own society. The reason is, of course, that it cannot be done without flagrantly contradicting what Marx said. Hegel's sense of the importance of institutions seems altogether more realistic than Marx's illusion of their dispensability, which has deprived a large part of humanity of the ways of openly discussing its own social predicament.

Taylor is somewhat indulgent to this disastrous Marxian error, and he curiously credits this mistake of Marx's – probably his gravest one – to Hegel's influence.

> Marx's. . .inability to see this rift was already implicit in
> his original position, in the transposition on to man of
> Hegel's notion of a self-positioning *Geist*. The powers of a
> Spirit who creates his own embodiment, once attributed to
> man, yield a conception of freedom as self-creation more
> radical than any previous one. . .a leap to free self-activity
> of generic man limited only by the (ever receding)
> refractory bounds of unsubdued nature [p. 555].

If you believe that you will believe anything, and institutional checks are then clearly neither necessary nor feasible 'after the revolution'. I should hardly hold it to Hegel's credit that he inspired this notion of Marx's; Marx's misguided sociological beliefs about the sources of basic conflict, it seems to me, also played their part in producing this egregious mistake.

Taylor is both too harsh and too kind to Marxism. It seems to me eminently doubtful whether Russian post-revolutionary history can fairly be blamed on the ideological deficiencies of Marxism. Russian society had strong centralist tendencies, and one could hardly expect these to be weakened after a ferocious civil war. The supposition that the available conceptual tools made any odds at that stage seems to me quite fanciful. But the issue is different in a period such as the present, when the Soviet state is stable, and a relative affluence gives it a certain elbow-room for manoeuvre. It is then that the total lack of warrant or recipe for pluralism and for effective institutional liberty within Marxism becomes truly disastrous. By anticipating only a total, role-less and institution-less freedom, Marx made it that much harder for societies invoking his word to achieve more limited and realistic liberties. The best – if indeed Marx's exaggerated vision was the best (and Taylor rightly has some doubts on this score) – is the enemy of the good. All of this would seem to make Marx an appallingly bad guide either to the internal mechanics or to the appropriate moral norms of late industrial societies.

But let me now consider the tradition as a whole rather than its internal differences – the tradition as presented by Taylor, that is, with its Hegelianised Marx, and with Taylor as its modern spokesman.

Like most members or fellow-travellers of the Hegelian tradition, Taylor derides what might be called the liberal way of legitimating values – that is, the presumption to stand outside the world so as to judge it, or to select within it. The extraordinary presumption inherent in an individual's claim so to be able to 'stand outside' does indeed constitute a very major argument on behalf of this tradition. Taylor asks 'Why does Hegel want to speak of a spirit which is larger than the individual?', and replies, severely (p. 380):

> These ideas only appear mysterious because of the powerful
> hold on us of atomistic prejudices, which have been very
> important in modern political thought and culture.

But an individual really does not transcend his community. He is

> a being who can think, feel, decide, be moved, respond,
> enter into relations with others; and all this implies a
> language, a related set of ways of experiencing the
> world. . .It is the particular way he situates himself within
> his cultural world that we call his identity.

This is the very core of Taylor's position and also of what he finds of most value in Hegel. This is 'expressivism'. Man is, it appears, a culture-sharing animal. But, like other 'expressivists' of this kind, Taylor is neither consistent in his position, nor does he properly understand his anti-expressivist, transcendence-seeking adversaries.

They, or the best among them, do *not* say that an individual can divest himself of his culture, and then take a kind of space-flight in extra-cultural space, so as to survey the scene and select his option. They say that certain *principles*, not individuals, can so transcend the local cultural cocoon. The Utilitarian principle of maximising the sum of satisfactions, or the Kantian principle of requiring symmetry of consideration for everyone, claims precisely this kind of authority – that of being capable of commanding assent quite independently of the way in which this, that, or the other culture happens to see things. They are meant to judge cultures, not presuppose them. So the position does not require the weird assumption that an individual can divest himself of his cultural clothing, but only the much less difficult contention that he can apprehend the authoritativeness of certain principles which stand outside the cultures to which they are applied.

Ironically, it is precisely the 'expressivists' like Taylor who covertly presuppose the possibility of cultural nakedness. Taylor and Marx repudiate the Robinson Crusoe way of doing moral philosophy, and both practise it surreptitiously. The argument that we only have identity through and thanks to our culture-cocoons leads to the conclusion which Taylor and many (though not all) expressivists cannot accept: namely, that all these cocoons are equally good, that they are all self-justifying. This of course would be an impossible position for any truly radical critic of contemporary society. Surely we must be able to say that some cocoons, notably our contemporary one, are gravely defective. But how? By what norms?

A few pages after the passage quoted we learn that the state is only fully rational if it expresses the ideas by which its individuals define their identity. But this, if it means anything, means that they somehow possess identities and ideals prior to the institutions which they then judge, and which they can consequently probe for conformity with those ideals! Even if in this particular passage Taylor is merely expounding Hegel (it is not fully clear), he makes no critical comment. His own expressivism does not endorse all cocoons; all societies are expressive but some more than others, and he clearly prefers some to others. And he plainly does not do so or wish to do so by assuming that prior human identity whose very possibility he also denies.

Taylor is, of course, right in saying that the 'liberal consensus' is an ideology like any other, in the sense that it is based on premises which are open to discussion, rather than exempt from it in virtue of being somehow beyond all ideology. It *is* an ideology; and, as it happens, a good one. He may even be right, though I'm not so sure, that it had an 'important support' in 'the view of man as primarily a producer'. The real essentials of liberalism, it would seem to me, could very well survive into a world which, as a consequence of affluence, and aware of the need to avoid exhaustion of resources, overcomes the compulsion towards ever greater productivity.

Expressivism is contrasted with 'those who feel fully at home in [modern Western society]. . .the heirs of Enlightenment mainstream, who proclaimed recently (and somewhat prematurely) the "end of ideology"' (p. 542). Clearly, the romantic–expressivist tradition is opposed to these.

Now it seems to me that these heirs to the mainstream of the Enlightenment offer an incomparably better guide to our world and our choices than do the expressivists. What was wrong with the 'end of ideology' was the assumption that it was readily available, and already in the possession of at least some of us. But the aspiration – a pluralist affluent society, in which people are free, economically and politically, to pursue their romantic fulfilment at home, while in the public sphere good instrumental institutions prevent tyranny and watch over the overall economic performance – seems to me vastly superior to either Marx's fantasy of stateless harmony, or Hegel's over-eager endorsement of existing polities (even if qualified by a lot of grousing in small print, carefully recorded by Taylor). It is also very much harder to attain, protect and diffuse such a system than we once supposed.

Unlike Taylor, I do not take the year 1968 too seriously; a shadow of a shadow, *ersatz* of *ersatz*, it re-enacted 1848, which in turn had re-enacted 1789. But the 1970s scare me stiff. The expressivists never made the *Financial Times* Index tremble. The miners and the oil sheikhs, who do have that power, are not activated by expressivist yearnings. All they want is a much bigger share of those post-Enlightenment goodies which expressivism spurns. Furthermore, it is not clear to me how advanced, large-scale societies can fulfil the requirements of expressivism, other than by holding Nürnberg rallies. I'd rather do without. What on earth is wrong with having one's expression at home (paperback classics, hi-fi) and leaving the public sphere to soulless pragmatism?

The expressivist alternative offers bad sociology and bad ethics.

It gives no illumination concerning the internal mechanics of any kind of industrial society. Man's romantic yearnings are not the key problem; it is the unromantic ones which matter.

A philosophy which gives us terms in which to speak of the dangers to liberty is more valuable than one which deprives us of such terms, even if it tells us how to bemoan our loss of togetherness and oneness with nature. A philosophy which gives us the means for an endless discussion of a *maladie imaginaire*, but none for the diagnosis of real, grave and perhaps fatal ailments, does not seem to me a worthwhile one. The diffusion and the price of affluence, the maintenance of political liberty – the criteria for, and the means of attaining, these ends are what we do need to think about. It is all very much harder than we supposed some decades ago. But 'Expressivism' is not an option which need tempt us. Thanks to Taylor, I understand it, and Hegel, better than I did before. I doubt whether they could find a better exposition or advocate.

2
Ethnomethodology:
the re-enchantment industry or the
Californian way of subjectivity

A quarter of a century or so ago there was a well-known eccentric in Edinburgh who used to accost passers-by on Prince's Street and ask them – are you sane? If any replied Yes, he would retort – ah, but can you *prove* it? And, as they could not, he proceeded triumphantly to show them that *he* at any rate could prove his sanity, by producing his own certificate of discharge from a mental hospital.

And so it is not merely with one's sanity, but also with one's inner and private life. Do you have an inner life? You protest you do, and a rich one to boot. Ah, but can you prove it? Of course you cannot. Anything you say in vindication of your own inner life is highly suspect, being partial and biased evidence at the very least, and to the sceptic, it is brazenly circular. As a lady once wrote to Bertrand Russell, she was a solipsist and was amazed that so few people were moved by the cogency of her views.

Your own reports do not establish the existence of your inner life: on the contrary they only derive such trustworthiness as they may possess from the prior assumption of your possession of such an inner life, and thus cannot vindicate it without circularity. This is 'the scandal' of solipsism, as Kant called it.

But though the unaided citizen, challenged on his walk on Prince's Street to provide good evidence of his own inner life, will fail to do so, the scandal of undemonstrated privacy no longer exists in sociology. There the inner life has at long last been put on a sound scientific basis. For this, if I understand it right, is the aim, essence, and achievement of Ethnomethodology.

It would be hypocritical to claim that the writings of Harold Garfinkel are a model of lucidity. Not only are many of his sentences and arguments utterly obscure, in what can only be described as a wilful manner, but his very standards in this field would seem to be eccentric. He observes (*Studies in Ethnomethodology*, 1967, p. ix):

> Parsons' work, particularly, remains awesome for the. . .
> unfailing precision of its. . .sociological reasoning.

It is possible to admire Parsons for his personal modesty and charm, for the manner in which he has sensitised an American sociological generation to a set of ideas and problems, or the way in which he has provided post-1945 America, all of a sudden inheriting the white man's burden, with some tools for the new task of thinking about societies other than their own and that of the Navajo. But to admire him for *precision* of thought suggests that the person saying this has no idea what precision of thought means. But the remark is, I think, significant for the understanding of Garfinkel's movement. It emerged in a milieu in which thought is not expected to be finely honed.

Though hardly a model of lucidity, two facts at any rate emerge quite clearly from *Studies in Ethnomethodology*: it is pre-occupied with the inner meanings, to the actors, of their actions; and secondly, it places the study of those inner meanings within the sociological tradition, of which it sees itself as a continuation. It does not abrogate or supplant sociology; it perpetuates and completes it, by an approach which stresses the subjective meaning of conduct.

It has of course its own way of referring to that inner meaning of human conduct: 'Ethnomethodological studies analyse everyday activities as members' methods for making. . .activities visibly-rational-and-reportable-for-all-practical-purposes, i.e., "accountable"' (p. vii). *Accountability* appears to be the key word; reflexivity, indexicality, and rationality also turn out to be important. The terminology and its nuances are not irrelevant to the understanding of the movement and its ideas. (The undefined term 'member', incidentally, seems to refer to *anyo*ne – presumably any member of a society or culture.) The most significant point in the above quotation is perhaps the reference to 'member's *methods* for making. . . activities. . ."accountable"' (italics mine).

What is significant about this is that 'accountability', which seems to mean the fact that our actions are such that we can give *accounts* of them to ourselves and others – that, as we used to say, they 'have a meaning' for us – is not something God-given or inherent in the nature of things, but requires *methods* for its accomplishment. Accountability is not self-explanatory. Nor is it. In fact, it is not at all clear to me that ethnomethodologists either succeed or even strive to show how this accountability really is achieved; they seem rather, as one would expect from avowed members of the phenomenological tradition, to concentrate on showing what those inner meanings *are*: description, not explanation of the manner of this achievement, seems to be their line in practice.

Secondly, it does not seem obvious to me that men do use, on individual occasions, any *methods* at all to make their actions 'accountable'. A perfectly possible view, one possessing at any rate *prima facie* plausibility, would be this: it is culture, or language, which provides the ready-made material potential for giving an account of this act or that, and, on individual occasions, men simply draw upon this available wealth of characterisations. They draw on an available stock of accounts. If this is so, it would follow that a *culture* (or a language) perhaps does employ some 'methods' to make such and such a set of 'accounts' available to those who have learned its rules, but that individuals do not use any methods at all to make things accountable – they just fall back on available accounts, without further ado. This is a query about the whole programme which perhaps deserves to be put on record. The voluntaristic element in the movement's ideas, the suggestion that *we* use 'method' to give 'accounts', may be significant for understanding its social roots. Does it not spring forth in a society in which, much more than anywhere else perhaps, cultural traits are optional and contingent? Does it not reflect this characteristic?

But leave that aside. Irrespective of whether they have rightly or unambiguously identified *the way* in which accountability, in their sense, is problematical, there clearly is merit in seeing and stressing *that* it is problematical. This property of conduct – that we can give accounts of what we do – is not always either noted, or seen to raise the problems which in fact it raises. It is an 'accomplishment... known, used, and taken for granted' (Garfinkel, op. cit., p. vii). He goes on to say, plausibly, that it is a 'fundamental phenomenon'. It is not entirely clear *how* fundamental, how exhaustive and how exclusive. Are the limits of either sociology or ethnomethodology defined by it? Or are other, non-accountable phenomena *also* to be encountered within the limits of either subject? And if so, is there a theory of the relationship between the accountable and the non-accountable? (If there were, would it be a kind of Marxism in reverse, in which the 'accountable', the inner, becomes fundamental, rather than being relegated to the superstructure? And – a question which will inevitably reappear – does this cult of subjectivity, like others, have great difficulty in allowing for 'false consciousness', for error? Are the 'accounts' self-guaranteeing, self-authenticating, self-sufficient?) These questions spring to mind. Whilst the nature of Harold Garfinkel's prose makes it impossible ever to be sure just what topics are or are not really dealt with in any given passage, nevertheless one has the impression that these questions remain unanswered.[1]

But still, two points at any rate are clearly visible: this subject is about what actions mean to us, and it remains within the wider bounds of sociology. Now there is a paradox here. Subjectivity used to be always with us, like original sin or B.O., a predicament, encumbrance or embarrassment, and not a privilege or an achievement. It was an inescapable feature of the human condition, which we knew only too well, too intimately. Some of us might yearn to escape from it, and seek techniques for overcoming it, but we had no need whatever to *establish* it. Like the strollers on Prince's Street, we thought we knew full well we were sane, and when challenged to *prove* it, found the challenge redundant, offensive, or amusing. What we needed least of all were special methods for establishing, identifying, or discovering the features of our own subjectivity. We had privileged access to our own private selves and meanings, and though some philosophers tried (not at all convincingly) to tell us we had nothing of the kind, at least they did not insult us further by telling us that *they* had privileged access to *our* subjectivity...No, no, that would really have been too much.

Here one might say, with that snide mixture of resentment and envy which characterises Europeans talking about America, that Americans really do not do things by halves. As a character in a *New Yorker* cartoon might have observed, by Jove, if we are going to have subjectivity, we sure *are* going to have some subjectivity. No half measures here. Subjectivity is going to be put on a proper scientific basis. No longer will it be handled in that impressionistic, slapdash, literary, well...subjective way, in which it used to be handled, if handled at all, Before Garfinkel.

Note that it is all rather like Watsonian Behaviourism in reverse. And it has just the same drive, panache, and messianism. The Behaviourists said that 'consciousness' had no meaning; there was no such thing. Now we are told, with similar fervour, that consciousness

---

[1] For an excellent discussion of such problems, see Bill McSweeney, 'Meaning, Context and Situation', *European Journal of Sociology*, 14, 1973, 137–53.

(renamed accountability), is all over the place, there is no end of it, it's coming out of everyone's ears. It is indeed not entirely clear whether *anything else* exists. Perhaps it is objectivity which has no meaning now? Anyway, whether or not the new subjectivity is exhaustive and all-embracing or not, it is absolutely clear that there is lots and lots of it about, enough to keep us all going for ever, whether as its investigators or as men ('members'), and so without fear of it being some time absorbed into some impersonal, cold objectivity. This warranty, I suspect, is a very important element in the appeal of Ethnomethodology. And note that, of course, it is central that subjectivity is not merely vindicated, as *a* realm amongst others: on the contrary, it is made, if not quite exhaustive, at least very crucial and creative. It is our subjectivity which *makes* the external world. Its independence and externality, its hard *given* quality, are illusory. We, or at least our meaning-conferring activities, are really the masters and creators. This is a very old doctrine in a very new idiom. The movement stands squarely in the Idealist tradition.

Nevertheless – and this also is important, and is what gives the ideas and style of the movement its distinctive flavour – this is a cult of subjectivity *in the idiom of that scientism which has for some time been the dominant language of the American social sciences.* This is why that reference to Parsons's precision of thought was so significant. These guys are, one might say, the romantic reaction to Parsons's classicism, but within the same language.

Phenomenology is like prose, we've all been speaking it for ages, though apparently it takes a guru to tell us of it. 'James bring me my slippers' is indeed ethnomethodology par excellence. It uses accountable, indexical methods to create a world. . .indeed.

First, American sociologists made a big fuss about the scientific nature of their methods, concepts, language, techniques. They were certainly stilted and possibly bore some resemblance to science. Later, some of them decided to abandon the aspiration to objectivity, impersonality and abstractness, associated with science. They could of course simply say – we are abandoning those aspirations. But no, they call it *phenomenology* instead. The abandonment of striving for method becomes *one further method*, even deeper, more mysterious and esoteric than those which preceded it, and retaining arcane language.

The idea that each man creates his own world, presumably as he wills, precludes the imposition of extraneous rules (e.g. of logic) on him. Furthermore, creating one's own world, and scientific study of the creation of that world, are the same thing: that is what 'ethno-methodology' *means* (i.e. using the methods of the ethnos which is being investigated, instead of imposing extraneous ones). So the charity or courtesy which tolerates any abandonment of logical or other order in the object of inquiry, is, in a sense quite properly, extended to the inquiry itself, which then combines all the wildness of a private unconstrained world with all the abstruse obscurity of sociological 'theory'. The accounts are both private and abstruse, wild and jargon-ridden. They freely violate the logic and grammar of the terms employed. This doubly based unintelligibility endows them with a depth which inspires awe and admiration in the adepts.

Though they do resemble the romantic poets in their fondness for the humble, ordinary aspects of life, in their penchant for somewhat self-consciously seeing these homely things 'for the first time, really', the continuities of their idiom with the scientistic style of thought and expression are at least as important as the revolutionary breaks which they bring. Let us face it, they do not write well, and their stylistic failings spring from these very features – careless neologism, a slapdash indifference to precision and rigour in exposition, an eager willingness to say more and to say it again rather than refining what one had already said, and so forth – which have been noticeable in the sociological world from which they sprang long before their own particular twist was ever heard of. The 1960s were indeed a revolutionary and romantic period, for well known reasons, at least on the major campuses and in California. If one wanted to project or translate its distinctive mood, the cult of subjectivity, the rejection of external structures, into the language and *problematik* of sociology, then one should quite naturally end up with something just like Ethnomethodology.

So this movement would be the manner in which the subjective, 'Californian' mood enters the otherwise sober, scientistic, sociological segments of the groves of academe. If this social location of the movement is correct, it is dramatically symbolised by various external characteristics of the movement – for instance, its distinctive lecturing style, which certainly owes more to Elvis Presley than it does to Talcott Parsons – the tendency to twist and writhe, to make love to the microphone, to convey by every gesture that spontaneity, subjectivity and self-generated continuity and flow are everything, as opposed to formal structure and extraneous rules. Or again, when I had the unforgettable pleasure of attending a Conference on

Ethnomethodology in Edinburgh, it was noticeable, and I think significant, that the quality and quantity of ethno-chicks surpassed by far those of chicks of any other movement which I have ever observed – even Far Out Left Chicks, not to mention ordinary anthropo-chicks, socio-chicks or (dreadful thought) philosophy chicks. All this must indicate that there is a great continuity between the culture of this movement and that of the rising youth culture, which supplies it with these perks. The movement has magic, and it has it for the young.

Though continuous with the culture of the *seccesio iuventutis*, it is worth making a reservation here: the opting out from square and objective values is, as indeed is most of the dissidence of the young generation itself, *far* from total or definitive.

At a very earthy level, there is not the least suggestion that the movement or its members spurn secure positions or material rewards. Not at all. In general, there is only a stress on subjectivity, not on rebellion. Dissidence only enters, if at all, in as far as it is implied by subjectivity: the appeal of the movement and of its ideas in the field of criminology and related studies is clearly connected with the view that deviance is in the eye of the beholder, or rather in the concepts, the labelling practices of the beholders. This facilitates, not so much a re-valuation of values directly, as reconceptualization of concepts. . .and this may be directed primarily and naturally at those acts of classification of square society which seem harsh, punitive and censorious. Thus rebelliousness enters only in so far as there is a tendency to loosen, corrode, undermine the order-imposing and order-enforcing ideas of society. In other ways, the establishment order does not appear to be seriously questioned. It is indeed difficult to see how it could be questioned, for criticism would seem to presuppose some objective norm or vantage-point, and it is not clear how such a thing could become available to spirits so deeply attached to their own subjectivity. The movement confers liberation and a kind of sense of superiority on its adherents, but does not require or encourage them to assault the established order.

This absence of any kind of sustained subversiveness is interesting. (The dissidence is largely restricted to hairstyle, lecturing posture and methodology.) No-one knows whether the dissident mood of an important segment of youth in the 1960s was a foretaste of a more general and radical coming dissidence of nearly *everyone*, as ever more and more people benefit from and become sated with affluence, or whether on the contrary it was merely part of a permanent

American pendulum, due to be followed by another wave of McCarthyite conformity, as of the late 1940s and the 1950s. Just suppose that the latter alternative is the correct one, and that we are due for another period of conservatism: the particular movement under discussion has little to fear from an eventual backlash, unlike some other elements in the life of recent years. It is not actually committed to denying any article of the American constitution or credo (or at any rate, no more than is required by an implicit need to cast doubt on any assertions aspiring to objectivity); and more important, it is certainly in no way committed to any un-American loyalty. If the witchhunts come again, its members ought, in all logic at least, to be safe and out of harm's way. In this respect, as in some others, the movement is reminiscent of American Freudianism, and the strictures made on it by Erich Fromm.[2] It offers a moral and conceptual bolthole in each person's subjectivity, but, over and above the implicit devaluation of the objective, external order, it is not subversive, but quietistic and a-political. In somewhat phenomenological spirit, perhaps, it suspends or brackets the external order, rather than inciting to violence against it.

Our contention, that the movement represents the projection, into the language and institutions of North American sociology, of the cultural posture of semi-dissident youth of the 1960s, can also be illustrated from the most celebrated of the ethnomethodological innovations in method – the device which could be described as *throwing* someone (conceptually) by suddenly acting on assumptions quite other than those which the other person takes as self-evident: the son behaves as if he were a lodger, or vice versa. The otherwise invisibly translucent subjective assumptions, pervading the world, are *made* visibly by being made 'anthropologically strange', through being deliberately defied and flouted by wilfully 'inappropriate' conduct.

The point of such an exercise is fairly obvious: it highlights the interpretative, meaning-conferring activities of participants, by shocking them out of treating these tacit assumptions as self-evident, and this it does by blandly defying them. The irritation engendered by the defiance of a tacit assumption (this is not how *sons* behave. . .) has as its effect that at least the assumption thereafter ceases to be tacit.

Now this famous device, which is virtually the heraldic emblem of the movement, is clearly an application of a general principle

[2] Cf. Erich Fromm: *Sigmund Freud's Mission* (London, 1959), pp. 105 and 106.

which underlies most of the sartorial and other customs of the dissident generation. One wears, blandly and without any stressed irony even, clothes whose historic significance was once definite, formalised and circumscribed, and one does so in contexts which are different from or opposed to the rules which had once governed the use of the habit in question. Thus for instance the anti-Vietnam-war generation had a special penchant for the use of military uniforms, notably the uniform of the army to whose activities it was most opposed, with NCO's stripes and all. As a writer in a Sunday paper chat column observed, the rules for dressing up are simply that you must dress as for an occasion, but *not* the occasion to which you are actually going. For instance, a full dress SS uniform (preferably worn with a Star of David), is acceptable virtually anywhere, *except* at a reunion of old comrades in Munich. The similarity between these sartorial principles and the methodological device under discussion is obvious. Clothes are roles and roles are clothes. There is a quiet defiance of a rigid, 'objectifying' system of roles, displayed by deliberate behaviour such as could only seem wildly incongruous *if* that objective system of roles and norms still retained its full authority. But by quietly and systematically defying it, one thus deprives that system of its authority. This can be and is also practised in spheres other than dress. American girls from the more expensive colleges sometimes indulge a kind of polite, wide-eyed, light-hearted, un-argumentative non-comprehension or non-comment on the assumptions of other generations, and a similarly *voulu* un-troubled concern-free spontaneity in implementing some weird alternative conventions; all this is accompanied by a marked refusal to send out the signals which normally indicate reception or recognition of message – which is meant to convey both total liberation from the conceptual constraints of others, and easy comfort, at-home-ness, in some other and more natural set. In a way, this is a democratisation of the aristocratic maxim – *Never explain!* It is indeed important for this particular technique, to refrain from argument or attempt at persuasion, for that implies anxiety and the existence of some shared and obligatory norms in terms of which the argument would proceed. They neither explain nor question, but proceed in their wide-eyed way. There is no need to explain or to justify, only for each party to do and to think its own thing, in the secure knowledge that no common law binds us all and all kinds of convention are equally possible.

The ethnomethodologists have taken this spirit and device and turned it into a research ploy. This is the sociology of *drag*, extended from apparel to concepts and roles – plausibly enough. In a sense, this sociology stands Durkheim on his head. Durkheim's central preoccupation was the problem of conceptual constraint – the social constraint *on* concepts, and concepts *as* social constraint. This sociology is preoccupied, not with the constraint, but on the contrary with the *contingency* of concepts, roles and norms. It employs their easy and light-hearted substitutability to bring home that very contingency. It is perhaps a little unclear whether its central point is the sheer existence of a human world created by our own labelling activities, or whether the stress is, in somewhat existentialist spirit, on the freely chosen, un-compulsory, contingent nature of those humanly-created worlds. ('Le *self service* de sa conscience libre', as J.-F. Revel characterised Sartre's early position.) Presumably it is a bit of both.

Something should perhaps be said about what seem to be the implications of the method for the style and organisation of the movement. This is a matter of interpreting the meaning of their conduct, as it strikes one, in the light of what one knows about their ideas: perhaps a regrettably impressionistic procedure, though it is unclear on what grounds, from its own premisses, the movement could object to it. Perhaps it could. Be that as it may, for better or worse, it may be worth while to record and interpret one's impressions.

The consequence of the meaningful, 'accountable' nature of human and social reality is that there is endlessly rich material ever at one's disposal: one need merely *look* and record the plethora of meaning in every situation that surrounds one, and comment on it, and there you are. . .Practitioners of the art do indeed give one the impression that they do not prepare their performances carefully, but prefer to *ad lib* on whatever is is front of them, in front of their mental vision, and then to go on and on and on and on. To come prepared with a well-organised argument might perhaps be seen as a kind of treason (all structures were treason for the young of the 1960s); and it would indicate, presumably, an insensitivity to the indexical nature of human/social reality, to the here-now, 'reflexive' and 'incarnate' character of 'accountable' practices. The consequence is that the performances of these practitioners do indeed tend to be very 'reflexive' indeed, in the sense of being largely about themselves. Here there is a further parallel with psycho-analysis and its pre-occupation with its own therapeutic relationship. As ethnomethodology does not claim to cure anything, one cannot say that it is itself the disease which it endeavours to cure, but one wonders whether it does not consist largely of the phenomenological account of itself.

So it is reasonable, in terms of their own ideas, that the practitioners should improvise rather than come prepared, and that they should talk about themselves and their own immediate *Lebenswelt*: they bring us what is obvious, and yet it is meant to have the great freshness of that which is *really* seen for the first time. Previously we had ignored it, just because it is so close, intimate, and seemingly obvious. If what the practitioner tells you seems to you obvious but not fresh, well then – is it not because you *still* haven't *really* seen it? Here once again there is a host of parallels, logical and stylistic, with psycho-analysis.

It is not quite so immediately obvious why the practitioners should have this tendency to go on and on and on and on, the marked unstoppability trait. From inside their ideas, one could extract the following rationale: anyone who stops, displays remarkable poverty of his own *Lebenswelt*! He has run out of things to see and comment, with all the freshness of that which is obvious yet seen for the first time, really. . .so that to trail off into silence is to betray defeat, exhaustion of vision or perception. This reasoning, tacit or other, may well be *a* factor; but I suspect there are others.

There is an aphorism about the difference between American and British styles of conversation. British talk is meant to be like tennis, with the ball going forward and back, the harder, faster and more accurate, the better. American conversation is like cricket: he who holds the floor acts like a batsman, hanging on as long as he can, the longer the better, till the hostess rules him *out*. The lecturing style of the practitioners is certainly of this latter kind. They hang on like grim death, resisting fiercely all attempts to bowl them out.

But there are probably reasons for this comportment over and above it being part of a wider culture. One has the impression that the movement is fairly *tense*, anticipating and resisting aggression, both inside but also, and above all, from the outside. This is a messianic movement, possessed of much charisma and magic, and in exclusive possession of an important new revelation. The magic which it has for so many followers clearly means that there is much to gain and lose, in terms of admiration, devotion and all the rewards, psychic or other, of charisma. In one way it is a protestant movement (every man a clerk, for every man has access to the new world of 'accountability'), but it uses catholic means (i.e., it is ecstatic and experiential rather than sober and scripturalist). This combination must presumably lead to internal tensions. A whole community of charisma-endowed mediators-with-the-obvious-but-newly-revealed-world cannot but tread on each other's toes. The protestant principle gives free entry into the priesthood (can there be privileged access to the *Lebenswelt?*), but the catholic techniques prevent the use of rational–legal sober methods of settlement of demarcation and priority disputes and conflicts. So the seeds of tension must be there, internally. And that there is fear of and hostility to external critics, is only too manifest.

Now look at the defensive tactics available. Hanging on and batting on relentlessly is a fairly good device, as long as you hold the attention of the audience; if you do, you have passed the ordeal. This is further rationalised by seeing the critic and questioner as one further role, one further artful device, and describing it and him in that style which comes naturally to the movement, rather than concentrating on the *content* of his queries or criticisms. One participant in the Edinburgh Conference commended the evasion of posed questions, by stressing the 'dangerous role of the questioner', for it is he who *chooses the questions*. . .(who else could?)

Under criticism, there is a shift to, so to speak, the third person: instead of discussing the criticism and its logical merits, you switch to *describing* the conflict situation, the critic, his stance, and so on. This in a way neutralises him, at worst puts him and the position he criticised on the same level, as fellow participants in the same social, 'accountable' situation; but in the end it does even better than this – it by-passes the issue of the content and logical validity of the criticism, which is demoted, so to speak, from the extra-territorial status of a critic, to becoming but one further character inside the play, and the play is then interpreted by the rules *of* the movement itself.

This tendency to switch from considering the critic's argument, to *describing* him and the conflict situation is of course strikingly parallel with psycho-analytic procedures for dealing with criticism, but it also fits in well with the *ad lib*, here–now descriptive style favoured by the movement. Instead of a prepared lecture, the practitioner seems to prefer the stance – a meaningful thing happened to me on the way to the lecture. . .and then he goes on and on; and any criticism can then be treated as one further meaningful, 'accountable' event. Thus every assertion put forward by a member of the movement has a double status: as an assertion it is, presumably, true or false, and liable to confrontation with argument or evidence. But, as an *event* in the lives and world-constructions both of the propounder and of the critic, it must be seen as such, and the criticism interpreted as an attempt by the critic to impose himself on the original propounder. Seen in this light, the force of the counter-argument or counter-evidence to the assertion is no longer relevant. The original propounder, as qualified practitioner of the movement, is of course entitled to decide which level is to be invoked, and of course he can and does invoke the second level when in trouble. Moreover, to clinch and cover the whole procedure, there is a meta-theory which asserts that what happens at the second level is legiti-mate and perhaps the only subject matter of sociology, so that the criticism-avoiding ploy, far from being objectionable, is perfectly justified, indeed the very model of sound method. All this is of course perfectly paralleled in depth psychology.

This strong *reflexive* tendency means that the objective world evaporates, asymptotically approaches zero, as perhaps it is meant to, just as psycho-analysis tends to retreat from theory or interpretation to stress on the therapeutic here–now relationship itself. It is like the man who was so entranced with watching his reactions to the play that he failed to watch the play. In the end, is there any play? The movement has not merely discovered indexicality for sociology, it is itself the most indexical thing going.

One should add that despite the mystical–communicative stance of its relation to its chosen reality (as opposed to the use of pre-estab-lished rules for determining what is to count as true), which must encourage free-lance individual messianism, one nevertheless has the strong impression that the important practitioners have a well developed, and at least partially enforced, sense of hierarchy and of ranking among themselves. The most conspicuous unwillingness to formulate and articulate the abstract, general principles of the doctrine (rationalised variously, e.g., by appeal to its rapid develop-ment which makes *everything* out of date), seems inspired at least in part by the fact that licences to articulate versions of doctrine are only granted very sparingly by leaders, and are seldom delegated, or practised in their absence. The leader's authority would seem sufficient to discourage defiance of this custom. In any case, caught between the danger of such disapproval and disavowal from above, which involves losing face inside the movement, and on the other hand perhaps being verbally defeated by an outside critic, the practitioner may in any case have little temptation to transgress in this matter. Also the subjective nature both of the reality under investigation, and the methods employed for investigating it, give the practitioner, if tempted to make a bid for doctrinal independence from his leader or leaders, little confidence in having some independent outside norm to which he could appeal to sustain and defend his stand. Heretics in this Church have no scripture which they could invoke against some Council of Constance. As stated, this movement is protestant only in its implicit egalitarianism, the inevitably universal accessibility of the realm of 'accountable acts' which it has discovered; but it is *not* protestant in possessing some unambiguous external repository of truth, some Scripture, to which the man accused of heresy could appeal in order to defend himself. They have discovered accountability, but it is not clear that they are accountable to anyone or anything. The world which validates assertions is a private world. The lack of extraneous norms, as reactionaries often remind us, can make us *less* rather than more free.

The movement is a species of idealism, with its stress on a world-creating subjectivity, and like others of its kind, it faces a problem when it comes to the notion of *error*. How can we be in error about a world which we ourselves have made? The problem is only accentuated by a specific feature which we have already commented on, namely the ubiquity, pervasiveness, and contrast-lessness of its material: an ethnomethodologist does not need to prepare and bring his material, it is always to hand, always underfoot. But if so, what could count as *not* being material? Not only is error itself a bit of a mystery, but even the mere absence of the proper kind of cognition is barely conceivable. When would we be without this material? – and when could it ever be mistaken?

At this specific level, there is once again a parallel between ethnomethodology and psycho-analysis. The ubiquity of psycho-analytic material is explained differently, it is true, by means of a theory concerning the revealing role of free-association. In ethnomethodology, it is the pervasiveness of meaning, 'accounting', which does the same job. But how, in principle, does or can psycho-analysis distinguish between raw free association and valid interpretation? Similarly, how can ethnomethodology distinguish between any old bit of accounting, and the kind of accounting that can be hailed as a piece of *science*? In these systems, the very boundary between *knowing* and *being* would seem to disappear. Knowing would seem to reduce to exemplification, to the concrete presence, so to speak, or perhaps only one which is authoritatively conjured up by the Master

Practitioner of the new technique? How can one distinguish? How indeed. In psycho-analysis, this problem of demarcation or distinction between the raw object and interpreted understanding of it is solved through ritual status: the movement distinguishes various sacramental states, and valid interpretations can be distinguished from raw free association in terms of the identity of the propounder. *Formally*, ethnomethodology cannot do this, for, as far as I know, it lacks any such theory of sacramental states or priestly status. In practice, one has the impression that nevertheless, it does employ such a method: that its hierarchy and structure, though unformalised and not underpinned by any explicit theory, is very clearly articulated and present to the minds of its members, who can tell the status of an 'account' from the status of the accoun*ter*.

So much for one's impressionistic profile of the movement. To be properly understood, however it needs also to be set against a wider background. It does not stand alone in the world; on the contrary, it is but one specimen or example of much wider and more important trends.

As stated, it can usefully be seen as Behaviourism-in-reverse – the enthusiastic resuscitation, the 'scientific' vindication of the fact that we all live in our private worlds. Privacy is no longer abandoned to the Joyces and Prousts of this world, but can be formally taught and most scientifically authenticated.

But the contemporary resuscitation of the human world, of life as lived and conceptualised, as it is 'accounted', *in* life rather than in abstract explanation, has certain distinctive features, which are exemplified not merely by this movement, but also by others. The formulation of the Inner/Outer opposition is no longer individual and sensuous, but collective and conceptual. This might be characterised as the Husserlian rather than the Berkeleian way to re-enchantment, to the vindication of the *lived world*, against the impersonality of non-indexical science. Berkeley, wishing to avoid a cold and scientific/materialistic world, stressed that the real is what is perceived, and thus gave us a warm world of sensuous consciousness-only. But that was also, notoriously, a lonely and individualistic world, within which it became very difficult to give an account of the existence of *other* consciousnesses. Now *that* is not at all the contemporary way to re-enchantment: the characteristic contemporary way is through *concepts*, not through sensations. Our daily concepts are vindicated by appealing to the alleged fact that they constitute, pervade or construct the world we live in. The Lebenswelt is not the sensory screen of a lonely individual, but the shared conceptual wealth of a society, culture, or language. .

Behaviourism, through its dramatic exaggerations, symbolised that cold disenchanted world in which, supposedly, only scientific concepts were allowed, and others, especially those connected with introspection and consciousness, were proscribed. Movements such as ethnomethodology re-legitimate our daily notions, by making them simultaneously the object *and* the tool of a reputedly respectable scientific inquiry. (It is of course the fact that they are simultaneously both objects and tools which leads to the vertiginous confusion of object and method, in which the inquiry generates that which it would investigate, and in which the object of inquiry disappears into the investigation, and in which it is difficult to see how any investigation could ever be falsified, or how the investigator's authority could ever be challenged. This is one of the ways in which they acquire immunity, a benefit of clergy which is evidently claimed by the practitioners of this mystery.) If sociologists study this, or use it in their inquiries, then, plainly, it *must* be real. Thus the movement in effect offers a comforting, reassuring, home-restoring ontology. There is a story about German students who were told by their Professor of Philosophy that they, the students, had a *real existence*, and who went wild with joy on being given this information. Ethnomethodology also teaches us that our daily lived world and experience are real, and we can and do rejoice in this.

But note that it is done by vindicating our daily concepts. (I am not suggesting for one moment that Berkeley's way, achieving a similar end by absolutising the world of our senses, was a better way.) And here there are some problems and dangers.

Our world is indeed socially generated by the concepts we employ. The concepts we employ therefore also constrain us, for they 'make' the world in which we act. So be it. There is obviously some degree of truth in all this.

The conceptual generation and saturation of our world is of course ethnomethodology's debt to phenomenology. It is the stress on concepts, rather than sensations, as world-bricks, or at least the bricks of *our* world, which sharply distinguishes this tradition from that of empiricism.[3] It is our concepts which make our world, and so constrain us.

[3] Cf. Michael Phillipson and Maurice Roche: 'Phenomenology, Sociology and the Study of Deviance', published in *Deviance and*

But consider the dangers here. There is a kind of a slide.

(1) Concepts *constrain*.

(2) *Concepts* constrain.

(3) It is *mere* concepts which constrain.

(4) *Only* concepts ever constrain.

There is a tendency to slide from 1 through 2 and 3 to 4. There is thus a tendency to end in a position which might be characterised, paraphrasing Freud, as the fantasy of the *Allmacht des Begriffes*, the omnipotence of the concept.

It is not at all clear that the movement under discussion does slide, unambiguously and irrevocably, into any such position. For one thing, its own formulations of its own position are simply not clear enough to enable one to tell just where it stands on this crucial issue. More positively, there are passages in Garfinkel's 'What is Ethnomethodology?' which could bear the interpretation that they are designed to ward off this very danger. But, whether or not it can be shown that the movement is guilty of this extreme position, it is also not easy to show that it is innocent of it. And, most certainly, it cannot, given the topics and problems which interest it, evade the question. What then is the relation of conceptual to *other* constraints? If it has failed to deal with it in a lucid manner, then this must be held against it. It simply is not an issue which it can evade.

The truth of the matter seems to me this: concepts do indeed constrain us. But they are not the *only* things which constrain us. Our life is lived in an environment whose constraints are at least in part physical, in the sense of being independent of the conventions, ideas, and expectations of the society which harbours us. Concepts do not kill or nourish; but killing and nourishing are socially important. The two kinds of constraint, conceptual and extraneous, pervade each other and are fused with each other in a complex and bewildering manner. For instance, a physical imperative may leave open a number of ways of executing its demands, not all of which however are socially permissible, 'conceivable'. Or a conceptual

Social Control, edited by Paul Rock and Mary McIntosh, London, 1973.

This paper is a remarkable demonstration of the possibility of stating the ideas of this movement with admirable lucidity. In other words, the smoke-screen of obscurity and gobbledygook which accompanies, alas, some of the official, authorised manifestos of the movement, may possibly be indispensable for inducing the reverent trance of some of the followers, but is not actually inherent in the ideas themselves.

imperative may be disguised as a physical one, to give it an extraneous authority. And so on. The complications are endless. It is no doubt one of the tasks of sociology to disentangle this. But how well can it be done by a 'methodology' which seems to have so strong a predilection towards the conceptual? Even if it does not formally preclude the Other, does it retain any real sensitivity for it?

And it is open to the suspicion that it is indeed defective in such sensitivity. This point has been forcefully made by Professor Zygmunt Bauman:

> Ethnomethodologists claim to have a particular knack for descending to the level of 'everyday life' from the abstract heights of the official sociology inhabited by imaginary homunculi. But it is a strange everyday life they descend to: hardly anybody eats there his everyday bread, even less bakes it, let alone earns it – though, as a naïve observer would say: eating and baking and earning bread seem to constitute eighty percent of the everyday life of eighty percent of everyday people.[4]

Perhaps Bauman's hypothetical observer is indeed naïve: in California, where the movement is based, baking bread certainly, and earning it most probably, do *not* take up eighty percent of the time of that segment of the population which provides ethnomethodology with its avid clientele. We shall have occasion to return to this point, for the local and specific roots of the movement are interesting and significant. Still, in as far as the movement claims to have a universal human validity, Bauman's point is important. This is not *everyone's* Lebenswelt. In Leeds and in Poland, people still need to earn their daily bread, and in Poland daily bread can perhaps still be, as it is in the Lord's Prayer, problematical. But all this highlights the movement's lack of sensitivity to constraints other than conceptual ones.

There is a further point. It is important to distinguish between concepts *as* constraints, and the constraints *on* concepts. Concepts (or their absence) are indeed *a* means of social control: they inhibit options by making them unthinkable, or only thinkable with opprobrium. But concepts and their authority, such as it is, are not

---

[4] 'Culture, Values and Science of Society'. Inaugural lecture delivered by Professor Z. Bauman on 7 February 1972, and published in *The University of Leeds Review*, 15, no. 2, October 1972.

self-explanatory: the bounds of applicability of a notion needs itself to be explained.

Cancerous semantic growths are happily not common, but they can and do occur: the problem of deviance and conformity arises *for* the delimitation of meanings, as it does for any other human activity. This boundary-maintenance needs to be explained, not taken for granted. Again, the movement under discussion is ironically open to the suspicion that it encourages us to take this for granted, that it obscures the very existence of the problem. The world of meanings or accounts is not endlessly permissive – but how are the limits set?

That these dangers or insensitivities are present, as dangers, in the general attitude adopted and encouraged by the movement, can hardly be in dispute. It cannot be demonstrated that these are more than dangers, more than mere possibilities. But the reason why it cannot be *shown* is not so much because the dangers have been carefully avoided, as because the slapdash, wilfully obscure and undisciplined verbosity makes it impossible to be sure just precisely what it is that is being said. In such conditions, neither guilt nor innocence are evident.

It is worth considering the general and specific roots of this cult of subjectivity. The subjective tends to become an object of a cult only when it has become precarious. The cult of the subjective, the human, the conceptual, the Lebenswelt, gains in importance as a reaction to an external, mechanical, mathematised, impersonal world.

All this merely helps locate the movement within a much wider, indeed an immense tradition, which starts perhaps with Vico's reaction to Descartes, and reaches its height with the romantic and idealist reaction to the Enlightenment. Fichte, telling us how the ego rolls its own world, rather than accepting it ready-supplied in conventional realist fashion by some external Other, might well be claimed as a key ancestor by the contemporary representatives of this attitude. But the really important and formative influence behind them is of course phenomenology.

Edmund Husserl's central idea was simple. It was to put philosophy on a scientific basis, and to endow it with a special field of inquiry at the same time, by giving it as its special area the world 'bracketed', the world as we experience/conceptualise it, but so to speak *suspended*, without reference to its reality or lack of it. We were to look at our world *as* our world, and no more.

Now the whole idea of 'bracketing' the world, of looking at it as
we live it, seems to imply that someone else is doing something else,
is somehow refraining from bracketing, and *is* judging the world.
And, indeed, this is so. The phenomenological suspension, which is to
give us the world as we live it, in a kind of pure state, does stand
contrasted with some other attitude, which *does* have its doubts
about the reality of the Lebenswelt.

It is here that phenomenology makes its crucial mistake.

When the Lebenswelt really *was* a Lebenswelt, no-one called it by
any such name. Try to convey to a member of a primitive society the
need to see the world he lives in *as* the world he lives in: he does
indeed live in it, but he would have difficulty in grasping what *other*
world he is meant to contrast it with. The Lebenswelt and the world
are then one.

The Lebenswelt has only become conceptualisable as such, has
become so to speak visible, just because we no longer altogether live
in it. We do *not* live in our Lebenswelt – not altogether. It has
become, as the ethnomethodologists might say, anthropologically
strange. It is no longer *the* world; it is already a *mere* 'Lebenswelt',
it is *already* bracketed, not by phenomenology, but by life itself.
We already see it as *a* vision, amongst others, and a somewhat suspect
one, which is authoritative only in its own terms and by its own
interior standards, but about whose standing as a whole we have
our doubts. We know that it *was* our world; we are not sure whether
it is *the* world. We suspect that ultimate and effective reality is
articulated in some other idiom, that the world which can claim
our real cognitive allegiance is not the old inherited Lebenswelt, but
contains it, as one very partial, selective, perspective-distorted vision
within it.

The Lebenswelt is now like a living-room in a house in which there
are many other rooms. It is a kind of parlour which contains the
family's antiques and which has a pleasing olde worlde air about it.
This is perhaps where the family meets on formal occasions but this
is not where important work is done or important business transacted.

Such is the Lebenswelt. The irony is, we have only come to be
aware of it when we no longer live in it, at any rate not exclusively
or predominantly. Phenomenology claims to 'suspend' it, to suspend judgement about its reality-status, to see it simply *as* a
Lebenswelt. But that, precisely, is what it no longer is. And by
pretending to 'suspend' it, phenomenology in fact covertly fortifies
it, it ratifies it by a kind of sleight-of-hand; by seeming to exempt it

from even entering and competing in the scientific reality-stakes, it implies that at least simply *qua* Lebenswelt, in its more modest pretensions, its status cannot be in any doubt. Qua Lebenswelt at least it is secure and vindicated...But that is not so. The world we 'live' in is itself unstable, shifting, multiple, complex and ramified. Trivial day-to-day decisions may *perhaps* be taken against a background picture articulated in old, homely, inherited, Lebenswelty terms; but when it comes to important decisions, we look to the reality behind the muddled shorthand of daily convenience.

Ethnomethodology has inherited this unintended and half-covert ambiguity from phenomenology. Does it *ratify* the 'accountable' world of daily experience, or does it highlight its optional, problematical nature? It does both, in effect. It makes a fuss of its importance, but also stresses its problematical nature. Yet it stresses the ultimacy of that world more than its problematical nature. Thereby it ratifies it.

But within this general tradition, what distinguishes ethnomethodology perhaps is that there seems to be a special stress on the contingent, self-created nature of the world we inhabit. It is an artful achievement, that it appears to erect such a world at all...but the artfulness could equally be deployed at constructing some other world. The fragility or contingency of the effects achieved by this 'artfulness' seem to be something specially highlighted by the practitioners of this technique and style. And this would bring us to the specific social roots of this movement. Its general roots are the need for re-enchantment, for ratification of the old human world. But there are also specific roots.

Max Weber thought that rational industrial production brought with it the cold 'disenchanted' vision of the world, from which a few self-indulgent intellectuals escaped by means of decorating their private chapels with all kinds of exotica and antiques. Daniel Bell has argued[5] that there is an incoherence between the orderly and rational organisation of our production, and current culture, with its rejection of structure and discipline. But that may be a mistake. Perhaps the two are quite congruent now. A really advanced industrial society does not any longer require cold rationality from its consumers; at most, it may demand it of its producers. But as it gets more advanced, the ratio both of personnel and of their time is

---

[5] 'The Cultural Contradictions of Capitalism' in *The Public Interest*, no. 21, Autumn 1970, republished in *Capitalism Today*, ed. D. Bell and I. Kristol, Basic Books, 1971.

tilted progressively more and more in favour of consumption, as against production. More consumers, fewer producers; less time at work, more at leisure. And in consumption, all tends towards ease and facility of manipulation rather than rigour and coldness. A modern piece of machinery may be a marvel of sustained, abstract, rigorous engineering thought; but its operating controls must be such that they can easily and rapidly be internalised by the average user, without arduousness or strain. So the user lives in a world in which most things have an air of easy 'natural', 'spontaneous' manipulability. And why should not the world itself be conceived in this manner? Why should cognition, conceptual construction, not come just as easily as handling the now so-simple controls of a car? The culture of undisciplined spontaneity mirrors, rather than defies, the economic base of our society.

Why not indeed? This general *facility* of the world and of cognition, inherent in the tilting of the balance in favour of the life of consumers rather than producers, is further reinforced in America by the populist, anti-intellectual tradition, the protestantism of the heart rather than of the Book, which has prepared the ground for such doctrines. So when the general need to re-enchant the world is felt, when warm individuality, privacy, subjectivity are to be vindicated against the external, the abstract, the impersonal, then a cult of easy, spontaneous, immediate cognition or erection-of-the-world comes naturally as the expected thing. The modernist theologians have already habituated us to an Instant God, created in no time by mere 'concern', or by the mere act of worship. Here we also have an Instant World, and an Instant Subjectivity, the two supplied jointly as two complementary products.

Thus the very general roots are the widely shared need, to vindicate the human world as lived (or rather as it *used* to be lived) – against the encroachment of the world as seen through those cold abstract concepts which confer explanatory and manipulative control, at the cost of ignoring the individual, the specific, the private. But, in the most 'modern' state of the richest and most industrially advanced country in the world, the private and the subjective is both in greater danger, and *also* more free from constraint, than it is anywhere else. The combination of rootlessness and willingness to innovate, the American freedom from excessive deference to some keepers of Cultural Norms (all traits acclaimed as an American birth-right), in a very newly settled and very rich land, have led to a situation where *anything* is possible, anything goes. The homogeneity of car, freeway, supermarket, suburb and countryside, the impersonal grid landscape, somehow coexists with an extraordinary liberation, permitting any spiritual, sartorial, architectural, sexual fantasy. On the sub-structure of the most advanced and most standardised industrial society, there emerges a kind of luxuriant and luxurious, willing anomie...And who is to say in the end which is superstructure and which is substructure?

Official sociology (which on the whole the ethnomethodologists do not claim to supersede, but only to complement), with its somewhat stilted terminology, its search of general theory constructed on a rectilinear and abstract design, is like that linear system of freeways and grid suburban streets and houses; whilst these wild techniques for seizing or eliciting the hidden private life are like those oriental esoteric shrines and practices which yet flourish in the impersonal concrete wilderness. So the privacy which is investigated here is not so much human subjectivity in general, which is often constrained, anguished, and fused, harmoniously or painfully, with the externalised aspects of human life; rather it is this very specific, volatile, unconstrained, *fantaisiste*, Californian kind of subjectivity. It seizes the spirit of a conceptual constraint which is more conceptual than constraining, in which the optional aspect of roles or concepts is more conspicuous than their compulsiveness.

The research devices they employ would, in a caste society, mean pollution; in an estate society, breach of the law; and in an old class society, social solecism. But here, they are possible. The lid is off: neither poverty nor deference to authority constrain cultural expression which is both expansive and luxurious, and yet is somehow haunted by a sense of its own contingency. The Durkheimian problem of conceptual necessity is replaced by the account of conceptual 'artfulness' and contingency; and this is perhaps symbolised by the flamboyant manner in which the practitioners conflate or oscillate between a professorial and a pop or DJ style of exposition. Yet, at the same time, they do not altogether defy or forget the socio-economic base of their own liberation, of *le* self service *de leur conscience libre*. Their method offers a kind of do-it-yourself-kit for everyone to make/find their own subjectivity: and the need to supply such a thing at all suggests that the recipients are no longer all too sure that they really have a privacy or subjectivity at all. They need to be *shown* their own subjectivity, to have it supplied like those prefabricated ethnic meals which emulate, say, the menu of the Mexican peasant, but come all ready on tin foil, so that all you need do is put it in the oven for 15 minutes and then eat it in front of your TV.

The pre-packaged ready-cooked and so very contingent subjectivity is similarly convenient; is, so to speak, an industrial, supermarket, ready-to-eat subjectivity. You just warm it up. When Max Weber spoke scathingly of the intellectuals who furnished their private chapels with spiritual exotica and indulged in intellectual antiquarianism, he clearly had in mind an élite hobby, which presupposed privileged access to leisure and resources. It was hand-made Re-enchantment for the Few. But one of the advantages of the affluent society, of the further advance in the equalisation of conditions, is that re-enchantment itself is now mass-produced, standardised, and rationalised. Subjectivity, like the Mexican peasant's meal, is no longer produced in the mud hut of the pueblo; specialists will prepare and package for mass-consumption a variant of it which, when all is said and done is almost as palatable and perhaps much more hygienic. So let us welcome the day when we can be reassured of the existence of our own subjectivity, and be supplied with tools for locating or erecting it, in a way which is no longer restricted to a privileged élite, nursing its nostalgia for enchantment like a badge of rank; but, on the contrary, which is supplied so as to make both the nostalgia and its solace available to *all*.

3

A Wittgensteinian philosophy of (or against) the social sciences

People who philosophise about the social sciences generally tend to assume their legitimacy, as an aspiration if not as a reality. Many of us have a vested interest in their existence. What would happen to our livelihoods if there were no such thing? So we tend to ask a kind of Kantian question: *How* are the social sciences possible at all?

It is refreshing to come across someone who asks a more radical question – *Are* they possible? – and who asks this question not ironically, but in all seriousness. That this is so is only too evident from his conclusion, which is negative: they are *not* possible. The activities which fall under that description are either logically illegitimate, or, if warranted, do not differ significantly from many activities practised anyway by ordinary people in the course of their ordinary lives, who would not dream of claiming any 'scientific' status for them.

Over a decade ago, a highly interesting book appeared which did in fact argue such a case.[1] Its argument deserves to be remembered. Personally, I have a penchant for sustained scepticisms, and am not at all swayed by the recent fashion which would rule generalised scepticisms out of court. Secondly, scepticism about the social sciences may claim that, far from being eccentric, it simply articulates a widely diffused feeling or suspicion. Also: instead of, as is the fashion, proposing programmes for the social or human sciences, should we not turn the tables for once, and look at how cogently the case for their dismissal can be argued? Let us for once put the burden of proof on the sceptic – especially as he seems most eager to bear it. Thirdly, this particular dismissal is presented as the corollary of a recently very influential philosophy. It thus has the

[1] A. R. Louch, *Explanation and Human Action*, Oxford, 1966.

interest of a set of putative implications of a position which had numerous convinced and voluble followers in the fairly recent past. Furthermore, their dismissal of the social sciences is argued as a logically integral part of an overall social and political attitude, and one which is by no means unattractive. For all these reasons, the book deserves our continued attention.

A. R. Louch's *Explanation and Human Action* is an exceedingly strange book, but it is not an unattractive one. Its attraction resides in its courage and candour. Some members of the movement to which Mr Louch proclaims adherence are conspicuous for bet-hedging formulations, for presenting hunches as definitions under the guise of conclusions and so on. No such charges could be made against Louch's book. Its main points are breathtakingly daring and far-reaching. The author himself frankly announces in some cases that he has failed to establish his contentions, and only hopes that he may do so in the future. In other words, there is a freshness and unpretentiousness about the presentation, whilst the content continuously gives one the impression of genuine intellectual groping, and of sincere curiosity. I feel little sympathy with most of the conclusions (though I feel a great deal of it with some of them), but I am impressed by the manner. There are, admittedly, extensive parts of the book where I find it difficult or impossible to understand what the author is driving at: but I have the feeling that this is due to the fact that some of the author's tacit assumptions and conventions are so unlike my own, that when he condenses the argument I do not make the right connections or fill the gaps correctly. It is not due to deliberate smokescreens and evasions.

Mr Louch's main contention, were it true, would have revolutionary, or rather suicidal, implications for all or most social scientists. 'My main intent has been to show that the idea of a science of man or society is untenable' (p. viii). Those of us who think that such a science exists or is emerging, are deluded. This conclusion Mr Louch derives, as he tells us, from the philosophy of Ludwig Wittgenstein and his school. In fact, this idea or attitude pervades the school in question, though it has not hitherto been formulated with such welcome and brutal frankness. (For instance, Mr Louch himself invokes, on p. 224, the remarkable doctrine to be found in Professor Gilbert Ryle's *The Concept of Mind*, to the effect that psychology can or need only explain abnormal behaviour, but is irrelevant to normal conduct.) Both the premiss and the conclusion of Mr Louch's work make it natural to compare his with the work of

Professor Peter Winch, notwithstanding the fact that, at least superficially, Winch's conclusions are formulated in a much gentler
manner. In fact, there are striking similarities and some interesting
contrasts between this book and *The Idea of a Social Science*, and
the two books deserve to occupy adjoining places on the shelf.
Louch's own attitude to Winch is an attempt to correct Winch's
position, more in sorrow than in anger: Winch in Louch's view was
aiming in the right direction, but did not get it quite right. The two
criticisms he makes of Winch on p. 164 are based on two shrewd,
valid and important points, though I am not quite clear whether
in fact Winch himself is open to the first of these criticisms. (He
certainly is open to the second one, and other erstwhile Wittgensteinians, notably Professor Alasdair MacIntyre, at least were at one
stage also conspicuously guilty of the second.)

The first of these points is that we should not rely too easily in the
explanation of human conduct on the alleged 'conventions', or 'ideas
behind the conduct', for, as Louch suggestively puts it, 'for every
convention in the hand, there are two in the bush'. In fact, not two
but legion: as I prefer to put this point, there is a Principle of
Ideological Meretriciousness at work in human societies, which ensures that at any given time there is a variety of (as it were) scriptural
warrants available for quite diverse courses of conduct. Louch's stress
on the ambiguities both of the conventional climate and of conduct
is salutary, and constitutes an insight which should have a place of
honour in the science whose existence he denies. I am not clear
whether Winch, for all his talk about the conventions and concepts
which guide conduct, or rather constitute it on his view, is really
committed, as Louch suggests, to the view that a unique, unambiguous and easily accessible set of conventions is operative in any one
context. MacIntyre, whom Louch does not mention, was once
guilty of such a view, through his aprioristic doctrine of social
causation,[2] to the effect that if we grasp the logical connection
between a set of ideas and the resultant conduct, no further comparative, causal-nexus-establishing research is necessary or relevant.
This only makes sense if we can ever rely on a set of ideas to be, so
to speak, in exclusive possession of an agent. (In fact, we cannot rely
on this. We all behave, in matters of belief and adherence to convention, like governments who assign an ambassador to the official

[2] 'A Mistake About Causality in Social Science', in *Philosophy,
Politics and Society: Second Series*, eds. P. Laslett and W. G.
Runciman, Oxford, 1962.

foreign ruler in his capital, whilst sending less overt but still accredited agents to keep in touch with the various rival revolutionary groups and governments-in-exile. You never can tell.)

The second charge, of which Winch *is* guilty, is, as Louch puts it, giving 'the impression that the sociologist or anthropologist is concerned only with intra-cultural or intra-conventional actions'. Indeed: when Winch does come across inter-cultural conduct, all he can do is either condemn it (as if this made it less of a reality), or, most implausibly, force it into an intra-cultural mould. This comes out most clearly in the case of an example which Winch himself records with commendable honesty but without realising how disastrous it is for his position, and which Louch also discusses (p. 176), viz., war and violent conflict. We need not even assume two roving bands, totally ignorant of each others' concepts, locked in conflict about some piece of nourishment (though such cases must occur). Assume instead two sailors in a shipwreck, fighting over a single piece of wreckage which can save one of them but not both. Even if it so happens that the two sailors 'speak the same language', literally and figuratively, their shared, or unshared, conventions are quite irrelevant to the situation, characterised by a *breakdown* of conventions. This is merely an extreme case. Ordinary social life is probably characterised by a pretty continuous series of minor or partial breakdowns of such a kind, and they interest the sociologist as much as convention-bound behaviour. To say all this is not to deny that *some* violence is highly conventionalised, indeed ritualised; but not all. But Winch is forced to obscure the distinction between (say) a duel or a feud, in which the conventional element is all-important, and a brute conflict in which all conventions lapse. Total war differs from, say, eighteenth-century warfare. If, as Winch would have it, everything is convention, we miss the most important social fact that some things are *much* less conventional than others.

Though Louch notes that this Winchian 'conceptual' account of war would lead us to treat, for instance, the Crusades too much in terms of their own propaganda, too much at face value so to speak, his criticism of the 'conceptual' account is that in fact it does not go far enough. He seems to think (p. 177) that Winch's account only fails with respect to the occasion of war (for the real motives may be less edifying than the propaganda would suggest), but is nevertheless applicable to the manner of its conduct. But it does not always, or generally, apply to the manner either. Louch says (p. 176): 'It is clear...why a soldier operates a machine-gun...His nation is at war, and this *means*, among other things, that soldiers will act in this way. All well and good, but one wonders: if this is sociology, why does it need to be written at all? Assuredly, the concept war includes the notion of people trying...to kill one another' (italics mine). All is *not* well and good. Unwittingly, Louch here underscores the need for that sociology which, according to him, is so redundant and only restates the obvious. Real sociology does *not* explain warlike conduct (though both Louch and Winch are willing to do so) in terms of the implications of the *concept* of war. The concept may be there, but some soldiers will run away, some refuse to fight, and some fight. Any sociologist would look not merely at what is involved in the 'concept' (and bearing in mind Louch's point that more than one concept may be available), but also at the social controls or pressures available and operative. If sociology were merely conceptual, perhaps Louch's strictures could be justified. But clearly, theoretical sociology is not as platitudinous and redundant as Louch elsewhere insists, for it does at least preserve its devotees from howlers such as the supposition that warlike conduct can generally be explained by *concepts*.

Louch uses his own criticisms of Winch, incomplete though they are, to make the following point: Winch is wrong in claiming that sociology is a philosophical, conceptual inquiry. It is (says Louch) an empirical inquiry. Winch is quite right (the argument runs) to reject theory, statistics and prediction, but wrong in supposing that a 'conceptual' inquiry presents the only alternative. (He does this, in Louch's view, because he is still imprisoned in the Humean dichotomies which Louch rejects.) Thus Winch, on this account, is right in what he is endeavouring to do, but wrong in his manner of formulating it.

From the viewpoint of a real, working sociologist, the moral of it all is this: there is not really any substantial difference between what these various Wittgensteinians say about the social sciences, great as the differences may seem to them. In practice it matters little whether one is told that there is a correct method in sociology, but that it is conceptual–philosophical, and that comparison and prediction are out (Winch); or that there is nothing like *a* method at all, but that what knowledge there is, is empirical, though at the same time theory, statistics and prediction are out (Louch); or that connections between belief and action are to be discovered conceptually, without empirical checking, whilst statistics still have a place in sociology, in the form of a truly surrealist pursuit of the owners of hitherto ownerless acts (MacIntyre). For anyone concerned with what actually happens, how, and through what constraints (amongst which conceptual ones are only one group amongst many), these diverse forms of idealism are much of a muchness.

There *are* some interesting differences between these various Wittgensteinians, but these are of interest to philosophers rather than sociologists. Leaving aside the rather *tutti-frutti* amalgam of late Wittgenstein and young Marx (1844 vintage, sweet and heavy), once attempted by MacIntyre, there are interesting differences between Louch and Winch, other than those stressed by Louch himself. These differences arise from stressing different aspects of Wittgenstein's thought. There are various intertwining themes in Wittgenstein, and the implications drawn for the social sciences differ a bit according to which of these themes is uppermost. For Winch, the crucial part is the meaningful nature of conduct, where the meaning of an act (or utterance) is its place, its function within a language, a 'form of life', a culture. (Louch indeed comments perceptively on this genesis of Winch's attitude, on pp. 162 and 174). By contrast, Louch's vision is inspired primarily by the Wittgensteinian rejection of generality, by the stress on diversity, which, for Louch, warrants the rejection of the ideal of *generality* in explanation. It is the (allegedly hopeless) pursuit of this which is the main sin of social scientists. Within Wittgensteinian exegesis, this point has often been formulated in terms of saying that description rather than explanation is the philosopher's job. Louch does not use this terminology: instead of 'description', he says '*ad hoc* explanations', using this expression, of course, in a way which is the very opposite to the usual pejorative way. Ad hoc explanations are good, the misguided pursuit of general explanations is bad. Apart from this stress on irreducible complexity and diversity, Louch is also in some measure inspired by the Wittgensteinian doctrine of what may be called the Contrast Theory of Meaning (which reinforces the stress on diversity: if everything is unified under one set of concepts, those concepts lose their effectiveness, according to this argument), and also, pervasively, by a very unusual view of the relationship of fact and value.

These differences in inspiration between Louch and Winch make little if any difference to their (in my view entirely mistaken) recommendations to working sociologists, but it does make some difference to the substantive picture of society conveyed by their work. Winch's claustrophilic insistence on meaning-within-a-culture-only leads to that characteristic *Drang* towards a cosy, self-contained conceptual cocoon, a rather Betjemanish, William-Morrisy world, back-to-the-cottage-and-craft (surreptitiously fed, however, by a modern electrical grid). Hence Winch faces an insuperable difficulty when required to account for the modern pluralistic world, of which his own affectionate account of the cocoon is a part.

This difficulty does not arise for Louch, who seems to revel in tough-minded style in all kinds of diversity. He does, however, have to face another difficulty (as does Winch), namely, that of accounting for the *demand* for homogeneity, notably in explanation, in the modern world. This problem is not overcome, as Louch supposes, simply by denouncing this demand as a mistake. But before discussing this, it is necessary to look at Louch's general position, as outlined in his book.

Louch's book is not merely about the social sciences. It also outlines a general philosophical position. His central point about the social sciences – that the pursuit or hope of generality is a cardinal error – is a corollary of that position. As he observes, were that position orthodox, it could be taken for granted. It is, however, a highly unusual position (and, in my view, an incorrect one), and consequently it must be defended so as to provide the basis for his more specific observations about the social sciences. I shall try to sketch out this general position, and then make some comments on the various elements found in it. These elements are,

(*a*) Generality does not even generally enter explanations of events in the physical world;

(*b*) It never enters into explanations of human conduct, which are and ought to be ad hoc;

(*c*) They are not merely ad hoc, but are such in a special way. They do not establish a regular connection, but show that a situation 'entitles' an action;[3]

(*d*) Moreover, or consequently, explanations of actions are not merely ad hoc, but also invariably, and essentially, evaluative;

---

[3] 'Desires and emotions, pleasures and pains, are identified in ourselves and others, in the light of what we regard or infer or see as desirable, appropriate, or entailed by the situations in which we find ourselves. As a consequence, such terms explain actions, not by showing a regular connection. . .but by seeing the situation as entitling the action. And this, as we shall now see, provides a *formula* for an account of what has more traditionally been thought of as reasons for acting.' (p. 93, italics mine).

(*e*) For these reasons, amongst others no doubt, the atomistic metaphysics associated with empiricism is false. The world does not consist of disjointed little bits;

(*f*) Hence the model of explanation associated with this metaphysic – generalisations covering conjunctions of the little bits, generalisation validated not by the content of what is observed but by statistical evidence of actual association – is also not generally valid;

(*g*) Other dichotomies associated with this metaphysic, notably that between fact and value (but also apparently that between conceptual and empirical), are invalid.

Some of these positions have, of course, already been touched on in the previous discussion of Louch's view of sociology. The perception of the various individual props in their place in his system as a whole is, however, essential for their proper understanding. I have schematised his total position with a view to making it intelligible, but with full awareness of the fact that these various assertions in some measure overlap with each other. Furthermore, an author who rejects generalisation as vehemently as does Mr Louch may object that any brief summary must be both general and misleading. As against this, one can only reply that these formulations follow his own as closely as possible. A hostile critic might observe that (*b*) and (*c*) are incompatible: (*b*) seems to claim that each explanation is sui generis, whilst (*c*), in Louch's own words, provides a *formula* for the explanation of action. I should not myself press this criticism too hard. Louch's ideal of ad hoc explanation, untainted by even tacit generality, whether applied to customary explanations of conduct or to Louch's own work (I am not clear whether he intends it to be reflexive in this way), seems to me so absurd that I do not expect him to stick to it consistently, and feel no surprise when he fails to live up to it. It would be interesting to count the number of general statements in his own book, and compare this with the number of ad hoc explanations (if any), and see how he accounts for the disproportion. Ad hoc explanation seems to me as absurd as general explanation seems to him. (There are no *intending* ad hoc explanations, so to speak: there are only sinful would-be general ones which have slipped into being ad hoc by excessive self-indulgence.)

(*a*) This is one of those truly daring theses which Louch puts forward, with an endearing temerity which scorns camouflage or escape-clauses. Louch here sets out to overturn all that Hume has taught about causation. It seems that, Louch argues, we do in at least some important cases actually *see* causal connections (pp. 40

and 41), without having to infer them from regular succession. 'Explanatory terms are frequently given a use, not by rule or criterion, but by paradigm. The movements of colliding billiard balls is what we mean by causal interaction...When we talk about hitting and striking...we are not (normally) making inferences about the probable consequences of certain kinds of events, we are *describing something we observe as a whole*. I *see* one car colliding with another...when I explain a case of causal interaction it is not in a normal sense an inference from general sequences *at all*, but a statement of *what I have observed*. To treat an instance of collision as a special case of generalisation, is to generalise...artificially.' Louch goes on to describe how, when he witnesses a car collision, he *sees* a causal connection, without any implicit reference to any generalisation. 'Observed collision, in short, provides a paradigm of causal interaction. We may be said to *see*, not merely *what* happens in such cases, but *why* it happens.' (Italics mine throughout, except for the last two emphasised words, where the emphasis is Louch's.)

It is perhaps difficult to convey to non-philosophical readers just *how* great a revolution this would constitute, if true.[4] One can say, with no irony whatever, that Louch's courage in putting forward such a position without hedging is admirable.

But his account of the situation happens to be demonstrably and technically mistaken. I shall discuss the matter in terms of his own, and highly suggestive example of a car collision, an example which does indeed give the 'direct perception of causal connection' thesis a maximum run for its money.

Phenomenologically, describing simply what happens when we witness a collision, Louch is of course right. We do not necessarily or generally invoke theories in so many words: we see the impact of one car on another, or even if we arrive after the event, see how the dent in one vehicle corresponds to the outline of the relevant part of the other, and immediately conclude to what is happening or has happened. But: are we necessarily right in our conclusion? The fact

---

4 Admittedly, Louch is not the only linguistic philosopher to credit himself with the strange and remarkable cognitive power of perceiving causal connections without stooping to further research, for we have seen Alasdair MacIntyre to have claimed the same. But I suspect that the latter, who in any case no longer holds this view, would have found some ways of asserting that his capacity to discern the nexus between ideas and subsequent action does not violate Hume's principle that there is no observable nexus between discrete events.

that so very frequently we are indeed right in this kind of case is simply a consequence of the very high reliability of certain *generalisations*, notably about the behaviour of the type of metal and other material involved in car construction, the consequences of impact on fairly rigid structures at certain speeds, and so on. But for the tacit reliance on these generalisations, we should not be able to 'see' the causal connection. In fact we do not *see* it at all, for all that we actually see might remain unchanged and yet the causal connection be quite other than we suppose, if the generalisations we tacitly use in interpreting what we see turned out to be false after all, in the light not of what we see but of extraneous evidence. When we see the collision of (say) two gas clouds, or even two solid bodies with properties we are not familiar with, we do *not* know what consequences to expect and we do not see any causal connection, paradigmatically or in any other way.

There are numerous factors which contribute to Louch's error here. For one thing, the innocently descriptive-looking term 'collision' is in fact already a theoretical concept, covertly containing a *general* idea which interprets that which is actually 'seen'. 'Collision' implies contact of fairly hard, impenetrable bodies. This is 'general' at least twice over: it implies subsumption under the general notion of hardness, and the sharing of the properties of members of that class, and secondly, even each individual case of a hard object implies permanent (hence, general over time) possession of resistance, impenetrability.

Secondly, when two unusual events follow each other in close succession, or are simultaneous, this does (according to circumstances) create some presumption of a causal connection. It does so by a kind of crude argument by elimination: when in 'normal circumstances' B never happens, and then it does occur in circumstances made abnormal only by A, we naturally first look to A for an explanation. But, of course, we may be mistaken: only a theoretical, and hence general, explanation of how A and B connect – an explanation only validated by further, extraneous evidence – really clinches the matter. We do not really *see* the connection, though it may seem so on occasions. (I have noticed children making conspicuous mistakes in this kind of case. Trying to start a bonfire with wet wood, I pour paraffin over the wood. Then I throw a match on it, and it flares up. Children, who, like Louch, 'saw' the causal connection between the match and the flaring up, but had not observed or understood the significance of the previous pouring of paraffin, clamour that I should throw another match. They suppose that the throwing of a lit match, which they *saw* causing a flare-up, is a sufficient cause of it. Only further research, or theoretical information which covertly contains it, can enlighten them about the error.)

Thirdly, there is what might be called the Evidence from Fit. We 'know' that only the elephant's foot could have made that particular imprint on the concrete before it set; the police 'know' that only this man's finger could have left that particular fingerprint on the safe; and Mr Louch 'knows', seeing the correspondence between the bonnet of one car and the dent in another, that the former caused the latter. (This greatly reinforces the argument from simultaneity or quick succession of two events.) But once again – is this a genuine case of *seeing*, in other words of knowing-from-one-observed-instance, that one thing has caused another? Once again, generality and theory are covertly present. Dovetailings, 'fits', are only evidence on the assumption of certain general, theoretically established properties, about hardness, impact, and so on. If two gaseous clouds had fitting outlines, we should *not* make the same inference as we do from two 'complementary' bits of broken pottery (where we promptly infer that they were parts of the same jar). The complementary coastlines of America and Africa, are evidence of 'continental drift' only if it is shown that land masses can indeed 'float' on the surface of the globe.

All these factors, superimposed on each other in the case of a car crash, mislead Louch into supposing that he can *see* a causal nexus. But Hume was right: he can see nothing of the kind. In each case, what shows up the error is the consideration of how easily and frequently we can be mistaken about the nexus which, in a loose sense, we 'see', and concerning the kind of additional evidence which can confirm or disconfirm our supposed perception. This additional evidence is always comparative, general, theoretical.

Louch's only answer to this kind of extraction of covert generality is that it is 'artificial'. Certainly, our assumptions about the general properties of solids are so ingrained, so built into our every expectation, that we are barely conscious of them, and do consider it the height of artificiality to spell them out. But this hardly shows that they do not exist. For special purposes, we *need* to make them explicit. Explaining the logic of our understanding of causation is one such purpose. Explaining to a child why it cannot touch the rainbow is another. We can only do this by stating that a certain tacitly assumed generalisation – visually perceptible shapes with apparent location also have certain properties such as hardness – has certain limitations: notwithstanding what we 'see', it does not apply to rainbows.

The failure of Louch's anti-Humean revolution concerning causation in nature has a double interest. Its minor interest lies in counteracting what Louch himself, with commendable candour, describes (p. 50) as its role in this book – to be 'a softening-up move'. It was 'important to recognize that often we do see why things happen without benefit of laws, models, or generalizations', not only for the intrinsic interest of this alleged discovery (which would indeed be tremendous, were it true), but also in order to make it easier for us to accept a similar thesis concerning human conduct.

If we can sometimes understand nature without any implicit generalisation, then why not allow the same for man? Why indeed? My own reaction to this softening-up process is, unfortunately, that I become hardened-up. I am prepared to look with some sympathetic attention at special cases in favour of anthropomorphic interpretations of *man*, at pleas for a special status of human understanding, but find myself getting counter-suggestible if these are preceded by covert appeals for anthropomorphism and apriorism in *nature*, claims that our alleged perceptions (in fact, our preconceptions) give us immediate access to natural knowledge, without benefit of any research and, in effect, without corrigibility.

But the failure has another deeper significance. Louch's willingness, indeed his eagerness, to reject what he calls the atomistic metaphysic, and explanation-by-generality, and his fondness for what he openly calls ad hoc explanations, are profoundly significant for his misunderstanding of the social sciences. For the social sciences have a double connection with the ideal of generality, the rejection of the ad hoc. Like any other science, they are born of this requirement. But unlike other sciences, they are quite specially concerned with this requirement as a phenomenon. Sociology is not merely a fruit of the Enlightenment, it is quite specially concerned with understanding of the Enlightenment, with understanding why and how men come to be dissatisfied with the ad hoc justifications found in any one society. This is a crucial point, and we shall return to it.

(*b*) and (*c*) The theory that explanation of human conduct is and ought to be ad hoc.

Louch's affection for ad hoc explanations is of course the obverse of his distaste for generality. He knows full well where this penchant leads to: no predictive power, and moral relativism. Where others might dislike these consequences and try to avoid them, Louch embraces them with alacrity. 'Desires and emotions, pleasures and pains, are identified in ourselves and others, in the light of what we regard or infer or see as desirable, appropriate, or entailed by the situations in which we find ourselves. As a consequence, such terms explain actions...by seeing the situation as entitling the action. And this, as we shall now see, provides a formula for an account of what has more traditionally been thought of as reasons for acting' (p. 93). The relativism to which this leads is acknowledged openly. 'Psychoanalysts and psychologists, writers, critics and philosophers, cannot...be said to provide the lineaments of human nature, conceived as permanent and enduring features of man's life. They deal instead in the changeable patterns by which behaviour is justified. What counts as grounds for the moralist varies from time to time, person to person, and circumstance to circumstance' (p. 103). 'Relativism thus means that actions can only be judged in context, and that there happens to be no universal context. Explanation of human action is context-bound. This should not be surprising. Human conduct is a response to an incalculable variety of situations. What is important is the variety, the detail, not the general features which afford grounds for the statement of laws...We cannot look... for a basic moral principle...or an empirical law from which particular actions can be inferred' (p. 207).

A number of fairly obvious objections can be raised to Louch's doctrine of ad hoc explanations and their desirability, though I fear none of them will move Louch. (1) Being ad hoc, these explanations have low power, or none at all. But as we have seen, Louch believes he can *see* a solitary nexus, and abhors prediction anyway. So the fact that the explanation explains nothing but the case for which it is invoked, and does not predict, does not worry Louch. That is just how he likes it. (2) As these explanations only explain by referring to what someone considers to 'entitle' an action, and views of this vary from man to man, group to group, and so on, all explanations are entirely relative, before we even reach the problem of moral relativity. Once again, Louch seems entirely willing to accept this consequence of explanatory or descriptive relativism. (3) All this talk about situations 'entitling' actions seems to confuse (at least) three distinct levels. At the lowest level, a situation 'entitles' an action, when I can see, in terms of the customs and assumptions of an age, how the situation might well lead to it. In this sense, I see how an unguarded valuable object 'entitles' the theft. In as far as I do not, however, endorse the act, there must presumably be another and stronger sense of 'entitlement', reserved for actions more genuinely 'entitled', in a sense closer to the ordinary meaning of the term. And in as far as there is disagreement about what is or is not entitled in this second and stronger sense, there is also a third sense, corresponding to what is normally conceived of as moral philosophy: the formulation of general criteria, those which, if you like, entitle (sense 3) entitlement (sense 2) and distinguish it from the weakest sense (1).

Louch's answer here is partly that he considers the pursuit of the third sense to be a mistake. But surely he must distinguish the first two senses? He seems to think that he does have an answer to this problem (formulating it in the second complete paragraph on p. 102), but I am afraid I simply do not understand what he is saying here – unless he is simply obliterating this distinction as well, and embracing an extreme relativism, one which would no longer allow us to distinguish between 'understanding' an action in the sense of seeing that it might occur in such and such circumstances, and condoning it. *Tout comprendre ad hoc, c'est tout pardonner*, it seems.

Be it noted that Louch's tolerance for all contexts and all norms, both in explanations and evaluation (which two he fuses), plays a role similar within his version of Wittgensteinianism to that which Winch's sense of cultural relativity plays in *his* version. Though their vision is different – Winch likes his cultural islands, where Louch revels in a most pluralistic, open, diversified, Babel-like society – both end at a conceptual and moral relativism. Louch's is more extreme, however. Winch is careful to limit his relativism to cultures and to deny it to individuals. Louch's knows no limits.

(*d*) The tie-up of explanation and evaluation.

It is only for purposes of exposition to readers who possibly do not share Louch's views, that this point is presented separately from the previous one. For Louch, the moral saturation of explanation, the fact that 'value and fact merge' (p. 54), is closely connected with, or virtually identical with, the necessarily ad hoc nature of explanation of conduct, and the fact that explanation is concerned with how, in anyone's (freely relative) view, a situation 'entitles' an action. Hence the distinction between (*c*) and (*d*) is for expository convenience only. Anyone converted to Louch's viewpoint can obliterate the distinction.

I feel a good deal of sympathy with Louch's perceptions concerning the intimate nature of the fact–value connection. The intimacy of this connection is something which follows logically, it seems to me, from certain key doctrines of Wittgenstein's. It is consequently rather odd that it is conspicuously contradicted by the public posture of most Wittgensteinians, and Louch is an honourable exception. The public stance of most Wittgensteinians is something as follows: philosophy is *wertfrei*. We analyse concepts, clarify issues, solve or dissolve puzzles; we do *not* – with very great emphasis – meddle with substantive issues, which are properly left to the inspired prophet, theologian, and so forth. Indeed our clear-minded neutrality is what, above all, differentiates us from our muddled predecessors, and it is this which irritates the general public against us. But this irritation is based on a misunderstanding, a failure to appreciate the truly and properly *wertfrei* nature of philosophy.

This attitude is absurd, for in fact, of course, the whole practice and procedure of these philosophers is pervaded by a variety of theory-and-value-loaded assumptions. But above all, it is in blatant contradiction with Wittgenstein's central doctrine of the denial of the possibility of a 'perfect language'. If a 'perfect language' were possible – one describing the world without redundancy and omission, and in a manner which always made clear that which is objective and that which is added by the notation – then indeed we could speak in a *wertfrei* manner. We would know what *a fact* is, and evaluation would be either absent, or if present, clearly insulated from the chemically pure facts that are being evaluated.

But, indeed, such a perfect language, capable of apprehending facts in their purity, is impossible. There are only context-bound ways of speaking, tied in their selection, their emphasis, their categorisation, to this or that purpose, this or that set of priorities. For these obvious reasons, one can only sympathise with Louch when he stresses that the characterisation and explanation (these two hardly being distinct for him) of human conduct are also essentially and inescapably evaluations.

Louch sums up his position well on page 56: 'scientists feel that if they set their values to one side, articulate them, and isolate them in a preface all will be well. But values do not enter descriptions of human affairs as disruptive influences; rather, they allow us to describe human behaviour in terms of action. Inasmuch as units of examination of human behaviour are actions, they cannot be observed, identified, or isolated except through categories of assessment and appraisal. There are not two stages, an identification of properties and qualities in nature and then an assessment of them, stages which could then become the business of different experts. There is only one stage, the delineation and description of occurrences in value terms.' I only hope that Mr Louch's philosophical colleagues will read and ponder this passage, and reflect on the plausibility of supposing that there are two separable activities, the description and the assessment of a concept (for instance, a religious concept), enabling them to separate the responsibility for description and for assessment.

Yet the use Louch makes of this valid perception, when applying it to the characterisation of human conduct, seems to me excessive. Where the more usual Idealist insight is that an 'action' can only be isolated from the continuum of behaviour by means of the *meaning* it has to the agent and the participants in the situation, and hence cannot be defined in abstraction from meaning, the twist given to this perception by Louch is that an action is only isolated as such by means of an *evaluative* concept. This seems to me, roughly speaking, true. (There are complications, concerning actions with a negative evaluative charge, so to speak; consider the act of, say, 'treason'.) Generally speaking, the norms of identity are also norms of excellence (or, sometimes, of the opposite): the criteria determine not merely whether or not some piece of behaviour falls into a given class, but also whether it is being commended or not. Moreover, this is not an accident: we are indeed, as Louch would insist, interested in human conduct from the viewpoint of its merit, and the reasons for isolating some behaviour as an 'action' at all are also the reasons for being interested in it from the viewpoint of adequacy as a performance.

So far, so good. But it seems to me that Louch both oversimplifies and exaggerates. He oversimplifies, in that he ignores, by implication, one interesting piece of complexity present in many, if not all, societies: they are richer in norms than they are in roles. For instance, pacifism and militarism co-exist in some societies. Hawks and doves differ in values, but they share the same identificatory concepts: they can both unambiguously single out the type of conduct concerning the merit of which they disagree. There are subtler and more complex cases: roles and acts in which the criteria to be satisfied are so multiple, and perhaps so changeable, that a kind of relative *Wertfreiheit* is imposed already by the ordinary use of the concept.

And if this is possible, or necessary, in the ordinary unreflective use of the concept, how much easier it is for the sociological observer! To recognise an action, he must know the criteria which identify and evaluate it, but he is certainly not compelled to share those criteria. Though Louch has little time for the doctrine which says that a historian must re-live the thoughts of his subjects, he appears to be, by implication, guilty of a variant of this doctrine: to perceive and understand an act, we must share the values which lead to the activity-in-question's being seen as an action at all. But this seems to me absurd. I can perceive, indeed understand, many acts of which I thoroughly disapprove. And I refuse to be bullied by Louch into a totally relativistic moral philosophy (p. 102), in the interests of equating all description with evaluation, by the threat which insists that to refrain from such relativism is, inevitably, to misdescribe an action. On the contrary, it seems to me to be Louch who misdescribes the manner in which we recognise actions.

(*e*) The atomistic metaphysic.

This is perhaps the crux of the matter. It is moreover intimately bound up with (*f*), the generality-model of explanation, and (*g*) the rejection of what may be called the empiricists' dichotomies. These themes must be discussed jointly.

The atomistic metaphysic says, roughly, that the world is made up of small, hard, isolable little facts. These are isolable from each other and distinguishable from any evaluation of which they may be the object.

One can see how this picture immediately leads to the generality model of explanation, and to the Humean views both of causation and of evaluation. What else can explanation be, but the summary of the patterns of succession of the various atoms? The same holds for causation: there is no glue between the atoms; 'causation' must simply be, once again, the pattern of succession. Evaluation, again, is no part of the objects, but is superimposed on them.

The atomistic metaphysic and these various theses are indeed so closely interconnected that one may wonder whether the 'atomistic metaphysic' is anything more than a kind of pictorial, concretised version of those doctrines. Whether this is so, or whether it has some existence of its own over and above these doctrines, I shall not discuss here. Suffice it to say that when the hard little atoms are identified with bits of 'experience', in other words with sensations, we have the familiar world-picture of empiricism; and that Louch rejects the whole set of these doctrines, with full awareness of their interconnectedness. We have indeed seen in some detail how he rejects the generality-view of explanation, and the Humean view of causation and of evaluation.

What, one may ask, has all this to do with sociology? In fact, the connection is close, important and interesting. It will perhaps emerge best if we look at what Louch puts in the place of the rejected doctrines.

He offers us a knowledge and understanding of human and social life which, in alleged conformity with our normal, ordinary thought is totally ad hoc, morally saturated and context-bound. If any specialised, professional, scientific inquiry is to be added to what we claim to know and understand about human conduct in daily life, it is not to go far beyond that ordinary understanding or differ from it in principle. 'Psychologists and social scientists, keen on achieving status among the natural sciences, have been led to suppose that they could refine action-descriptions into quantitative descriptions... What is needed in...psychology...is not measurement, experiment, prediction and formal argument, but appraisal, detailed description, reflection and rhetoric. If science is characterized by discovery and prediction, there are no sciences like psychology and the social sciences. For the study of action does not require new and hidden events and processes, but reflection upon and reordering of what we see men doing' (p. 235). 'I have claimed that there is no such science as non-physiological psychology, and that the social studies are not sciences characterized by their own laws, but a heterogeneous collection of inquiries strung together on the common theme of human action' (p. 236).

Why is this wrong? And, more significantly, what light does this error throw on sociology?

Note that Louch's argument is not, or at least not primarily, a philosophically orchestrated version of the popular view that sociological generalisation is impossible because human behaviour is hopelessly diversified and unpredictable. He does, admittedly, say this as well on occasion (for instance, on p. 207); but the point he really stresses and uses as a premiss is a second-level one. It is that there is irreducible variety, adhocness, relativity to context, non-generality and non-predictiveness in the way in which we explain, describe and evaluate action (these three aspects being, of course, fused). This is the premiss which appears again and again and which is central to his argument.

I do not believe that this premiss is correct, in as far as there is a fair amount of generality even in ordinary, day-to-day explanation of human action. But what I wish to challenge is not so much the premiss, as the inference based on it. Let us suppose the premiss to be correct (and there *is* a significant element of truth in it): the inference Louch bases on it is nevertheless invalid. If it were true that our customary accounts of human conduct were ad hoc, non-general, and so forth, it nevertheless does not follow that the social sciences, in a strong sense, are impossible.

What does follow from the premiss is that these ordinary explanations, if indeed they are so ad hoc and so forth, are unworthy of inclusion in a social science, if such a science can exist. It does not, however, provide any grounds for supposing either that it can or cannot exist. To establish his point, Louch would have to argue at both levels: he would have to show not merely that our customary explanations are ad hoc, but also that the material of the social sciences is inherently non-amenable to genuine, general explanation. The former he does do, whether successfully or not, at least at some length. If the former were true, and the latter not true, it would still be possible, or even plausible, that a genuinely generalising social science is possible, but that it must not borrow its concepts from ordinary explanation, or from the societies it investigates.[5] In effect, Louch leaves this possibility open.

Louch would probably deny that he has left this possibility – the possibility that whilst ordinary explanatory concepts cannot serve to provide a generalising social science, *other* concepts may be found which will do the job – open. But surveying carefully the arguments found in the book which can be mustered to show that such a possibility does not arise, I find that they fall under three headings:

(i) The argument on page 207;
(ii) The argument from the failure of the various social sciences;
(iii) The general structure of the book with its, to my mind, circular argument.

Let us take each of these in turn:

(i) 'Human conduct is a response to an incalculable variety of situations. What is important is the variety, the detail, not the general features which afford grounds for the statement of laws. One can on occasion imagine or even discover a case in which the context is universal, perhaps, for example, loyalty to friends or tribe,

[5] Precisely this position has been forcefully argued by Professor Walter Goldschmidt, in *Comparative Functionalism*, Berkeley and Los Angeles, 1966.

safeguards of life, or protection of children. But we cannot look to such cases for. . .empirical law from which particular actions can be inferred. In the first place, the case embodying universals does not normally arise, nor is it as a rule a determining factor in human choice. Human choices are made with respect to that variety of situations in which these universals play a progressively more anaemic role.'

There are some oddities about this argument. The thing which in a way puzzles me most is the hint, in the last sentence, that we have here an *evolutionist* doctrine, that things are getting 'progressively' more and more diversified in the way Louch likes. The examples with which the imaginary opponent and protagonist of nomothetic science is credited are not strong ones. But above all, we are faced here with simple assertion, circular repetition – the variety of contexts is there at the beginning and the end – and not evidence.

(ii) This provides, naturally, one of the most piquant parts of the book. Louch has little trouble with showing that much sociological theory (as well as much in other social sciences) is tautological, vacuous, pretentious. I am entirely with him here – or, *almost* entirely. My qualifications are just these: the often appalling pretentiousness and verbosity of recent 'theory' has at least one merit: like hypocrisy, it is the compliment paid by vice to virtue. It is the implicit recognition by the cognitively feeble that they should try to mend their ways. They only do it in externals: they strive to emulate the outward garb of genuine science. But though they fail to emulate the substance, and indeed parody it most appallingly, they at least underscore, underwrite, some important virtues.

The important comments on Louch's argument here are these: for one thing, he exaggerates the failures of social scientists. We do have some general knowledge. Secondly, past failure does not entail future failure, unless Louch's interpretation of the reasons for the failure be granted. The reason Louch offers is of course the inherent impossibility of generalising social science. A minor piece of evidence I should like to offer Louch, in support of a rival interpretation, is this: he should consider the extent to which the pretentiousness of philosophers and literary critics resembles that of sociological theorists. Is there not a *sociological* explanation for all this, in terms of expansion of higher education, the new needs made of it, and so forth, which force university teachers to dress up their wares?

And, perhaps most persuasive, an ad hominem argument. Mr Louch appears to dislike statistics in any form. (It is not quite clear why, and why he should consider them so very discontinuous from ordinary empirical observation which he commends. To treat them with quite such abhorrence borders on treating them with excessive reverence.) Hence in the course of his discussion of political science he attacks pollsters (p. 183). His attack takes the form of a *general* sociological analysis of the consequences of public opinion polls! His argument is that the immediate testing of the popularity of any policy by polls will lead, through the desire of governments for re-election, to a political system possessing the undesirable character-istics which Plato credited to democracy. Now this sociological theory seems to me wrong: it ignores not merely technical facts about various political constitutions, which cause elections to happen only periodically; more significantly, it ignores certain sociologically crucial traits about the type of industrial society in which polls are practicable. There may be strong forces at work in such a society which will not tolerate capricious policy-making. (Louch may, however, have unwittingly hit on one reason neither polls nor elections are easily practicable in 'underdeveloped' societies.) But the truth of Louch's theory is not the point. What *is* the point is its logical form. It is itself general, context-free and value-free! It argues from certain general premisses, and not from this or that concrete case; the merit of the argument depends on whether the implications of those premisses are correctly and exhaustively followed out; and the argument can be understood and evaluated by anyone, quite independently of political values. It is, in fact, a specimen of just the kind of sociological theory which, according to Louch, we do not possess. It happens to be an unsuccessful attempt, but does not the attempt imply that Louch (who, in any case, did not consider it unsuccessful) believes success to be possible?

But the question of the interpretation of the relative failure of sociology brings us to Louch's third argument.

(iii) The overall structure of the book is, of course, this: general explanation of human conduct is impossible; it is tied up with the atomistic metaphysic which is false; its falsity can be seen by demon-strating the direct perception of causal connection, by seeing the fact–value fusion; sociologists fail in their endeavours to generalise; plausible explanation for their failure is, that generalisation in sociology is impossible, for reasons stated; hence, this impossibility-thesis is further strengthened by one further piece of evidence – the failure of sociologists; thus, further strengthened, the thesis of impossibility of generalisation becomes not a possible explanation of the alleged failure of sociologists, but *the* explanation. This again clinches the matter.

One's overall acceptance of this circle of reasons (and here I use 'circle' non-pejoratively) will depend, of course, on how persuasive one finds each of the elements in it. If one finds each element in the circle independently persuasive, as Louch does, and if one then starts going the rounds of the circle – this is what the book consists of, in effect – one will of course end up with one's faith very powerfully reinforced. When inherently plausible bits dovetail so nicely, the resulting structure has a great strength and resilience indeed. Above, all, one will be willing to make the transition – if indeed one *notices* that an inference is being made, at all – from the fact, if such it be, of the relative failure of social scientists, to the interpretation or explanation of this fact, in terms of the alleged inherent impossibility of their aim. But, after all, other explanations are available for the fact in question.

For my own part, of course, I find neither the circle nor its elements persuasive. If anything, I find the over-neat dovetailing of the various elements in the circle somewhat off-putting and suspicion-stimulating, and I find the circle *less* appealing than its parts. Still, I do have some sympathy for limited aspects of parts of the circle: it is true that the social sciences have not been conspicuously and unquestionably successful. It is true that some theorists in these subjects, including some men with celebrated names, are pompous, pretentious humbugs. It is true that some explanations in ordinary life are ad hoc and context-bound. It is true that facts and values are not always as neatly separable as the positivist model would suggest.

But the facts which constitute Louch's starting-point are open to an interpretation quite different from the one he offers.

Quite unwittingly, Louch has provided us with a highly simplified ideal type of a certain type of thought. I shall call it Traditional/ Primitive thought, or TP for short. I do not wish to be credited with any crude theories, or any theories at all, concerning the historical or other distribution of TP, or with any assumption to the effect that TP is wholly or permanently in possession of the thought of any group, or wholly and permanently absent. All I do require for my argument is that TP should be an ideal type recognisably approximated by many actual ways of thought, and be seen to be logically incompatible with another style, which I shall call the Generalising/ Scientific, or GS for short. The two are logically, but not socially, incompatible. In other words, they can co-exist in the same person, at the same time, and even be applied to the same phenomenon: but the contents of a TP explanation will be inconsistent with that of a GS one.

The main characteristic of TP explanations is that they operate with a notion of the customary, in a way such that anything customary requires *no* explanation (can be deemed to be self-explanatory, if you wish), and only that which goes beyond or against the customary requires a specific explanation at all. The customary is connected with the habitual life of the community in question. The 'explanation' of the non-customary is somehow an account, or just a formula, which somehow restores it to the customary. It has no predictive power and does not seek an effective unifying principle for the various deviants requiring explanation, either as between each other, or binding them with the customary cases.

By contrast, GS thought is characterised, above all, by a symmetrical treatment of the customary and the unusual: both require explanation *in equal measure*. It almost follows from this that it is committed to explanation-by-generalisation, for it is debarred from appealing either to the customary/normal or to some 'restoration' of it.

Now it seems to me that TP and GS present, no doubt in crude and simplified form, the central distinction between pre-scientific and scientific thought. This is not the place to attempt to explore fully how this distinction relates to the other favoured criteria of science (attention to experience, testability, mathematical formulation, experiment, cumulativeness, or any other). We are concerned with its relevance to sociology.

Since the days of Comte, if not longer, sociology has been concerned with GS thought – or, if you like, positive science – twice over. It is, like any other science, an *instance* of the pursuit of the general, non-ad-hoc, non-custom-invoking explanation. But it is also concerned with such custom-free, generalising knowledge, or the mere ideal of such knowledge, as a very crucial *phenomenon*. For a natural science, the TP attitude, the failure to be puzzled by the 'normal' and the willingness to accept any old ad hoc explanation, is simply an obstacle to be overcome, to be replaced by a more sensitive logical nose for what is and is not puzzling, and a more discriminating palate for what is or is not an explanation. But that is all. For sociology, it is more: the acquisition of greater logical sensitivity, the intolerance of the ad hoc and custom-bound, is at the same time the revelation of an *object* of study. By no longer taking the customary for granted – with all its implicit beliefs and norms – it reveals it, and the custom of other societies and belief-systems, as an object for investigation.

Louch asserts that there is a connection between the generalising ideal of explanation and the atomistic metaphysic. There is indeed a connection, and it deserves further examination at this point. When TP thought, with its invocation of the customary and normal, is replaced by GS thought, which is no respecter of any custom and treats everything as equally in need of explanation (or, if you like, legitimation), a certain vertigo is the inevitable consequence. It is all very well at the beginning, when only some bits of the normal are drawn out, as it were, and subjected to the indignity of attempts at explanation: but what happens when it is seen that *everything* is open to question? Where do we begin, where do we end, what remains for us to rest on whilst all else is in flux?

It is in the light of this that certain major philosophic doctrines must be understood – notably that 'atomistic metaphysic' which is so much (and from his viewpoint, so rightly) an object of Louch's attack. The atomistic world-picture, notably in its best-known version, as elaborated by the great British Empiricists, is in effect an attempt to present a reasoned set of criteria of what is and what is not puzzling, of what does and does not require explanation, of showing what explanations are available and where they can or must come to an end. The argument runs as follows.

The world comes to us in little bits, bits of experience, that is, sensations. Each of these is quite independent of all the others. All we can do by way of explanation is to sum up the patterns in which these little atoms turn up. There is a sense in which each individual one is beyond all explanation: they just turn up. Experience is ultimate and sovereign. Within its realm, we can, however, discern patterns, and these in a way explain the individual occurrences falling under them.

This theory may have no great merit as a genetic account of how a baby comes to build up a picture of the world. Moreover, I do not wish to discuss its merits as an account of what the world is really like. But it does have one role, of supreme importance both for its philosophic appreciation and for the appreciation of the part it has played in the history of thought and science: it provided a neat and a non-arbitrary criterion for what is and what is not puzzling, for what is and what is not to be explained. It provides a start-line for puzzlement, when the customary or religious base-line ones are there no more.[6]

For Louch (as for Wittgenstein), such a requirement of generality is simply a mistake. Generality in itself is a snare, but generality in philosophy in particular, concerning criteria of what requires to be explained[7] and what does not, is especially bad!

[6] It is important that atomistic empiricism is not the only great theory to have played this role in Western thought. The other theory which has played this role is Materialism. The essential thing about materialism, as about atomistic empiricism, is that it provides a general and more or less defensible − intuitively and by argument − criterion for what is and what is not puzzling, for what needs to be explained and what can be treated as self-explanatory, as the bedrock at which the regress of explanation can and must come to a stop.

These two great theories are normally supposed to be in conflict. Superficially, they certainly are: for the materialist, the sensations and their characteristics, which are the empiricists' bedrock, are secondary qualities; for the empiricist, the extended impenetrable stuff and its properties, the bedrock of the materialist, are but a construct. In fact, they are complementary, and each does convey an essential feature of the scientific tradition of which each claims to be, wrongly, the whole essence. But that is another story.

In detail, Louch does have some appreciation of how these two great regulators of explanation worked: of how (p. 42) the materialist model calls for explanation of action at a distance, whilst the empiricist one tolerates it and any other brute correlations. (In a covert kind of way, Louch's own doctrine of perceptible, single-case causation, owes something to the materialist model. Causation 'seen' in the dent made by one car on another is seen because the basic, primary qualities of extended stuff, as admitted by the materialist, are taken for granted.)

[7] P. 48: 'The supposition that only general and precise criteria for what counts as a datum will preserve empirical knowledge from the taint of the *a priori*. [By contrast] I have tried to suggest, first that what counts as a datum or evidence is governed by contexts; the attempt to define it generally leads to the incoherence of atomistic or sense-datum theories.' Louch is thus quite clear about the kind of reasoning which generates the appeal to 'atomistic or sense-datum theories' but, like other members of his movement, fails to see the force of that reasoning.

Similarly, there is nothing general for him about explanations. 'Explanation, in Wittgenstein's phrase, is a family of cases, joined together only by a common aim, to make something plain or clear. This suggests that a coherent account of explanation could not be given without attending to the audience to whom an explanation is offered or the source of puzzlement that requires an explanation to

This mistake has as its consequence the misguided attempts to create a social or psychological *science*. 'For the behavioural scientist, however, the rationale for his activity is the univocal theory of explanation that all explanation consists in bringing a case under a law. This view has an initial plausibility...within...the science of mechanics (though even here there are some doubts...), but as applied to human performance it is totally irrelevant, producing, to the extent that its form is religiously followed, the sterile research that characterizes much of modern psychology and social science' (p. 233).

My view happens to be the very opposite: it is a mistake to suppose that the pursuit of generality is a mistake. But it is a mistake of a very special and interesting kind, connected with sociology in more ways than Louch supposes. Louch supposes that the connection is simply that this alleged mistake generates the to him misguided pursuit of a social science. He is quite right in the supposition that, indeed, the ideal of generality underlies the social sciences, as it does other sciences. But there is a further connection: the emergence of GS thought is not merely a logical, and historical, precondition of the social sciences, it is also (jointly with its contrast, TP thought) a crucial phenomenon *for* the social sciences. It is also a crucial phenomenon for philosophy. And at both levels, Louch quite misunderstands this phenomenon (as does Winch).

At this point, I shall attempt to give what seems to me the *correct* view of the situation. In as far as this view is manifestly incompatible with Louch's picture, it will constitute a refutation of the Louch–Wittgenstein view, provided of course it can be shown that it is indeed the correct view. But for the purposes of exposition, the specification of this view will precede the attempted demonstration of its truth.

The correct view: at a low level of civilisation, characterised above all by TP thought, explanations do indeed often tend to be ad hoc, context-relative, heterogeneous in logic. There is a tacit, or open, assumption of a 'normal' order, both with respect to society and to nature. Explanations are indeed attempts to show that the apparently abnormal 'fits in' after all. Civilisation, the development of thought and the emergence of science, on the other hand, are

> be given. There are many audiences, many puzzles, and a variety of paradigmatically clear cases that give rise, by contrast, to puzzles about other cases. The means of explaining are thus quite heterogeneous' (p. 233).

characterised by GS thought – by the increase in relative importance of explanations which are general and context-free. This advance, however, tends also to corrode the previous normalcy-invoking world-views and their credibility. The pursuit of alternatives is generally known as 'philosophy', and an important role of philosophic theories is to provide not merely recipes for the finding of explanations, but criteria for what is to count as an explanation – again, in a context-free manner. The requirement of context-freedom is dictated not merely by logic, but equally by the instability of contexts: in plural and unstable societies, there is no normal state of affairs which conceivably could provoke its own 'base-line' for explanations. Sociology is born of the attempt to understand this flux, as well as from the simple extension of the ideal of general explanation to human conduct. The contrast between TP thought and the societies which harbour it, and GS thought and societies permitting it, is itself the first and most important distinction within the subject matter of sociology. It is not merely its precondition, it is also the centre of its subject matter.

What reasons can one invoke in support of this picture, as against Louch's? This picture (1) makes sense of the enormous difference we do indeed observe between scientific–industrial societies and the rest; (2) it makes sense of the generality which is, his protestations notwithstanding, found even in Louch's own arguments, and also in all human thought. The idiographic context-relativism preached by Louch is simply mistaken; (3) it makes sense of the admittedly modest and undramatic successes of nomothetic social sciences; and (4) it makes sense of the very great successes of natural sciences.

By contrast, Louch gives us a picture of the world, in which even the success of natural science is a bit of a puzzle, in which no account can be given of the drive to generality (in morals, social sciences), other than that it is a mistake, and in which the great cognitive and productive differences between societies are barely perceptible. He does score in one respect: he offers an explanation of why the social scientists have not done all that well.

The superiority of what I call the correct view over Louch's view is not a matter of formal proof. Each of the features better explained by the correct view might also be otherwise explicable; each of the features highlighted by it might be better left ignored. (Similarly, of course, the feature invoked by Louch, the backwardness of social science, can be explained by assumptions other than their impossibility, and, of course, it normally *is* explained in other ways. The existence of some ad hoc, context-bound explanations in our normal daily references to human conduct are explicable as signs of intellectual backwardness.)

It would be idle to pretend that anything can be formally clinched, one way or the other. I have no doubt in my own mind that a view which distinguishes between science and superstition, which recognises the amount of generality present even in daily accounts of conduct, and which aims at more, is the better view. The advantage attaching to this view in fact seems to me quite overwhelming, though I have done my best to state both views in a low-keyed, un-question-begging way – indeed, falling over backwards to give the ad hoc view not merely a fair run, but to make it seem at least a starter. Having tried so hard, it seems to me in the end that I have failed. It is a non-starter.

Something more should be said both about Louch's views on morals, and about the moral inspiration of his views in general. What makes Louch attractive as a thinker is that he seems to be all of a piece: though many topics and points are discussed or touched on in his book, there is an underlying coherence, a consistency which is only seldom sinned against. Happily, Louch is not self-exemplifying: there is little that is opportunist and ad hoc about the various opinions put forward in his book. Much as it goes against his own doctrine, there is great internal homogeneity in it, the application of a fairly small set of general principles. He may preach the doctrine of the fox, but he is in fact a hedgehog.

This comes out well in his views on morals. His context-relativism and cult of the ad hoc leads him, for instance, to deny distinctions which other moralists have supposed inherent in the nature of things and independent of context – such as the distinction between principle and desire. Following out the logic of his premises, and without tongue in cheek, he reaches rather Oscar Wilde heights on this point: 'Desire is a species of acting on principle' (p. 69). For Louch this is not a paradox but a simple consequence of his premises. Neither desire nor principle are causal; neither is general; both connect an act with circumstances which warrant it. So where could there be a difference?

One of the dark sayings of Wittgenstein's youth was that ethics and aesthetics were one. Louch's moral philosophy could be summed up by saying that ethics and the social sciences are one. Neither is allowed to generalise (Kantianism is *out* in morals, just as the nomothetic ideal is *out* for the social sciences), both are relativistic. In all this, Louch is entirely consistent with his own premisses. 'Appraisal is the means for identifying the object of inquiry...' (pp. 57–8). Thus ethics absorbs psychology, but the reverse is equally true. 'The study of ethics is empty without the detail of particular human actions...' (p. 235). At this point, Louch is very close to the Existentialists.

But more interesting even than his views *about* morals and the philosophic status of ethics are his substantive pieces of moralising. Two passages in particular I found very striking, one at the end of Chapter 8, the other in the concluding (tenth) chapter. The first of these follows on one of his rejections of both nomothetic sociology and moral Kantianism. 'A universal moral principle presupposes a common life, which our differences of occupation, age, sex and income deny...It could emerge only if men truly shared a common life in which distinctions of employment, wealth and status have disappeared. The changes in society envisaged to achieve that end are messianic, whether the messianic hope is Christian or Marxist. And perhaps this suggests that moral agreement is not worth the price of such uniformity' (p. 208).

And then he goes on to tell us what he *does* approve of: 'And so the only moral recommendations, as the only recommendations for the empirical study of man, come to the same thing – a move here, a move there, zig and zag, after the manner of Aristotle's recommendations with regard to the Mean, everything tentative and subject to change. It is in both overweening generalizations in ethics and the pretensions of general theory in behavioural science that we stand most to fear the sorts of impositions on our lives that make for totalitarian regimes. Things, so to say, are always bad, or at least not nearly so good as we could imagine them being; but wholesale changes, whether backed by Plato's ethics, Marx's historicism or Skinner's laws of conditioning, will most likely make matters worse. For men and situations represent a variety and a changing variety, which makes the application of general laws trivial or false and universal moral principles a positive evil.' How very similar this rather moving passage is to the views of Michael Oakeshott, who, however, is not mentioned in the book. But whilst containing the same perception of life – no salvation is to be had, but the pursuit of it will make things worse – it seems to me superior on two counts: stylistically, it is free from a certain excessive mellifluousness, and logically, it is more consistent. There are too many theorists these days who invent charges against Marxism which, though indeed applicable to it, apply at least as much to Christianity, a point which the authors choose to ignore. If you dislike general principles, absolutist claims, the idea of real salvation, and prefer instead the acceptance of diversity and adversity, then indeed you should dislike Plato and Christianity and Kant, as well as Marxism. Louch's clear-sightedness and honesty here show that, to his credit (though in contradiction with some of his own professed beliefs), he is a man who follows out the implications of his ideas with integrity and consistency.

The moralising of the final section of the book has a different kind of interest.

In those final passages (pp. 238–9), Louch makes plain the moral purposes which led him to his views. 'The...attitude evinced by behavioural scientists, conscious or not...is rather the engineers' attitude.' 'Perhaps we shall find it [the most efficient means for manipulating people] in Skinner's laboratory, in a military camp, or in a circus, or perhaps in the methods of thought control and forced confession that Stalin and Mao Tse-tung may or may not have borrowed from Pavlov. The scientific or engineering attitude forces us to acknowledge, even to admire, the successes of such methods. For it leaves us no way of placing these *efficient* techniques in the larger context of a less laboratory-like society, in which men, *conceived* of as autonomous agents, pursue both harmonious and conflicting aims. The laboratory *success* is dangled in front of us.' 'Totalitarianism is too weak a word and too inefficient an instrument to describe the perfect scientific society...In the engineers' society, perhaps unwittingly promoted by psychologists and sociologists bent on being scientists, we should have to give up the concept of an open or civil society...A programme *having* such ultimate consequences cries out for refutation' (italics mine throughout).

Let me say to begin with that I share Louch's values here. I, too, dislike the Brave New World. I am a little puzzled about how *he* manages to hold these values so firmly and why he should be so eager to convert us to them, given his protestations about the inevitability and desirability of moral relativism. For a plausible case can also be made out for what Louch calls, with a shudder, 'the perfect scientific society'. The author of *Brave New World*, though he too shared Louch's reaction, had the generosity of heart to state those arguments, fairly and forcefully, through the mouths of some of his characters, which is one of the things which makes the novel so powerful. (It would not have had the impact which deservedly it has had were the cards stacked too heavily on one side.)

But this is not the main point which must be made against Louch here. The main point is that he evidently considers the horrific programme of the 'engineers' to be *feasible*. He speaks, too often for it to be a mere slip of the pen, about the *successes* of such methods. It these methods *can* be successful, does it not follow that human conduct is, after all, subject to general laws? 'These methods' can only apply their lever, so to speak, if provided with the fulcrum of regular, reliable responses by the people destined for manipulation. If people's responses were inescapably, irreducibly ad hoc, idiosyncratic, context-bound, autonomous, no such manipulation would be possible. Is, then, that vaunted autonomy of ours a mere *conception*, sustained, it is true, by our normal, traditional habit of ad hoc, logically feeble explanations (which undermine no autonomous self-image, through being so very feeble), but liable to be destroyed by determined teams of social engineers?

Louch's very fears seem to give him away. If what he fears is even a possibility, then what he asserts elsewhere is not true. Admittedly, these final passages are not entirely unambiguous. Though the sentences and phrases I have quoted seem to indicate, unambiguously, that he does consider what he fears to be a realisable condition, there are other passages which are open to a different and contrary interpretation. (If indeed they are meant to be so interpreted, they are in blatant contradiction with the other passages quoted.) But he also says (p. 239), 'the world is not just *in fact* immeasurably more complicated than the laboratory; the complexity is a condition of any life we would think worth living' (italics Louch's). Here he seems to be saying, in the course of asserting the value of complexity, that it also obtains 'in fact', which might be taken to imply that the engineers cannot succeed after all. And the very last sentence of the book, which again is none too clear, could be interpreted in a similar way.

At this point, as so often, Louch's position is very similar to Oakeshott's. But it is noteworthy that he does not take the same way as Oakeshott does from a similar dilemma. Oakeshott, too, is caught between saying that 'Rationalism' (which corresponds pretty closely to the engineers' science execrated by Louch) is (*a*) a very bad thing, and (*b*) impossible, in the sense that its aims can never be achieved. There would seem to be some tension between these two views, for something which cannot happen is not normally also something which need be greatly feared and denigrated. Oakeshott's principal way of surmounting this dilemma is to say that whilst it cannot happen, nevertheless a good deal of harm can be done in the unsuccessful *attempts* by Rationalists to make it happen. His main thesis is in the indicative mood: the moral thesis is almost incidental – or so it is claimed. It is interesting to note that Louch *could* easily adopt this way out, but that he does not. His failure to do so greatly weakens his case, for by admitting that the danger is a real one, he appears to contradict some of his most cherished theses – namely, that the feared programme is unrealistic.

But as indicated, in fairness to Louch, his position at this point is not quite unambiguous. The most plausible interpretation – taking into account both the number of assertions supporting it, and their unequivocal nature, as opposed to the equivocation on the other side – is, however, that he considers a Brave New World to be a possibility, though of course an undesirable one. (It seems to me that he is right, on both counts.) But if this terror is a genuine danger, the defence he is proposing is the feeblest imaginable: it is like setting up a paper wall to stop a real tank. If human nature and society *are* manipulable by means of general laws formulated in (presumably) a new language devised for that purpose, it is no defence against the social order based on such manipulation, to scream that, in the old language, all explanations were ad hoc and feeble, and that by its rules (if indeed it be allowed to have any rules) the new language is improper!

An interesting point in Louch's general position is one at which he disagrees with Wittgenstein and presumes to criticise him. Such open-mindedness is refreshing.[8] The point at issue is the relevance of the notion of *games* to human conduct and society.

What Louch in effect does here is to invoke one Wittgensteinian idea against another. The idea under attack is the 'game' or strategic intepretation of human conduct. 'Sometimes it looks as if Peters, Melden and Szasz, and behind them Wittgenstein, are arguing that

---

[8] This might simply be a sign of the times. Writing about philosophers, 'in Britain at any rate', Mr Anthony Quinton observes (*The New York Review of Books*, 12 January 1967, p. 26), 'Wittgenstein and Austin are not so reverently regarded now as they were ten years ago...' The reverence has, however, spread to new regions, more significant for the social sciences, if Professor T. Burns is to be believed: 'In America, the new generation of sociologists, ardent students of Wittgenstein, Austin...' (*The British Journal of Sociology*, 17, no. 4, December 1966, p. 430).

if behaviour can be identified as action, we are logically compelled to follow the explanatory road toward games and strategies' (p. 229). Earlier (p. 20) Winch was also cited as a person holding this view, also under the inspiration of Wittgenstein. But this view, which would assimilate all human action to making-moves-in-games, and thus open the way to a homogeneous social science, albeit of a non-causal kind, is untenable, because (p. 229) 'an ulcer can serve as a move in a game. . .It also has causal ancestry. At least, we should not be inclined to suppose that the effect of tracing such an ancestry is to commit a logical blunder. Similarly. . .amnesia, anaesthesia, paralysis. . .can be regarded as links in a chain of physical events.'

The immediate evidence Louch uses here against Wittgenstein and his followers (or rather, especially his followers: one may suspect that Wittgenstein might not have gone with them on this point, and would have agreed with Louch) is a commendable recognition that causes do play some part in human life, that we cannot consider ourselves guided entirely by our ideas or concepts, that Wittgensteinianism does not provide a warrant for a kind of highbrow version of Christian Science, of opting out of the physical world and its causal laws. But the underlying argument here invoked by Louch is another Wittgensteinian idea – the denial that *any* model has general applicability, the insistence on the diversity of things or concepts. If this is so, *games* cannot be the universal key either. They cannot be invoked to exclude causal explanations everywhere, and all the time. Thus Louch uses one part of the doctrine to check another. His insistence on diversity flows over into an insistence on *contrast* – any type of explanation becomes vacuous, he argues, if all-embracing – a point he invokes very much, for instance, against Goffman's extension of the notion of play-acting (pp. 215 *et seq.*), or even against unifying ideas, when treated seriously, in history (p. 222). His argument here seems to me to commit a very serious error. From the correct observation that a theory is vacuous if it is all-embracing in the sense of following all possible facts, he carelessly slides over to a quite different doctrine, to the effect that a theory is vacuous if it is all-embracing in the sense of subsuming all actual phenomena under a limited set of concepts. But the two things are quite distinct and, in the interesting cases, *inversely* related: often the simpler the theory, the more facts it excludes, and the more testable and *non*-vacuous it is. But quite apart from this mistaken use by Louch of the doctrine of the vacuity of theories which exclude nothing, it is very curious how much he harps on this (to my mind, valid) view: he constantly uses it to show the vacuity of sociologists' or psychologists' theories (for instance, he makes, on pp. 222 and 223, the familiar point that Freud is conspicuously open to this criticism). It is curious that *Louch* should invoke this view, for vacuity and explanatory impotence do not seem to bother him when they occur in those ad hoc, relative, context-bound 'explanations' of ordinary thought. *There*, he admits it and glories in it! He also does not seem to realise that by invoking the need for exclusion of some facts, as a criterion of non-vacuity, he is implicitly admitting the ideal of generality in explanation which, officially, he claims to reject.

All the same, when it comes to *games* and causes, Louch's desire to avoid any general model, even a Wittgenstein-inspired one, leads him to make some very important observations, observations which escape the other Wittgensteinians whom he cites, in their urge to show that life is lived entirely in a Realm of Meaning. This Mary Baker Eddy-tendency, as it were, is, of course, present not merely amongst the followers of Wittgenstein, but also amongst some followers of Freud. It is in connection with the latter that Louch castigates the view that we are exempt from physical causation (p. 229): 'Szasz views mental illness as a problem of living, and concludes that it cannot be the subject for mechanical treatment. But physical ailments are also problems in living. We should not conclude on these grounds that they must not be treated or explained by physical means. *Most of human behaviour is ambiguous in the same sense*. All sorts of actions may be moves in a game, looked at one way, and yet be shown to respond to the manipulation of the physical environment of which the action is a part, and thus be explained by reference to causes' (italics mine).

What Louch says here seems to me both conspicuously true and enormously important. (Incidentally: what Louch says here about the possibility of causal explanation and consequent manipulation supports the interpretation I have adopted of those slightly ambiguous final remarks of his. He fears the Brave New World as a real *possibility*.) Just this seems to me one of the crucial features of the human situation – the ambiguity, the double vision, of our life and conduct, the overlapping and incompatible visions of life as we live it in the first person and of life as understood impersonally by science. This is one of the crucial, perhaps the most crucial of, problems: it is probably the greatest weakness of the general philosophical movement of which Louch is part, that it simultaneously ignores, obscures and evades this problem, and provides facile and

inadequate vindications of our autonomy, of the legitimacy of our
traditional and first-person view of our life. It is interesting to find
Louch, in the course of correction of an error which is not really an
error at all (i.e., the drive toward generality of explanation), himself
stressing this genuine and disastrous mistake. Unfortunately he is not
consistent, and his wisdom at this point does not carry over to the
rest of his book. Whilst he perceives, at this point, the ambiguity of
our situation and the pervasiveness of the possibility of causal
explanation, elsewhere, both in the general position adopted and in
many specific assertions (for instance, at the top of p. 236), he falls
back into the conventional Wittgensteinian attitude, the vindication
of the anthropomorphic view of man through the uncritical acceptance of traditional language.

Something ought perhaps to be said about Louch's treatment of
detail and of the specific social sciences. Louch has evidently done a
fair amount of hard work. His book is rich in documented examples
drawn from the social sciences. The book is not merely much longer
than Winch's, it is also much less schematic.

Winch's book is rather aprioristic.[9] He knows what the social
sciences can be, what they must be, what they cannot be: he demon-
strates it by philosophic reasoning which establishes the desired
conclusions to his own satisfaction, and if a few unfortunate theorists
like Durkheim and a few tribesmen like the Azande get mixed up in
the argument, this is by way of illustration only. In the case of Louch,
the references to the concrete studies of social scientists are far more
genuinely an organic part of the book. The central thesis was, I
imagine, generated quite independently of the material assembled to
test it (and to say this is not in any way to criticise Louch); but the

---

[9] According to Louch, Winch also preaches apriorism for the social
sciences. So if Louch is right here, Winch's practice is consistent
with his theory: he does what he preaches. But I suspect that Louch
really misinterprets Winch here. Winch says that the social sciences
are *conceptual*, that they are about the concepts of societies, our
own or others. But for a Wittgensteinian, concepts are not observed
either by gazing at a Platonic heaven, or by looking into one's own
consciousness. They are observed by doing something rather like
anthropological fieldwork, by seeing concepts 'in use', though it
appears that in the case of philosophers, this fieldwork can be done
at home and restricted to office hours. Hence it is not aprioristic
(though, in fact, it is utterly impressionistic).

material *is* assembled with some effort at thoroughness for the purposes of testing it. We may not agree with Louch's view that the test was passed successfully, but he certainly does assemble a good lot of examples for us, and illuminates at least his own position in his attempts to show that these examples support it.

A good part of the book does in fact deal with individual social sciences from this viewpoint. The rest of the book deals largely with the 'philosophy of mind'. For the benefit of readers not familiar with philosophical terminology, I ought to say that the philosophy of mind is not about what you might suppose (i.e., mind), but about aches, qualms, twinges, twitches, quirks, itches, etc., about most if not all things liable to happen on or near our skins and describable by monosyllabic, and preferably Anglo-Saxon, terms, and treated in a manner designed to show that these etymologically earthy goings-on prove Descartes to be wrong. I find this a rather tedious subject, even when treated by the otherwise interesting Mr Louch, and it only comes to life for me when Louch sins against his own principles and generalises, e.g., to the effect that explanations of human action are generally justifications of them. So I shall not say much about this part, except to report that Louch holds that Descartes' influence in generating our mistakes has been exaggerated, and that he thinks (pp. 219–20) that Gilbert Ryle, the father of this subject as now practised, has not gone far enough in the piecemeal and context-relative direction.

Louch does spend a good deal of time actually discussing the social sciences. But whilst he clearly has done his best to immerse himself in them, the picture he brings us back is not in all cases one which would sound true to a practitioner. He adopts different strategies with different sciences. Economics, with its highly abstract and hence general theory, clearly presents a problem. Adam Smith is dealt with in a rather Oakeshottian way: it would be a mistake, it seems, to treat him as formulating general principles, applicable to all humanity. He was merely bringing into explicit consciousness special economic practices that happened to have grown up. A very strange picture of Keynes is presented (p. 75). On page 195, he makes very heavy weather of showing that formulae such as 'MV equals PT' derive their authority from 'the mechanics of book-keeping'. I was taught elementary economics over two decades ago by a tutor totally impatient of any philosophy, and even then, under such tuition, the idea that 'MV equals PT' is a tautology was a commonplace. Some kind of case could be made out for a Louch-ian view of the social sciences, by appealing to economics, and above all to the fact that theoretical and applied economics meet so seldom, that 'applied' is in fact a misnomer. There is something odd about a situation in which it is quite possible to be a good economic historian, or a financial operator, without knowing any theory, and without feeling the loss. But if there is a case to be made out here, Louch has not made it.

Again, his view of sociology (p. 18) is unconvincing. He seems to suppose that sociologists must be either what he calls 'neo-positivist' and static, or upholders of grand theories of the evolutionist or cyclical kind. Whatever successes the non-grand students of social change have achieved, or missed, they are sufficiently numerous to have their existence recognised. Louch's view of social anthropology is also odd. He offers the disastrous advice that diffusionism should be revived, repeatedly (pp. 169, 170, 181 and 182). Admittedly, it will be a feeble diffusionism, for it must not, any more than any other social science, have causal pretensions. This is a view which does indeed follow from Louch's general position: societies do not lend themselves to structural comparisons (for this would mean generality and causation); but there is no harm in seeing how this or that trait has spread, with or without context. Louch castigates Winch for not allowing comparisons at all (p. 182): he does not object to them himself, provided they are logically impotent. If anthropologists followed this advice, they would give up their interest in similarities and contrasts of structure, and go back to concern with similarities of 'traits'. I can hardly think of anything more retrogressive.

His formal view (p. 160) is that 'anthropology is only a collection of traveller's tales with no particular scientific significance', though he goes on to stress that the 'only', when used by him, is not pejorative. (In this he is certainly sincere. Indeed, the description is, in his mouth, an expression of praise. None of the social sciences are scientific in the sense of being genuinely theoretical, and if they were he would wish them to the devil.) The anthropologist is just a traveller who observes well and who has been to very strange places. Louch makes no attempt to give an account of anthropologists who have been to places that are not distant at all, or who, in distant places, were not interested specifically in the exotic. He unfortunately takes as his paradigm of an anthropologist, a report which, especially as presented by Louch (p. 161), panders to the now popular stereotype: the anthropologist is someone who tells you about a repulsive custom, but in so much detail that you end by seeing its point and sympathising.

In connection with Malinowski and Wittgenstein, Louch makes some quite interesting observations (p. 165) about the similarity between the two functionalisms. Certainly, both men stressed the role (of utterance or custom) as opposed to the models of either external reference, or imitation or inheritance. Louch fails to observe that whereas Malinowski's functionalism is fairly testable (having been tested and, on the whole, abandoned), Wittgenstein's contains a guarantee of its own success built in as a *definition*. (It is just this kind of practice that Louch derides amongst sociologists.) He fails to observe that whereas Malinowski's relativism is tenable, Wittgenstein's is not. The difference lies in the problems each man set himself. In answer to the question 'Why do societies have the institutions they do have?' it is legitimate, though perhaps neither precise nor true, to say 'They serve needs in various contexts, and are maintained by the other institutions in those contexts'. But Wittgenstein was not asking this de facto sociological question. He was inquiring into the origin, and by implication into the answers, of philosophical questions. And then the functionality of our language (if indeed it obtains) in this or that culture is irrelevant. It is totally irrelevant because philosophical questions do not arise (as Wittgensteinianism holds) from the failure to perceive that alleged functionality, but, on the contrary, from the breakdown of closed forms of life, and from attempts to find independent foundations for new forms of life or thought.

Most interesting of all, under the genuine but obvious similarity between Malinowski and Wittgenstein, he fails to notice another striking contrast, and one entirely in Malinowski's favour. Wittgenstein believed that philosophical error springs from the detachment of thought from its manifold concrete contexts, from a pursuit of generality; and in this, of course, Louch follows him, with fervour. Malinowski noticed that exactly the opposite is true. Ordinary thought is too diversified in its logic, too much ad hoc, too compromised with specific purposes and contexts, to have much validity. In saying this, he was merely reaffirming something fairly obvious. The denial of it by Wittgenstein and Louch is both paradoxical *and* mistaken. This apotheosis of the untidy, the ad hoc, the context-bound, and the denial of generality and science in human affairs, are all parts of one big and unacceptable paradox.

4
Period piece

There was a time during the winter of 1944/5 when I was taken about once a week on the back of a lorry to the public baths at St Omer for a quick shower, no doubt in the interests of hygiene. As the lorry entered the town and slowed down for the corners, it was possible to jump off, and by forgoing the shower, have half-an-hour or so on one's own. A number of soldiers would do just this and thereby gain enough time for a rapid visit to the local brothel. For my own part, urgent though the call of the flesh was at the age of nineteen (oh where are the snows of yesteryear?), I never saw the inside of the brothel, at any rate in St Omer. Instead, when I picked myself up from the cobbles, I beetled off to the bookshop. There I bought up the literary hebdomadaires, expecting them to be the equivalents of those English weeklies which had constituted the near-totality of my education as a schoolboy in England.

I soon reached the conclusion that the French ones were more numerous, more flimsy (physically and otherwise), more ephemeral and blatantly partisan than their English counterparts. I remember that there was a lefty one called, agreeably, *French Letters*. But within this proliferation of what seemed lightweight stuff, two names stood out: Sartre and Camus. An inner bell rang the very first time I read something – was it by or about them? – and I knew these two would become permanent parts of my intellectual furniture. And so it is. But with the passage of years, almost imperceptibly these pieces have moved to ever less central parts of the house. Being forced to re-examine the Sartre chest by the English translation of the *Critique of Dialectical Reason*,[1] I find it hidden in the

---

[1] Jean-Paul Sartre: *Critique of Dialectical Reason. I. Theory of Practical Ensembles.* Translated by Alan Sheridan-Smith. Edited by Jonathan Rée. NLB. London, 1976.

attic under a pile of papers and dust. I shall certainly *not* get rid of it. It means far too much...and anyway, it would not fetch anything. But I do not see it moving back to the central and functioning part of the house.

But what did it mean?

Sartre has now acquired the quality of a period piece. Both his brilliantly elegant and economic literary style, and his shamelessly prolix, undisciplined, self-indulgent, conceptually free-associative philosophic prose – the two being so effectively juxtaposed – are now part and parcel of that seedy, shabby, demoralised, inflation-haunted, impotent France of the end of the war, as far from the present as another planet.

Existentialism made its appearance as the philosophy of the human condition. In fact it made such a fuss of the human condition that it seemed to have invented it. It could be seen as a theory of the human condition, or alternatively as the abrogation of all theory in the name of the human condition: our condition comes first ('existence precedes essence'); it is we who, in our condition, invent, choose and commit ourselves to theories, which only derive their standing from that commitment (whether or not we admit this); and just this *is* our condition. No theory can save us, for it is we who make and choose our theories and our selves. To pretend otherwise is 'bad faith'.

If this is indeed our condition, why do we need to be told about it? Surely this would be the one thing with which we would be only too painfully familiar. And can a learned profession be kept going by the exegesis of the human condition which, when all is said and done, has only a limited number of things to be said about it? Do we need to buy and read difficult books to learn about that anguished condition which, according to those books, is our constant and inescapable companion? Existentialists would reply that bland, false philosophies had obscured the truth of our condition from us; that overt existentialism was born of a reaction to the Hegelian doctrine that an all-embracing, problem-resolving, cosmically guaranteed synthesis was available. Existentialism was a philosophy which not merely denied that this could be done, but gloried in this denial.

But ought not the human condition, whatever it is, be something universal? – is there not something odd in seeming to say that all conditions are human but some are more so than others? This is where the period flavour comes in. End-of-war and post-war France was like the human condition, but a damn sight *more so*. If ever there was a situation when men could not find external reassurance for their identity, dignity or conviction, this was it. Sartre and Camus made a philosophical virtue of necessity, or, rather, they softened the pain by teaching that a particularly acute condition was merely *the* universal human condition, and that those who suffered from less acute forms of it were in bad faith, and thus, though seemingly better off, really inferior as human beings.

The general features of the human condition which provide existentialism with its starting point – such as that we conceptualise and 'make' both ourselves and others, and thus mutually constrain each other, and hence 'hell is other people' – lend themselves to the generation of pleasing paradox. If Proust is the intellectuals' Dickens then Sartre is their Oscar Wilde. My favourite paradigm of Sartrian human relations occurs in his play *Le Diable et le Bon Dieu*, in which the hero, Goetz von Berlichingen, and his mistress Catherine sit cosily in front of the fire, Goetz in pantoufles and all, but looking somewhat ill at ease (I quote from memory)

> Goetz: Catherine, you have been acting strangely of late. Are you hiding something from me? Are you sure you still feel the same about me?
> Catherine: Yes, I swear. . .
> G: My dear, you do appreciate that what I love in you is the horror which I inspire in you. Are you sure you still loathe me sincerely?
> C: Yes, yes, I swear. . .each of your caresses inspires me with the deepest revulsion. . .my dearest fantasy is to kill you. . .I dream of it several times every night. . .
> G: (mollified) Ah well, in that case. . .

Peace is restored, *Gemütlichkeit* prevails, and Goetz puffs contentedly at his pipe.

Sartre is not merely expert on these stalemates of mutually constraining consciousness, he is also a specialist in the distinctive predicament of the intellectual. *Mains Sales* was not merely about Titoism and the morality of the vacillating party line, but also about the ambivalent prostration of the Hamlet/intellectual before the man of action and commitment. In his splendid trilogy of novels, Mathieu is the central character and, one supposes, expresses the author and his fantasies. In the final scene, during the collapse of France in 1940, Mathieu becomes involved with a group of Chasseurs Alpins who refuse to surrender, and engage the Germans in a desperate rearguard action. At last he finds commitment and decision, and disavows his past vacillations. *Bang!* A Jerry bites the dust. That one was for one of the books I never wrote. *Bang!* Another one. That was for that woman I never made...And so on, for quite a bit. (By those criteria, I could decimate a regiment.)

The fourth volume of that *roman fleuve* never appeared. One can only suppose that it would be embarrassing to have Mathieu survive that situation, and difficult to continue the novel without him. In literature, as in life, when caught between inconvenience and bathos, the rest is silence...

Apart from capturing the spirit of an age in the idiom of a would-be universal metaphysic, what did he achieve? It would be idle to pretend that he did not exemplify, encourage, and ratify some of the worst traits of the Left Bank spirit: obscurity, prolixity, apriorism and indifference to fact, ponderousness, pretentiousness, dogmatism, cliquishness, insularity, a silly idealisation of the proletariat combined with a *de facto* intellectual elitism, the attempt to underpin the most specific and local of prejudices by the most abstruse and universal-seeming arguments...and above all, a certain dreadful knowingness and confidence in the presentation of argument. This last can only be described as a kind of intellectual *machismo*: to betray the least doubt would be to show lack of manliness. The force of one's insight is conveyed by total confidence in uttering it. In Britain, this style was characteristic of Bernard Shaw and his generation, but happily seems to have gone out of fashion. Individuals and movements may in fact be dogmatic, but at least they hide their dogmatism rather than parading it as a badge of depth.

The *Critique of Dialectical Reason*, all of its 800-odd pages, does alas display these traits to the full. It is the fruit, as so much of Sartre's later work, of the marriage of his existentialism and his Marxism. The existentialist supplies some very abstract premisses or concepts about the human condition, the Marxist somehow extracts from them values, conclusions, interpretations concerning the concrete processes of history and society. The common existentialist stock of notions about our condition reappears in a new formal language which borrows more and more from the metaphysics of Marxism, and provides the machinery with which one is to get somewhere. The editor has thoughtfully provided a glossary which he frankly admits is unsatisfactory, and in this he is indeed right. The definitions themselves are utterly obscure, and if one substitutes the definiens for the definiendum – as one is encouraged to do by the fact that the concepts form a kind of circle – one gets real mumbo-jumbo. These notions are related with the utmost looseness to each other and to reality. The propositions articulated with their help are very often quite unintelligible. He is a *grand mystificateur* more than a *grand simplificateur*.

Despite the great length, the book is not even meant to be conclusive. It is merely part I of a work of which the second, conclusive part II has not yet appeared, though the French original of part I dates back to 1960. This forthcoming volume – on which Sartre was said to be working feverishly – 'will attempt to establish that there is one *human* history, with *one* truth and *one* intelligibility – and not by considering the material content of this history, but by demonstrating that a practical multiplicity, whatever it may be, must unceasingly totalise itself through interiorising its multiplicity at all levels' (p. 69).

The above sentence is far above the average level of intelligibility of the present volume. It seems to mean that it is possible to show, by formal logical argument, that in the end there will be one single interpretation of human history, which will become increasingly available to all the individual participants; it will sum up ('totalise') all the fragmentary data and come out with one and the same final sum for all men, who 'interiorise' it. Now if it is indeed possible to 'demonstrate' any such thing, it does look as if some abstract Logic was dictating the course of human history after all...This reinforces the old suspicion that what they do on the Left Bank is to stand Marx on his head, ending up with some version of Hegel.

Sartre would not accept this, of course. In an interesting and relatively clear passage (p. 23), which also throws a good deal of light on what he thinks he is doing, he distinguishes the Hegelian, Marxist and 'Positivist' positions. He thinks he is really showing how it is possible to be both inside history, as one participant with a partial vision, and yet also to aspire towards a total and uniquely correct view which covers the future. Positivists, in his sense, are those who, in pedestrian manner, make predictions about the future merely on the basis of assumed continuities with the past; and Hegel only 'proves' the necessity of the past, but refrains from speaking about the future; only Marxists attempt the more heroic task of telling us right now at least something about the great All: 'It is...necessary to demonstrate, in opposition to Positivism, how, *at this very moment*, dialectical Reason can assert certain totalising truths – if not the whole Truth' (p. 23).

This is an interesting claim, for it is a proud admission that Marxism is indeed 'historicist' in the sense of claiming to know, right now, what will come to pass. As Sartre observes 'Positivists often ask Marxists how they can claim. . .to detect the 'ruses' of History, the 'secret' of the proletariat, and the direction of historical development' (p. 23).

So Sartre indicates that he will show that this indeed can be done. Yet almost at once, he also remembers his materialist manners, and Marx-the-right-way-up makes his reappearance: 'Marx. . .began by positing that material existence was irreducible to knowledge, that *praxis* outstrips Knowledge in its real efficacy. Needless to say, this is my own position' (p. 24).

So knowledge (even in its privileged 'dialectical' form) does not after all cover the way things are really going. Practice goes its own way. As David Downes put it, praxis makes perfect. Our thought is merely a part of 'the real as a particular form of human activity'. But then, why should the dialectical Marxist thought be any truer than that of other men, whose thought is *also* part and parcel of that 'real'? This question bothers Sartre, and rightly so. He repudiates a facile solution: 'Of course dialectical materialism has a practical advantage over contemporary ideologies in that it is the ideology of the rising class. But if it were merely the inert expression of this rise. . .how could we speak of a progress of *consciousness*? Like philosophical liberalism today, it would be no more than a mythical reflection' (pp. 25–6). Well that sure puts me in my place.

We can now see his central problem: how can one, as a good historical materialist, both accept one's place inside history with all its limitations, and yet also claim at least partial understanding of the Whole *as it truly is*?

Leaving him with this grand problem which he does not yet claim to have solved, the performance of dialectical reason in the more accessible spheres of the past and present does not inspire confidence. When this volume appeared, the Algerian war was not yet finished, and Sartre naturally alludes to the problems of colonialism, and North Africa: 'In reality, racism is the colonial interest lived as a link of all the colonialists of the colony through serial flight of alterity. As such, like the living Idea it presents itself as infinite depth. But its depth is both petrified and strictly formal, because it is limited to producing itself as a negation of everyone by serial infinity' (p. 300).

Leaving aside the mumbo-jumbo, which alas is typical of much of the book, the passage does make one clear claim at least – that racism is a by-product of the colonial situation. To believe that racism only came to North Africa with colonialism is a sad example of apriorism and indifference to fact.

Students of the French scene may want to know how Sartre himself views the relationship of his own existentialism to his Marxism. Marxism now seems to be granted priority. He only speaks reluctantly of existentialism, sometimes re-naming it 'the ideology of existence': 'I do not like speaking about existentialism...A past peripheral cultural fashion, not unlike a brand of soap [p. 821]... I regard Marxism as the untranscendable philosophy for our time, and I believe that the ideology of existence...is an enclave within Marxism itself, both produced and rejected by Marxism' (p. 822).

That puts existentialism in *its* place. It also hints obscurely at some background meta-theory which decrees that Marxism is mandatory *now*, but not forever (so may the final 'totalisation' be different after all?). But it seems that his erstwhile Existentialism is now superseded, in as far as an overall 'totalisation', an authoritative overview, is after all attainable by *Reason*. In plainer English, this would seem to mean that a kind of all-embracing truth about man and history can be worked out by just *thinking*. Despite the Kantian sound of the title of the volume, there is no question of a *critique*, a sustained delimitation of what this Reason can or cannot do, and why. There is instead a painful and somewhat circular groping, as of a blind rat in a maze, successively feeling its way up a succession of unpalatable dead ends, and yet unwilling to resign itself to its predicament. Repelled and attracted by each of these blind alleys in turn, it makes the rounds and promises a solution in the next volume. All this does at least give his thinking a certain tension. He makes the round of Marxist–materialist requirements (primacy of our *praxis*), the self-choice and reflexive view of man inherited from Existentialism and phenomenology, and the curiously Idealist aspiration for a 'totalising', conclusive vision.

Dialectical Reason differs from Analytical Reason in that the former deals with self-conscious and mutually conscious antagonists, whereas the latter deals with inert nature. (Actually, Sartre does not exclude the possibility of a 'dialectic of nature' either, but prefers to remain agnostic about it.) Who are those inter-locking antagonists who provide material for the dialectic? Classes, naturally. But they seem to generate each other by their mutual awareness:

> it is conceivable – as a pure, formal, logical hypothesis – that there should be a Universe in which practical multiplicities would not form themselves into classes. . . But *if classes do exist*. . .if the unity of each is not directly occasioned by the *praxis* of the Other. . .everything will scatter to infinity. . .This means that the unity of each class depends on that of the Other, and, above all, that this dependence is due not to some dialectical magic but to a real project of violence which incorporates the other unity as a practical factor of its own (p. 794).

In English: there *must* be class conflict so that he may have his Total Story (otherwise everything will 'scatter to infinity'). It must be violent (this seems part revolutionary mystique, part concession to materialism, avoidance of idealist 'magic'); yet the mechanics of the violence hinges on mutual and hostile consciousness.

Thus Sartre's Existentialism now seems seriously modified: if a 'totalisation' is attainable by Reason, even if it be 'dialectical', then does not a kind of Essence precede Existence after all? (For that rationally established story must impose itself on reality.) That sounds Idealist/Hegelian rather than Marxist. But at the same time, he insists that the totalisation is only reached through classes and their practice and violence. But the Marxism in turn is suffused with Existentialism, with self-creation through consciousness and above all, through the mutually hostile consciousness of rival classes. So we go round the mulberry bush. The final message, which takes over 800 pages to reach (and the end is yet to come) is this: History is the story of class struggle, but in the idiom of *Huis Clos*.

5
Chomsky

In *Reflections on Language*,[1] Chomsky is addressing the wider world rather than merely his fellow linguists:

> I will sketch what seems to me an appropriate framework within which language may prove to have a more general intellectual interest, and will consider the possibilities for constructing a kind of theory of human nature on a model of this sort.

Not that we really need to be convinced that language is of more general intellectual interst. Any pretence to studying language as merely one thing among others is a mere affectation, or at best a methodological ploy. Language, man and the world are so intertwined that theories about any one of them inevitably presuppose a good deal about each of the others. The currently most fashionable way of supporting this point is to insist that the world is conceptually, hence linguistically, saturated. Chomsky has brought home to us, more than any other man perhaps, another aspect of this interlocking man–world–language liaison: our very capacity to use language at all is not self-evident or self-explanatory, and cannot possibly be explained in terms of the repeated use of such easily accessible, introspective processes as association or its supposedly tough-minded variants, Stimulus, Response and Reinforcement. The ability to generate and recognise an infinite number of unpredictable sentences simply cannot be explained by the loose and feeble explanatory power of notions such as 'analogy'. To pretend otherwise is to cling to a low and infantile standard of what may count as an explanation. Thus

[1] Noam Chomsky, *Reflections on Language*, London, 1976.

our capacity to speak, and hence to think, is rooted in our internal organisation, which is a far-away country of which we know little.

Chomsky's firm formulation of the problem and clear indication or exemplification of the kind of thing that might count as its solution, lies at the heart of his achievement. The actual execution of the programme for which he has shown the norms is quite another matter – technical, contentious and evidently in flux.

If in this book Chomsky tries to spell out more explicitly the general and philosophic implications of his work, he is in a way repaying a certain debt. The central intuition underlying his work is really a philosophical or methodological one, concerning what may or may not count as an explanation. His basic idea was certainly available before him, and he would be the last to deny it. On the contrary, he delights in exploring its pre-history. But it is almost certainly true that his idea would not have had its great impact, had it not been launched as part and parcel of a technical, operational attempt to work out a generative grammar. In a way, he is an operationalised Plotinus. Plotinus observed that the eye must contain something sun-like, if it is to be capable of perceiving the sun. Chomsky has formulated the problem and a research strategy which has begun to dig at the roots of findings, in the depth of our cognitive and linguistic capacities, that internal capacity which they must possess which makes them ready to perceive or to articulate that rich range of objects which, in fact, we can note or express.

There is a certain paradox here: an idea which is old can only make its mark if married to a specific enterprise which, in itself, is contentious and inconclusive. There is also a certain parallel with Freud. The elements in Freud's vision which seem valid were not new and can be found, in a more exciting literary form, in Nietzsche, as well as perhaps elsewhere. Yet they made their enormous impact thanks to being fused with more specific doctrines and a clinical practice whose merits are eminently questionable. In each case, an old idea becomes persuasive by being married to a concrete programme. In each case, this gives it a seriousness to which philosophy on its own cannot nowadays aspire.

Those interested in a crisp and succinct formulation of Chomsky's basic position would probably still be best advised to turn to his earlier *Language and Mind*. The present volume is however of distinct interest in as far as in it Chomsky also discusses specific points raised by others against his formulations. Chomsky continues to be puzzled by the vehemence of the hostility to his 'innatist' or 'rationalist' view of our capacity to learn and use a language, and he notes, plausibly enough, that the vigour and persistence of the opposition seem to indicate some very deep sources. His speculations about these sources are interesting, but I do not think he identifies them with precision, partly because he puts too much blame on an 'empiricism', a notion which is left in a somewhat unrefined state.

> The claims of empiricism have often been put forth not as
> speculation, but as established fact, as if they must be
> true. . .Such claims must be evaluated on their merits, but
> if they are found to be without support, plain wrong, or
> seriously exaggerated, as I believe invariably proves to be
> the case, then it is appropriate to search elsewhere for their
> appeal and power.

Certainly. But note that they 'must be evaluated'. By what criteria? Chomsky's implied and tacit answer – tacit because to him it is too obvious to need stating, and because, as he has erroneously observed elsewhere, all rational men would agree to it – is that these claims of empiricism must be evaluated by the criteria which empiricism itself has codified. The claims must, as the saying goes, fit the facts. That is the clue to the profound hold which empiricism has over the minds of so many (including Chomsky, but not, as he sometimes seems to think, all mankind), and makes some of his formulations *seem* so offensive.

The really significant aspect of empiricism is that it sets up an ultimate, so to speak terminal, norm for decision-procedures in cognitive disputes. It identifies the final court of appeal. This does not mean that we may not discuss its authority; but it does mean that if we attempt to do so, we are discussing the merits of total alternative and incommensurate worlds, with all the attendant philosophic difficulties. (Within which world is the debate to take place?) There are at least two kinds of world: one, in which the procedural rules of the final court of appeal are rules of evidence and of evidence alone; and the other, a world in which the final arbiter is compatibility with some substantive conviction. Most of mankind has, I believe, lived in the latter kind of world. Modern man has, at least in part, migrated to the former. Chomsky himself has done it so completely that he is not very clearly aware that any other kind of world, any other kind of cognitive authority, is conceivable. His seeming repudiation of empiricism springs ironically from a commitment to it so complete that it is unaware of its own existence.

Once one distinguishes clearly between empiricism as a formulation of norms for the settlement of cognitive disputes (in which sense he endorses it), and empiricism as a schema for explanatory models for our behaviour or competence (in which sense he repudiates it), the compulsiveness of empiricism in the latter sense can perhaps be exorcised. The present volume is of interest, amongst other things, because in it Chomsky comes closer than he has previously, as far as I know, to spelling this out:

> We can agree that classical rationalist and empiricist doctrines should be recast. . .so as to be more directly susceptible to empirical test. . .Descartes, Hume and Kant were grappling with problems at the borders of scientific knowledge. . .and sought such evidence as they could muster to justify their theoretical speculations. But from a justifiable concern for empirical confirmation, we cannot argue to a commitment to empiricist doctrine.

Indeed not, if empiricist doctrine means an explanatory schema for performance or competence. The above passage gets it right, yet one is bothered by various features: the failure to stress and underscore the crucial ambiguity of 'empiricism'; the *en passant* tone, hardly suggesting that we have reached the heart of the matter: and that misleading remark about Descartes, Kant and Hume, which makes it sound as if they were primarily concerned with constructing models of our intellectual competence, seeking whatever evidence might come to hand. In fact, they were primarily working in the theory of knowledge (even if Hume was unclear about the distinction), and concerned with establishing what could count as evidence at all, and why. Those who do not wish to throw away the achievements of empiricism in this field sometimes erroneously suppose that this obliges them to oppose Chomsky in the area in which his real achievement lies. This is an error, but one encouraged by some of his own formulations of his views.

Another deep reason for opposition to Chomsky's ideas springs from the fact that he, more than anyone else perhaps, has rammed home the fact that it is never true to say *I speak*; the correct formulation must be *it speaks*. We are unaware of the principles which lead us to form our sentences and sequences of sentences, and thus we know not how we 'think'. It is not quite clear how or why we take responsibility for it. Lichtenberg may have said it, but Chomsky really brings it home, by struggling to identify the mechanics of that logico-linguistic *id*. The kind of Unconscious presupposed by the Chomskian approach is quite different from its Freudian namesake, but, appearances notwithstanding, it requires an even more drastic re-thinking of our picture of man. The Freudian Unconscious may have been unhousetrained and randy, but otherwise it was quite familiar, jolly and clubbable. We get used to it with ease, or even alacrity. I am much less at ease about those inner strings and pulleys which are the subject of the generative grammarians, and which are recorded in a truly hideous notation in Chomsky's book. (Could not something be done about this? It leaps neither to eye nor tongue. It is no aid to exposition or comprehension. I refuse to believe that no more elegant solution to this technical problem is available.)

The issue which arises through all this controversy between Chomsky and one important segment of his critics concerns whether or not man is transparent to himself, whether or not he is best described or explained in a human idiom. Chomsky sees this issue and takes a firm stand on it: the human or familiar idiom is neither adequate nor privileged. But for some reason he treats these global or pan-human populists, the defenders of the Old Human Vision, as a species of empiricist. In fact they are quite distinct. They are often opposed, sometimes bitterly, to empiricism, which when radical also ends up with a counter-intuitive picture of man, far removed from the cosy, familiar *Lebenswelt*. Radical empiricists and our pan-populists may indeed share a distaste for the invocation of hidden structures in the explanation of human conduct, but their reasons for the distaste are different, and their sharing it does not make one of them a sub-species of the other.

The minor reasons Chomsky picks out for the appeal of empiricism and the resistance to his views are interesting but incomplete: though in fairness it must be said that he himself notes that 'the issues can be perceived along many dimensions and in quite different ways'. Thus he speaks of 'the appeal of empiricist ideology in Marxist thought, a commitment which has often been expressed in the most extreme forms'. Here 'empiricism' seems to mean the doctrine of the malleability of human nature. Chomsky illustrates his point by quoting from Gramsci:

> the most fundamental innovation introduced by Marxism
> into the science of politics and history is the proof that
> there does not exist an abstract, fixed and immutable

'human nature'. . .but that human nature is the totality
of historically determined social relations.

This statement is surely false, comments Chomsky. So? He hints at
the fascinating and vertiginous possibility, recently re-stated by
Gunther Stent, that there is a biological underpinning to the limits
of human thought. I have some difficulty in imagining how we could
ascertain these limits without at the same time transcending them:
any idiom which can articulate these limits must presumably also
be able to articulate alternative possibilities. Whatever the truth
about these difficult matters, Chomsky sketches out amusingly some
of the possible social consequences of mankind's advance towards
these conceptual Last Frontiers:

> As creative minds approach the limits of cognitive capacity,
> not only will the act of creation be limited to a talented
> few, but even the appreciation and comprehension of what
> has been created. . .Such limits might be approached more
> or less at the same time in various domains, giving rise to
> a 'crisis of modernism'. . .blurring. . .the distinction
> between art and puzzle. . .Mockery of conventions that are,
> ultimately, grounded in human cognitive capacity might
> be expected to become virtually an art form in itself. . .
> It may be that something of the sort has been happening
> in recent history.

Have those bricks at the Tate Gallery been hammering at the
very limits of our cognitive structures?

6

Notes towards a theory of ideology

Offence
> If I were to imagine. . .a day-labourer, and the mightiest
> Emperor that ever lived. . .sent for the poor man. . .
> and informed him that he wished to have him for his
> son-in-law. . .what then?. . .the labourer. . .would become
> somewhat or very much puzzled, shame-faced and em-
> barrassed, and it would seem to him. . .quite mad, the
> last thing in the world about which he would say a word
> to anybody else, since he in his own mind was not far
> from explaining it by supposing. . .that the Emperor wanted
> to make a fool of him, so that the poor man would be the
> laughing stock of the whole town. . .This thing. . .of
> becoming the Emperor's son-in-law might readily be
> subjected to the test of reality, so that the labourer would
> be able to ascertain how far the Emperor was serious. . .
> or whether. . .he merely wanted to. . .help him. . .find his
> way to the mad-house. . .And suppose now that this was
> not an external reality but an inward thing, so that factual
> proofs could not help the labourer.

> Søren Kierkegaard, *The Sickness unto Death*
> (*Fear and Trembling* and *The Sickness unto Death*,
> edited by Walter Lowrie, Doubleday Anchor,
> New York, 1955, p. 215)

Ideologies are systems of ideas or beliefs. This is hardly contentious
and does not tell us very much, partly because we do not know, from
the definition, just how much is to be read into the words occurring
in it. Moreover, whilst ideologies are systems of ideas, not all systems

of ideas are ideologies. What is the specific differentia? What is it, within the (nebulously defined) wider class of systems of ideas, which turns some of them into ideologies?

Offensiveness, in the quasi-technical sense which Kierkegaard here gives it, seems part of the answer. Ideologies contain hypotheses, but they are not simply hypotheses. They are hypotheses full of both menace and sex-appeal. They threaten and they promise; they demand assent with menaces; they re-classify the moral identity of the believer and sceptic: and they generate a somewhat new world. The world is different according to whether one looks at it from within or without a given ideology.

It might be objected that any idea whatever can be exciting or terrifying for someone, in some context. Indeed. *Anything* whatever can be the object of sexual desire, as a character in Sartre observes in self-defence, and I have a feeling that it says somewhere or other in the works of Talcott Parsons that anything whatever can be the object of cathexis. So it is.

It seems to me an essential characteristic of ideologies that this offence-generating property is *inherent* in them, that it is implied in their very intellectual content. It is not contingent. Any fact, in a suitable context, may indeed be overwhelmingly significant and exciting to someone, somewhere. But ideologies contain contentions which are inherently fear- and hope-inspiring and are meant to be such to anyone, anywhere. This does not necessarily mean that they always succeed in eliciting such powerful reactions in the people exposed to them. Kierkegaard clearly believed that it was of the very nature of Christianity that it gave offence, but, in the work in which he introduces the notion, he also displays some irritation with and contempt for those who stubbornly refuse to be offended. They clearly are, for him, a lower form of humanity, a kind of human vegetable: 'The degree of offense depends on what passion a man has for admiration. The more prosaic men, devoid of imagination and passion, and who therefore are not apt to admire, they too may be offended, but they confine themselves to saying, "Such a thing I cannot get through my head, I let it alone"' (p. 217). And earlier on, discussing despair, which for him is the failure to embrace the offence-giving faith, he says:

> In consciousness of being in despair a man is furthest from
> being conscious of himself as spirit. But precisely. . .not
> being conscious of oneself as spirit is despair. . .whether the

> condition be that of complete deadness, a merely vegetative
> life, or a life of higher potency...In the latter case the
> man is like the sufferer from consumption: he feels well,
> considers himself in the best of health...precisely when the
> sickness is most dangerous [p. 178].

All this amounts to an admirable explication of the concept of
offence. Kierkegaard's own favoured belief system promises salvation,
but only on condition that one 'believes in' the system in question.
The system also overtly proclaims itself offensive, and this offensiveness is of its essence, if Kierkegaard is to be trusted. The tension
which this offensiveness induces in the souls of some is then treated
as a kind of confirmation of the system itself. No truth, indeed no
identity, without offence. Nevertheless, the indisputable fact that the
tension-generating offensiveness fails to work for *some*, is also accommodated and invoked: the despair of those who do not even know
they are in despair, is deeper, more noxious, than the condition of
more conscious sufferers.

One can of course see the origin of Existentialism at this point, and
also understand the manner of its bifurcation into religious and
atheist varieties. The latter kind invokes a premiss drawn from the
theory of knowledge or from an account of the human condition: all
belief systems are offensive, in the appropriate sense, and hence all
are tension-generating, simply because men never have the evidence
adequate for a viable system of ideas. A viable system can be defined
in various ways, but basically what is at stake is a picture of one's
environment good enough to warrant action. In practice, we can
never have such a picture with a logical warranty, and hence action
and life are always a gamble, a leap, a device without safeguards of
correctness. Q.E.D. Religious Existentialism contains a further
nuance: it points an accusing finger at philosophies which claim that
they *can* warrant our vision of things, and proceed from the falsity
of this claim to stress the greater psychological truth of religions,
with their frank demand for non-rational commitment, and from
this it somehow slides to a putative vindication of religion itself.
Religious irrationality lays bare or exemplifies the human condition,
therefore those irrational beliefs are valid.

These questions in the history of ideas do not concern us here.
I have begun with Kierkegaard's concept of offence simply because
it seems to me to offer an admirable starting point to the understanding of ideology, to what it is that distinguishes what in practice we

recognise as ideology, from *any* old system of ideas. Ideologies attract and repel; they do both at once; and, I suspect, they can generally function only if indeed they do both: 'the mightiest Emperor... informed the labourer that he wished to have him for his son-in-law...and suppose now...that factual proofs could not help the labourer' (pp. 215–16). This seems to me of the essence of the predicament of man-in-face-of-an-ideology: he has cause to be attracted and to be afraid, and has no way of telling *which*.

The threat or menace in an ideology is in some ways like a painful rite de passage, which restricts entry, makes membership valuable to those who have gained it, ensures that membership does not become devalued by becoming too easy; it is a source of pride to the initiates, and gives them a psychic investment in retaining and restricting membership. But it has the advantage over an initiation rite in that it is timeless and ever-present. The Queen in *Alice* claimed to believe at least three impossible things before breakfast. Believers in offence-giving faiths perpetually carry such impossible convictions with them.

A community of believers is defined by shared belief, but this could hardly work if the membership-conferring belief were something anyone could simply stumble on or work out for himself. It must be *different*. There is no way of patenting ideas or convictions, other than, perhaps, by making them simultaneously eccentric, demanding, difficult and authoritative. Their eccentricity disconnects them from other ideas: and if they positively contradict commonsense notions, there can be no way of deriving them from such ordinary notions.

The strain generated by offensiveness has at least two functions: it is diacritical, serving to separate believers from unbelievers, and it helps enforce discipline and ranking within the community of the faithful. No man is tied to another by an unstressful conviction which he can understand and establish by his own unaided efforts. Precarious, and above all offensive ideas, are different. If one man presents an idea of this kind to another, with the full backing of his own authority, he is really issuing a challenge: submit, or defy me. And if the man submits, he is henceforth tied to the idea he accepted by his own pride and dignity. If it is subsequently discarded as absurd, he himself is also thereby demeaned.

But offence is not generated by unacceptability alone. The world is too full of absurd ideas; not all of them are embraced, and not all of them define a community of the faithful. Something else is required. In Kierkegaard's illuminating story, the promise or offer made by the Emperor is not merely implausible – it is also *tempting*.

If the repulsiveness, the offensiveness, is the *trap*, then an ideology also needs *bait*. In fact, I do suspect that all ideologies need both a trap and a bait: an entry-inducing and an exit-hampering mechanism; usually these take the form of commitment to an absurdity, and of some positive, unproblematical *appeal*, which attracts potential believers initially. The trap may prevent them from leaving once they are in, but what is also required is something to lure them in in the first place. In Kierkegaard's story, we can feel that the labourer, terrified of his own presumption, nevertheless does rather fancy himself as in-law to the Emperor. It is absurd, of course. . .but not *so* absurd as not to be rather attractive, all the same.

The bait can be a promise or an idea, or both. A unifying idea, with a genuine or putative explanatory power, which illuminates what had previously been obscure or disconnected, will do very well; and at the same time, it is good if some kind of salvation is also implied. The idea generally *clicks*: this, we feel, at last makes sense of it all, we had always vaguely suspected that something of this order was the underlying truth. A promise of salvation does click: can the world be such as to justify despair? We are inclined to think not. The *offence* of which Kierkegaard speaks so eloquently clearly springs from the co-presence of both the click and the revulsion.

The revulsion seems necessary for production of that tension without which there would be no price, no value, no discipline, no commitment. It seems built into ideologies by some hidden hand, some cunning of reason, to ensure that they can function as such; let us leave aside just *how*, for the moment. But how is it ensured that we are vulnerable to the seduction of the promise, to the bait?

The answer is of course that we are not all of us equally and at all times so vulnerable. In the work with which I have chosen to start, Kierkegaard does of course employ a simple device for making sure that we are so vulnerable. Despair, which in his language means amongst other things susceptibility to faith, is universal, of course. If some men are not aware of being in despair, well that only shows that their despair is that much deeper, that they are at a lower level of consciousness, approximating to a merely vegetative existence. Within this system, despair is clearly not to be escaped, other than through faith.

Other writers choose different definitions and valuations. Nietzsche and the pragmatists valued robust confidence and instinct higher precisely because it is not vulnerable to the bait and the trap, because it does not need to sustain life by faith, because its life is allegedly self-sustaining or is its own faith. Nietzsche spoke with derision of Pascal as a man who tried to induce despair in us all.

Arguments exist which claim that we are all vulnerable, and which are less tautological than Kierkegaard's. Death, uncertainty, contingency, the limitations of our power and our knowledge, and the inherently incomplete and/or uncertain status of our ideas – all these, and perhaps other features of the human condition seem to ensure that we are ever vulnerable. Anyway, there seems to be no doubt at any rate about the vulnerability of some men or groups, at least those less favoured or protected by good fortune, temperament or fortitude.

Perhaps, in those pessimistic accounts of the human condition which purport to show that we are all vulnerable and in need of faith, we can find a clue to why both the bait and the trap are ever-present: if the objective situation is such that we can never be confident, either morally or cognitively, or in any other way, why then that ensures that any faith which promises to reassure us will also be false to the facts of the case and thus generate offence. Any coherent picture will be less than adequately justified, and thus at risk, open to doubt, and hence offensive.

Double status

It is a well-known feature of ideologies that they claim to be intellectually sovereign. The truth, Spinoza said, is the touchstone both of itself and of falsehood. From the inside, ideologies are not merely true: what is far more important is that they provide the very criterion for telling truth from falsehood. They monopolise validation.

They can provide the promised salvation to their believers only on condition that they are treated as logically terminal: they are to be the final touchstones of truth and falsehood, it is in them that cognitive sovereignty resides. Questions are ultimately resolved by appeal to *them*.

This is a well-known, conspicuous trait of ideologies. But certain odd, and indeed most significant, consequences follow if one sees this trait in conjunction with their offensiveness, discussed above.

A claim can only give offence, in the sense intended, within the context of some *other* and wider world, of some other set of rules, which it manages to offend, and which it did not itself invent or sanction. The promise of sublime elevation made to Kierkegaard's humble day-labourer is offensive precisely because it is made in a given world in which it goes against all social expectations, against all social norms, for day labourers to be so promoted. Both the bait and the trap, indeed, can only have their efficacy in terms of some prior world, a world *preceding* the one to be defined and logically dominated by the ideology in question. So, in a curious way, ideologies tacitly and implicitly admit that they do not dominate or fill out the world after all. They function within a world they did not themselves make.

This admission can, in a simple religious form, be quite naïve and unselfconscious. Robertson Smith's work on the religion of the Semites consists precisely of spelling out tacit assumptions of this *ante*-world, a world which traditions such as the biblical one simply took for granted, and within which they naïvely, unselfconsciously operated. At the same time, I would not wish to claim that a sophisticated theology could not overcome this seeming contradiction, somewhat along the following lines: perhaps of course, the offence operates in a prior world, one which the believer had inhabited before his full conversion, and it made its initial impact in terms of the ideas and conventions of that world. But this does mean that this prior world has some basic or ultimate authority. It was a provisional and illusory habitat, from which the believer had to propel himself to the version of truth; but once that is attained, the ladder by which he has ascended is rightly pushed away and discarded and is *then* seen to be redundant. Just because Grace first makes its appearance to the unregenerated in terms of their erstwhile condition, and impels them in those terms to seek their own salvation, it does not follow that those terms are ultimate or even sound. Not at all.

We shall not here (or anywhere else, for that matter) solve the question of the legitimacy or ultimacy of either outlook – of the internal vision of soteriological belief, or the external, dispassionate, faith-suspending scrutiny which preceded it (or followed it again, in the case of renegades). We are here concerned with the sociological, not the normative aspect of the matter. And sociologically, this situation has most important implications.

Ideologies are indeed ultimate, normative, sovereign, and offence-giving in their total claims; but at the same time, they do *not* altogether conceptually define and dominate a world. They are articulated in a language wider than the world which they themselves would define and authorise to exist. It is from *that* richer world that they recruit the neophyte, and it is also *in* that world that they are offensive. Hence they are bi-lingual or bi-conceptual. The ultimacy-claim commits them to treating their own conceptual scheme as all-embracing, terminal, as the very touchstone both of truth and falsehood; but the crucial mechanisms of offering bait and closing the trap work in an idiom and by standards external to the ideology itself, which has its own standards of truth and falsehood, of conclusiveness, of evidence, and of proper presentation.

This dualism or ambivalence is an extremely important trait of ideologies. Its most obvious explanation lies in the fact that they propose monopolistic solutions in contexts in which they do not, or do not altogether, monopolise power.

Even in cases when they possess the political power to proscribe rivals, they do not really have the conceptual power to make rival positions *unthinkable*. There is a certain fashionable philosophy of culture (with quite diverse roots in contemporary philosophy, sociology and anthropology) which would make culture ultimate, as the only necessary, and sufficient, ground of the norms and cosmological ideas which pervade it. Quite apart from the devastating objections one can raise against this philosophically and morally – it is an attempt to browbeat us into accepting culture, or even accepting a specific given culture, as self-validating and authoritative – this is quite mistaken on a straightforward descriptive, sociological level. It is a most interesting and important trait of many, perhaps of all conceptual systems, that, unlike the artificial *Newspeak* of Orwell's *1984*, they do *not* succeed in making dissent or heresy unsayable, unconceptualisable.

If I am right in my stress on this trait of ideologies – they claim ultimacy and at the same time naïvely accept the rules, conventions and norms of some other world within which they operate, attract clients and endeavour to peddle themselves – then this also shows the misguided nature of certain modern theological reformulations of religious belief. Take, for instance, Barthian religious fundamentalism. It defends religion by pointing out, correctly enough, that it is above or beyond all defence. Its claims have so elevated and ultimate a status that to *defend* them, from some other premises or assumptions, would be to contradict religion itself – for such a defence or justification would implicitly give those other premises or assumptions, whatever they might be, an even higher and more ultimate a status. The argument is perfectly cogent as far as it goes. It faces one or two difficulties which do not concern us here –

notably, that it applies with equal force and indeed equal facility to *any* belief system which takes the trouble to incorporate in itself the simple assertion that it itself is ultimate. It makes things too easy for too many claims.[1] What does concern us here is the phenomenology of religion, as a form of ideology. The Barthian defence is quite untrue to the facts of the case, to the very spirit of that which it would defend. Logically or not, actual faiths have in fact *both* claimed ultimacy *and* are defended, argued for, from extraneous premisses drawn from an antecedent world which is naïvely taken for granted, as given.

The rival wing of modernist theology, exemplified by Tillich and others, travestied the nature of the defended faith in another way. It totally *removes* all offence. If God is equated with one's ultimate concern (whatever it may be), it only needs the fairly trite premisses that men do have concerns, and that these concerns can be ranked (at least at any given time) in order of urgency, to establish, by a terrifyingly simple argument, the existence of God, or at least of *a* God per man. (A man who, at the top of his list of concerns, has a number of equally urgent or ultimate concerns, ipso facto becomes a polytheist, I suppose.)

World-generator or world-apex?

The conceptual bi-lingualism of ideologies, or their double status as defining the limits and norms of the world and at the same time inhabiting a world which they share with their infidel rivals, brings one to a further point of importance in the study of this topic:

There are two distinct, though interrelated questions, which are sometimes confused or at any rate not distinguished with adequate emphasis.

(*a*) The social construction of reality.

(*b*) The role of ideology *within* reality.

---

[1] *Nur mit ein bisschen anderen Worten*, a similar argument is nowadays often found in fashionable Marxist theology. At one point, we learn that Marxism cannot be transcended (as long as the conditions which engendered it obtain, or because it is *the* philosophy of our age, etc., arguments which curiously imply that conditions of its transcendence *are* conceivable, even if they are not yet our conditions); this established, we take from the philosophy of science the trendy claim that no theory is at the mercy of mere fact; and we reinforce the package by noting that the putative refutations are in any case in the idiom of a bourgeois vision which we *have* transcended, and the case is established.

The social-construction-of-reality theme has had a certain vogue of late, and has been fed by a variety of philosophical and sociological streams, similar to those which encourage the idea of culture as normatively sovereign, ultimate, and beyond challenge. Indeed, the two sets of ideas appeal to similar tastes and are often conflated. The ultimacy of cultural norms protects those norms (or those which one most fancies amongst them) from criticism and challenge; the social construction of reality ensures that reality, being man-made, cannot be alien to man, cannot be icy, impersonal, cannot exemplify the theses which are pejoratively known as scientism or reductionism. Things are as we fancy them. Thus (*a*) our beliefs are true, and (*b*) our world is as we wish it. The two arguments converge like pincers on the same objective.

Discerning the motives which lead men to find pleasure in these views does not of course undermine, let alone refute, these views. These views have a simple and powerful basis. One premiss is provided by the contention that any picture of reality must be conceptually saturated: 'things' can only be 'grasped' in terms of some system of ideas. The second premiss is provided by the contention that the carriers of such systems of ideas are not individuals but 'languages' or cultures, which are internalised by individuals in the process of their education, of their 'formation' as human beings with a cultural identity and a capacity to use a cultural medium. (One need not here face the question of the extent to which such a process of internalising a language or culture presupposes a pre-existing, 'innate' equipment.) Each of these premisses is very powerful (even if not necessarily very precise), and jointly they certainly encourage the conviction that reality is 'socially constructed'. This view then agreeably opens the way *both* to endorsing a given view of reality irrespective of logical objections to it (because that is what reality *is*, and one could not expect it to be more than our social vision), and *also*, if one wishes, of rejecting uncongenial views, however well supported by facts, simply because they allegedly are no more than artefacts of a social order which one happens not to endorse.

The idea has received further encouragement in the recent past from the at least partial successes of Chomskian linguistics. The tacitly unquestioned pre-Chomskian view of language was as of an accumulation and an echo: we accumulated our linguistic wealth like a squirrel amassing nuts, 'from experience'. The essence of the Chomskian view is to see the wealth of sentences which an individual can utter and understand as *generated* by some central, persisting mechanism, whose mode of operation can hopefully be reconstructed by working back from a delimitation of the range of performances of which it is capable. If this can be done for language, for recognising sentences, why not also for the rest of psychology, for our capacity to recognise *anything*, for the range of things which 'are' our world, or for the range of actions and meanings which are our social world?

For various reasons, it seems to me that this task, of explaining the 'generation' of our social or our total worlds, is much much harder even than the task of specifying the 'generative grammar' of a language. For one thing, discipline or social control in linguistic behaviour seems, interestingly, to be much stricter and more effective than in other spheres. Speech eccentricities are much easier to detect than eccentricities of conduct, and people seem much less inclined to commit them. The linguist seems to have access to much more clear-cut material at the basis of his work. But is there such a thing as ungrammatical *conduct*? You might say that a solecism such as wearing a black tie with tails is a sartorial-grammatical slip. But it is easy to identify such slips only in spheres such as these, e.g. 'formal dress', which are, precisely, distinct from the rest of life, and recognised as such, by being heavily 'ritualised'. In language we do have grammar, but in conduct we have only morality or custom; and immoral conduct, far from being hard to interpret in a given culture, may in fact be its statistical norm, and perfectly intelligible to all participants. Really bad grammar verges on incomprehensibility, but improper conduct is perfectly comprehensible. Is there then some deeper moral grammar which excludes some physically possible actions, and which effectively precludes them even when they are technically efficient and carried out by powerful people? It seems doubtful. The large majority of sane normal adults have no difficulty in internalising the grammar of their language to a point at which they commit fairly few solecisms. But this is not so in the field of norms of conduct, outside a man's home circle: people need to tread warily, and their fear of ridicule is an important factor in social control. They are not sure of the moral grammar; but if they are powerful enough, they also do not respect its bounds. The powerful defy etiquette with impunity. Social conduct does not have as firm a grammar as language does. It is often *technical*: it chooses effective *means*, not codified symbols. If this is so, much modern *structuralism* may be inspired by quite the wrong model, and Pierre Bourdieu may be giving us a wrong hint from Chomsky for his *Esquisse d'une théorie de la pratique* (Genève 1972) which runs as follows:

> When we discuss the levels of descriptive and explanatory adequacy, questions immediately arise concerning the firmness of the data in terms of which success is to be judged...For example...one might ask how we can establish that the two are sentences of different types, or that 'John's eagerness to please...' is well-formed, while 'John's easiness to please...' is not, and so on. There is no very satisfying answer to this question; data of this sort are simply what constitute the subject matter for linguistic theory. We neglect such data at the cost of destroying the subject [Noam Chomsky, *Current Issues in Linguistic Theory*, 1964].

In the world of conduct, the conventional and the technical *compete* with each other. Means–ends (technical) effectiveness makes itself felt, whether or not it conforms to the conventions ('grammar') of the culture. A man with the more powerful weapon can impose his will, whether or not the social syntax condones it. It is not so with language. Breath is cheap, the opportunity cost of utterance is very small; so the means need not be costed carefully. Men very seldom display their status or power by eccentricities of speech. On the one hand it is generally too easy (even if penalties may exist to sanction verbal or phonetic unconventionality), so that it doesn't prove very much; and at the same time, by hampering intelligibility, it may undermine whatever end the utterance was meant to satisfy. Words generally do not have any effect directly; such effects as they have, they normally attain through being *understood*. So there is neither need nor incentive, generally speaking, to break the rules, to violate the 'grammar'. Hence a 'structural' approach, which makes such good sense for the study of language, cannot easily and without great reservations be transferred to the study of social behaviour. One does wonder whether the failure to see this does not make a great deal of *structuralisme* irrelevant. Specimens of actual conduct are *not* evidence for a 'structure' in the same sense as utterances – or the boundary between acceptable and unacceptable utterances in a given language – constitute evidence for the structure of the generative mechanism of that language. (It is also not at all clear just where in 'society' such a mechanism could possibly be located.) Actual conduct, unlike speech, is a by-product of two quite different sets of factors – the cultural conventions within which the conduct takes place, and the real-world causal connections which are quite independent of those conventions. In speech, the same is true of the choice of meanings to be conveyed; but it is *not* true of the manner in which these meanings are articulated, conveyed and understood. But linguists are concerned with this latter process, which is significantly different from the choice of either actions or of meanings.

Another obvious difficulty faced by anyone attempting to extend and apply the Chomskian strategy to our 'reality-construction' is this: language, however important and central, is nevertheless *a* thing in the world amongst others, and does not fill out the world. A linguist attempting to specify the mechanisms which generate a given language may without circularity assume a certain world with given properties, within which and in terms of which he is endeavouring to complete his task of specifying the mechanisms. But an epistemic-sociologist endeavouring to tell us how we 'construct our world' is a man who has sawn off the branch on which he is sitting. Which prior world is left in terms of which he could do it? And what precisely is the status of that more ultimate world or idiom? The practitioners of this art, of giving us conceptual frissons by telling us *we* have made our world, do not seem unduly worried by this painful regress, but this seems to be so only because they do not aspire to any very high level of explanatory precision or rigour. They seem to be quite content with a general indication that such construction must be taking place, and with a fairly nebulous specification of just *how* it is done. The whole thing is then illustrated with alleged examples of the end-products of the process, without any genuine, concrete and precise theory of 'social world-construction'.

My own guess is that for various reasons, over and above the ones indicated, the task of indicating just *how* we construct 'our' reality will be well beyond our powers for a long time to come. What Sir Peter Medawar says about the related problem of the genetics of behaviour is also applicable here: 'the problem is very, very difficult. Goodness knows how it is to be got at. It may be outflanked or yield to attrition, but probably not to direct assault' (*The Art of the Soluble*, Harmondsworth, 1969, p. 97).

Our present purpose does not require us to decide either how or whether such construction takes place. It *does* require us to separate this question firmly from the problem of ideology in a narrower (but still broad and important) sense. Ideology, in the sense in which I am here approaching a tentative sketch of it, is something *within* the world, and *not* co-existensive with it, or with the world of any individual or group. It is a set of ideas with claims to intellectual authority and sovereignty *in* the world, and with a consequent strong tendency towards eliciting offence in Kierkegaard's sense – promising much but also inspiring fear of deception. It is something operating *in* our world, even if it claims a high status in it, and not something which actually *makes* the world and is presupposed by it. The two problems are inter-related. We must of course take seriously the Durkheimian thesis (of *The Elementary Forms of Religious Life*), which runs as follows: the main function or effect of the central belief system of a society is to inculcate, to make compulsive, the pivotal concepts, moral, cognitive and other, of that society. Those pivotal concepts then organise, direct, the perception and under-standing of anything else in the world of the members of the society. Without them, we would not have a world *at all*.

This thesis may or may not be true. But if true, that means that 'ideology', in the somewhat narrower sense, which I am trying to define, is also crucial for the wider question concerning how we 'construct our world'. The concepts which it makes central also dominate and organise all others. But that wider question – how do the central categories make the world – is as yet beyond our powers. The narrower question – how do they comport themselves in the world – may be more manageable. It seems to me best to try and deal with it first, without sliding over into the wider one, notwith-standing their inter-connection.[2]

What else is not *ideology*?

I have endeavoured to exclude from 'ideology' the very big thing, namely our total vision of reality (avoiding the question of whether we do live within a single such totality). But there may also be much *smaller* things which deserve to be excluded from it.

It seems to me pointless to include pre-literate, tribal religions

---

[2] In his interesting recent Malinowski Memorial lecture (*Man* (N.S.), 12, 1977, 278–92) Dr Maurice Bloch has argued that anthropologists have been too ready to accept what I have called the Durkheimian thesis, and to assume that the solemn concepts of the official faith do dominate, and are exemplified in, the concepts of daily use. (May not ritual solemnity create a kind of conceptual ghetto, insulated from the notions of daily life?) He has shown that some of the debate about the alleged social relativity of rationality hinges on the insufficiently examined assumption of the correctness of this thesis.

within the class of 'ideologies'. These religions tend to be 'Durkheimian' in the sense of being a heightening of the ordinary social life and its confirmation; but the relatively low level of religious specialisation and of doctrinal codification and of the independent power of doctrinal propositions make them, in important ways, unlike that which we normally classify as ideology. No doubt, there are grave problems of demarcation. Cargo cults have made it amply obvious that traditional faiths of this kind can easily be adapted to transform rather than ratify and perpetuate a social order. Or again, tribal religions can compete with clearly doctrinal, 'ideological' world religions on something at least approaching equal terms:

> A long time ago, the lama, the putchu, the khlivri and the brahmin agreed to organise a contest to decide which one of them had the most potent knowledge. The losers would have to pierce their drums and burn their books. To win it was necessary to reach a certain Tibetan lake by next morning. The lama and the brahmin travelled on a ray of the rising sun. The other two priests, voyaging on their drums, arrived but a few instants later, and failed the test. The putchu and the khlivri burnt their books and pierced their drums. [Story about conflict of four religious cults, two local and two representing higher literate religions, translated from Bernard Pignède's *Les Gurungs* (Paris, La Haye, 1966), p. 387.]

Tests of rival magical power of course also take place between contestants within a single faith:

> The Alawite sultan, Moulay Ismail, having heard that Sidi Lahcen was a great scholar, invited him to the capital. . .at the palace, and each. . .night, Sidi Lahcen smashed the dinner plates. The sultan was enraged. . .and demanded an explanation. The saint told the sultan that he was only breaking clay dishes, whereas he, Moulay Ismail, was breaking the dishes of Allah (i.e. the workers). . .
> Humiliated, the sultan, his sword raised, charged Sidi Lahcen. Suddenly his arm froze above his head, and his horse began to sink into the ground. A wall of fire sprang up. Terrified, the sultan begged for his life, offering his kingdom to Sidi Lahcen. Sidi Lahcen refused the kingdom but told the sultan to have his scribe draft a decree freeing

the shurfa. Decree in hand, Sidi Lahcen left Meknes
[A legend recording competition in relative power of *baraka* between a local saint and the central ruler (narrated by local followers of a descendant of the saint. . .) in *Symbolic Domination* (Chicago, 1975) by Paul Rabinow, p. 19].

But one is disinclined to consider these spiritual-athletic contests as ideological ones. No doctrine is being tested: what is at issue is only priority or power or the excellence of given religious *performers*. Ideological conflict arises when doctrines, not men or shrines, are in opposition. But indisputably, this boundary is one which is very difficult to trace on the ground: there will be many borderline and ambiguous cases.

These notes are notes towards a theory, and not a theory; and hence, naturally, they are not complete.

Part II
The cognitive predicament

7

Options of belief

Relativism is a doctrine, or rather a class of doctrines; it is also a problem, a state of mind, and sometimes an affectation. It is an affectation in as far as there is always something slightly suspect about a man who asserts relativism with an entirely straight face and in a calm, assured tone. He is always a little like the good lady who wrote to Bertrand Russell – I quote from memory – a letter which went roughly as follows:

> Dear Lord Russell, I am a solipsist. I find the arguments
> for solipsism irresistible and convincing. What puzzles me
> is that so few other people accept their irresistible force.
> Can you explain this? Yours sincerely, X.

One feels naturally that if she was so firmly convinced, she ought not to have worried about whether or not she received assent from what were, after all, mere figments of her own imagination, nor to have sought explanation of this logical obtuseness from another such figment, however distinguished.

Relativism notoriously faces the same problem. The relativist affirms his own position. Thereby and at the same time, he asserts the falsehood of the rival position, which denies and contradicts his own. He denies what might be called absolutism. Thus in the very act of formulating his own position, he also exemplifies his own commitment to at least one exception to relativism, namely the non-relative, absolute truth of relativism, as against absolutism.

I once heard a thinker who was quite influential at the time, expound relativism and then defend himself, when this obvious objection was raised, by saying this objection would only hold if he had asserted relativism in a dogmatic manner. A certain urbane tolerance in the manner of asserting the position, he seemed to be saying, protected the view from such a charge. Now this won't do. Certainly, if the position is asserted dogmatically and intolerantly, this may well be morally or politically objectionable, and the fact that the position contains a logical incoherence may then justly be used to ironise it. A becomingly tentative and tolerant relativist may be that much more likeable and thereby escape ridicule. But the problem itself did not hinge at all on the tone or dogmatism of the propounder. It is independent of it. It arises equally if the position is written out on a piece of paper, and presented without any information about the state of mind or the other beliefs of the person asserting it, or indeed, without knowledge of whether it is being *asserted* at all. The difficulty is logically internal to the position.

And yet, at the same time, though internal to the logic of the assertion itself, it is not just a logical puzzle. It is not simply one of those logical conundrums whose significance, if indeed they are significant at all, derives from the light they may throw on the system of logic or language within which they occur. The paradox of relativism has obvious affinities with the problem of the Cretan who said that all Cretans were liars or the Viennese who said that all Viennese talked nonsense; it may indeed be just an instance or a reformulation of these paradoxes. It may indeed be that such logical mind-twisters are of profound importance – that, as Russell thought, mathematics rocks when we ask whether the class of all classes not members of themselves is a member of itself. But it seems that the ordinary man in the street, and even the ordinary intellectual in the street, does not often ask himself this question. It does not impinge on him unless he either is a specialist, say in the foundation of mathematics, or has an idiosyncratic penchant for logical puzzles.

Not so with relativism. Relativism shares various obvious formal logical properties with those puzzles, but differs from them in that men are impelled to worry about it by other, weightier or perhaps just more pervasive, common-human considerations.

So here is an interesting position which it is impossible or improper to hold with an entirely straight face, and which, at the same time, it is difficult to refrain from entertaining altogether. One holds it, or rejects it, or merely contemplates it, but one does it uncomfortably, either way. Steven Lukes is indeed, most commendably, uncomfortable twice over. In his 'Relativism: cognitive and moral' (*Aristotelian Society Proceedings, Supplementary Volume* XLVIII 1974, p. 185) he says

I have argued that there is (or rather that we must assume there to be) an Archimedean point in matters of knowledge but that there appears to be no such Archimedean point in matters of morality. Why, then, do I find this double claim uncomfortable?

There appears to be discomfort in either position. There is much merit in such discomfort. Lukes ends his essay by an overall observation on the 'temptations of relativism'.

> These can be overcome either by resisting them *in toto* or by giving in to them with abandon. The situations of the consistent Puritan and of the uninhibited voluptuary are at least unambiguous.

One wonders. However, he goes on:

> It is the *partial* resistance to temptation that causes anxiety and a lingering sense of dissatisfaction.

Why 'lingering'? In as far as this suggests that the dissatisfaction will not disappear quickly or easily, I warmly agree: but in as far as it also seems to imply that the dissatisfaction is not all that strong, I feel dismayed. It sounds like some kind of sentimental nostalgia, a kind of lingering Proustian after-pain which one endures with a wistful pleasure. That may be the proper way to view an unhappily terminated emotional attachment. If such a pain did not linger, why that might be positively rude, and one would also deprive oneself of a certain enjoyment. But relativism is a more serious matter. This is no bitter-sweet chagrin. It ought to be felt and understood with lucidity.

What is it that impels one towards relativism? There are various overlapping considerations, negative and positive. It is customary to invoke the fact of diversity of belief. This seems to me an over-rated consideration, both as a matter of psychology and of logic. The sheer perception of the diversity of ideas does not seem to shake the firm, non-relative, absolutistic conviction of many individuals and communities. Sometimes indeed confidence and dogmatism feed on such an awareness. Does not our Faith itself tell us that there are pagans and heretics? Their very existence confirms or illustrates the faith which they would deny. The manner in which pagans and heretics cling to their errors eloquently exemplifies what the faith itself tells us about the perversity of the human heart or about the social bases of knowledge. We are not so easily shaken. That the truth *seems* different on the other side of the Pyrenees only highlights what we have always known about the deplorable state of affairs on the other side of the mountains.

And as a matter of logic, the sheer existence of divergent opinions, and even the wide diffusion of error, even the quantitative predominance of erroneous opinion, in no way undermine the uniqueness and absoluteness of truth. The existence of true propositions presupposes the existence of their erroneous negations. True propositions can be negated in many ways, and for every predicate truly attributed to a subject, there are countless false ones ready to usurp its place. So, in all logic, the population of false assertions is incomparably larger than that of true ones, a kind of horrifyingly numerous mob of barbarians pressing on the beleaguered citadel of Truth. And truth is not easy to attain; science would not be the glorious thing it is if it were. Hence it is quite natural that this monstrous population of falsehoods not merely exists, but is embraced by many. This only highlights the shining virtue of those who attain truth.

So it is not the sheer awareness of diversity which leads us to relativism. It is something else. Two things, in fact:

1. Absence of criteria for evaluating that diversity, for choosing from amongst rival claimants within the multitude of positions.

2. A sophistication about what might be called the machinery or underpinning of knowledge or opinion. Knowledge is not, as might naïvely be thought, an unmediated contact with pure reality. The articulation of propositions or the perception of data presuppose a conceptual-linguistic structure which makes possible the assertion of that proposition, or a complex sensibility which is as it were receptive to that datum. Even, or especially, the sensitive skin is a most complex thing. But these frameworks, which make possible the assertion or registration of an idea or a perception, are not neutral. How could one transcend their norms or their assumptions?

There is also the supposed need to provide a philosophical base for tolerance. (This is perceptively discussed by Ian Jarvie in 'Cultural Relativism Again', *Philosophy of the Social Sciences*, vol. 5, 1975, 343–53.)

I shall concentrate on the argument from lack of norms.

Absence of general criteria, for evaluating rival claims to our faith, may be felt as a regrettable *lack* of something we would fain have but, alas, do not possess. Equally, however, it is nowadays often acclaimed as a *positive* doctrine, something asserted joyfully, almost triumphantly, and not at all as a despairing admission of a deficiency. There are a number of fashionable doctrines which tell us that criteria of correctness are endlessly various and idiosyncratic, that they are inherent in each practice, institution, art, concept, or culture, and are *not* reducible to common principles. All cases are to be judged on their own merits; all bridges are to be crossed only when reached. We are told that even political liberalism and tolerance are conditional on such a plurality and its willing recognition.

Perhaps so. But whether we reach the doctrine of the absence of general criteria by the high road or by the low road, as a joyful liberation and underpinning of political liberalism, or as a despairing lack of a guiding light and norm, either way the inescapable consequence is the same: if there are no general criteria to guide us in choosing even between neighbouring practices within one culture or society, let alone across cultural boundaries, then relativism would seem to be our doom and destiny. There is not *merely* diversity, there is a diversity which does not allow of rational or demonstrable or binding choice between the elements it covers.

The argument from lack of overall criteria has an important variant: the argument from regress. Who guards the guardians? Even if there are or were criteria, how could one choose between rival criteria, if someone sets up a rival? Or if there were second-level criteria to arbitrate in such cases, the problem would still reappear at the next stage. The regress of validation or justification raises its disturbing head.

It is interesting that the argument from regress does not operate with equal persuasiveness in all fields. In the paper by Steven Lukes on Relativism from which I have already quoted, the author admits that he inclines, with discomfort, towards relativism in morals, and towards its denial in matters of knowledge. I have some observations on this asymmetry.

In morals, or at any rate in academic moral philosophy, the argument from regress receives a kind of confirmation from the highly influential and somewhat mis-named Naturalistic Fallacy argument, formulated by G. E. Moore early in the century, and for a long time widely accepted in the trade. In substance, and when reformulated in less scholastic terminology and style than was favoured by its original propounder, the argument amounts to this: the essence of moral merit cannot be equated with some determinate, specified thing, such as for instance the Greatest Happiness of the Greatest Number, commended by the Utilitarians. For if we did so *equate* it, we would thereby automatically deprive ourselves of any means of even asking whether indeed that one specified and favoured thing, such as for example the welfare of humanity, is good, or is the only good. For you cannot ask a sensible question about an identity or a tautology. It answers itself, and the answer is trivial. But we do not wish this question to be trite, and will not allow it to be so. Even if we did agree on some unique overall moral criterion, as good liberals we shall not allow ourselves to be deprived of the very tools for even *asking the question*, or for querying its answer. The *Newspeak* of Orwell's *1984* may have been so constructed as to render heretical thoughts and questions unsayable and unthinkable: but we shall not put up with the imposition of such shackles on our language and thought.

An admirable liberal sentiment, with which I warmly concur. The present formulation of the Naturalistic Fallacy argument, incidentally, has to my mind the great merit of presenting the conclusion as a corollary of a determination to have an open and liberal language or conceptual scheme, one which does not prejudge our values, rather than as a weird report on the behaviour of some mysterious entities called ideas, or, as some of Moore's later followers present it, as a highly impressionistic and suspect report on the alleged habits of users of the English or of other languages.

What matters for the present purpose is, however, that the argument, as a price of a free and open language, hands us over to the predicament of regress and to relativism. No overall criterion (for that would silence moral questioning), so – no way of settling disputes between minor, culturally or situationally more specific criteria; hence diversity is terminal. Hence relativism. And it is not surprising that this should be the price of liberalism.

Now it is curious that this is far more persuasive in the sphere of morals than it is in the sphere of knowledge. An identity established between the ultimate criterion of moral merit and something specific is repellent precisely because it would bind us henceforth to *that* something specific, whatever it be. On the other hand, if we propose an identity between the ultimate criterion of *truth* and something specific (not just a paraphrase), the result is less repugnant. Take as a simple example, just for the sake of argument, a theory of truth which says that truth *is* that which corresponds to the facts. (I'm not here arguing the merits of this definition, but using it as an example.) The consequence of accepting such an equation is that henceforth, in the linguistic or conceptual community which has accepted it, one can no longer even ask whether, in general, that which corresponds to the facts is also true. The affirmative answer has been predetermined and prejudged, thereby rendering the question itself trivial.

But I don't think we mind this. No liberal hackles rise in our throats. Quite right too. No conceptual tyranny seems to descend on us at that point; the Open Society is not threatened.

Why not? Not only is the open, liberal society *not* threatened by this conceptual measure – by the possibility that the overall, general nature of truth will henceforth be frozen, through the provision of a general criterion of it; I think rather that a free society actually benefits from this. I should go further; I suspect that a free society in the sense in which we understand it – an intellectually free society – could only have emerged through such a codification of the idea of truth, through the provision of a independent criterion.

Why so? To attempt to explain this, let me turn to one of the much-discussed recent theories of truth, namely the so-called Semantic Theory of Truth. It is generally conveyed by the formula ' "*S*" is true if and only if *S*'. We can assert '*S* is true' only if we also assert *S*, and vice versa. To sum up the comments of a very distinguished contemporary logician, Professor Quine of Harvard – I quote from memory – what it boils down to is that the attribution of truth to statements does not really presuppose any notions other than those already used inside the statement itself. We understand no more when we claim that a statement is true, than we do when we understand that statement itself. Another most distinguished and influential contemporary philosopher, Sir Karl Popper, treats this theory as a vindication of the Correspondence view of truth, and of the idea of objectivity.

I shall not discuss the merits of this theory within formal logic. But in a wider context, when considering the problem of objectivity which is of course the obverse of the problem of relativism, it is sadly unhelpful or even badly misleading. Let us approach the problem in this way:

Imagine that an invisible or camouflaged Martian anthropologist of great longevity has been, without any of us knowing it, investigating various human communities on earth for quite a few centuries. He has noted the crucial institution of language. He has also noted the existence of sentences: speech is not continuous, it tends to break up into often (not always) separable units. These units are reproducible on distinct occasions and the separate occurrences are sometimes treated as in some way identical and interchangeable. In literate cultures, these conventions of writing contain signs, such as full stops, to indicate the ending of such sentences, such repeatable and isolable units.

Having noted all this, our Martian anthropologist will also note something else: people have favourable and unfavourable attitudes towards these linguistic units or sentences. Some are good, some are bad. Bearers of good sentences, authors of books or articles or manuscripts containing good sentences are rewarded in various ways, and conversely, authors of bad sentences are discouraged and penalised. Moreover, the grading of sentences seems bi-polar. There is not some continuity of marks. They are, on the whole, like *good* and *bad*, polarised. They go into one of two large boxes.

My guess is that this anthropologist will have a strong feeling that the *way* in which sentences are graded as good or bad is fairly systematic, rather than arbitrary or idiosyncratic, though at the same time he will experience much difficulty in discerning what underlying principles govern this grading. And at this point, he will have to become a differential, comparative anthropologist, and start noting that the grading works differently in different human communities.

At this point, allow him to simplify a bit, just so as to formulate his first general theory on this most intriguing point. He will notice that a certain shift has taken place over a given historic period. It wasn't so much that the *terms* for praising clusters of communicative noises have changed: the terms of praise and blame for these clusters used to be 'true' and 'false', and their equivalents and corresponding terms in non-English speaking communities. What *has* happened is a certain curious and enormously important shift in the centre of gravity, so to speak, of the criteria which appear to be applied before these seals of approval or disapproval are attached to noises.

Roughly: once upon a time, 'truth' seemed, especially in the case of *reverently* uttered sentences to be a matter of authority, status and loyalty. (The German word *treu* still bears testimony to this connection.) A noise cluster was often graded positively as 'true' when it was uttered by the powerful and/or prestigious members of the community, or when it had a hallowed place in its traditions or holy books. Later, this particular connection seems to become attenuated, and another connection emerged: noise clusters could more often receive the blessing of being called 'true' even when contradicting some that were revered, and even if first propounded by individuals of low power and status.

In brief: this merit-conferring appellation, whatever it may 'really' mean, came to be connected *more* with something outside the system, and less with the authority and status system inside it.

So far, I have tried to describe this simplified situation as it would appear to our hypothetical and hidden Martian anthropologist/ observer; and I have tried to assume as little as possible about his own preconceptions and intellectual apparatus. But now let us describe the situation as it appears to us, in our own terms.

Once upon a time the earth was inhabited by communities with a very low rate of scientific growth, and a strong tendency to impose intellectual orthodoxy on their own members. For the past few centuries, we have seen first the occurrence and then the diffusion of the scientific revolution, and an amazing rate of scientific growth, and, very roughly and unevenly accompanying this, a diminution of reverence, in other words a slackening of the ties between perceived truth on the one hand and status and authority on the other.

Basically, this has been a shift from a pluralistic notion of truth, subject to many social pressures and a variety of criteria, to a more single-purpose criterion – and the most striking feature of this new criterion is that it places the ultimate point of decision, the power of attributing good marks and bad, *outside* the society itself. The idea of 'empirical inquiry', of 'experiment', is a way of conveying that the decision lies outside human power.

Or, switching back to the imagined language of our extra-terrestrial observer: in the past as now, human communities were observed grading the noises they make. In each case, the grading seemed to be bi-polar rather than continuous. Evaluation of sentences was not like temperature or the football league table, but rather there was always a tendency to have a simple two-term grading for sentences; or at least, the most important and influential form of grading has this form. In English, the marks employed are 'true' and 'false'. All this is shared by the old and the new societies. Our Martian ethnographer will also have noted that in both periods, the procedures which precede or accompany grading are very complex and involve appeals to externals, be they portents or experiments or whatnot. But there is a difference between Then and Now. What is it?

The decision procedure which determines Salvation or Damnation for statements, for noise clusters treated as identical, has lost both a certain pluralism *and* a certain involvement in the wider society; once it served many purposes, including the maintenance of order and the prestige hierarchy, *and* it used *multiple* criteria. Now it is increasingly concentrated in the hands of one institution, known as 'science', which is largely divorced, in its manner of reaching verdicts, from most social purposes. It calls its single purpose 'truth' or 'explanation'. These are old words, but their effective, operational meaning now appears to be more homogeneous. The theoreticians of science tell us that it works roughly as follows: members of this community of science construct pictures which are very abstract and have many, indeed infinite, consequences, and these consequences are then tested against reality. This testing is known as 'experiment'.

This account may be a simplification, and many have challenged it. But let us accept it for a moment and deal with possible modifications if necessary.

Traditional, pre-scientific societies were not devoid of empirical knowledge. In some ways, they were richer in this respect than we are: a lower division of labour, a smaller administrative–bureaucratic tail, a proportionately greater involvement of the population in agriculture, meant that by some criteria more people knew a great deal more about the natural environment than is the case today. But their empirical knowledge was enmeshed in other activities, and the noises men made in the course of those activities were subject, inevitably, to a multiplicity of socially-oriented criteria of assessment. In other words, truth was not one but many.

Today, truth is a specialist business; it seems to be one, not many; and the institution or sub-community ('science') devoted to its pursuit seems to use a fairly homogenous criterion. It is difficult to formulate this criterion in an illuminating, meaty, non-question-begging way; but what does seem obvious about it is that it is distinct from other socially operative criteria of merit. Truth is *not* beauty; nor virtue, nor utility, nor the advancement of any political cause.

This, incidentally, is the reason why I hold those philosophers who hail the 'Semantic Theory of Truth' to be misguided. Quine's informal observation, that the notion of truth does not add anything to the notions already contained in a sentence declared to be true, needs itself to be stood on its head. The 'Semantic Theory' is acceptable in a sphere, such as formal logic, in which the single-criterion idea of truth is already taken for granted. But this is not self-evident; the idea of this kind of truth is something which humanity had to

discover and learn. Individual sentences are only understood nowadays because we interpret them in the light of *this* particular idea of
truth; as an externally, extra-socially validated claim. We understand sentences in this way because we have learnt *this* idea, which is
diffused as it were, throughout all sentences; the reverse suggestion,
that the idea of truth is simply parasitic on understanding sentences,
is wrong. One can only hold it in consequence of a kind of insensitivity to historical change, to the great Change which has overtaken
humanity in the way it grades its own noises. There are many ways
of grading noises. There are many, many alternative ways of grading
noise clusters (sentences) along two-valued scales, as is the custom of
so many societies. For instance, one could grade as T all noise clusters
satisfying the criterion of having been approved by the High Priest
or by the Central Committee, and grade as F all those which, in the
given language system, are held incompatible with the first class.
Historically real noise-grading systems tend to be complex and have
composite criteria.

The problem of truth is a *differential* problem. What we require
from a theory of truth is an identification of one particular method
of noise grading, an identification which highlights what makes that
particular system distinctive. When we have seized this, we have
some understanding of what we mean by 'truth'. So it is totally
unilluminating to say that characterising a statement as 'true' adds
nothing to the assertion of the statement itself. This is indeed so, but
only because, precisely, the assertion of the statement tacitly presupposes the overall grading method used by the system of which the
statement is part. It is the criteria employed by that method which
really interest us. They are not self-evident. There are diverse
alternative ways of grading. And there is *one* amongst these which
we wish to define and understand.

Once again: what does this imply for the problem of relativism?
Let me sum up my conclusions, with no illusion that I have demonstrated them. I have merely indicated the path along which one may
reach them.

There is no *overall* solution for the problem of relativism for there
are *three* such problems. If one formulates the problem in the
abstract, one gets nowhere. The abstract formulation runs: there are
diverse societies with diverse cognitive systems and diverse criteria.
How could one judge between them, without employing one of those
very criteria which are to be judged? How can the litigant judge in
his own case? And how can a criterion not be *someone's* criterion,

emanate from some society and its habits of thought and its norms, and thus be, precisely, a litigant? How indeed?

The overall formulation of the problem must be replaced by another one, which recognises that not all the ditches between societies are the same. They are of quite unequal depth. There is *one* colossal, or should I say abysmal, chasm. It separates not two individual societies, but two large classes of societies.

To the one side of the Big Ditch lie societies which have firmly separated the grading of noises for truth in the single-aim external-verdict sense, from other types of evaluation. On the other side of the ditch lie societies which have not done this.

This is of course a simplified model: most societies are complex. Nevertheless, if one speaks of the centre of gravity of their attitude, and ignores subsidiary strains in their life, it is this picture that one ends up with.

Positivism – both of the nineteenth-century variety and of the more recent kind – had at least the merit of seeing the importance of the Big Ditch and trying to characterise it; even if it over-simplified the matter, and in its recent formulations suffered from blindness to the social context of the question.

Once we note and understand the distinctive character of the Big Ditch, we can also take an interest in the minor ditches in the lands on either side of it. We end up with *three* problems of relativism, where we previously had one. Is this a gain? I think it is; for the three separated problems may, in isolation, prove more tractable than when they are conflated into one overall problem.

1. The Big Ditch. This is relativism with two terms only. This is the problem of the validation of scientific method. Or, if you prefer, this is the question: Is the scientific world picture more valid than the non-scientific, traditional or Revelationist one?

2. The problem of the small ditches within the pre-scientific world. Here I am prepared to surrender to relativism. A comparative anthropologist or sociologist may and will find fascinating differences in cognitive power between diverse traditional societies; to say that 'they are all alike' is silly. But though they do differ greatly, and their differences deserve study, there seems to me no point in establishing League Tables or Top Twenty. Grading here is pointless. Accept relativism.

3. The small ditches between scientific communities. What is at issue here is of course not the difference between mere rival theories, but between incommensurate rival paradigms – what might be called

Thomas Kuhn's problem. Here grading is not pointless, but, on the contrary, mandatory. We inevitably do it anyway; there *is* scientific progress, not just meaningless changes of fashion. The problem is to show how we do it, and with what justification.

My main point is that (1), (2) and (3) are very different problems and require quite different approaches. Recent theorists have tended not to distinguish them, and this is a great error.

8
The pure enquirer[1]

In the beginning there was Descartes. Descartes turned the world inside out. Before Descartes, knowledge was one thing in the world amongst others. After Descartes, the world is but a thing within knowledge. B.D., men lived with a given world, indulging in a variety of activities, such as making war, money, or love, and some of them also on occasion indulged in the less colourful activity of acquiring knowledge. A.D., however, things have to be known first, and can only exist thereafter and are so to speak established and legitimated *by being known in a proper manner*. Know first, live after. Living *before* you know is but a provisional, makeshift rehearsal or preparation, but it is not serious and does not count.

There has long existed a well-established Descartes-refuting industry. Descartes is overcome at least once every twenty-five years, and the rate of Descartes-transcendence has been accelerating of late. Like the man who said that there was nothing at all to giving up smoking, he had done it so very many times, philosophy finds it easy to refute Descartes with finality, and does it ever so often. Bertrand Russell told me that there was a special circle in hell reserved for those who claim to refute David Hume. The circle of those who have overcome Descartes must resemble Wembley arena on Cup Final day.

The consequence of these multiple and diverse refutations is that 'Cartesian' has come to have a diversity of senses, not exactly abusive but in the main mildly pejorative, and signifying a variety of 'overcome' doctrines, varying with the viewpoint of the new outlook. At the same time, Bernard Williams observes in the final words of

[1] Bernard Williams: *Descartes: The Project of Pure Enquiry*, Penguin Books, 1978.

this important new study of Descartes, his intellectual 'project, its conception and its execution, are all of a piece'. Yet within this unity, there are diverse strands. What are the various Cartesian ideas which are available for such varied if definitive refutations?

(1) An acute distrust of the historically accidental assemblage of opinions embodied in any given culture at any given time, including Descartes' own. He noted that there is no rubbish which men have not endorsed with confidence – and they are encouraged in their cultures. One might add that, conversely, most of what men have endorsed with confidence was rubbish. He is thus the philosopher of, if not cosmic exile, then at the very least of cultural exile, of inner emigration from one's cultural assumptions.

(2) The resulting cognitive predicament can be overcome however, by making an entirely *fresh start*. A wholly new departure, which thereby disconnects itself from past error, is both necessary and feasible. Professor Bernard Williams in his new study of Descartes very properly names the Cartesian enterprise that of *The Pure Enquirer*. (This is not the name of a new daily newspaper run by Mary Whitehouse.)

This belief in the both mandatory and feasible nature of the fresh start (a pessimist may hold it to be mandatory but not feasible) makes Descartes into the philosopher of the crucial break, a *coupure*, in the epistemic history of mankind, though the *coupure* is not to be interpreted in an Althusserian sense. There happens to be one qualitative change in the intellectual history of mankind (not necessarily concentrated into a single event or even period) which is quite incommensurate with other intellectual revolutions, far deeper than any of them, and which marks the beginning of such cognitive salvation as may be available to us.

(3) Within the large corpus of dubitable and untrustworthy opinion, there is hidden a redoubt of uncontaminated, struggling to get out, pure certainty, if we can but find and release it. A purification, a quarantine operation is thus given a base from which it can safely operate.

(4) From this safe base or redoubt, exiguous in itself, a cognitive *reconquista* can then be mounted, which will then restore unto us an entire and habitable world, one which will however not become re-infected with doubt, but possess a certainty similar to that previously possessed only by the redoubt. A safe, though nevertheless reasonably speedy, method is available for effecting this expansion-without-new-danger.

(5) The location of this redoubt, which is to play so strategic a part in our reconquest of a trustworthy world, is our thought, our self-consciousness, including our doubt itself.

The *cogito ergo sum* is open to at least three interpretations: it can be read as an argument from self-exemplification (doubt is thought, thought is self, so doubt itself exemplifies and establishes the existence of self); or as a much more questionable argument from agency to agent; or as the invocation of the indubitable nature of immediate consciousness.

Thus the cogito must be read in the first person singular: *I* cannot doubt the existence of *my own* thought, consciousness. This makes him the philosopher of cognitive individualism, of inner-directedness. Crusoe rebuilt his world because he was ship-wrecked. Descartes chose to simulate such a fate in thought, so as to re-build a world unbeholden to outside sources and thus trustworthy. Thus, within Catholicism, he practises a kind of ultra-Protestantism. This is a sovereignty of consciousness rather than conscience.

(6) The position also contains an inescapable stress on *consciousness* as such, irrespective of the individual units in which it appears. The crucial role it occupies in the whole enterprise makes it necessary to give it a special status, quite distinct from the rest of existence. In this way, Descartes also becomes the philosopher of mind–matter dualism.

(7) Though the redoubt (individual consciousness) was there, it had to be located and its credentials established. This was done by the method of radical doubt. Anything that could be doubted at all had its candidacy eliminated. What remained? Only one Cinderella, the self-conscious ego, could fit the very narrow shoe designed by Descartes for his end. This assumes that generalised doubt makes sense, and makes him in one way the philosopher of scepticism.

(8) The quality which however was to be revealed by this stringent test was that of certainty, and this also makes him the philosopher of the search for certainty.

(9) The expansion from the safe bridgehead had itself to be safe and certainty-preserving. There was to be no retracing of steps. This makes him the philosopher who conceives knowledge as a progression without retreats, linear, irreversible, deductive. (Williams points out that this conventional interpretation of Descartes needs some modification.)

(10) The expansion proceeds by discrete, isolable steps. In fact, Descartes recommends that it be broken up into as many distinct

steps as possible. Their isolability is assumed. Things are done more securely if they are done one at a time. Orderly, tidy procedure is mandatory. Nothwithstanding his aristocratic name, he was a bourgeois stickler for order and tidiness. His Rules of Method sound exactly like a recipe for inculcating what Professor Basil Bernstein calls the elaborated code of speech, that distinctive middle-class style, which used to pervade education, and thus favoured middle-class children. I am always surprised that no-one has attacked Descartes as the philosopher of class bias in the educational system. In this sense, Descartes was an atomistic rather than holistic philosopher.

(11) The items employed in this step-by-step progression were to be clear and distinct. This is the commonest sense of 'Cartesian', and makes him the philosopher of clarity.

Note that these central traits or commandments of Cartesianism can be stated without obscurity or technicality, and in some ways this is of their essence. If they depended for their articulation on some specialised jargon, whether of the seventeenth or twentieth century, this would contradict the stated purpose of providing a clean, fresh world. The jargon would bring its own infection with it.

The world of the Cartesian is different from that of the non-Cartesian. Though, for instance, it may contain God – as it does in Descartes' own version – He too may only enter after prior cognitive clearance. No-one is allowed in without the humiliation of prior scrutiny. No-one except the doubting ego has right of citizenship by birth. No-one and nothing is above the Law of Knowledge. Even though God has an important position in Descartes' world, running a kind of cognitive central bank which underwrites all other and special operations, nevertheless He too must submit to vetting before taking up His post. Once Descartes establishes God, Descartes and his God become symbiotic – Descartes establishes God's existence, and God guarantees Descartes' further ratiocinations. So they propel each other like two skaters, moving each other along the ice by alternate pushes and pulls. The first step, the cogito, had a logical structure which was transparent and genuinely self-guaranteeing: the relationship to God is intended to extend this luminous certainty to the whole system.

It is not so much, as Williams says (p. 201), that the Pure Enquiry is a secular enterprise, in a world containing other options: it is an activity which in the end makes all other options secular. The essence of religion is not, as is supposed, transcendence or authority: it is making some *substantive* belief ultimate and sovereign. This then generates transcendence and authority. Conversely, Descartes' elevation of formal-epistemic criteria to a position of ultimate sovereignty, eventually generates both immanence and individualism. Nothing substantive in the world retains certainty or sacredness.

The diversity of Cartesian ideas within the unity gives his opponents a range of choice for dissent. Michael Oakeshott, with a fine turn of phrase, castigated the very aspiration for *coupure*: 'With almost poetic fancy, he strives to live each day as if it were his first.' Marxists can have a field day with the way in which his conception of knowledge mirrors possessive individualism. He was indeed the Samuel Smiles of cognitive possessive individualism. He taught us how we could make it on our own, he loathed being in cognitive debt, and he would only trade with capital he had personally accumulated – the very model of a self-made-man. Pragmatists and Popperians reject the idea of *coupure*, the great discontinuity in cognitive history, the linear conception of cognitive growth, the requirement of certainty, and of prior foundations.

But perhaps the most virulent anti-Cartesians are to be found among the adherents of the recently dominant fashions in academic philosophy in this country. Both the spirit of his whole enterprise and the steps undertaken in its execution seem to them not just wrong, but the very paradigm of error, the very thing which philosophy should *cure*. Descartes wanted all things to be made a-new, Wittgenstein taught that philosophy left everything as it was. Descartes separated mind and matter, Ryle thought the separation a grand mistake and J. L. Austin claimed that the Argument from Illusion cut no ice with him. Generalised doubt was declared absurd. The aspiration to 'cosmic exile' is derided. The list could be prolonged.

Professor Williams has had a distinguished career at Oxford, London and Cambridge, ever close to the philosophic establishment, and one approaches his book with great expectations. That he has become at least lukewarm about these recent fashions adds a welcome element of unpredictability. He tells us that the work has been a long time a-writing, and that as much as 14 years separates some passages from others – which tempts one into stratigraphic speculation about the volume.

So we do get a dramatic confrontation? On the surface, very little. Most of the leaders of the recent movement are mentioned at best tangentially and in footnotes. Gilbert Ryle suffers the humiliating fate of being cited as an example of a feeble argument in a minor work, whilst his main book, proudly and overtly an anti-Cartesian tract claiming to destroy the entire Cartesian vision of man, is totally ignored. Wittgenstein occurs in a couple of footnotes, G. E. Moore gets little more, J. L. Austin does not occur at all, though he believed himself to have shown the Argument from Illusion, and hence general doubt, to be baseless. (Chomsky, about whose warm and positive self-identification with Descartes Williams rightly has his doubts, is mentioned in a footnote which has escaped the attention of the index-compiler.)

Deeper down, however, the answer is more complex. There are thinkers who throw away the ladder by which they have ascended, at the end of their enterprise, having first used it to the full; and there are others who throw away the ladder at the start, scorning to use that for which they cannot vouch. Descartes of course belongs to the latter, Wittgenstein to the former. The bewildering thing about Williams is that he expounds Descartes in the manner apposite to the *other* camp. The ladder which Descartes threw away was the world itself. Any world is conceptually saturated, concepts are cultural, cultures are suspect, so any un-pasteurised world is in all probability cognitively unhygienic. The nastiest rung on the repudiated ladder was the scholastic terminology of his own time. Did he cut himself off from the scholasticism of the seventeenth century so as to be subjected to that of the twentieth, with the whole outside world thrown in for good measure?

That is what it sounds like at first. The Pure Enquirer is introduced (p. 48) in a somewhat patronising tone: 'it can be said that it is not an obviously absurd undertaking. It might well be...that devoting oneself for a while exclusively and intensively to trying to raise the truth-ratio would offer some large benefits.' The purity of the P.E. seems to me to be at first misdescribed. Williams makes it hinge on singleness of motive (concern with truth only, the truth-ratio, the proportion of true beliefs to the rest), as distinct from the multi-purpose conduct of life. But what was really at issue was purity from current cultural assumptions, which for Williams however seems to be but a corollary of the temporary single-mindedness. This gives the mistaken impression that the Project is separate from life, rather than life, temporarily, *par provision*, being disconnected from *it*. This Descartes, of the early parts of the book, sounds to me like a compromise between the real one and what recent fashions would have grudgingly allowed.

Still, it is better than saying that the enterprise *is* absurd. All the same, it is an odd Descartes. He is trying to raise his 'truth-ratio'

– it sounds like a golf handicap. He seems somewhat of a nut – displaying manic single-mindedness in one sphere, though remaining cosily commonsensical in private life. With his eagerness to collect true propositions, never mind what they are about, whilst remaining embedded in a context of sturdy common sense, he does remind me of those philosophers of the 1950s, but not of the Descartes I have read.

This early treatment seems to me to do great injustice to the spirit of his argument. There may always be a case against treating a historic thinker as a contemporary (though Williams has argued the other way, interestingly, in a debate with and edited by Bryan Magee, in *Men of Ideas*, published by BBC publications, 1978), but there is a special case against doing it to Descartes. When a man is trying to stand outside the world or at its edge, don't confront him with your entire paraphernalia including the kitchen sink. As Wittgenstein might have said (cf. *Tractatus*, 5.452), the world may not be introduced in epistemology with an entirely innocent face. The subjection of Descartes to torment by a thousand subtleties with an innocent face seems to me almost as bizarre as that recent philosopher who expounded Descartes' Project by saying that it was like trying to find out what Adam thought just when God had created him – when, in fact, the point of the project is precisely that it subjects God, Adam, and (with very special pleasure) those philosophic paraphernalia to doubt. Why cannot Descartes be expounded with the same clarity and simplicity with which he explains himself?

Happily, this treatment does not last. In due course, we get something far better and more interesting. Descartes plunges us into the Valley of Doubt in order eventually to lead us up the sunny Slopes of Certainty. Williams expounds him the other way round, which really is putting Descartes before the horse. The irony is that in the end, Williams descends far deeper into the Valley of Doubt, if not of Despair, and in dead earnest, than Descartes ever did by way of thought-experiment. As I find the Valley of Doubt far more interesting than the Pastures of Complacency, I naturally like Williams' book better and better the further it gets. Whether his opening moves and their tone follow from a perverse strategy of exposition, or constitute a survival from the 14-year-old stratum of the book, I cannot tell.

He soon comes to explain to us some of the good and sound reasons for Descartes' project. So we leave behind the weird maniac with an idée fixe about his batting average, who is nonetheless a sturdy commonsensical bloke the rest of the time, who might coach the Magdalen crew in his spare time, and meet a more interesting and recognisable Descartes. Williams expounds the deep problem in one of the most interesting passages of the book (pp. 64–8), which I here attempt to summarise in my own words: knowledge is haunted by relativism. The very idea of knowledge requires that there be something independent of knowledge which is there to be known. But what we know is affected by the cognitive apparatus (conceptual, sensory, linguistic, cultural, what have you). Descartes thinks, therefore the daemon exists, you might say. Of course we can try to find out about that apparatus, but that is just one further piece of knowledge, and hence the initial point applies once again. So how do we break out? Williams' general interpretation of Descartes is that this is what he was trying to do, by means of acquiring knowledge that was absolute (not tied to any perspective), and hence also certain. In as far as Williams recognises this as a perfectly genuine problem, there is no further need to condescend to Descartes by saying that his project is not obviously absurd.

Williams admits that his formulation of the problem is somewhat anachronistic, in as far as it draws on post-Cartesian thinkers. Indeed, this anachronism does not matter, for Williams does identify the problem which inspired Descartes' project. Yet I would qualify the account. Descartes was not so worried by the perspectival quality of knowledge, which in itself is not necessarily problematic. If diverse perspectives are reasonably coherent, if they fit into a scheme which explains why they diverge (even if that scheme is itself perspective-bound), this on its own does not generate scepticism. Many traditional belief-systems have such a 'stratified' distribution of visions amongst segments of the population. This isn't troublesome, as long as you know who is tops. Plato was content with such a vision. Alternatively, perspectives don't matter if we all have the same one (as Kant thought).

What did bother Descartes was not the existence of perspectives alone, but the fact that some of them were so patently dreadful. And one might add – the more dreadful, the more confident. 'The worst are full of passionate intensity.' He did not suppose that all perspectives could be fitted into a coherent evolutionary chain (a much later solution to this problem). He was worried by the argument from illusion in its correct, cultural form: look at the drivel which communities embrace with confidence, and ask yourself whether you can trust your own!

One might put it this way: did Descartes indulge in pervasive doubt in order to raise the quality of his cognitive luggage, or did he raise the standards of cognitive acceptability, because there were good grounds for pervasive doubt? Each of these statements is correct, but the stress should be on the *second*.

He tried to go it *alone*, and he tried to stand *outside*. He was the philosopher of cognitive inner emigration, and the stress can be on the inner or on the opting out, the need to disown an inheritance. The individualism fits in with a society which was also becoming individualist in other ways, the aspiration to stand outside marked the radical discontinuity in the intellectual history of mankind which was taking place in his century. The discontinuity and the solitude were deeply linked, and accentuated each other.

Inner conceptual compulsion, which had survived the purification by pervasive doubt, was the method of attaining both the break with the past and with culture, and of providing the individual with his safe inviolable redoubt. Eventually, over two centuries later, the wheel was to turn full circle and Emile Durkheim was to claim that inner conceptual compulsion was itself but the voice of society and culture; but that was a long way off. The idea that conceptual custom was authoritative simply in virtue of being custom was further off still, and would have struck him – rightly – as absurd.

Descartes stood somewhere near the start of the great Cognitive Miracle, the emergence of a tradition which for once acquired genuine and cumulative knowledge, thereby also highlighting the cognitive poverty of other traditions, and he contributed to it and to its self-consciousness and codification. His work is a kind of Magna Carta of the commonwealth of cognition. However partial and incomplete and unsatisfactory in detail, it points the way to the rules of a civilised polity. He singled out the crucial differentia: henceforth, sovereignty, the entrenched constitutional law, lies not in any content, but in the form or manner of knowing.

The problem which led him to this was simply: how can we know that our way is not as dreadful as the others? The problem of the theory of knowledge is a differential problem. What we need to explain is not why everyone has knowledge, or why no-one has it; what we need to explain is why some cultures, some cognitive styles, attain so much of it, and why others attain so very little. It is the unsymmetrical distribution of cognitive wealth which constitutes the problem. As Williams puts it (p. 301): 'The requirement was that we should be able to overcome relativism...through having a view of

the world. . .which contains a theory of error: which can explain the
existence of rival views, and of itself.' Williams does not explain
how a sense of perspectives on its own should produce the craving
for certainty. It only does so in conjunction with a deep sense of the
awfulness of many (perhaps, all but one) perspectives. This leads to
another questionable interpretation of Descartes, the identification
of his question with Meno's (p. 38). Was Descartes so preoccupied
with truth, knowledge, or certainty, for their own sakes? (This was
only true of the maniac with whom we started, given his obsession
with his golf handicap.) He was after something simpler and
homelier, after knowledge-*of-the-world*. When illusion patently
abounds, *then* certainty becomes a precondition of it. He was only
obsessed with certainty in the way in which an otherwise un-
obsessional man might become obsessed with cleanliness during a
plague. (Camus' *problematik* is not so far from Descartes'.) He wanted
a world which he could call his own and respect. The *cultural*
argument from illusion makes it impossible to accord respect to the
conceptual ancien régimes. It is this and this alone which leads to the
Project: for once, the foundations must be certain!

Williams pays too much heed to Descartes' distinction between the
pursuit of truth and the conduct of life. This makes him sound like
a Cartesian in his study, but a man of common sense outside, who
perhaps needs telling to take his common sense back into his study.
But, as Descartes makes plain in his discussion of his own private
morality, the rules of conduct in life are *par provision* only. This is
not for real. Whilst erecting a decent edifice, which will deserve our
respect, we must needs live in a shack, possibly holding our nose
whilst we do it. The old *Lebenswelt* is just a public convenience.

Do not be misled by the fact that Descartes re-incorporated a lot
of the ancien régime in his own version of the new edifice. That was
just a mistake, soon corrected by his philosophic progeny. The idea
that the ancien régime as such and as a whole could be respected,
because elements within it were functional in it, would have struck
him as bizarre. Those who uphold it now can only do so precisely
because they are parasitic on the work of Descartes and his followers,
because the newly pruned perspectives are no longer so patently
dreadful.

Williams is right in using the term *Project* for Descartes' enterprise, in as far as it is indeed true that Descartes was attempting to
do something quite distinctive – even if Williams does not altogether
succeed in identifying what that distinctive enterprise is. For

Williams, what distinguishes Descartes is motivation or interest: where other men follow a plurality of aims or criteria when engaged in acquiring knowledge, Descartes, at least in philosophical office hours, has but one aim – to increase his 'truth ratio'.

But this isn't quite correct. It sounds as if Descartes wanted *more* truth, in proportion to non-truth. But what he really wanted was a qualitatively different and new *kind* of truth – namely, culture-proof or culture-free truth.

He needed it because he was imbued by the sense that cultures are capable of inspiring unwarranted confidence in us all, concerning what are in fact non-truths. This being so, it follows that our whole cognitive edifice is suspect, at least in as far as it is supported by nothing but culturally shared and encouraged confidence. The way out? Find culture-resistant convictions and identify their distinguishing marks. Just as logical truths can be defined as that which remains true in any possible world, so scientific truth is perhaps that which remains true in any possible culture. Descartes thought such truth could be located by means of the assumption of the most unfavourable culture – the malignant daemon, i.e. a very powerful and malevolent brainwashing device – and then seeing which convictions *still* evaded dubitability, even on this deliberately unfavourable assumption. Thus the pursuit of certainty, and the temporary single-minded concentration on one-aim-only, are but a means, in handling a problem situation which is still with us. Cosmic exile, or rather Cultural Exile, was the solution offered. We are clearer perhaps about how very difficult it is to implement this strategy, but we still have to try. The other solutions which have since been offered for this problem are even more problematic, or circular and question-begging.

Williams' failure to identify Descartes' Project with accuracy is connected with his failure to bring out the full force of the conflict between Descartes' vision and recently fashionable philosophy. That fashion consisted of saying (in somewhat different terminology) that there was no need to seek culture-free knowledge at all; that cultural permeation, far from contaminating knowledge, is the only validation it can or need have; and consequently, that the Cartesian aspiration towards culture-transcendence is *the* philosophic error par excellence. Where Descartes insisted that cultures must not be judges in their own case, this view insists that they may and must do precisely that. There could hardly be a greater incompatibility than that which exists between this vision and Descartes'.

In Williams' book, this conflict is not absent, but it is rather toned down. Admittedly the Cartesian enterprise is no longer derided, but is half-apologetically defended as a kind of eccentricity which may have good reasons for its excuse. These reasons are well stated but their full force is not underscored, and one may well wonder whether their full implications are perceived.

There is nothing unrealistic and unworldly about Descartes' Project. Imagine the President of a great Republic, convinced that his chief intelligence agency pursues policies of its own, inimical to himself. Or imagine the Prime Minister of an old constitutional monarch, convinced that the central police force is corrupt. They can appoint someone to set things right. But if the rot has gone far enough, how can they trust this appointee? How indeed. If the rot has gone far enough, they must start the job themselves, and sack the lot. This is what Descartes did to his own ideas. He then needed a watertight selection procedure for the first new appointee, who could be relied upon to choose new officials as trustworthy as himself. Or imagine the citizen of a totalitarian country, who knows, not that some journalists fib or boob, but that the entire press is slanted. He too cannot but adopt a Cartesian strategy. The cognitive plague is not an uncommon feature of the human condition. It may even be the normal state of affairs.

In the twentieth century, most cultures are in a Cartesian condition. Those which became Cartesian early, now live under his rules of sovereignty, and the Cartesian tradition dominates their cognitive morality. This does not mean that everything they believe can be deduced from the rules of knowledge or the principle of individual scrutiny; but it does mean that substantive convictions which persistently defy these dual sovereigns lose authority. There is of course a close parallel at this point with democracy in politics. The general will is not at the root of all policies; but policies which persistently defy it, do not easily survive. We are all Cartesians now.

So is Williams. The most fascinating parts of the volume are the tantalisingly condensed, profoundly intriguing, highly elliptical and occasionally obscure final six paragraphs (*not* the appendices), where we get a sketch of what is presumably Williams' own world, and it is patently the product of three centuries of Cartesian pruning and self-examination. It is a new *Lebenswelt*, a world to live and think in, not a piece of speculation detachable from a man's identity. This shows how wrong it was to treat the separation of the Project and of life as serious and permanent. It was a highly practical Project, with nothing nutty about it.

In this world, what has happened, for instance, to the Cartesian dualism of mind and matter? From two substances to the Two Cultures, you might say. Matter remains the object of the natural sciences and of an absolute, non-perspectival vision, in the light of the 'intercultural success' of science (p. 248); but the absoluteness is now, plausibly, divorced from certainty. (In other words, we continue to face Descartes' *problem*, the need for a unique non-perspectival vision, whilst giving up the quest for certainty which was Descartes' *means* towards the solution of that problem.) We hold on to the absoluteness 'rather grimly' (p. 303). But, by contrast, the world of mind, philosophy, the social sciences, lacks both absoluteness and certainty, even determinacy itself perhaps. There, everything is 'liable to radical indeterminacy of interpretation' (p. 302). Thus private pains, aches, twinges, philosophy, the social sciences, all belong to the same Realm of Being. I always feared as much.

Thus our world is a dualistic one. A trans-cultural natural science inspires confidence, notwithstanding the fact that it is not stable or linear and does occasionally retrace its own steps. It appears capable of inspiring confidence despite its own instability in time, and its capacity for sustained growth is indeed its glory. But it has another great disadvantage: the world it offers is not the world we live in, as flesh-and-blood social and individual beings.

This dual citizenship of ours is most awkward. The ordinary world in which we live and have our identity, and which contains 'social science, common perceptual experience and so forth' (p. 302), apparently cannot, in Williams' view, aspire to absolute, un-perspectival knowledge in the way in which natural science does. So human beings, whose lives and identities are forged in a perspectival and interpretation-bound world, within which, as Descartes saw, they have to make their cognitive beginning (for once upon a time we had nothing else), nevertheless eventually attain a totally different world. . .which then however helps to corrode their faith in the one in which they originally began and in which they continue to live and identify themselves. It corrodes it by showing it to be a distorted aspect, one into which perspective has injected much illusion, and from which it has subtracted much that is real. Awkward indeed!

If only philosophy – which is a part of *our* world – were itself absolute, *and* explained how both absolute and perspectival knowledge comes to exist, that would be a solution: but, as Williams rightly observes, in our time the supposition 'that philosophy itself is absolute knowledge – perhaps even the highest form of absolute knowledge. . .must reasonably [be seen] as a *reductio ad absurdum*' (p. 302). Indeed. The most characteristic, and perhaps from Williams' viewpoint the most dated, aspect of Descartes' project is that it aimed at doing just this: to provide objective knowledge with a subjective base, which would indeed also have to be absolute if it were to carry the burden placed upon it.

If this cannot be, the situation is indeed a stalemate: the two worlds to which we have entry-permits, each holds the other in thrall. The private or culturally idiosyncratic world, in which we live, consists presumably of merely perspectival, secondary-quality reflections of the absolute reality, and is thus as it were demoted by it, and is indeed commonly seen as having a much lower status – important decisions are taken in the idiom of the other world, whenever possible. But at the same time, the absolute or objective world is only known by *people* who live in, and who start from, the private world; and they alone make the cognitive evaluations, such as this one. . .The substantive and the epistemic ranking contradict each other. The non-perspectival world is at the mercy of perspectival men – *and* vice versa. So where does the final decision or authority lie?

Williams' solution, as formulated in this volume, is alas far too brief and condensed to do justice to him. He repudiates the old answer, which would make philosophy into the broker between the two worlds – because it claimed to be on the one hand human, *ours*, but on the other, authoritative, and capable of putting science in its place. It is indeed human, all-too-human, and as for its authoritativeness. . .who are you kidding? So if this won't do, what is the alternative? Williams' reply is strange:

> The absolute status of philosophy would not be required
> just by there being some absolute conception of the world,
> but rather by our knowing that there was and what it
> was. We have agreed all along that we should need some
> reasonable idea of what such a conception would be like,
> but. . .not. . .that if we have that conception, we have to
> know that we have it. . .To ask [for that]. . .is. . .to ask for
> more – very probably for too much [p. 302].

If I understand this correctly, it means that we have or presuppose a conception of absolute knowledge, but that we probably cannot know that we have it, and hence can hardly know what it is. If we knew we had it and knew what it was, that *would* be philosophy, but what we can actually do under that name clearly doesn't rise to any such heights. So we hope we have it, but don't know just where we put it...So we are like freeholders who have lost their deeds, don't know where they are or even have any clear idea of what they would look like, but hope that the very idea of possessing them, without knowing that we do, will save us from eviction. It seems a thin hope. This would seem both a most tortuous and despairing solution – but as Williams states it in so condensed and obscure a way, we can only hope that he will yet expand it and thus enable us to assess it better.

But this problem is indeed absolutely central. The tension between our being and our knowledge, between culture and cognition, between human individuality and cognitive order, underlies most philosophical positions. Every philosophical baby that is born alive is either a little Romantic or a little Reductionist, and there are deep reasons why this dilemma is imposed on us. There is no facile escape from it, though many are offered on the market. Descartes' actual solution – which would transcend deceptive culture by means of a purified self, base an outer world on that self, and establish a continuity between the two – may not tempt us any longer.

But Descartes' use of the purified individual self as a means of escaping one's culture remains an excellent dramatic way of conveying or symbolising the profundity and uniqueness of *the* great Discontinuity in the cognitive history of mankind, and the fact that it is connected with the shift of authority to the manner, and away from the content, of knowledge – and with the realisation that claims to authority are, in the end, examined by private individuals, and cannot evade such examination. The Crusoe myth symbolises both individualism and the great historic discontinuity, the fresh start. So the question he tried to answer is inescapably and pervasively with us. Williams provides us with only the briefest possible glimpse of his own reaction to them.

But if his fascinating dualistic sketch of his own world is correct (and it bears resemblance to my own), note how very justified Descartes was in his generalised doubt, his distrust of culture. If this, or something like it, is true, then none of those conceptual anciens régimes could be correct, not merely in what they said, but above all in the confident way in which they said it. They too offered a continuous picture of nature and man, which was part of their appeal. The 'unified science of man and nature' was not only a 'positivist fantasy' (p. 302). Positivism assimilated man to nature, they did it the other way round. They have now been eroded by the Project. We have abandoned them, and inhabit the world produced by the Project, which has become our new *Lebenswelt*. But if *they* were wrong, then, a fortiori, a philosophy which would endorse or underwrite them all, simply because they were a 'form of life', must itself also be wrong.

This would seem implicit in Williams' conclusion, but it is not underscored. I have heard Descartes accused of cautiously refraining from spelling out conclusions, whilst hoping that the reader might tumble to them. Does the Inquisition stalk the Moral Sciences Club?

9

An ethic of cognition

The following argument can be put against all and any methodology: presumably a methodology contains prescriptions which are more than just the requirement to observe the formal commands of logic. No-one who writes a book on method thinks he is merely replicating the precepts of consistency, non-contradiction and so forth. So, a methodology must have some meat which is not merely logic. But if it asserts, or presupposes, something over and above the formal requirements of logic, will not that *something else*, whatever it may be, have some implications concerning *the world*? And if so, can one not imagine or construct a possible world within which those implications are false, and within which consequently those recommendations are misguided? And if such a world is conceivable, obviously we cannot say, in advance of all inquiry, that such a world is not the *real* world. But what use is a methodology which prejudges the nature of the world we are in, before we have investigated the matter, and before we have any right to an opinion about it? So we cannot use it *before* we inquire, as a tool of investigation, or as a guide to what tools to use. And we certainly do not wish to use it *after* our inquiry is over. For one thing, it is too late by then; for another, by then we can presumably enjoy some much more meaty conclusions, and will hardly have much time for the relatively thin and abstract doctrines of methodology, even if, from another viewpoint, they evidently were not thin and abstract enough.[1]

This argument can be used and I think has been used as an attack on the very idea of method: method, purporting to be more than

---

[1] Dr E. Zahar of the LSE drew my attention to the argument and to roughly this formulation of it, and cited Paul Feyerabend as its source.

mere logic, must have some substance. But method, being method, must also be neutral, and hence must have no substance. An enterprise which is simultaneously required both to have some substance and to have none, cannot satisfy the demands made of it. Hence, no method is possible.

I wish to accept the argument, but use it, not as an attack on the very idea of method, not as a reductio ad absurdum of the very notion of method (which is the spirit in which I think it was used), but on the contrary as a means of highlighting the true nature of methodology. Yes, method is more than logic; consequently it does indeed prejudge some results of inquiry prior to the very start of the inquiry, eliminating certain possibilities, excluding certain imaginable worlds; *and rightly so*. Some worlds are indeed eliminated, in an a priori fashion, by philosophical methodology. The aprioristic exclusion of those worlds is of the essence of the thing. But, though method is aprioristic, and on points of substance at that, this admission should not be worn as a badge of shame. It is, on the contrary, a badge of honour. Certain worlds are *out*. We exclude them, not because we can know in advance (or, perhaps, ever) that the world we actually inhabit is not one of these excluded ones, but for some other reason or reasons. I for one think that those reasons happen to be good ones.

Which are the excluded worlds?

I am not sure I can give a general characterisation of *all* such excluded worlds; but it is I think possible to offer a general outline of *some* of them, of an important sub-class of the excluded worlds. Let us call them, without prejudice, the Ideologist's Worlds.

The world of an ideologist, the world satisfying the requirement of some well-constructed Ideology, has certain general traits. It is always a non-alienated world, in the important sense that in it the Real and the Rational sustain and support each other; the realm of fact and the realm of value are not separated from each other. The True and Good and the Beautiful converge and ratify each other. Such a world has a basic plot, in which the Good faces its opposite. Within it, this cannot be doubted, for this is central to the belief system in question, and were it to be in doubt, all else would tumble. But it need not be doubted, either: for the plot of our cognitive adventure neatly dovetails with the story of moral, political and other confrontation. In essence, within it, the story of our cognitive and exploratory adventures is this: the good men have cognitive equipment or attitudes or whatnot which make them perceive the real plot, whereas the evil and accursed ones are blinded, by forces or mechanisms specified in the overall story itself. So, the sheer distribution of faith and disbelief itself confirms the truth of faith. Only those devoid of Grace doubt the existence of God; only neurotic resisters doubt the insights of depth psychology; only class enemies fail to see the cogency of scientific historical materialism; only victims of rigid models of how language works spurn the mature Wittgenstein, etc.

You may say that there is a certain circularity in such forms of reasoning, and no doubt this is so. But note that this in no way constitutes a conclusive refutation of any vision of this kind. It isn't only that, from the inside, to a true believer, the circularity does not in the very least seem like a *circularity*; one has to be a nasty minded outsider-sceptic to see it as such. From the inside, it does not look like circularity at all, it looks like the consensus and convergence of so many manifest signs and indications, which one would have to be blind or wicked to ignore. Indeed it is precisely those wicked ones who insist perversely on casting doubt, and supporting their cussedness by specious reasoning about circularity!

But the important point is not that, from the inside, it does not look or feel circular at all. What *is* important is the fact that we have *no* logical or independent way of proving that such a 'circular' world, or strictly speaking a world sustained by reasoning which seems circular to an outside and hostile critic (or outside and *hence* hostile), cannot exist. On the contrary: it could well exist. A world so constructed as to make its most important features manifest to the good, and obscured from the wicked, might well exist. Perhaps, indeed, it does exist: and perhaps *this* world is just such a world. There is nothing in the very least logically self-contradictory in such a supposition. It cannot be excluded by logic. And it cannot be excluded by fact either, for it is constructed precisely in a way such that all facts can be accommodated. It is only to the outsider or, in its own terms, to the wicked, that facts are 'accommodated', an expression which suggests wilful manipulation. From the inside, for a healthy undisturbed vision, all facts support and endorse the vision.

So a world of this kind *is* possible, and there is no purely logical reason for excluding it a priori. There is nothing self-contradictory about the idea of such a world. It is true that there is a certain suspicion-enhancing consideration, which runs as follows: if the real world is *not* like that, nonetheless a movement which possesses a well-constructed belief-system of this kind, will never have to admit that it is in error, even though, on our supposition, it *is* in error. But this merely shows that *if* the world is indeed different, then nevertheless believers in an ideologically neat world need never admit defeat. But that in no way proves that the world is not as they claim it to be.

Furthermore, there is a certain consideration on their side, which I shall call the Argument from Elementary Decency. Decent people live decent orderly lives in decent homes and good districts. People who live in filthy houses in areas of ill repute can hardly be surprised if some of that ill repute rubs off on them. What goes for houses and districts also goes for universes. Decent people live in decent universes. A decent universe is one with some measure of propriety and order. Knowledge and morality are not, in such a universe, strangers to each other. They dovetail. Even people not too sure that the universe is like that often feel that it ought to be, or that society ought to be such, or that, if things are not like that, philosophy really ought to do something about it.

I am not saying that this is a cogent argument. It is open to the objection that we did not make the universe. I for instance personally disclaim all responsibility either for the existence of the universe or for its general character. I had nothing whatever to do with it. I was not even consulted. Things are as they are. I did not make them. I just tell it like what it is, but that does not make me responsible. Still, though this would seem cogent, people are curiously sensitive to the view that you can tell whether a man is a bastard by the kind of universe he inhabits. The quality of badness rubs off onto bearers of bad news. So, there is a certain moral sentiment on the side of the assumption of an ideological universe.

When people speak of 'alienation' one of the things they nebulously mean is the overcoming of a world in which life and meaning diverge, in which there is a lack of fittingness and justice. The Hegelian–Marxist tradition for instance, sees the plot of human history in the overcoming of such alienation. Marx's transcendence of philosophy is not a form of positivism but means, if I understand it, that henceforth alienation will no longer be overcome by mere words and in a fictitious world, but in real life and in this world.

The idea or feeling of a 'meaningful' world seems rooted deep in our minds and moral expectations, perhaps in virtue of our earliest family experiences, perhaps through some cultural traditions, or perhaps for other reasons. Whatever the basis of these anticipations, they provide a powerful impulse towards the acceptance of an ideological world; for only such a world, in the sense here defined, can satisfy this craving.

The substantive content of certain methodologies in fact excludes (whatever else it may exclude as well) such worlds. Consider, in the simplest possible terms, what these methodologies actually prescribe. Take the Baconian version. It commands us to read the book of nature with attentive care and to find what is actually there, rather than what some other consideration may lead us to wish, expect, or deem appropriate. The Popperian variant allows us, indeed encourages us, to anticipate whatever we may wish, for any reason whatever; this doctrine professes total indifference to our motives and our sources of inspiration. All that matters is that, once we have been inspired, never mind how and never mind for what reason, that then our anticipation should be subjected to trial by the book of nature. Generically, it would be fair to class the inductivist and the Popperian philosophies together as species of *empiricism*, and no doubt there are further kinds.

What *is* empiricism, in general?

The rough but correct definition, i.e. the one which brings out what really matters about the doctrine, is also highly paradoxical. It runs approximately as follows: empiricism is the a priori exclusion of a certain class of possible worlds, namely those worlds which satisfy some very deep general moral yearnings, roughly indicated above.

The definition is paradoxical in as far as it underscores, as seems to me entirely proper, that empiricism is indeed itself an a priori doctrine. To attempt to establish it empirically, as Hume did (as a kind of finding about how the human mind happens to work), is not merely circular but more seriously objectionable. As a piece of genetic psychology it is blatantly false, for reasons which ought to have been obvious though they have only become familiar thanks to Noam Chomsky; as a schema for the construction of psychological theories it is quite outstandingly sterile. The merits of empiricism, which are very considerable, lie entirely in the field of normative epistemology. It is a cognitive ethic, a code of intellectual comportment. But even within this sphere, there are great and well-known difficulties about defining it correctly or in a satisfactory manner.

The most natural way of defining it is by invoking the notion of *experience*. I remember, at the time of the height of confidence of the linguistic school in philosophy and of rampant 'common sense', a very prominent linguistic philosopher ironising empiricism and its philosophical systematisation in roughly the following words: are these thinkers saying any more than that we learn by experience? So what is new? (The answer to this question is of course that empiricism does not say merely that we learn from experience; it says we can learn *in no other way*. And that is very new, radical, and contentious.) Another prominent thinker of this persuasion thought he had solved or dissolved the problem of induction as follows: of course we learn from experience. (No folk saying could be false.) But learning from experience is not using some funny kind of argument. So there is no induction (for its principles would have been the principles of that unusual type of argument, and there is no such type). But if there is no such thing, there cannot be a problem of how to justify it. Problem solved. (In those days, problems were generally solved with such breath-taking simplicity and speed, though all this was sometimes spun out to article or book length.)

The key idea in empiricism is the sovereignty of experience, and above all the exclusive and sole sovereignty of experience, in cognitive matters. What seems a trite truism (we learn by experience) becomes an unbelievably daring, radical, destructive, and difficult doctrine if reformulated more strongly so as to say – we learn in no other way. Let us leave aside for a moment the problem of how such a doctrine, or rather, such an ethic, can be justified or supported. There are grave enough problems concerning the definition of this view. These problems hinge on the definition of the notion of 'experience', which is used by our preliminary account of 'empiricism'. Intuitively and naturally, 'experience' is what we actually 'encounter', come across, sense, etc., that which we can't stop coming, before we start 'adding' to it. The trouble with this natural and intuitive notion of experience is well known.

The trouble is, to put it in a simple way, that what is simply there and in front of us, 'experienced' by us, is absolutely saturated by our expectations, our concepts, our culture. It is not wholly determined by these things, of course; we cannot altogether think away or transform reality by our thoughts. The cultural relativity of reality, like the death of Mark Twain, has been very much exaggerated of late. But though events are given, the *kind* of events they are, the way they are classified and interpreted, is not given, but made by men, their language, their culture. This is a familiar and well-supported theme and there is no need to expand it.

Empiricists who wish to articulate and refine their position, either in pursuit of precision for its own sake, or as a step on the way towards defending their philosophy, have one obvious strategy open to them: they can try to isolate, define, characterise that *given* element which plays such an important role in their philosophy, which is the ultimate cognitive sovereign, the intellectual arbiter. I do not think they have been successful in this. It is easy enough to convey, in a rough and ready way, what we mean by experience; but it is difficult to do so in a non-metaphorical, and more than sketchy way. Perhaps empiricist philosophers will be more successful in the future in this endeavour.

But I doubt it. I suspect the boot is on the other foot. It is not so much that we need to define 'experience' or 'the given', so as to identify that which we have made into our cognitive sovereign, so as to make all theoretical structures subject to this master, and ultimately accountable to his judgement. It is the other way round. We need to identify that which is being excluded, generically, and we may need to resign ourselves to not being able to identify sharply and unambiguously that residual sovereign in whose name and under whose authority the exclusion takes place. The essence of empiricism is that all, but *all*, theoretical structures are accountable; that none can claim such an awful majesty as to be exempt from the indignity of inquiry and judgement; and that substantive theoretical systems so constructed as to elude and evade this indignity, are out. *Out*.

What we can define and exclude are the world pictures which are, by an a priori decree, *excluded*. We can so exclude a whole class of them, by indicating certain formal features which they possess – for instance that kind of dovetailing of moral and cognitive ideas which evades testing by morally disqualifying the sceptic. There are of course other devices such as the characteristic one of demanding assent with menaces. No attempt is made here to list them all. 'Experience' of 'the given' is then defined or identified only negatively, as that which is not under the control of any theoretical system, but independent of them all. This is metaphorical and formally unsatisfactory, but I doubt whether we can do much better. Professor H. H. Price's celebrated account of the meaning of 'sense data', in his *Perception*, really amounts to this. The term or notion of 'sense data' is of course an attempt to give a philosophic account of experience, breaking it up into its alleged constituents, and using a term which has both a singular and a plural. The granular or atomic character of experience is a marked feature of the empiricist account of it. Is it based on 'experience' as we actually know it? Many novelists, painters, and philosophers anxious to capture the real texture of our experience would vigorously deny this. Perhaps the clue to this atomism lies in its role or function, which is *not* to represent experience faithfully. Suppose that this role consists of undermining, puncturing, torpedoing falsification-evading belief systems, and suppose that these are sustained and kept going above all by the fact that they are indeed systems made up of mutually supporting parts, such that the various parts come to the help of any one of their number which is being threatened by falsification or refutation. Atomistic empiricism insists that these systems appear at the bar of knowledge not as corporate units, but as far as possible one by one, in isolation, and present their credentials singly. The empiricist metaphysic operates like those turnstiles at the entry points to underground stations or football arenas, which in effect break up the crowd into its constituent members. The transition from a traditional thought style to one dominated by empiricism is rather like the change experienced not so very long ago by many tribesmen incorporated in a modern state. Under tribal law, they turned up at a legal confrontation as a clan, and performed a *collective* oath. Now, subjected to a modern legal code, they are obliged to turn up *alone*, and to testify alone.

Thus empiricism is normally present as an account of how in fact we know (through experience), or sometimes as a metaphysic (the world is made up of experiences), such that, on either interpretation, certain worlds which defy or evade experience are, as a corollary or consequence of the initial position, excluded. On my account, all this is back-to-front. The essence or real starting point of the position is *the exclusion of certain kinds of world*, in quite an a priori manner. A certain possible misunderstanding should perhaps here be prevented: people may assume that describing a theory as quite an aprioristic one, is an attempt to denigrate it. This is no way intended. Empiricism is an a priori doctrine; and it is also a *good* doctrine.

The question now arises as to how one can know that a doctrine normally read one way, should 'really' be read in another and reversed way. The answer is roughly that it is this reading of the theory which really brings us the reasons why the theory is as persuasive as it is.

Let us return to the general consideration of ideologies or belief systems. It is they who create the problems to which empiricism offers a putative solution. We have stressed one trait of ideologies, a trait

in terms of which we have in fact defined them: they are so constructed that they are not refutable from inside. They generate, each
of them, a world so neatly rounded off that, though it is well fed by
confirmations, no refutation can occur within it. But, though this is
an important characteristic of ideologies, it is not the only one.
Another one of the first importance is: they are bi-lingual. Though
they speak a language which is closed and generates a full-circle
world, they must invariably – if only for the purposes of proselytising,
defence, and so forth – also entertain diplomatic-conceptual relations
with other worlds, and meet on more or less neutral ground, or at
any rate ground not wholly controlled by either side.

For practical reasons, they have no choice but to do this, though it
inevitably makes them look naïve, childish and contradictory. Inter-
ideological détente inevitably involves double-think. A belief system
within which certain principles are sacred and define the very
criterion of reality or truth, so that their recognition is the very
touchstone of the integrity of thought, an entry qualification to any
debate, will at the same time, when meeting outsiders on relatively
neutral ground, argue for or defend those principles...But *arguing*
in their favour of course presupposes that there are some more
authoritative principles, some more authoritative sources of evidence,
in terms of which the sacred axioms of the system are justified;
which automatically make those previously sacred principles less
than ultimate and hence less than sacred. Some theologians like
Barth have noticed this and tried to turn it to good account: to
defend the faith would be to contradict it; hence it is true without
any defence. Neat and simple. Unfortunately (*a*) this itself is an
argument, however brief, and thus sins against its own premiss; and
if you sin, you might as well sin strongly, and give us some better
arguments, and (*b*) *qua* argument, it is easily and automatically
applicable, if applicable at all, to *any* faith, and not exclusively to
to *the* faith.

In fact, most belief systems are not so summary and Barthian.
They generally do argue, often at great length, sometimes with
enormous scholastic elaboration. When they notice, as sometimes
they do, the contradiction between the total and ultimate nature of
their claims on the one hand, and the willingness to argue at all and
thus appeal to more ultimate standards on the other, they develop
elaborate and sophisticated second-level theories to explain it all.
Only Grace can give you faith but reason can help in this way or
that. (This doesn't really solve the problem: either this help is not

essential, in which case it is irrelevant, or it is essential, in which case the problem reappears with all its initial force.)

However, the point which concerns us here is not so much just what ideologists say when they speak in the outside or neutral language, but the fact that they speak it at all. The language has certain norms and conventions. Whilst conversing in Neutral-speak, the ideologists must at least seem to observe its rules and procedures. Prominent amongst these, perhaps paramount, is the requirement not to beg the question, not to proceed in a circular manner. Your premises must not, at least blatantly, contain that which you wish to establish. The premises must be acceptable to both sides to the dispute. The game then proceeds in accordance with a rule which grants victory to him who establishes his own point from shared premises. If the shared premises do not already contain the conclusion, at least in a covert way, how can you ever get there? In fact, the contest is rather like those card games in which players, in addition to being dealt a certain number of cards at the start, also receive further ones in the course of the game. The subsequently dealt cards are known as 'evidence'. It turns up, and can favour one side or the other, notwithstanding their shared general premises.

One way of looking at empiricism is as an attempt to codify and make general, absolute, the conventions of Neutral-speak. Hence that need to define 'experience', i.e. what counts as a legitimate card which can be dealt in the course of the game. But leaving aside the technical difficulties of properly codifying empiricism, by adequately defining its key terms, what are the reasons for holding it valid? It says, on this interpretation, that Neutral-speak is good speak, the best speak, not just an interim lingua franca for use in buffer zones; and that all Closed-speaks are bad speaks, and should be eschewed even when the power and diplomatic situation does not actually compel us to do so. We should give up Closed-speak even when we can get away with not doing so.

Why should we obey such an injunction? It *is* an injunction rather than a theory. It cannot really be translated into a positive world-picture (though of course the doctrine of the world-made-of-sense-data is an attempt to do so), for its substantive descriptive content is negative – it excludes certain kinds of worlds, as indicated. But anyway: what is the authority of this injunction?

Here one gets into those final stages of the regress of validation where things get very difficult and elusive. Above all it becomes hard to maintain a distinction between description and prescription or endorsement. I am inclined to use descriptive language and simply indicate the various factors which, in my view, incline us in a certain direction (i.e. towards the acceptance of the empiricist injunction); but I should be the first to admit that this is a bit spurious, that the descriptive account is accompanied by a sotto voce 'and rightly so'. Anyway, which are those considerations which so incline us (and rightly so) towards empiricism?

(1) The plausibility of the empiricist model.

(2) The correct (sociological) argument from illusion.

(3) The lessons of the Big Divide.

(4) The extension of Neutral-speak.

(5) Kantian–Protestant ethics.

Each of these needs to be spelt out. I should find it difficult to assess their relative importance of persuasiveness. No significance attaches to the way in which they are ordered in this list.

(1) The key image in the empiricist model of cognition is very simple. It sees knowledge as built up from bits, 'data', which come and arrive 'from the outside', or are 'given'. The validity of knowledge hinges on this 'given' status. Truth is a kind of fidelity to the facts as supplied. Now any non-empiricist, apriorist theory faces a very difficult problem whatever other reasons may support it: it must claim that there is some kind of pre-established harmony between mind and reality. There are occasionally ways out of this: it may resign itself to a kind of autism and refrain from claiming external reference for our convictions at all, or it may claim that the harmony is ensured not by any constraint on the facts, but only by constraint on how *we* handle the facts. (In areas in which I hold apriorism to be valid, this is how I justify it.) But these recherché cases apart, apriorism must explain or justify this surprising harmony. It can only do as a corollary of some wider theory – and what reasons can we have for holding such a wider theory to be true? (Some such theories seem attractive. The benevolence of God constituted such a theory for Descartes; natural selection and evolutionary adaptation provided a similar background premiss for various kinds of pragmatist.)

But on the whole, it is difficult to find, let alone justify, such background warrants for pre-established harmony.

No pre-established harmony; we are given what we are given, and cannot go beyond that. What we call knowledge consists of shorthand summaries of that which is given, that which is given comes in isolable little bits, and truth consists in a kind of fidelity of the summaries to these bits. These are the persuasive insights, which supply the empiricist model with its strong, albeit not irresistible, appeal.

(2) The correct formulation of the argument from illusion runs as follows: we observe fervently held belief systems which contain blatant and pervasive error. In fact we see many such, denouncing each other, and indeed often disavowing their own past. Why should *we* be exempt? (The incorrect formulation of the argument from illusion is about straight sticks which look bent in water, or is it the other way round?) This being so, should we not subject belief systems to scrutiny? – and how can they be tested, other than by the 'given', i.e. that which, whatever it be, is not controlled by *them*?

(3) The biggest, most conspicuous single fact about the human world is the Big Divide between what may roughly be called the industrial–scientific societies and the Rest. The former possess, for good and ill, enormous manipulative and predictive powers over nature (though not over social processes), endowing them with the means both of mass destruction and of mass affluence and leisure. The latter miserably scrape a precarious living by agriculture or even cruder methods. Their techniques for either feeding or killing people are slow, inefficient, and labour-intensive.

It would be idle to pretend that the Big Divide is properly understood; but it is widely and plausibly held to depend on the growth of 'science'; and science in turn is widely and plausibly held to depend on the systematic application of the 'experimental method' (and no doubt other factors, such as standardised and operationalisable notation and measurement).

But the experimental method and its rationale can best be expressed in terms of, or as a corollary of, the empiricist model. The two appear but aspects of each other, and they seem to confirm each other. Thus the cognitive history of mankind, the radical growth in knowledge and control of nature since the seventeenth century, and the contrast with other periods and regions of cognitive stagnation, seem to confirm a model which in any case has a great deal of intrinsic plausibility.

The importance of original, Comtian positivism was that it combined an articulation of the model with a historico-sociological awareness of the Big Divide. The trite and scholastic nature of many twentieth-century formulations of positivism are a consequence of an interest restricted to the model alone. The empiricist story of how an individual accumulates information about the world, is only useful if treated as an account of how some societies (but some only) have learned to investigate nature, and so as a parable of the Big Divide.

(4) As stated earlier, ideologists are bi-lingual and meet in neutral territory and converse in Neutral-speak. This on its own does not necessarily convict them of hypocrisy. They often possess quite elaborate theories explaining why all this is allowed, why a language permitting or imposing doubt may on occasion be employed notwithstanding the fact that in the True Language, doubt is inarticulable. They possess conceptual exit permits, rather the way in which authoritarian regimes grant temporary exit visas to their more trusted citizens.

But, in the modern world, the area in which the conventions of Neutral-speak apply has been steadily growing, and the spheres in which the Closed languages are spoken have been contracting. In fact, one more often hears apologetic and tortuous, devious justifications for the occasional, Sunday employment of faith-language, than for the daily employment of Neutral-speak. Modern ideologies are a bit like central banks in dictatorships which employ quite different exchange rates in different markets and diverse circumstances. (Modernist theology, for instance, does not believe in anything, but merely debases the conceptual currency.) But the occasions on which they dare use the 'real' exchange rate as they officially see it, use their 'internal' concepts, have been steadily contracting.

Looking at their comportment can only strengthen the doubts one already has in virtue of the Argument from illusion.

(5) The appeal underlying the closed vision is, as stressed, the moral gratification of seeing a coherent, un-'alienated' world. But this is not the only moral vision operative amongst us. There is also what might be called the Protestant–Kantian ethic, which spurns extraneous confirmations and sanctions. We hold certain values, it says, and we do not need nature to confirm them for us. Let the facts be what they will; our norms are not at their mercy. We take no bribes – not even from the Top Management.

Thus there is an important ethic which actually encourages an expectation that facts will not fit in with a closed, integrated world, but will form their own patterns which need not be, and in all probability will not be, such as would somehow dovetail with human aims. Whether it is a sour grapes doctrine, which merely accommodates itself to this disagreeable world, or an independently held and persuasive morality (as I hold), we need not here discuss. But I am sure that either way it is, by now, an additional prop of the empiricist vision.

I have now sketched out what I think empiricism 'truly' is, and why we hold it or at least are attracted by it. Now for a certain admission, and some comments on the implications of this view.

The admission is of course that in a sense, empiricism is an ideology amongst others, though it is an ethic of cognition, and its substantive prejudgements are indirect and negative – a *differentia* which is all we can invoke to save empiricism from falling under its own axe. It is ideology, though, in my view, a very very good one. As already conceded, it cannot refute its rivals from neutral, shared premisses. Like the hero of the fairy tale who cannot be harmed by the ferocious evil spirits, as long as he does not step out of the chalk circle sanctified by holy water, they cannot be demolished as long as they remain within their own circle of ideas. Secondly, the empiricist model is itself a kind of complete circle. Data, whatever they be, are sovereign, and cognitive contentions are either about nothing at all (autistic in some way or other), or about the data; and only the data can decide. This simple and persuasive model, underlying empiricist epistemologies and metaphysics, can hardly be destroyed on its own terms. Furthermore – and this is perhaps the most crucial part of the admission – empiricism is, in practice, fluently bi-lingual. Its bi-lingual fluency is so great that it is almost a bit worrying.

What basically happens is this. As a 'prior philosophy', in Quine's sense – an independently established self-sustaining principle, prior to any specific inquiry, and one conferring legitimacy on more specific procedures – empiricism derives its authority from consideration (1), from the plausible and persuasive abstract model, the repudiation of either autism or pre-established harmony. But it would be dishonest to pretend that those of us who are highly sensitive to the claims of empiricism are persuaded by this philosophically pure consideration *alone*. We are swayed by it in part; but we are also significantly influenced by considerations of what we know *in* and *about* the world, by specific information, notably the historic record of various belief systems, cognitive styles, and diverse societies and traditions. It is the argument from illusion, so copiously fed and encouraged by the record of human credulity and its institutionalisations, and the conspicuous difference between successful and abortive styles of knowing, which encourage our empiricist faith. In other words, we are influenced by the track record of different styles of thinking; but this assessment can only be done within a given world, a given way of conceptualising things, and any such given way is of course itself the product of one style of thinking amongst others. Thus any such 'in the world' assessment is inevitably circular. So the empiricist faith is sustained by two considerations, which are so to speak in quite different idioms and which, if they do not contradict each other, at least stylistically jar with each other: one (the empiricist metaphysic) consists of trying to stand outside the world and not taking the world for granted, and the other consists of very much taking our current world for granted and then, from within it, having a look at the performance of certain concrete historical traditions of intellectual activity.

Philosophically, this is untidy and messy. In as far as empiricism is a recipe for constructing a world, a touchstone for what bricks of evidence may be used in erecting a universe, it seems a bit circular and illogical also to be swayed by evidence *inside* the world. But, circular and inelegant or not, this is how in fact we think. I do not for one moment accept Quine's oft-repeated belief that we can do without prior philosophy altogether, and trust the world which we seem to inhabit, the 'aggregate of existing science'; this may describe a possible course of conduct in periods of civil peace in the realm of our ideas, but it does not describe any possible course whatever in cases of dramatic revolutionary discontinuity, and these do happen. The Quinian view corresponds to a political philosopher who holds that history records *continuous* change, and the legitimate line of succession is always reasonably manifest! At times it is nothing of the kind, and some crises are quite unique and are not illuminated by the previous ones. In such situations of conceptual anarchy or the dissolution of cognitive norms, we absolutely need a 'prior philosophy'. (Empiricism happened to be a very good one.) We then absolutely need something like an extraneous vantage point. Our world has dissolved. Moreover, there is no meta-theory or meta-world, such as Quine tacitly or otherwise takes for granted, which guarantees the more general properties of the world, and provides, under the name of 'scientific method', ever-valid principles for the re-establishment of cognitive order. It was the establishment of that kind of general meta-world, a set of assumptions within which alone scientific method can operate, which was precisely the achievement of the empiricist tradition. It achieved this as a 'prior philosophy'.

The illusion that we do not need a prior philosophy at all is simply a consequence of the fact that it had done its job too well. It is both a compliment and a piece of dreadful ingratitude that its achievements should be so completely taken for granted.

But at the same time, man cannot live by prior philosophy alone. For better or for worse, we do shuttle-cock, in choosing our position, between independent and prior considerations on the one hand, and evidence drawn from within the world, about the comportment of human societies and ideologies. The appeal of empiricism derives, inelegantly, from such a double, strictly-speaking incommensurate, type of support.

So much by way of concession. What are the implications of this account of empiricism? There may be many; but some are of immediate interest.

The central element in empiricism, on this account, is a substantive, a priori and negative principle – the exclusion of certain logically possible and historically upheld visions. In the more elaborate account of what empiricism is, which admits our shuttle-cocking between prior-philosophic and intra-mundane historical considerations, this exclusion is seen to be both aprioristic (in as far as derived from the ultimate model of what knowledge must be), and in part based on evidence which, admittedly, is strong but never conclusive. (The fact that many closed visions are, when characterised in Neutral-speak, meretricious frauds, cannot establish that *all* such visions must be humbugs. Perhaps, who knows, the world is a Big Cosy Meaningful Unity after all, only we haven't hit on it yet; or perhaps even – excuse my shudder – one of the existing faiths is the true one.)

But if this is so – if the central idea in empiricism is paradoxically the a priori substantive exclusion of certain worlds – then certain more narrowly philosophical implications follow. If it is of the essence of a very important philosophy that it excludes certain visions, then the view that philosophy is, could be or ought to be 'neutral', is absurd. Another one is that falsificationists are wrong to spurn, as they tend to do, verificationism and Baconian inductivism. The difference between the two is not so very significant. The really important element in both forms is the deprivation of all positive, concrete visions, of the status of final norms of truth. (In their non-bilingual state, this is what ideologies do claim, even though they half-suspend the claim when talking to outsiders.) This end is achieved equally by a positive insistence on the sovereignty of experience (verificationism) as by a negative insistence on the right of experience to dethrone any particular theory (falsificationism). Historically and psychologically, it may well have been inevitable that the verificationist formulation should have been earlier, more influential and persuasive than the falsificationist one, whatever technical advantages the latter may possess; a revolutionary movement which promises a positive alternative and a deliverance is more attractive than a merely negative one.

This leads to another and closely related question. As W. W. Bartley pointed out, there is a certain development in Popper's thought from the problem of demarcation to the problem of rationality, from the cult of falsification to the cult of criticism. There are indeed certain passages in the later Popper which read as if the notion of criticism has replaced that of falsification, which seem to suggest that what matters is the critical spirit, and not any particular method it employs, and which seems to lose interest in the delimitation of rightful methods of criticism. (The earlier position still seems articulated in something akin to the empiricist metaphysic, in terms of a vision of the world made up of facts which eliminate the theories floating above them; the latter position is spelt out rather in a non-prior-philosophical idiom of the ordinary *Lebenswelt*. This evolution is curiously parallel to that which other philosophers went through, when they moved from pure prior philosophy of logical positivism, to the comforting and joyful return to the ordinary world of daily speech.)

Now this difference corresponds to a question which pervades this paper – namely, is the real meat of empiricism contained in its *exclusion* of closed worlds, with the talk of 'experience' merely a picturesque way of achieving that end, or is the actual stress on experience as that which is now sovereign, of the very essence of the position? I find myself vacillating on this. The grave difficulties facing any attempt to define or even indicate what 'experience' is, other than metaphorically or in a circular manner, incline me to think that what is at the heart of the matter is the exclusion of closed worlds. (In other words that it is the critical spirit which matters.) On the other hand, it is also difficult to give a good account of 'criticism'. One can imagine conditions of mere instability and rapid change, which are yet cognitively most unsatisfactory. The positive identification of the ultimate arbiter *does* seem to matter: it is *experience*, and not the last speaker, or the most powerful or eloquent one. This consideration inclines me to favour the formulation of empiricism in terms which do stress the independent and extraneous nature of the source of confirmations or refutations. It also suggests that it is historically ungrateful to spurn that empiricist metaphysics which habituated us to this idea and to its appeal.

10
Beyond truth and falsehood, or no method in my madness

Paul Feyerabend's rather idiosyncratic *Against Method* contains a number of theses or themes, interdependent and intertwined in various ways. Some of these themes are openly, conspicuously and deliberately personal, and we are plainly invited to see them as such. The personal aspect has a number of elements: a dialogue with the late Imre Lakatos, a settlement of scores with Sir Karl Popper and his followers, and a personal manifesto/self-portrait by Paul Feyerabend.

The volume is dedicated to Imre Lakatos, described as 'fellow-anarchist', and the introductory note specifies that 'every wicked phrase' in the book was written in anticipation of 'an even more wicked reply' from Lakatos. This may well give the impression that Imre Lakatos shared the author's 'anarchist' views and style, at least in some measure. For the record, and in fairness to the memory of Imre Lakatos, it is important to state that this fostered impression bears no relation to the truth. What is the case is that, in his private life, Lakatos was much given to agreeable clowning, which gave pleasure to his friends, and such clowning *in private life* may perhaps resemble, to some extent, the clowning found *in print* and within hard covers in Feyerabend's book. But in his work, his writings and lectures, Lakatos observed the highest standards of rigour, lucidity and responsibility. Not only did he observe such standards, he was, as Feyerabend himself reports in another part of the volume, deeply and systematically concerned with the maintenance of such standards in the face of current sloppy trends (anarchistic in Feyerabend's sense). Lakatos's élitism in educational policy, which he had the opportunity of supporting both under a Communist and under a Western regime, sprang precisely from this concern. It did not arise from some over-all right-wing position; he continued to be left-wing on economic issues, and did not seem unduly interested in hierarchy and authority, one way or the other, in society at large. It was the threat to *intellectual* standards which aroused him to strong feeling, whether it came from Communist egalitarianism or from Western permissiveness. By contrast, Feyerabend's book, if taken at all seriously, can only be a charter for the abandonment of all and every standard. It is inconceivable that Lakatos would have allowed himself to be hailed as a 'fellow anarchist' in this sense. The dialogue which did indeed go on between him and the author concerned certain specific issues about scientific method.

The claim that Lakatos's position was 'anarchism in disguise' is totally unfounded. It might perhaps be true that Lakatos has not solved the problem which arises from the divergence between the real practice of science on the one hand, and the picture of it offered by writers on method on the other. But it is totally irresponsible to present this failure (if such it was) as a tacit or camouflaged admission that the problem is insoluble, and that consequently 'anything goes'. For it is *this* argument which is at the heart of Feyerabend's book. There is nothing to show that Lakatos either embraced this conclusion or was logically obliged to do so.

The relationship to Popper is different. Popper and his followers are attacked on various grounds, over and above holding erroneous views:

> Popper's philosophy, which some people would like to lay
> on us as the one and only humanitarian rationalism in
> existence today, is but a pale reflection of Mill's *On Liberty*.
> It is. . .much more formalistic and elitist, and quite devoid
> of concern for individual happiness. . .We can understand
> its peculiarities when we consider. . .the unrelenting
> puritanism of its author (and of most of his followers), and
> when we remember the influence of Harriet Taylor on
> Mill's life and on his philosophy. There is no Harriet
> Taylor in Popper's life [p. 48n].

This is a piquant passage. My own liberalism is such that I hold that even puritans are not debarred from truth (some of my best friends are puritans) and that even professors of philosophy are free to refrain from having mistresses, if their inclinations are so eccentric. This should not lay them open to censure or render their views suspect. But perhaps I push liberalism too far.

But there is a serious element in all this. Feyerabend is not the only man of talent, closely associated with the Popperite movement, who after some time displays a need to lash out against it. W. W. Bartley III and Imre Lakatos himself are other names which spring to mind. It is difficult not to suppose that excessive demands for conformity and involvement, made by the master, are at the root of such subsequent revulsions. It is ironical that the foremost proponent of critical philosophy should have formed a movement so intolerant of criticism that it drives its own members to such outbursts. Those of us who admire Popperian ideas without having been involved in the movement, can only deplore the way in which, logically or not, the ideas come to be tarnished by such an atmosphere. Feyerabend's suggestion that this could be avoided by diversifying one's emotional involvements has its plausibility, though people should perhaps be free to choose the form which the diversification takes. In fact, not all single-minded people are necessarily intolerant, and even the possession of a harem does not necessarily make a ruler liberal. So Feyerabend's characteristically Viennese cure for the closed society can hardly be the whole answer.

Feyerabend's attitude to himself, which is affectionate and admiring, is the third markedly personal theme in the book. It is relevant in as far as the author repeatedly makes plain that this book is not to be judged by the normal conventions, such as are generally taken for granted by the authors, readers and reviewers of books. It is a *happening*. It makes its own conventions or rather it suspends a lot of them, and switches them on and off, and above all it invokes the meta-convention that no conventions are binding. The game is played by the author's own rules, which moreover he is free to change as he wishes. This naturally makes it somewhat difficult for the reader to assess or argue with the author's ideas. Just what kind of happening this book is meant to be, and by what criteria if any it could be judged according to its author, we can only guess at in the light of what he says about himself and his endeavour.

> Puritanical dedication and seriousness. . .I detest. . .I now
> prefer. . .the term *Dadaism*. . .A Dadaist is utterly un-
> impressed by any serious enterprise. . .is convinced that a
> worthwhile life will arise only when we start taking things
> *lightly*. . .is prepared to initiate joyful experiments even
> in those domains where change and experiments seem to
> be out of the question. . .I hope. . .the reader will remember
> me as a flippant Dadaist [p. 21n].

> . . .the epistemological anarchist has no compunction to
> defend the most trite, or the most outrageous statement. . .
> His aims remain stable, or change as a result of argument,
> or of boredom, or of a conversion experience, or to impress
> a mistress, and so on. . .The one thing he opposes positively
> and absolutely are universal standards, universal laws,
> universal ideas such as 'Truth', 'Reason', 'Justice', 'Love'
> [p. 189].

We can hardly complain that we have not been given the self-imposed terms of reference of the work. More of this hereafter.

In fact, the book contains a number of related theses and attitudes, some of which are of interest. In addition, there are secondary theses elaborated by way of support or defence for the main ones, a kind of intellectual spin-off from the main argument. What I would select as the primary theses, the backbone of the book, form a kind of series or progression. It is worth while enumerating the vertebrae in this spinal column, summed up in my own words:

(1) The actual history of science shows that the real advances of knowledge contradict all available methodologies.

(2) This shows that all methodological doctrines or principles are false.

(3) This is not because the existing theories of scientific method aren't good enough, but because *no* principles of method could ever be good enough.

(4) As it is difficult to distinguish very general principles of method from criteria of truth, it follows not merely that we cannot distinguish between good and bad methods, but equally that we cannot distinguish between good and bad substantive theories.

(5) Hence let a million flowers bloom, for at least two reasons (which to me seem contradictory): we cannot tell the good ones from the bad ones, *and* the proliferation aids the emergence of good ones.

(6) In our intellectual and cultural and other activities, there are many aims more important than truth, and for this reason, in addition to the above, we should not bother with truth and the uniqueness of truth. (This argument would seem to me otiose if we cannot in any case identify truth.)

(7) All this being so, we should just fool around as the fancy takes us. I, Paul Feyerabend, am fooling and clowning for all I'm worth, at this very moment, and all the time.

This seems to me the central plot, though, as I say, there are side-arguments and spin-offs which also deserve consideration. The elements in this spinal column are related to each other in various ways which give the book its organic unity. (1) is clearly the nucleus from which the whole thing grew. This is the area of Feyerabend's professional expertise, and where a claim that he is engaged in sustained debate with serious scholars (even if he himself also disclaims seriousness) can be upheld. One way to treat this book would be to concentrate on the extensive parts which argue this viewpoint in connection with the history of modern physics, and to ignore the rest as off-duty clowning, which had, through temperamental idiosyncracy, and encouraged by the spirit of the times, been allowed to intrude within the covers of the book. Such a procedure would be reasonable, and perhaps the most sensible one to adopt. I shall not adopt it, partly because it could only be usefully carried out by a historian and/or philosopher of physics, and partly because the rest of the book does seem to me of some interest, even if only as a phenomenon rather than a serious position, and I do feel competent to discuss it.

(2), (3), (4) and (5) are developments of (1), through various forms of strengthening or extension. Where (1) has a certain plausibility, these extensions or extrapolations lack it, but nevertheless they deserve some discussion. The most obvious criticism is of the step from (1) to (2) and (3): if existing methodologies do not do justice to the actual process of the advancement of knowledge, why can we not improve on these methodologies, and how could we know that it cannot in principle be done? (Perhaps I may at this point state my own view of the matter. I doubt whether any methodology can fully capture the complexity of the transition from one theory to another, or from one style or paradigm to another. The transition will always hinge on the *content* of the theory or paradigm, which of course must be ignored by an abstract and general theory of method, meant to be applicable impartially to all such advances. On the other hand, theories of scientific method *can* do the important job of singling out worlds amenable to science from those which are not. This is important because not all worlds or thought-styles are amenable to science. Cf. chapter 9.)

Feyerabend tries to establish (3) with the help of some additional tributary considerations which feed into the mainstream of the argument. History is far too complex to be encompassed within the simple bounds of any theory of method; and secondly, *reasons* are never sufficient to effect changes, of opinions or of anything else, and the inevitable *causes* cannot be incorporated in methodologies which can only specify reasons. On the first point, he invokes the authority of Lenin. All this seems to me to prove too much. There is a methodology for solving quadratic equations, which many schoolboys and others frequently implement. Of course, each real occasion of such implementation is more complex, *and* can also be interpreted causally. But this well-known general consideration can be invoked to exclude the possibility of *any* rational or norm-governed action. Are we to conclude that no-one ever really solved quadratic equations? This problem is in no way specific to the question of whether scientific methodology actually governs the history of science. Feyerabend makes no cross-reference to the relevant philosophical history of this much wider problem, but proceeds, here as elsewhere, as if he'd just discovered the point, and as if it were *specifically* relevant. His awareness of the relevant parts of general philosophy seems highly limited. Elsewhere, on the other hand, he blithely carries on as if no such impediment to human fulfilment existed, and reasons could liberate us. In brief, (3) neither follows from (1), nor is cogently, or even consistently, supported by additional arguments.

By contrast, at the next stage, *if* (3) be granted, then (4) does follow, and, given some not very contentious additional premisses, or tastes, so does (5). If there are no methods and hence no criteria, it follows that all substantive propositions are equally good or bad. If this is so, then in turn we only need a preference for activity as against passivity, to end up with anarchism rather than with scepticism. Given our alleged inability to distinguish between good and bad ideas, we can refrain from all of them (scepticism), or capriciously indulge in any that take our fancy (Feyerabendian anarchism). It would seem a matter of taste. Feyerabend notices that his argument could equally lead to scepticism, and it is in fact at many points indistinguishable from it. We seem to owe the preference for anarchism to his temperamental exuberance:

> Epistemological anarchism. . .differs from scepticism. . .
> While the sceptic. . .regards every view as equally good,
> or equally bad. . .the epistemological anarchist has no
> compunction to defend the most trite, or the most
> outrageous statement [p. 189].

Given (5), i.e. given anarchism/scepticism (choose your option, and presumably anarchist freedom includes scepticism as one of its own freely available internal options), the further transition to (6) also seems to me quite natural. Moreover, (6) has a certain independent plausibility, and many thinkers have reached it, or some position similar to it, without having come to it by the questionable path trodden by Feyerabend. Moreover, (6) can be supported by some additional considerations which are also present in the book. These are the arguments from the human condition, and from diverse cultural styles of life. (These are my terms, not Feyerabend's.)

The argument from the human condition runs as follows (when summed up in my own words): those of us who are honest, know that our intellectual life is a mess. Epistemologies pretend that each of us inhabits a coherent world, and that we reached it for good reasons, and know it to be rationally preferable to any other world open to us. In fact, we inhabit an incoherent chaos, we don't quite know how we acquired all the bric-à-brac that comes to make it up, though we do know that some bits of it we acquired improperly or even shamefully, by means we could not defend; and we also opportunistically keep all kinds of alternative visions and strategies in reserve, and hope to get by somehow. Coherent, clear and rigid visions are fraudulent façades, as are strong and consistent moral characters; and ideologies which try to bully us into pretending that things are otherwise, that good and manifest reasons are available to justify their own advertised options, commit violence against us and against the truth of the matter. All this is so, and constitutes the grain of truth in Feyerabend's more general anarchism (as opposed to his more specific thesis about divergence between methodology and the real history of science). This strengthens his case: he reminds us in a salutary manner of the way things really are, and of the amount of pretence involved in the official theories. But it is one thing to say that in a complex and difficult world, almost anything might contain some truth, and therefore it behoves us to be humble; and quite another to say that anything goes and therefore we should be arrogant.

Then there is the argument from culture and thought-styles. The point is familiar. There are many rival cultures and values in this world, often competing within single societies and within the breasts of single individuals. The choice between such styles or cultures is difficult, and certainly there are no easy or self-evident choices. But each culture or style of life tends to carry with it, and internally validate, its own world-picture and its own cognitive norms. Hence cultural relativism, or liberalism as between cultures, also forces us into relativism. This view is reinforced by the notorious difficulty or impossibility of proving basic premisses of world-pictures (a consideration which also strengthens the argument from the human condition).

Thus amongst the more plausible of Feyerabend's premisses are the view of the irrelevance of methodologies to the actual progress of science, and the idea that diverse cultures or values are incommensurate, and that the superiority of one of them (e.g. science) should not too easily be taken for granted. He uses *each* of them to support the view that anything goes, that an extreme form of relativism is valid. My own view is that the two problems in some measure cancel each other out in the sense that the main point of epistemologies is precisely that they provide a way of making inter-cultural comparisons. Epistemologies are indeed, I suspect, irrelevant to the manner in which *specific* cognitive advances are reached. Their real use lies in helping us make inter-cultural comparisons. A culture which subjects its cognitive capital to testing by arbiters *who are not under its own control*, seems to me superior to one which does not do so. Epistemological theories thus do give us some insight into how one could choose between whole styles of thought. But I do not expect them to apply mechanically to individual discoveries or advances, even *within* the culture which, as a whole, satisfies this or that epistemology.

All this is worth discussing. My complaint here is that, quite contrary to all appearances, Feyerabend, far from being too extreme (which is how he delights to present himself), is not nearly extreme enough; or, to put it another way, that his extremism fails through its frivolity. The trouble is, he reaches the problem of how we choose between different styles of life and their associated cognitive norms not, as the problem deserves, because it is important, relevant and intriguing; he reaches it by a process of wilfully exaggerating the implications of his conclusions about the relation of methodologies to the real life of science. Even then, he does not really reach the *problem* or discuss it properly, he merely reaches the anarchistic or relativistic solution of it, and he does that far more for the sake of trying to extract every ounce of *épatement* from it, than because he is seriously concerned with the question to which it might be a (regrettable) answer. The question is not properly discussed, nor the implications of the answer seriously explored. It is all just part of the clowning, an exaggeration of certain views, pushed to an extreme to achieve an effect or to avert boredom or to satisfy a jaded intellectual palate. As he tells us, his

> aims. . .change as a result of argument, or boredom, or of
> a conversion experience, or to impress a mistress [p. 189].

I only hope that she was more impressed than I am. There are some gullible mistresses about, but that I knew anyway.

One might however, object that the argument from the existence of rival cultural styles of knowing, between which it is difficult to arbitrate, only justifies *cultural* relativism (with whole cultures as the units to which truth is 'relative'); whereas Feyerabend's anarchism is relativistic in a more extreme form, going beyond even individual relativism and reaching to the justification of the autonomy of every mood, every caprice, and every individual – which must never be eliminated simply because some rival and incompatible belief has better support. . .

However, if this extreme individual-occasion anarchism/relativism of (5) and (6) be granted, then (7), an attitude rather than a belief ('I'm clowning, and clowning is best'), *does* seem to follow. In a world as described in (5) and (6), clowning does seem to make more sense than any alternative. But if clowning is the only permissible strategy ('anything goes'), as Feyerabend delights to repeat, then of course all the logical inadequacies in the previous build-up, not to mention the lack of seriousness, receive *ex post* clearance. It was all clowning, it proved that only clowning is the right method, and as no reasoning can fall below the standards of clowning, then by the very standards which we have now established, the reasoning which led us here was entirely sound. The circle is complete. The final step of the argument conclusively, by its own norms, underwrites all the steps which led up to it. Of course, some other clown might clown differently, and so might *this* clown when the mood takes him; but then, Feyerabend does not deny this. He says of himself:

> To be a true Dadaist, one must also be an anti-Dadaist.
> His [the epistemological anarchist's] favourite pastime is
> to confuse rationalists by inventing compelling reasons for
> unreasonable doctrines. There is no view, however 'absurd'
> or 'immoral', he refuses to consider or act upon. . .The one
> thing he opposes positively. . .are universal standards. . .
> though he does not deny that it is often good policy to act as
> if such laws. . .existed [p. 189].

Clearly Feyerabend has invented a game at which he cannot lose.

Of course, it is not internally coherent: the conclusion that all ideas have equal right to our assent, is supported, over and over, by arguments which presuppose that on the contrary we do know some of them to be true; that we know, for instance, the truth of certain generalisations, such as that all scientific theories are contradicted by some facts, or that some scientific theories continue to be upheld even when falsified. But a conclusion which claims to show that the requirement of coherence, like all other requirements, is illegitimate, obviously cannot be refuted by the demonstration that the approach to it contained incoherent steps...

So shall we leave it at that?

No. There are things to be said about the inadequacy of Feyerabend's *Problemstellung*, about his solutions, about the sources of that solution, and about his style.

We are in effect presented with the choice between two possible worlds. Each of these worlds is attained and ratified by a distinct cognitive strategy. Each has its own epistemology as its Founding Charter. The first world is the one normally inhabited by most Western academics. It is a world which historically owes something to the jealous and exclusive Jehovah, to the Platonic ideal of unique mathematical truth, to the rigour of Roman law, and to the scripturalism of the Reformation. These traditions all converge on the crucial idea that truth is *unique*, and is surrounded by a vast sea of variegated error. The idea of *method* which accompanies this vision, is that of a narrow and perilous path which leads, and which alone leads, to cognitive salvation. Science as conventionally conceived has taken over this picture. *Extra scientiam nulla salus* is how Feyerabend wittily and appositely [p. 306] sums up this conception.

Within this conventional world, the practice of clowning is also known, and is governed by certain conventions. These conventions preclude us from subjecting a clown's pronouncements to the same kind of scrutiny and criticism as we should apply to serious contention. To violate Clown's Licence is to show oneself a boor.

Then there is another and Alternative World, so warmly commended by Feyerabend. This world is infinitely rich and manifold and, according to Feyerabend, contains human beings greatly superior, freer and more fulfilled, than those who reside in the normal world. The underlying epistemology of this other world, its key and entrance, is the principle – *anything goes*.

These are the *dramatis personae*. What is the plot? This, alas, depends on what the reader does. If he carefully examines – as I think he should – this fascinatingly radical challenge to our usual assumptions, the idea that this Other World is indeed superior to the one we normally take for granted, and if in the course of doing so he dares raise some objections – he is scornfully dismissed as one who pedantically and meanly fails to observe a rule of *this* world, which exempts clowns from logical scrutiny...

If, however, he allows himself to be browbeaten by this into going along with the joke, he suddenly finds himself, not in the presence of a *jeu d'esprit*, but under summary judgement from a People's Court set up by the New Regime to root out all reactionary survivals from the Old World...

So clowning is, all at once, both a criticism-evading ploy within *this* world and one invoking its conventions, *and* the Founding Epistemology of *another* world which would supplant this one, and excoriate the adherents of a rigid and oppressive orthodoxy. It is all at once an argument-suspending evasion, and a warrant for condemnation of others.

Feyerabend's clowning is not total and unremitting, nor is his preaching of capricious incoherence self-exemplifying. Or perhaps one should say instead that he *is* consistent in self-exemplifying his secondary rejection of all consistency, which excludes even the consistency of inconsistency. (You can't win.) Anyway, contrary to his primary commendation of inconsistency, and consistently with his secondary denial of consistency even in inconsistency (this regress has the form of a kind of recursive wobble), he does argue with a measure of coherence. Let us consider for instance his handling of epistemology.

Perhaps an epistemology must do justice both to the good grounds for doubt *and* to at least the strong presumption that we do have some knowledge. Feyerabend does a good job on the first requirement, but is hopeless on the second. Epistemology has to explain, or explain away, the *differential* problem – that some bits of putative knowledge seem so much better than others. This occurs at both individual and at social level. Some cognitive traditions seem conspicuously more effective than others. Consider the individual and social problems in turn.

We are notoriously confident about certain predictions, such as that we shall die if we step out of the window of a 50-storey building. Feyerabend reports Lakatos as insistently invoking this argument. In fact, Lakatos liked using the argument against Popper's views as well as Feyerabend's:

> Where is the epistemological anarchist who out of sheer
> contrariness walks out the window of a 50-storey building?
> [p. 221]

Feyerabend thinks he can answer this in terms of irrational com-
pulsions of the reluctant anarchist.

> He may readily admit that he is a coward, that he cannot
> control his fear, and that his fear keeps him from the
> windows. . .What he *does* deny is that he can give reasons
> for his fear [pp. 221 and 222].

People who genuinely have fears which they also sincerely consider
irrational, have no objection to being cured of those fears, if a pain-
less cure is available. In fact, certain drugs are said to induce fearless-
ness in people in such circumstances. I am, however, convinced
(not irrationally, I believe) that the reluctant anarchist, when offered
the appropriate drug on the 50th floor, will also firmly refuse it.

Except for the more modern psychological idiom, this is of course
a new version of that aspect of Hume's theory which gave a psycho-
logistic account of our causal beliefs, for lack of a rational one.
Feyerabend presents his summary psychologism in a cavalier manner
as a new discovery, without the least hint that it may possess either
difficulties or a prior history.

Let us move from his failure to deal with the difference between
our *individual* firm convictions and our genuine doubts, and move
on to the difference between technologically effective and powerless
styles of thought.

If we adopted his principle 'anything goes', would not the consequence be a collapse of that science and technology on which we
have come to rely for affluence, and without which the world's
swollen population would both starve and tear each other apart in a
far more savage conflict than we endure at present? Interestingly,
Feyerabend does not deny the dependence of technology on that
kind of square science in which it is *not* the case that 'anything goes'.
This is an enormously significant concession: most people, when
asked to say why it is *not* true that 'anything goes', would invoke
the supremely important pragmatic consideration that some thought
styles lead to effective control over nature, and others do not.
No epistemology which ignores this Big Divide can claim to have
asked the right question. Feyerabend does ignore it in the mainstream of his argument, but, curiously, accepts it when dealing with

the (for him) tangential matter of the social consequences of his own position:

> while an American can now choose the religion he
> likes, he is still not permitted to demand that his children
> learn magic rather than science at school. . .The separation
> between state and church must therefore be complemented
> by the separation between state and science.
>
> We need not fear that such a separation will lead to a
> breakdown of technology. There will always be people who
> prefer being scientists to being the masters of their fate. . .
> Greece developed. . .because it could rely on the services
> of unwilling slaves. We shall develop. . .with the help of
> numerous *willing* slaves in universities and laboratories
> who provide us with pills, gas, electricity, atom bombs,
> frozen dinners. . .[pp. 299 and 300]

So, when it comes to securing these benefits, pills and all (the pills naturally come first on his list), there is a welcome admission that 'anything' evidently does *not* 'go'. With a coherent or coherence-recognising thinker, one might conclude that his épatant relativism is but skin deep: subjected to the acid test of practical effectiveness, relativism is abandoned. So perhaps it all boils down to the far less provocative and in effect mild contention, that there are aims other than truth, and that a scientific civilisation is in danger of ignoring or underestimating those other aims? A reasonable viewpoint, but hardly original, or deserving of all that Dadaist trumpet-blowing. In fact, it is a view often proposed by utterly square people. . . How ironic that a genteel platitude should lurk under all that apparent extravagance.

But note the social philosophy which accompanies it. It is a blatant recommendation of parasitism, Californian style. The opting out from cognitive and productive rationality is recommended on the basis of an open expectation that others will not do likewise, and that we can continue to benefit from their exertions. Though the helots are recognised as necessary for our comfort, we are at the same time invited to despise them. Arrogance and parasitism seem to lurk under the *gemütlich*, all-permissive liberation.

The position is parasitic twice over. The 'anything goes' principle is recommended partly as a piece of self-confirming anarchism, but partly also as a consequence of a more interesting claim – that the proliferation of rival viewpoints aids the advancement of knowledge.

But natural selection from amongst a host of contestants only works if there is, indeed, *selection*: it is not enough to say that the more contestants the merrier. If there is no selection, the multiplication of contestants on its own will have no effect whatever. The selection will only work if people do *not* accept incoherence, pointless pro-liferation of viewpoints, and so forth. So the effectiveness of the recommendation hinges on it being ignored, just as the material basis of the epistemological anarchist hinges on others not being anarchists – though they only get despised for their pains.

His doctrines about violence are similarly Californian. In a pro-nouncement early in the book, he tells us that

> A Dadaist would not hurt a fly – let alone a human being.

One is glad to hear it, though the persistent references to the pleasure that is to be had by confusing poor souls ('rationalists') who argue in good faith, does make one wonder. One's fears are later confirmed:

> Violence is *necessary* to overcome the impediments erected
> by a well-organised society. . .and it is *beneficial* for the
> individual, for it releases one's energies and makes one
> realise the powers at one's disposal [p. 187].

'Violence', if the word means anything, involves imposing one's will on a reluctant person who happens to be weaker. (Vigorous exercise with inanimate objects is not violence.) So violence does indeed help one person to realise the powers at his disposal, whilst giving another one a good taste of impotence and humiliation. The mystique of violence is justified as a reaction to a 'well-organised society', and not given any specified limits. It is conflated inco-herently with a pacifist no-fly-hurting posture, and goes with cog-nitive/productive parasitism.

His remarks on education are in the same tradition. In as far as a coherent doctrine can be extracted from his remarks, his view seems to be that education should be anarchist and tentative, not pre-judging such open issues as the relative merits of science and magic, but leaving choice to the individual. But, oddly enough, 'progressive' theories of education are abused, though contemporary 'progressive' educational theories come close to his kind of 'anarchism'. He notes that Lakatos was 'concerned with intellectual pollution', such as that

> empty verbiage full of strange and esoteric terms claims to
> express profound insights, 'expects'. . .tell us about our
> 'condition' and the means for improving it [p. 217].

Not a bad characterisation of *Against Method*, in which a melange of truisms and extravagances (hedged by self-characterisation as deliberate provocation) is presented as a recipe for our liberation.

His views about the general traits of our social condition are in the same style. For instance, whilst contemporary liberal society is apparently, as we saw, so oppressive that it justifies uncircumscribed violence on the part of the individual, *other* societies (generally far more oppressive) receive indiscriminate praise in this hysteria of protest. For instance

> primitive tribes. . .solve difficult problems in ways which are still not quite understood. . .there existed a highly developed and internationally known astronomy in the old Stone Age, this astronomy was factually adequate *as well as* emotionally satisfying, *it solved both physical and social problems* [p. 306].

Feyerabend appears to possess information about the emotional states and social organisation of old Stone Age man which has been withheld from more conventional anthropologists and archaeologists, no doubt because they are not aware of the methodological principle that 'anything goes'. In similar spirit, political interference in science in China and the USSR is commended, though apparently it was abortive in the case of Lysenko – who, by some most arbitrary decision within Feyerabend's terms of reference, does not benefit from the principle that anything goes.

Distant obscurantisms and authoritarianisms benefit from the principle – only the mild local liberal discrimination between reason and fantasy, and between the rule of law and chaos, does not. The history of the past four centuries is summed up as

> the suppression of non-Western tribes by Western invaders [p. 299].

So much for the non-tribal civilisations of the Eastern world. The ulama, Brahmins and mandarins are all relegated to the status of tribesmen. The only difference from the usual picture is that the poison brought by the conquerors is not capitalism and colonialism, but science and rationalism. Perhaps all this nonsense is simply a case of indulging his self-proclaimed 'favourite pastime' which is to 'confuse rationalists by inventing compelling reasons for unreasonable doctrines'. Unfortunately, this rationalist at any rate finds himself far from compelled – just embarrassed at seeing someone make such an exhibition of himself. Far from compelling anything, this stuff can only be saved by the catch-all defence that 'anything goes'.

Has he, to use the kind of colloquialism he enjoys, gone off his rocker? Or is it all an elaborate joke? No. It only falls back on being a joke when under criticism. It borrows its social attitudes from Californian dissent, and its motive from the need to lash out with maximum force against one specific academic closed society. This motive seems to drive the author to any position of supposed maximum outrage, in accordance with the well-known internal mechanics of tantrums, when the child looks round for the most potent verbal missile that may be to hand. The author appears so intoxicated with his own charm that he evidently thinks these antics are irresistible, and repeatedly nudges us to notice how liberated, daring, rich in ideas, and free of noxious constraints he is. Discussing a critic who dared note an inconsistency in his work, he writes:

> Machamer. . .raises the ghosts of papers I wrote centuries
> ago (subjective time!) to combat something I wrote more
> recently. In this he is no doubt influenced by philosophers
> who, having made some tiny discovery, come back to it
> again and again for want of anything new to say and who
> turn this failing – lack of ideas – into a supreme virtue,
> *viz.* consistency [p. 114].

No such weakness in our author, evidently: his ideas are not tiny, but big, and flow in so constant a stream that evidently we need not fear the pseudo-virtue of consistency. And look how truly big those ideas are: comparing primitive societies with scientific ones, in favour of the former of course, he notes

> true, there were no collective excursions to the moon, but
> single individuals. . .changed into animals and back into
> humans again [p. 307].

Scepticism about this truly amazing achievement would no doubt indicate failure to appreciate the principle that anything goes, and enslavement to the rigid thought-styles imposed by rationalism. The clowning posture he derives from some tradition which teaches that light-hearted *Gemütlichkeit* is the cure for the world's ills. The trouble is that clowning only has charm if it is good-natured, and has an element of humanity and humility. This clowning is persistently rasping, boastful, derisive and arrogant; its attitude to what is rejected is aggressive and holier-than-thou, and opponents are not allowed to benefit from the all-permissive anarchism; the frivolity contains a markedly sadistic streak, visible in the evident pleasure taken in trying (without success) to confuse and browbeat the 'rationalists', i.e. people who ask questions about knowledge in good faith. This is why what might otherwise seem a harmless piece of Californian–Viennese *Schmalz* leaves such a disagreeable taste in the mouth.

11

The last pragmatist, or the behaviourist Platonist

'Ontology' – the study of pure being – sounds faintly comic. Yet, within technical philosophy, there has in the past few decades been a certain revival of ontological discussion, somehow different from the old familiar styles. The highly distinguished Harvard logician and philosopher Willard Van Orman Quine is, perhaps more than anyone else, associated with what one might call Ontology, American Style. In his hands it is not at all ponderous or archaic; it is brisk, incisive and technical. His views constitute a fascinating philosophy of marked and distinctive character.

Quine is not interested merely in the question of *what there is* – his characteristically elegant formulation of the ontological problem – but also, and perhaps primarily, in *what is said to be*: what are the ontological commitments of this or that theory or assertion? This is ontology-in-the-third-person: one asks not what there is, but what kind of being is presupposed by this or that theory, without necessarily endorsing that theory.

This is itself a variant of a long-established species of philosophical reasoning: a kind of discourse is taken as given, and one then infers the existence of the entities presupposed by that kind of discourse. Any element in the discourse which is 'irreducible', which cannot be eliminated, then becomes a sign of something real. For instance, to take a celebrated example, G. E. Moore early in the century argued that, because statements about goodness were not 'reducible' to other kinds, therefore a quality called goodness existed. Moral discourse was his datum. Irreducibility of some element in it was then taken to establish the reality of what corresponds to that element.

What specially distinguishes Ontology, American Style, however, is that it is far more *wertfrei*, uncommitted, cool, detached and technical. The exercise is content, for a long time at least, to *remain* in the third person, to elicit the ontology underlying a particular theory, and relative to it, without striving to arrive at any final, definitive ontology of its own, valid for everyone. The ontology *of a given theory*, not a unique and absolute ontology, is what is sought.

This is an interesting and characteristic change in motivation. Once upon a time, the underlying motive of ontology was to find a safe stable resting place, to tell us what really and ultimately existed, to set out the bounds of being. This motive at least appears to be absent from the newly revived form of the subject. It is content to be tentative, experimental, and tolerant. In brief, this is a very *pragmatist* ontology:

> The question what ontology to adopt still stands open, and the obvious counsel is tolerance and an experimental spirit [*Word and Object*, p. 19].

Elsewhere we learn how this ontological scrutiny distributes its favours and grants certificates of existence:

> Numbers and classes are favoured by the power and facility which they contribute to theoretical physics...Propositions and attributes are disfavoured by some irregularity of behaviour in connection with identity and substitutions [*Ontological Relativity*, pp. 97–8].

Evidently existence is a privilege and not a right. It must be earned by long faithful service and by refraining from irregular conduct.

But the revived form of ontology does share a certain problem of method with the older kind. What people or assertions *say* doesn't on its own signify much; it is what they really *mean* which counts.

> The trouble is that there is no simple correlation between the outward form of ordinary affirmations and the existences implied [*Word and Object*, p. 242].

So, before you can elicit the ontic commitment of a statement, you must indulge in what R. G. Collingwood contemptuously described as the scholastic pedantry of reducing to logical form, or what a more recently fashionable idiom might describe as locating the deep under the surface structure. Quine feels none of the contempt which Collingwood felt, though there is a touch of inward-turned irony perhaps in the irreverent manner in which he speaks of the *canonical notation* of 'quantification', which is what, in his view, does give us the required entrée to ontology:

> In our canonical notation of quantification. . .we find the restoration of law and order. Insofar as we adhere to this notation, the objects we. . .admit are precisely the objects. . . over which the. . .variables. . .range. To paraphrase a sentence into the canonical notation of quantification is. . . to make its ontic content explicit [Ibid.].

'Quantification', in the logician's sense in which he here uses the term, means the use of the notational devices '(x)' and '$(\exists x)$', which are read as 'every object x such that' and 'there is an object x such that'. These devices occur at the beginning of statements and indicate the range of applicability of the assertion, the *things* to which the characterisation applies. The list of these 'things' is the ontology, the existential inventory, of the theory in question.

The logical technicalities need not for the moment detain us. What matters is that we here possess a device for telling what things exist, *according to this theory or that*. We translate the theory into canonical notation, and then see what values fit the 'quantified' variables – and there you are. ('Quantification' in this technical sense has nothing to do with its normal sense, i.e. the turning of qualitative characterisations into quantitatively expressed ones.) Schopenhauer once claimed: the world is my idea. This canonicism in effect says: *the world is my notation*.

Ah, but there is a snag: how do you know that the translation into canonical notation is a correct one? People articulate their beliefs in all kinds of idiom and notation. They may be illiterate, notation-wise; and who is to carry out the translation into that one special notation which alone can bring out, make explicit, their 'ontic content'? Here Quine turns out to be the impeccable liberal and gentleman:

> We cannot paraphrase our opponent's sentences into canonical notation for him. . .rather we must ask him what canonical sentences he is prepared to offer. . .If he declines to play the game, the argument terminates. . .our suppositious opponent is simply standing, however legalistically, on his rights [Ibid. pp. 242–3].

Most laudably, Quine supports a kind of Constitutional Amendment, guaranteeing every citizen's right not to incriminate himself ontologically. He is not obliged to speak in a manner which lays bare his ontic commitment. The time when this was written was a period in American history when its political equivalent was not always respected, and Quine set an admirable example. Ontologists in the past, let's face it, were often men of dogmatic and authoritarian temper, only too willing or alas eager to impose ontic commitment onto cowed audiences, and clearly Quine is anxious not to follow in their footsteps. No one may be convicted on the testimony of others, nor may he be forced to incriminate himself. It is pleasing to observe such high standards prevailing in the ontological inquisition.

But, liberal and correct though he is, Quine cannot altogether eliminate a note of irritation from his voice. The supposititious opponent is *legalistically* standing on his rights. The son of a bitch is lucky that we are so scrupulous. Let him not push his luck too far; he may come across someone less restrained and correct, and be *made* to speak in canonical notation, and betray his ontology. We have ways of making you talk about the values of your variables!

Quine's not quite controllable annoyance with people who won't squarely face the ontological music and own up to their ontic luggage also comes out elsewhere:

> We find philosophers allowing themselves not only abstract terms but pretty unmistakable quantification over abstract objects. . .and still blandly disavowing, within the paragraph, that there are such objects [*Word and Object*, p. 241].

People like that will obviously stop at nothing. Quine is visibly upset by such behaviour: 'pretty unmistakable quantification', and yet they won't admit the existence of the objects over which they quantify! That hurts. Only courtesy, one suspects, prevents him from calling them outright humbugs. As it is, he contents himself with referring to

> philosophical double talk, which would repudiate an ontology while enjoying its benefits [*Word and Object*, p. 242].

There you have it, straight from the shoulder.

Now why is ontology so serious? Why is this 'doubletalk', i.e. not owning up to the existence of the objects about which one talks, so grave an offence? If we answer this question, we shall perhaps understand some at least of the inward rules of Quine's rather idiosyncratic world.

Note first of all the lax standards prevailing elsewhere. For instance, I have always tended to be a nominalist, i.e. one denying the reality of abstract objects. But I have supported nominalism in the same lukewarm, unorganised, lackadaisical and lazy spirit in which I support, for instance, Portsmouth Football Club. I have not joined the Supporters' Club, never go to away matches, and do not own a scarf or rosette. A real supporter must feel the same contempt for me that Quine displays towards such feeble nominalists, men who 'pretty unmistakably quantify' over abstract objects and yet don't own up to their existence, nominalists–fainéants who do not go to away matches. I thought that I could be a nominalist simply in virtue of so to speak philosophic taste. It has never occurred to me that before I could claim to be a nominalist, I had to do some hard *work*, and that I had to watch my tongue. Quine insists that I must indeed do both.

The dreadful thing is, I haven't even tried to be a serious, card-carrying nominalist. I have never tried to eliminate 'quantification' over abstract objects from my discourse. I shamelessly 'quantify over' abstractions *and* deny their existence! I do not try to put what I say into canonical notation, and do not care what the notation looks like if someone else does it for me, and do not feel in the very least bound by whatever ontic commitments such a translation may disclose.

Why am I so totally lacking in logical *vergogne*? Why am I so frivolously lighthearted? The answer is of course that I believe neither in the existence of any canonical notation, nor in the possibility of reading ontic commitments from it. In this I am not eccentric but, on the contrary, a follower of local conventional wisdom. Another aspect of that recent conventional wisdom, the idea that ordinary language itself constitutes a kind of new canonical notation, I do not accept for one moment; but the negative part, the repudiation of the pursuit of an invented and authoritative canonical notation, strikes me as cogent. It is Quine who is unusual, in continuing, albeit with selfconscious irony, to talk of a canonical notation with ontic import, and to suppose that one special notation will throw into relief the relationship between theory and reality.

The repudiation of an ontologically authoritative canonical notation, and its replacement by reverent acceptance of the vernacular, is by now one of the best-explored stories in recent academic philosophy. It all happened roughly between the 1920s and the 1950s. Canonical reverence for logic came to be stood on its head, and it was the *vernacular* whose turn it then was to become sacred. It was just because the canonical notation had previously been taken so *very* seriously, that, when it was repudiated, the newly liberated, now free-floating aura and reverence attached itself to its implausible but apparently sole available successor, 'ordinary language'. It is the absolute monarch who leads to totalitarian democracy. It was the myth of a canonical notation which led to the mystique of ordinary speech.

If the canonical reverence led, in the fullness of time, to a revulsion, and a subsequent apotheosis for the vernacular, may we then expect Quine, or at least some followers of his, to retrace the same path? *No*: and not merely because history never repeats itself perfectly, nor just because Quine is in fact perfectly familiar with the well-trodden path from the worship of notation to the worship of ordinary language. There is another and more interesting reason.

Quine is not merely a person who believes, with or without a measure of irony, in the existence of a canonical notation with ontic involvement. He is not merely a philosopher who takes logic and its notation seriously. He is also a *pragmatist*, and is often characterised as a 'logical pragmatist'. This makes an enormous difference to the tone and spirit of what we might call his logical canonicism. Herein lies one of the distinctive traits of the Quinian return to ontology: the old canonicists were in pursuit of the absolute, they wanted an ontology because they wanted to rest on solid, reliable, final, and definitive *being*. His pragmatist acceptance of change and tentativeness precludes such a motive.

The old use of ontology – to endow our world with bedrock stability – is quite absent from Quine's employment of it. In his case, the ontological need springs from some quite different source, some other yearning; the erstwhile characteristic striving for the ontic absolute is conspicuous by its absence. This is a pragmatist trait, and Quine is indeed a pragmatist philosopher. A number of themes are generally involved in pragmatism, but two are specially relevant: a joyful acceptance of change, trial and error, impermanence (as opposed to the old pursuit of absolute repose), and a vision which considers human activities aid cognition in a biological perspective. Each of these themes is conspicuously present in Quine. The paradoxes do not end here – but they do begin here.

Ontology of a platonistic kind – the affirmation of the existence of abstract entities, in virtue of their place at the approved points of our canonical notation – is thus combined with a cult of impermanence, trial and error, all seen as essential parts of the biological history of the human race. Before studying Quine, I had never thought these particular themes could be fused, except perhaps by an incoherent, eclectic thinker. In Quine, they are fused, and in a philosophy which has a coherence and originality all its own.

It is this pragmatism which really explains why this particular logical canonicist will never retread the familiar path, taken by philosophy once before, in England between the 1920s and the 1950s. The dramatic inversion, the Gestalt-switch from seeking guidance from a canonical notation concerning What Is to an ecstatic repudiation of all such canons, combined with an uncritical, unselective re-endorsement of ordinary speech, could only happen because then the sought-after canons were revered in an absolutist, reverent, somewhat *verkrampt* spirit.

> The truth of the thoughts communicated here seems to me
> unassailable and definitive. I am therefore, of the opinion
> that the problems have in essentials been finally solved
> [*Tractatus Logico-Philosophicus*, Ogden translation, p. 29].

Thus spake Wittgenstein, in the preface to that classical case of canonicism, his *Tractatus*, dated 1918. This was not merely an expression of personal dogmatism, of which he always displayed an abundance. It was also the true voice of the old ontology: certainty and definitiveness were of the essence. Without them, conclusions were of no value. Here they were attained, at least in his own estimation. The method used was indeed canonicist – the discernment of real logical form under merely apparent surface form, used as a guide to What There Is. The form of reality was there, inferred from the real logical form. And the book went on to say:

> Philosophy is not one of the natural sciences. (4.111)
> The Darwinian theory has no more to do with philosophy
> than has any other hypothesis of natural science. (4.1122)

This also is the authentic voice of the old canonicist ontology; reaching out through the very forms of thought to the *general* forms of being, it disavows tentativeness, which only belongs to *specific* truths: at the same time also disavows any continuity between philosophy and science, which deals with such merely specific truths.

Continuity between animal activity and human thought was indeed the philosophically intoxicating aspect of Darwinism. The relevance of this had to be denied, for no specific scientific discovery could effect the general forms of thought and being; and all this continuity is, in marked contrast, and in true pragmatist spirit, *affirmed* by Quine. He affirms the tentative, temporary nature of all knowledge, including the thinker's own position and including the most abstract, canonicist ontology; and, similarly, he affirms the continuity between philosophy and science, seen as different parts of the same endeavour, and not radically distinct in kind. Above all, he affirms the Great Continuity, from inorganic life via the amoeba and via *Homo javanensis* to the most abstract piece of modern mathematical thought. All these are parts of one process, ultimately similar in underlying principle. These are characteristically pragmatist themes, and Quine upholds them with vigour and enthusiasm.

Thus we have here both a similarity and a difference; Quine *is* a canonicist (albeit an ironic and third-person one), but he is *also* a pragmatist. What follows from his pragmatism?

(1) A free-and-easy trial-and-error spirit is both preached *and* practised. The practice of it was not unknown in the past among canonicists: for instance, it was always much exemplified by Bertrand Russell, even in his canonicist ('logical atomist') phase. But with Russell, it was largely a matter of an irrepressible personal temperament. It was not ratified by any formal doctrine. Philosophically, Russell was a member of the Cartesian epistemological tradition, a passionate if sometimes discouraged seeker after certainty, definitiveness, and secure bases. Quine is different: temperamentally he also exemplifies the free-and-easy spirit (perhaps even a bit less than Russell did, for his world has less of that variety and instability which marks Russell's; his themes are more easily enumerated). But over and above *exemplifying* pragmatism in some measure, Quine has also elaborated an overt epistemological doctrine which actively preaches and justifies this attitude, which repudiates 'Cartesianism' in so many words.

A canonicism (ontology through logical form) which is yet so pliable and volatile, and which so consciously wishes itself to be such, and which proposes a rationale for why it should be such, can never build up that inner tension which had in Wittgenstein transformed logical canonicism into a worship and endorsement of uncanonical ordinary speech. Quine's canonicism may generate steam, but at the same time the free-and-easy pragmatism provides an ever-operative, ever-open safety valve. The pressure can never build up to explosion point, as once it had.

(2) An insistence on the continuity between man and nature, between human reason and biological phenomena. This might be called naturalism.

(3) An insistence on the continuity between philosophy and other forms of inquiry. This is somewhat contrary to the spirit of the age: philosophy once was *above* or can now be seen *below* other inquiries, but it is not normally allowed to be *alongside*. It switched from the pursuit of the ultimate and stable certainties to becoming, for instance, the cure of linguistic disease; this dramatic transformation and demotion was indeed connected with the equally radical switch from canonicism to the cult of ordinary speech. Canonicism justified the higher status, the inverted canonicism of ordinary-language philosophy justified the demotion. But either way continuity with other forms of cognition was denied. Quine affirms it.

The implications of these two continuity theses (man/nature, philosophy/science) are best considered together, Quine's philosophy is full of paradoxes: for, though a passionate naturalist, a man who insists on seeing man in the context of biological nature, in one important sense he is *not* an empiricist. This, once again, is most unusual: empiricism and naturalism normally go together. Quine, unconventionally, combines naturalism and platonism (his canonicism leads to the reality of abstract objects, i.e. platonism, because abstract objects are among the values of the variables about which we speak). Surprisingly, he also dissociates naturalism and empiricism.

He is altogether admirable in seeing, with the usual clarity and elegant simplicity, just what is involved in philosophical empiricism:

> The mistake comes. . .in seeking an implicit sub-basement of conceptualisation, or of language [*Word and Object*, p. 3].
>
> What perhaps basically distinguishes [my position] from the attitude of sense-datum philosophers is that I favour treating cognition from within our own evolving theory of a cognised world, not fancying that firmer ground exists somehow outside all that [Ibid., p. 235].
>
> The philosopher's task differs from the others. . .in detail; but in no such drastic way as those suppose who imagine for the philosopher a vantage point outside the conceptual

> scheme that he takes in charge. There is no such cosmic exile [Ibid.].
>
> With Dewey I hold that knowledge, mind, and meaning are part of the same world that they have to do with, and that they are to be studied in the same empirical spirit that animates natural science. There is no place for a prior philosophy [*Ontological Relativity and Other Essays*, p. 26].

The crucial issue is emphasised with brilliance. What is at stake is precisely the cosmic exile, the 'prior philosophy'. Philosophical empiricism is, as Quine sees, most unnaturalistic, indeed transcendental: such empiricism abstracts from the ordinary world which we normally inhabit, and would judge it from a stance of *cosmic exile*. It uses the idea of 'experience' in order to attain such an external vantage point: it is pure experience which is to be outside the world and sit in judgement on it.

Quine repudiates, not the invocation of experience, or even its uniqueness as a source of data, but its *use* for the purpose of such prior-philosophic, cosmic exile. No such exile is possible or necessary; no such priority, no such ante-world, as one might say, is available to us. Thus it is in the name of naturalism (i.e. the impossibility of ever standing outside the natural world) that he repudiates empiricism (i.e. the idea that 'experience' provides an independent and absolute set of data by which we could judge pictures of our world).

One might say that he repudiates, not the empiricist solution, but the empiricist *problem*. Thus Quine does not merely dissociate naturalism and empiricism: it is *because* of his naturalism that he dispenses with classical empiricism. We may not stand outside our own natural world – even if we use the idea of 'experience' to do so!

The old formulation ran roughly as follows: we need a judge, an arbiter between rival beliefs, rival worlds in effect. Pure *experience* is such a judge. Thus, paradoxically, classical empiricism does not treat experience as one further thing within the world, which is the way in which common sense sees it, but as, in effect, a transcendent thing outside all worlds and sitting in judgement on them all. Far from being 'in' the world, the world is 'constructed' from it. It is prior to that world, and in a sense has higher status – for it judges the world.

Why do we think we need such an extraneous and independent authority? To accept the testimony of the various world-pictures presented to us, is plainly, to proceed in a circular manner. These various competing litigants cannot be taken at face value: their testimony is biased, circular, self-interested and untrustworthy. What is really characteristic of world-pictures, belief-systems, is that they simply fill out the entire world and cannot be dislodged from the inside. They so to speak capture the wells of truth and starve out all opponents. They consist of theories which contain criteria of truth itself, and these are so manipulated as to ensure the reconfirmation of that set of theories itself. The concepts are so arranged that this is not visible, or only visible from the outside, to someone who can drink at some *other* well.

The only way in which we can decide between such systems is by possessing some oracle, some authority, outside and above them all. This is the formulation of the problem (which Quine rejects). 'Experience' is merely the solution of that problem (which otherwise Quine does not reject). How can one reject the formulation of the problem which would seem cogent? One thing only can help us evade the problem: if we do not need to distrust the litigants after all, if the rival world-pictures have good claims to our assent. Quine does have such trust. This is where his naturalistic evolutionism comes in. It constitutes a background theory which tells us that (and why) our successive world-pictures are sound, all in all if not in detail, and deserving of trust.

The empiricists' formulation of the problem goes back, at the very least, to Descartes' deep distrust of our intellectual inheritance and the consequent need to find an extraneous vantage point, a cosmic exile. Quine's repudiation of either the need or the possibility of such cosmic exile, the firm imposition, on our thought, of *residence surveillée* within this world, is made possible by his trust, all in all, in our conceptual inheritance. We need not stand outside it, partly because we cannot, and more significantly, because we need not: and we need not, because, all in all, that inheritance is under sound management.

And how do we *know* that it is sound? This conviction itself is a corollary of a wider, evolutionist–pragmatist picture of our thought, a picture which owes much, as the whole pragmatist tradition does, to the Natural Selection view of man and all his activities, including thought itself:

> Creatures inveterately wrong in their inductions have a pathetic but praiseworthy tendency to die before reproducing their kind [*Ontological Relativity*, p. 126].

Moreover:

> Scientific neologism is. . .just linguistic evolution
> gone self-conscious [*Word and Object*, p. 3].
> Our patterns of thought. . .have been evolving. . .since
> the dawn of language; and. . .we may confidently look
> forward to more of the same [*Ontological Relativity*, p. 24].

We see here a conceptual if not a social Darwinism. It is inescapably somewhat harsh, and perhaps ultimately owes something to Calvin as well as to Darwin.

> [T]he purpose of language. . .is efficacy. . .Such is the
> ultimate duty of language, science and philosophy, and it
> is in relation to that duty that a conceptual scheme has
> finally to be appraised [*From a Logical Point of View*,
> p. 79].

This is a very American and pragmatist tone, reminiscent of Veblen as well as the pragmatists. One wonders how one knows that a harsh nature has issued this severe edict about what our duty is, spurning more frivolous, less craftsmanlike criteria of merit. *Qui est donc cette dame?* As a concession to the softer mores of our time, there is also an admission of elegance for its own sake, but *only* when pragmatic considerations are absent:

> Elegance. . .engaging though it is, is secondary. . .[it] is
> simply a means to the end of a pragmatically acceptable
> conceptual scheme. But elegance also enters as an end in
> itself. . .quite properly so long as it is appealed to only in
> choices where the pragmatic standard prescribes no
> contrary descision [*From a Logical Point of View*, p. 79].

No encouragement to frivolity here. Life is real, life is pragmatic. There is indeed a marked – and, these days, endearing – Calvinist streak in Quine's epistemology.

But what really concerns us is his general strategy of validation. We can on his account trust our beliefs, by and large, not because we can step outside and validate them, but because we may remain inside the world and yet be confident that, all in all, human thought has generally obeyed the demanding pragmatist duty laid upon it by nature. (But how do we know that we are not among the damned? Though an epistemic Calvinist, Quine does not appear to be one of the tormented ones.)

The trust in the cosmic flow, that continuous progression from the amoeba via *Homo javanensis* to set theory, is not uncritical and total; it is not assumed that no errors are ever committed, or that we are free of them now. (Some or perhaps most are damned.) Such *static* complacency would be quite contrary to his pragmatist sense of flux, of eternal adjustment and impermanence; and such excessive complacency is indeed totally absent. But, if we do not endorse everything thrown up by the evolutionary pragmatic process of life and thought, how do we select *within* it?

Here, in answer to this inescapable question we come up against Quine's version of a 'prior philosophy', and an *independent*, extra-mundane standard in camouflaged form. It is something called 'scientific method'. Wisely, he makes no attempt at defining it closely:

> Scientific method was vaguely seen...as a matter of being
> guided by sensory stimuli, a taste for simplicity in some
> sense, and a taste for old things...a more detailed body of
> canons could be brought together; though it is customary
> to doubt that the thing could be done finally and defini-
> tively. At any rate scientific method, whatever its details,
> produces theory whose connection with all possible surface
> irritations consists solely in scientific method itself, un-
> supported by ulterior controls. This is the sense in which
> it is the last arbiter of truth [*Word and Object*, p. 23].

'Surface irritations' is of course decent third-person language for 'sense data'. The last two sentences in the above quotation are interesting and important. Ordinary theories, however abstract, are on this model open to two kinds of pressure – other theories, *and* data ('surface irritations'). 'Scientific method', whatever it may be in detail, is unique, in being, as Quine stresses, related to data alone and not to any other pressures ('ulterior controls') whatever, and thus constituting an independent and ultimate arbiter.

Thus we have here a body of canons (unspecified or loosely indicated) which possess an authority which is extraneous and in-dependent of all other theories. Clearly it cannot emanate from the 'surface irritations', which are mute, and ex hypothesi it owes no debt to (is not under the 'ulterior control' of) *other* theories. In other words, it seems to be exactly analogous to that '*prior* philosophy', which consists *precisely* of trying to formulate and establish a set of premisses prior to and independent of all specific theories, and which could consequently legitimate those theories by underwriting the manner in which they are extracted from data, without circularity.

Yet Quine has no option but to introduce this, or some similar, deus ex machina. Without it, one of two positions would become mandatory, and neither is acceptable: relativism (all systems equally true from inside, and there is no 'outside'), or a *total* acceptance of the authority of the evolutionary process (wherever it may lead us ipso facto constitutes truth). One of these options involves despairing of objective truth altogether; the other involves a worship of actual development, wherever it may be going, without any check. Each of these dreadful options seems repudiated in the following passage:

> Have we. . .so far lowered our sights as to settle for a
> relativistic theory of truth. . .brooking no higher criticism?
> Not so. The saving consideration is that we continue to take
> seriously our own particular aggregate science. . .whatever
> it may be. . . until by what is vaguely called scientific method
> we change them here or there for the better [*Word and
> Object*, pp. 24–5].

Note how absolutely essential is this messiah, vaguely called scientific method: without him, we are all either imprisoned in 'our own particular aggregate science', or, if we insist on change, we must without demur endorse the general de facto direction of change. But scientific method saves us from this, and makes the change valid not simply because it is change, but because it satisfies some *independent* criterion. Ask not for the price of this escape: it is, very simply, a 'prior philosophy' under another name.

Quine cannot be altogether unaware of the price he is paying, for, on occasion, perhaps in horror of seeming to pay this price, he comes close to accepting either one of the horns of the dilemma:

> Our patterns of thought and language have been evol-
> ving. . .since the dawn of language; and. . .we may con-
> fidently look forward to more of the same [*Ontological
> Relativity*, p. 24].

If indeed we can put our trust 'confidently' in the direction of evolution, then indeed we need no external guarantor or touchstone, no prior philosophy. But – aye, there's the rub – the idea that evolution is reliably progressing in a commendable direction is, after all, one theory among others, and surely not exempt from all doubt? The very idea of evolution is but part of our provincial conceptual scheme and scientific epoch. And so we read, a page after the preceding quotation:

> In saying this I philosophize from the vantage point only of our own provincial scheme and scientific epoch; true; but I know no better [Ibid., p. 25].

This lovely and – deliberately – teasing passage, coming at the very end of a lecture – the reader or listener is thereby forced to make his own exegesis, for none can be expected from the brusquely departing author – is open to *three* possible interpretations, each corresponding to one great philosophic possibility:

(1) Objectivism (prior philosophy): I have looked at the alternatives, *from the outside*, and our scheme is the best scheme, thank God.

(2) Relativism: this is my scheme, and I cannot jump out of my conceptual skin. My scheme, right or wrong. Each man to his own scheme; there is *no* truth for all.

(3) Evolutionism: 'Provincial conceptual schemes and scientific epochs' may, each of them, be trusted, for each plays its rightful part in a general and beneficient evolution.

Note that the ambiguity of the passage, allowing three quite divergent interpretations, is of a special kind. It is not an accidental, contingent ambiguity, such as arises when a statement is sloppily formulated, and uses words which are homonyms. Not at all. It is much more like those fascinating drawings which allow and indeed provoke more than one Gestalt and which, as we focus on them, periodically 'jump' from one to another, from an old woman's face to a young woman's head-and-shoulders, from a cat to a rabbit. But in this case the connexion between the successive Gestalten is even more intimate. We are presented with conceptual, not visual patterns. And each of the conceptual patterns has its own strains, and it is precisely those strains which impel one towards the next one...which then, in due course, perpetuates the merry-go-round one further turn, and so on.

This vertiginous rotating-ambiguity passage comes from the very end of a lecture [*Ontological Relativity and Other Essays*, p. 25], which accentuates its teasing quality: the lecturer brusquely if smilingly departs, the listener or reader knows he must do his own exegesis, and finds himself a spinning top. Elsewhere [*From a Logical Point of View*, pp. 78–9], also at an end of a paper – this seems the limit to which his thought can be pushed – we find the same rotating circle of ideas spelt out more fully step by step. The figures of relativism, evolutionism, pragmatism, rotate on the merry-go-round:

> The fundamental-seeming philosophical question, How much of our science is merely contributed by language and how much is a genuine reflection of reality? is perhaps a spurious question which itself arises wholly from a certain particular type of language. Certainly we are in a predicament if we try to answer the question...
>
> Yet we must not leap to the fatalistic conclusion that we are stuck with the conceptual scheme that we grew up in. We can change it bit by bit...
>
> [I]t is meaningless...to inquire into the absolute correctness of a conceptual scheme...Our standard...must be...a pragmatic standard...the purpose of concepts and of language is efficacy in communication and prediction. such is the ultimate duty of language, science and philosophy, and it is in relation to that duty that a conceptual scheme has finally to be appraised.

Thus we go round the mulberry bush: we start with the compulsive insight forcing one willy-nilly towards relativism (no exit from *our* world); we escape *that* by invoking the indisputable possibility of *change*; and we escape the danger that such change is merely arbitrary and pointless change, by crediting ourselves with insight into the ultimate purpose ('duty') of the universe and of human endeavour within it, *and* the confident expectation that, by and large, the changes we undergo do indeed satisfy that standard of appraisal; in other words, that we are among the saved. A Calvinist world in pragmatist idiom.

The dilemmas and alternatives between which Quine's pragmatist-evolutionism rotates and weaves its way are of course inherent in a certain starting point which Quine shares, interestingly enough, with the Hegelian–Marxist tradition, which of course has always exhibited parallels with pragmatism. The problem arises from a determination not to try and transcend this world, not to commit the hubris of any putatively extraneous stance, but to remain *within*. Quine is very proud of this aspect of the pragmatist inheritance:

> Philosophcally I am bound to Dewey by the naturalism that dominated his last three decades. With Dewey I hold

> that knowledge, mind and meaning are part of the same
> world that they have to do with. . .there is no place for a
> prior philosophy [*Ontological Relativity*, p. 26].

A philosopher like Hegel or Quine who is so determined to remain inside the play which he is writing inevitably ends up with this cluster of paradoxes, which jointly could be called the Pirandello Effect. Once the author agrees to engage in a dialogue with the Characters in Search of an Author, there is no further telling whether truth lies with *each* character (relativism), or with the author outside (objectivism) or with the movement of the play as a whole (evolutionism). So many Pirandellos in philosophy! – and we must leave this one to his vacillations. But note the striking similarity with Marx, whose repudiation of utopianism is parallel to Quine's rejection of a prior philosophy:

> The. . .doctrine that men are products of circumstances. . .
> forgets that circumstances are changed precisely by men
> and that the educator must himself be educated. Hence this
> doctrine necessarily arrives at dividing a society in two
> parts, of which one towers above society [*Theses on
> Feuerbach*].

These uncorrupted correctors of earthly error, towering above society, would fulfil precisely the same role as Quine's cosmic exiles. They would bring a prior philosophy. Marx called this utopianism. Marx and Quine, both determined not to stray out of earthly bounds, will have none of it.

These paradoxes and ambiguities are inherent in *any* attempt to manage without cosmic exile and without prior philosophy. It would be presumptuous to try and overcome them for him, and misguided to seek a clear resolution within the corpus of his work. But let us consider some other aspects of his pragmatist evolutionary naturalism.

The old pragmatists were, like all philosophical movements, selective in their inspiration. What inspired them above all was the biological history of life, and the close-to-home history of industrial civilization – but not much in between. These very distant vistas, and the immediate home environment, did indeed share certain conspicuous traits: change, progress, adaptation, diversity, competition. Both of them seemed success stories, leading somehow to improvement, through instability, diversification, growth, size, trial and error, adaptation. The history of life as such seemed to confirm the experience close to hand; and local experience seemed to provide instances of what had, apparently, always been the law of life. (Such use of biology as a charter of social organisation was ironised by Marx.)

The traits of this pragmatist spirit are indeed found in Quine: the most important inheritance from this tradition is that unmistakable blend of optimism, of confident trust in the general direction of things, with a very high valuation of instability, of perpetual change and diversity. (No doubt it is the confident optimism which makes the instability acceptable, indeed attractive.) What are the weaknesses of the outlook?

There might be a certain callousness, a willingness to see so many damned, an acceptance of cognitive Darwinism. But perhaps this is not a weakness; perhaps it is we who flinch from such doctrines who are weak and sentimental. But there is another possible charge: might not the optimism itself be facile and superficial, and based on a grossly selective attention to data? Biology may, in the very long run, show 'progress' or 'evolution' (though the 'lower' species are still with us, and who is to say who will last longest?) Again, *some* recent segments of the history of the new technological civilisation may indeed show 'progress'. But how about the long, long periods of stagnation, the tendency to social or cognitive stalemate, so much more typical of the human condition than is adaptive change? Men whose vision of the history of the world is based on biology plus the American nineteenth century may have been insufficiently aware of these stagnation phenomena, or too easily inclined to consider them atypical.

In consequence, they may greatly overrate the *continuity* of the story, and correspondingly underestimate the radical breaks, the uniqueness of key social or cognitive advances. Indeed, Quine's discussion of cognitive growth seems very much in this mould. There is very little about the dramatic birth of science or the highly specific inner tensions of pre-modern thought systems which, on a given occasion, generated our particular vision of an orderly, progressively intelligible, demystified world. (One rather feels such a world is taken for granted – as all too often it is taken for granted by philosophers of science – and the evolutionary story is then naïvely told *within* it.) The *Wissenschaftswunder* of the Western World is left almost unnoticed, for it is assumed to be simply the continuation, the natural sequel, of a long, long story. Instead, we have a rather biological vision of the growth of knowledge:

> The conceptual scheme in which we grew up is an eclectic heritage. . .Expressions for physical objects must have occupied a focal position from the earliest linguistic periods. . .General terms also must have appeared at an early stage. . .The adoption of abstract singular terms. . . is a further step and a philosophically revolutionary one. . . once abstract entities are admitted, our conceptual mechanism goes on and generates an unending hierarchy of further abstractions [*From a Logical Point of View*, pp. 77–8].

All this is very much a logician's evolutionary scheme of the history of mankind. If it has any crucial discontinuity at all, a Great Watershed, it is to be found in the arrival of abstraction or of abstract objects. This is the Incarnation, or perhaps the Disincarnation, of Quine's version of the Great Design. Quine's view of the age of ignorance which precedes it is conveyed in a truly delightful little poem:

> The unrefined and sluggish mind
> Of *Homo javanensis*
> Could only treat of things concrete
> And present to the senses.

This is very similar to Claude Lévi-Strauss's view as expounded in *The Savage Mind*, and much easier to follow.

So the logician sees human history, not as the story of liberty, of greater diversification, growth of energy consumption, or whatnot, but as the story of the discovery and diffusion of *abstraction*. At the same time, the pragmatist in Quine stresses the continuity, the utility, and the ultimate homogeneity of adaptive devices. Abstraction is treated as ultimately on the same level as other 'posits' (conceptual adaptive devices), such as the idea of material objects. It is this conflation of the platonist (for whom abstract ideas are real and the most treasured possession of man) with the naturalistic evolutionary pragmatist (who sees them as ephemeral or changeable devices, justified only by their utility and nothing else, and similar in status to all other adaptive devices), which gives Quine's thought its quite unique and puzzling flavour, and which makes him the Pragmatist Platonist. This is at the very centre of his thought.

The Logician's View of History and Cognitive Darwinism are

traits he shares with nineteenth-century predecessors (even if these traits were not previously combined in just this way). In contrast to these inherited themes, there are also aspects of his pragmatism which are new, which are not echoes of the past. In some ways Quine's pragmatism is indeed rather novel, and curiously expressive of the American climate of the 1950s. He is, of course, in no way a social philosopher. Yet the theory of knowledge sometimes unwittingly holds up a mirror to the mores of an age. Men's image of their own cognitive comportment may be an echo of their conduct in other fields.

One such trait of Quine's epistemology is its emphatic and self-stressed collision with classical empiricism. This arises in part through a certain brazen *collectivism* to be found in his epistemology:

> [o]ur statements about the external world face the tribunal of sense experience not individually but only as a corporate body...in taking the statement as a unit we have drawn our grid too finely. The unit of empirical significance is the whole of science [*From a Logical Point of View*, pp. 41–2].

Or, more discriminatingly:

> Sentences higher up in theories have no empirical consequences which they can call their own; they confront the tribunal of sensory evidence only in more or less inclusive aggregates [*Ontological Relativity*, p. 89].

The logician seems to credit propositions with a most powerful herd instinct, an inability to stand alone. This would not be surprising in one of those idealists who stressed the interdependence of everything; but Quine is a modern logician. The first principle of the calculus of propositions, an elementary part of modern logic, is that the truth or falsity of any proposition (unless *composed* of other propositions) is independent of the truth or falsity of any other. In other words, the assumptions of the calculus of propositions still reflect the old protestant loneliness and individualism. One is tempted to ask, if Quine's collectivist theory of knowledge is valid, how the calculus of propositions ever comes to have any application.

The contrast is indeed great with the rugged individualism of the old empiricist epistemology, which made the individual proposition behave like a protestant martyr – solitary, brave, independent,

defiant, accountable to his own conscience only, utterly contemptuous of the authority of either crowds or organisations, spurning ever
to look over his shoulder to see what the majority may say. Thou
shalt not follow a multitude to commit consensus. Such indeed was
the ultimate cognitive atom, the witness to truth, according to the
old empiricist parable of knowledge; and, if the empiricist fable were
to be believed, theoretical empires crumbled when defied by these
lonely heroes.

By the 1950s such rugged attitudes seemed, in the United States,
to belong to folklore rather than to reality. Senator Joseph Mac-
Carthy did not find many such defiant individualists crossing his
path. The dearth of the old ruggedness was not restricted to civic
and political life. W. H. Whyte's best-selling *The Organization Man*,
first published in 1956, deplored the disappearance of the protestant
ethic from economic life, and its replacement by the all-pervasive
ethos of corporate conformity. Men behaved as propositions do
according to Quine: they confronted their tribunals only in corporate bodies, as more or less inclusive aggregates.

In this way as in some others, Quine's epistemology, his theory of
the behaviour of cognitive units and aggregates, presented a remarkable parable for the America of the time. Take the philosophically
celebrated dispute about analytic/synthetic. Classical empiricism
sharply segregated these two species of proposition. 'Synthetic'
propositions were the workers, in direct contact with reality, at the
coal face so to speak; 'analytic' propositions were the management,
ensuring coordination and liaison, perhaps indispensable, but not
contributing directly to production. Thus classical empiricism, with
its sharply stratified population, offered a good allegory for a society
in which producers (peasants or workers) are clearly distinguishable
from rulers, managers or entrepreneurs.

But the United States is not and was not such a society. Its class
structure is gradual and unformalised rather than sharp and, more
important, the economic functions performed within it cannot be so
neatly segregated. It is the service sector which is growing. According to Quine, propositions in the body of science are like the em-
ployees of a corporation: there is a marked continuity and complexity of roles. The job of some is more supervisory, and of others
lies more in the handling of things, but it is a matter of degree rather
than of one great chasm. The sharp division between commissioned
and other ranks is only characteristic of some of those old-world
societies with their feudal hang-ups. An advanced corporation,

whether of men or of propositions, does not behave like that. It is gradual and continuous.

Whyte complained of the replacement of the protestant ethic by that of the Organization Man; David Riesman noted the shift from inner-directedness to other-directedness. These two themes are of course related, and they are strikingly reflected in the new-style pragmatism. The old pragmatist did in a certain sense preach opportunism – not under that name, but as flexibility, as sensitivity to the multiple purposes in life and to its complexities – but he still preached it *as a principle*. In spirit, the old pragmatists remained markedly inner-directed, high-principled and individualist/protestant. Their cult of practicality and concreteness was directed against the olympianism of the Ivory Tower Idealists, not against objectivity, which they tacitly took for granted.

The new pragmatist does not argue with Absolute Idealists; there are none of those left, to speak of. He *does* argue with classical empiricism with its over-neatly drawn division of labour in the field of knowledge. In the course of this the new pragmatism comes to deny the Inner Light, or inner-directedness altogether – in the sense idea of an *independent* and 'prior' inner judge, censor, the ultimate oasis of inner-directedness. Such 'prior philosophy' is repudiated. Instead, what is preached is a trust in the general direction in which things are going, in the confidence that the change is guided by good, consensual, shared norms ('scientific method') plus technicist gimmickry – any tool which works will do. No need for a fundamental Constitution ('prior philosophy'), nor any sense of the possibility of a fundamental alternative, of a really major parting of the ways in the evolutionary flow of things.

Finally, there is the style – which is, in the very best sense, of its time. It communicates by calculus or aphorism, by symbolism or by wisecrack. We have either a very high-powered and fully operational logico-mathematical technician, or a highly intelligent, totally informal, shirt-sleeved, open-necked man-of-the-world, who knows how to get across with brevity and punch, and sets no store at all by the pedantry and scholasticism of prolonged verbal exposition. A technique or a wisecrack, as may be appropriate: but no ponderousness. This again seems to me entirely typical of an advanced society which takes technicality for granted (in both senses: it cannot conceive its absence, but is not generally over-impressed by any one specimen of it – it can take it or leave it). Outside technical spheres one is content to communicate by impressionistic strokes. In this way as in others, where the old pragmatism represented an earthier and more severe, more self-reliant inner-directedness, arguing against Idealist intoxication with the Cosmic Unity, the new pragmatism, arguing against quite different opponents (over-stilted empiricists who would formalise unduly the division of labour between the facts which are recorded and the verbal conventions which record them) and in an entirely different context, tells another story.

How is this philosophy to be assessed? In some measure, the style is the thought; and the implications of the style itself must be considered. The style has two principal traits: the coexistence of powerful technicality with great verbal simplicity, the coexistence of formal operation and of the wise-crack; and, secondly, the pervasiveness of certain pragmatist, trail-and-error attitudes, which permeate the presentation and turn back on the thought itself.

A reader of Quine who is not a logician (and perhaps logicians too) has a curious feeling of moving in a bilingual world, in which two quite disparate languages are used simultaneously or intermittently without, however, much apparent awareness on the part of the user that their respective rules are very, very different. Switching the simile, it is as if he had intermittently to attend to some high-powered computer and also to play with some very elegant, but very, very simple shapes made of plasticine. The rules of making plasticine shapes are very obvious and familiar. The world of Quine's very abstract speculations about for instance the behaviour of those corporations of scientific propositions, about their surface and inner tensions, and so on, is simple, metaphorical and easily intelligible. They are intuitively accessible with the greatest ease. One may not agree, but one understands, perfectly. No strain is placed on one's powers of comprehension. The other technical world, on the other hand, is governed by the most mysterious conventions, which one can only make out with great difficulty.

But Quine does not treat them as two distinct languages at all. He switches from one to the other within one train of thought. Now there is, I am told, one sentence which is phonetically identical in Magyar and Turkish, and has the same meaning. Could one say that a man in Ankara who turns to his neighbour and says, 'I have an apple in my pocket' is, unwittingly, talking in good Hungarian? Can one say that a man in a Budapest bus who makes the same remark is talking fluent Turkish? I am inclined to say *not*.

Some of Quine's most celebrated philosophical theses are articulated in such Turko-Magyar. Take two of his tenets, incidentally related to each other: his denial of 'analyticity', and his attempt at doing ontology through canonicism, with which we started.

The denial by a logician of analyticity, of the idea that some propositions owe their truth only to the meaning of their constituent terms, has a wildly paradoxical air, like the denial of shoes by a cobbler, of the sea by a sailor. Quine's professional life is spent with precisely such propositions. However, let us leave aside the plausibility of his views here and look at his reasons. Some are drawn from his very abstract, biological pragmatism and holism: in the very long run, *all* our propositions are, on this pragmatist view, corrigible, if their systems come under strain. So be it. But analytic propositions were held to be *in*corrigible (not to be at the mercy of *any* fact). Hence it would follow that, if indeed *all* propositions are corrigible, then there can be *no* analytic ones.

So be it. What this really shows, as Barry Stroud has noted in *Words and Objections* (edited by Davidson and Hintikka, 1969), and as Burt Dreben pointed out in conversation as early as 1954, is that the problem of *explaining* incorrigibility simply does not arise, because no incorrigibility exists; but this does not actually invalidate the tools used for explaining it, had it existed. Quine denies that a certain *problem* arises, but presents this denial as a refusal of a *solution*.

But Quine also has quite other objections to analyticity. It does not fit into his notation. Logical inference in that notation is not analyticity-preserving the way it is truth-preserving. Moreover, the notion of analyticity offends both his platonism and his behaviourism: it invokes the notion of meaning, by hinging on the identity of meanings, and he does not want 'meaning' to exist, for meanings do not occur as values of his variables (this being his canonical test of existence); and at the same time it is very difficult to devise satisfactory behavioural tests for *identity* of meaning (a behaviourist objection).

All these arguments may have some measure of force, but that is not the point. What is relevant is that they are drawn from such *completely* different universes of discourse, such totally different – and often incompatible or incommensurate – contexts, that they really cannot be held to reinforce each other. The denial of analyticity from its technical inconvenience in a certain notation, and its denial from the ultimate flux of all things and the corrigibility of *all* human endeavour, are two such *totally* different things as to be only homonyms. To argue them as *one* thesis is to talk in Turko-Magyar.

Quine is often and very properly praised for his clarity. His style is indeed simple, elegant and clear. But the clarity is very deceptive. His background assumptions are not always spelt out, and they are not at all the ordinary or usual ones. What is obvious and unargued for Quine is not at all the same as that which is obvious and un-argued for the philosophical *homme moyen sensuel*. The fact that his assumptions are unusual, not to say eccentric, does not of course make them wrong: they may well be right, and at the very least it may be illuminating to see where they lead. The fact that they are not spelt out however, may lead the casual reader to be misled by the apparent simplicity, and fail to note their presence, and the subtle or important way in which they modify the very significance of the apparently simple conclusions. Both Quine's pragmatism and his canonicism may encourage him to refrain from spelling out his assumptions or highlighting their occasional eccentricity. The point about both these outlooks is that (paradoxically in the case of prag-matism) they lead one to see all assertions as part of basically the same universe of discourse; they do not lead one to have a sense of the fact that similar-sounding assertions may occur as parts of totally different kinds of game, and that they can then only be related to each other if the background assumptions of each game are fully spelt out. The levelling tendency of those two outlooks makes one talk, or makes Quine talk, as if there were only one conceptual currency in the world (notwithstanding his relativism in other contexts), and as if no exchange rates had to be specified. In fact, the exchange rates between conceptual currencies are very very complex.

He does sometimes talk as if the role and function of all our theoretical constructions and abstractions was to predict experiences. This comes very close to a return to the empiricist metaphysic which sees only experiences as ultimately real, and to seeing the rest of what makes up our mental life as but devices for the ordering and anticipation of experiences. The pragmatist tolerance both grants a reality, generously, to functionally essential abstractions by treating them all as equal and real, and yet also with another hand withdraws the gift of existence, by treating them as but devices and servants of a more restricted reality. Pragmatism, both in Quine's version and in general, vacillates ambivalently between a restrictive em-piricist puritanism, and a permissive pluralism which allows count-less ontic blooms to flower. But what is interesting is that the restricted empiricist world-picture is there somewhere in Quine's system: he doesn't really object to it as such when he objects to the 'dogmas of empiricism'; he merely objects to the very problem which, to my mind, most urgently calls for that restricted world as a solution – namely, the need to have a 'prior world' from the viewpoint of which we could assess and evaluate the various richer, cultural and scientific worlds which compete for our cognitive allegiance.

Quine's revival of ontology and his platonism are similarly Turko-Magyar. At least two arguments underlie Quine's platonism, his revival of ontology and his inclusion of abstract objects within it. One is the general pragmatism, at its terribly abstract level, with its very broad biological evolutionary vistas, which leads him to treat abstract objects as adaptive devices, and all adaptive devices as being in the end of the same kind: no need to distinguish concrete hard objects and abstract ones. Each is a form of conceptual adaptation. Here it is the notion of adaptive utility which is the great leveller: it equalises the condition of the concrete and the abstract:

> The myth of physical objects is epistemologically superior
> to most in that it has proved more efficacious than other
> myths as a device for working a manageable structure into
> the flux of experience...Forces are another example.
> Moreover, the abstract entities which are the substance of
> mathematics – ultimately classes and classes of classes and
> so on up – are another posit in the same spirit. Epistemo-
> logically these are myths on the same footing with physical
> objects and gods, neither better nor worse except for
> differences in the degree to which they expedite our
> dealings with sense experiences [*From a Logical Point of
> View*, pp. 44–5].

Quine is well known for his conceptual relativism, which involves him in the view that no really reliable translations may exist between different languages. This influential view follows quite naturally from his general Behaviourism. It is simply the special application of the widely held view that verification of an empirical proposition is an infinite process and can never be completed. If meaning is only identified through the behaviour of speakers, we can naturally never be sure that any two given meanings are really identical. You cannot put your foot in the same sentence twice. (It is not clear whether Quine endorses this view in general, but he certainly uses it both against the notion of translation and against analyticity.)

But it is curious to note that this relativism is but skin-deep. The manner in which he uses pragmatism as a great leveller, bringing abstract and concrete objects and everything else to the same level of a conceptual device for the ordering and prediction of experience, shows that he still assumes that *the same game* is being played throughout history, both biological and human. We were all after the same thing, from the amoeba to Einstein – it is just that some do it better than others. This assumption of the permanence and identity of the underlying aim is both extremely questionable and utterly *un-relativist*.

But Quine also works with another and quite different great leveller, his canonical notation:

> In our canonical notation. . .we find the restoration of
> law and order. Insofar as we adhere to this notation, the
> objects we are to be understood to admit are precisely the
> objects. . .over which the. . .variables of quantification. . .
> range. Such is simply the intended sense of. . .'every object
> is such that', 'there is an object such that'. The quantifiers
> are encapsulations of these. . .*unequivocally* referential
> idioms of ordinary language [*Word and Object*, p. 242,
> italics added].

Quine seldom loses his cool, but he does so with thinkers who would deny the 'unequivocal' nature of reference in the canonical notation (for instance on pp. 241–2 of *Word and Object*, or p. 99 of *Ontological Relativity and other Essays*) and insist on different *kinds* of existence.

> For us common men who believe in bodies and prime
> numbers the statements 'There is a rabbit in the yard' and
> 'There are prime numbers between 10 and 20' are free
> from double-talk. Quantification does them justice.

There is one ultimate criterion for the ontological commitment of a theory: when translated into the proper canonical idiom, what are the variables over which we range when we say things like 'There is an x such that. . .' And there's an end to it, so far as Quine is concerned. And it so happens that this criterion leads him to a certain kind of platonism, through the needs of mathematics, whose statements 'range over' abstract entities.

The platonism is unusual, as we have seen, in that it is experimental rather than definitive, and that its method is curiously and severely selective. Other thinkers who have argued from what we *say* to what there *is* (or to what we presuppose as existing) have taken the *totality* of our irreducible discourse as their premise: *any* elements in our discourse which we cannot eliminate, commit us to something 'out there' (excluding elements which are simply parts of the machinery of speech itself). Quine does not proceed in this way: not *anything* which we cannot help saying, but only the values over which our variables range, commit us to 'existence'. Our predicates, for instance, commit us to nothing. His philosophy is most unusual in that it is willing, indeed eager, to give a *behaviourist* account of predicates (that is how 'meanings' disappear), in terms of the behaviour of speakers, but a *platonistic* account of subjects (more accurately, of the 'values of bound variables'). Thus the platonism is both trial-and-error and curiously selective. Empiricists have tended to be phenomenalists in the first person and behaviourists in the third; Quine is, instead, behaviourist in the third person, but platonist in the first.

The whole idea of canonicist inference from the structure of language to what there is, or even to what-there-is-according-to-a-theory, seems open to a variety of objections. Take a very simple technical one first: Quine's criterion of existence, from the viewpoint of a given theory, hinges on what propositions are *true* within that theory.

> In general, entities of a given sort are assumed by a theory
> if and only if some of them must be counted among the
> values of the variables in order that the statements affirmed
> of the theory be true [*From a Logical Point of View*, p. 103].

So, if a theory contains a statement of the form:

$$(\exists x) F x \tag{i}$$

or, in English, there is an x such that it is characterised by F – then the theory is committed to the existence of those values of x which make the statement (i) true. But, if (i) is true, then so, by a very simple logical operation is

$$(x) F x \lor {\sim} F x \tag{ii}$$

– in English: *all* objects x are such that either they are, or are not, characterised by F. (ii) may not have originally been part of the theory whose ontic import we were concerned with, but there is no trouble at all about adding it! It follows, necessarily. Quine is clearly aware of this, in any case obvious, point:

> if the notation of the theory includes for each predicate a complementary predicate, its negation. For then, given any value of a variable, some predicate is true of it; viz, any predicate or its complement [*Ontological Relativity*, p. 95].

The trouble is, however, that *all* objects whatever make (ii) true; and thus all objects whatever are now added to our ontology – unless, of course, we restrict the range of (ii) to the *kind* of object to which *F* might *sensibly* apply. If *F*, for instance, were 'is a prime number', then cabbages, which neither are nor are not primes, for any man of sense, need not apply. But now we are back to the old way of ontology, which proceeded, roughly by asking, *prior* to any theory – what kind of object does it *make sense* to credit with existence? So we have, in fact, given up the Quinian programme of reading off the ontology of a theory by seeing what variables its affirmed statements 'range over'. Perhaps that was not the programme. But what was?

By and large, though I do not properly follow their reasoning, it is difficult not to agree with I. Scheffler and N. Chomsky (in *Aristotelian Society Proceedings, 1958–59*) when they ask in connexion with Quine:

> The question arises whether an adequate ontological criterion serves any philosophical purpose that cannot as economically be served by reference to the theories themselves.

Quine himself later seems to develop doubts about this when he observes, plausibly:

> The ontology of a theory. . .makes no sense unless relative to some background theory [*Ontological Relativity*, p. 60].

One wonders whether the whole approach to being via the 'range of variables' is not tied to a special kind of mathematical existence. The rest of us may well wonder at an ontological method which disposes of predicates by dissolving them in the behaviour of men, while sternly postulating existence for the subjects. Such logical schizophrenia seems hard to bear. On the other hand I have no difficulty with recognising different types of being, whether or not the notation can record the difference, an idea which plainly irritates Quine.

But the very idea of canonicist inference seems odd. Quine seems derisive when *others* use this principle. He writes:

> When Dewey was writing in. . .naturalistic vein, Wittgenstein still held his copy theory of language [*Ontological Relativity*, p. 27].

But is canonicism anything other than a version of the 'copy theory' of language – modified only by (a) arguing from a language to *its* view of the world, as opposed to *the* world, and (b) by the curious feature that only *some* bits of the language (range of variables) are allowed to mirror reality? These are nuances, but the principle would seem to be the same. Quine is a tentative, selective, canonicist platonist. There have been many canonicist platonists; it is only the tentativeness and the selectivity which make Quine unusual.

What is curious is that Quine's own favourite argument against classical empiricism seems usable, with at least the same force, against canonicism:

> Statements about the external world face. . .experience not individually but as a corporate body.
>
> It is misleading to speak of the empirical content of an individual statement. . .
>
> It is nonsense, and the root of much nonsense, to speak of a linguistic component and a factual component in the truth of any individual statement [*From a Logical Point of View*, pp. 41–2].

If collective responsibility applies to the goose of truth, why on earth does it not apply to the gander of ontic commitment? Truth about *what there is*, is, after all, only a kind of truth. Why can one amputate ontic commitment from one *part* of canonical sentences, while happily consigning the rest, including the meaning of predicates, to behaviourist reduction? One feels like exclaiming: could it not be that only whole languages, or at least large corporate bodies of propositions, face the tribunal of 'what there is', of ontic commitment, and that to compile inventories of what exists for this or that isolated assertion or part thereof, by seeing what it 'ranges over', is absurd. This is just what Quine argues for the *empirical* content of assertions; why is *ontic* content any different?

Yet Quine's devotion to this idea, that the 'range of bound

variables' of a theory is its ontic sacrament, seems firm and deep. We have seen some of the oddities it engenders: behaviourist reductionism for predicates, platonist realism for subject. There are others.

Quine makes it quite clear that the question of existence does not arise, for him, precisely in those cases which for most of us would constitute the very paradigm of an ontology: if, for instance, we had a finite list of existing objects, say, a list with two items, a thinking substance and an extended substance (there was once a famous ontology of this very form). But the conjunction – mind is a substance and extension is a substance – would not from him raise any question of existence. He concedes that his argument

> does not mean that theories. . .can get on *without* objects.
> I hold rather that the question of ontological commitment
> of a theory does not properly arise except as that theory
> is expressed in classical quantificational form, or in-so-far
> as one has in mind how to translate it into that form
> [*Ontological Relativity*, p. 106].

So take by contrast

> the case of a finite universe of named objects. Here there
> is no occasion for quantification, except as an inessential
> abbreviation; for we can expand quantification into finite
> conjunctions and alterations. Variables thus disappear. . .
> And the very distinction between names and other signs
> lapses. . .Ontology thus is emphatically meaningless to a
> finite theory of named objects [*Ontological Relativity*,
> p. 62].

Quite clearly, 'ontology' for him has to do with finding values for variables, the filling of certain gaps. Nothing else need apply. But what connexion has this question with any intuitively understood concern with 'what there is?'

The ontic commitment of a theory and its ability to do without objects seem somehow to be quite distinct issues. Clearly ontological commitment is for Quine indissolubly linked to 'quantification', to the availability of objects to fill gaps. One can only wonder why. One can only suppose that his ontological question has little overlap with the ordinary interpretation of the query concerning 'what there is' which *would* be answered by a finite list, articulable as a simple conjunction and hence without 'quantification' at all. 'Quantification' is like a slot machine, waiting for the right coins to make it work, to say 'true'. But, for every slot machine which affirms $(\exists x) Fx$, there must be another affirming $(\exists x) \sim Fx$; and jointly they must cover *everything* (even if possibly one of them hogs the lot). So where are we?

But all these oddities, interesting as they may be, are not what matters most at this point. What does matter is that these arguments for platonism from *canonicism*, and the argument for the same position from *pragmatism*, from the ultimate similarity of all adaptive devices, are *so* totally disparate as to provide another instance of Turko-Magyar. They are, to my mind, so completely incommensurate as not to be in any serious sense the same thesis at all: they cannot conceivably support each other. But in Quine's system, both the insensitive or weirdly sensitive canonical notation, *and* the stratospheric biological pragmatism which views everything (physical objects, gods, abstractions) as adaptive devices, to be judged as such and in no other way – *both* lead to a curious night in which cows, classes, classes of classes, etc., are the same shade of existential grey. For pragmatic reasons, I find this form of pragmatism unacceptable; and I find my reaction fortified when I see that it is supported by the convergence of at least two arguments, articulated in such diverse and totally incomparable idioms: all adaptive devices have the same status; and all values of bound quantified variables likewise have the same status. So, twice over, all existence is alike.

One may also worry about Quine's attitude to empiricism and behaviourism. Roughly speaking, he repudiates the former and endorses the latter. Strictly speaking, behaviourism is precisely that which he retains from empiricism; and what he really rejects in empiricism is not what it says, but the use to which it was once put, the question it was meant to answer, and the idiom in which it was articulated. The repudiated problem is that of 'prior philosophy', the extra-cosmic exile from which our world was to be built up without circularity; the idiom rejected is that inward language of sensing. So we get an empiricism without prior philosophy, and without that inwardness:

> Two cardinal tenets of empiricism remained unassailable. . .
> and so remain to this day. One is that whatever evidence
> there *is* for science *is* sensory evidence. The other. . .is that
> all inculcation of meanings of words must rest ultimately
> on sensory evidence [*Ontological Relativity*, p. 75].

This sounds in fact as if empiricism was being upheld, not repudiated. But it is only retained as a (most questionable) genetic theory, or a schema for the form which genetic theories are to have. Over and over again, he repudiates the ambition of 'seeking an implicit sub-basement of conceptualisation'. As he puts it:

> The old epistemology aspired to contain, in a sense, natural science; it would construct it somehow from sense data [*Ontological Relativity*, p. 83].

This ambition is disavowed:

> Unlike Descartes, we own and use our beliefs of the moment even in the midst of philosophizing [*Word and Object*, pp. 24–5].

In other words, we do not try to descend to that conceptual or sensory sub-basement. We retain our total cognitive wealth, unpurified and uncensored, though we may change bits of it here and there. Quine notices, with perceptiveness and irony, when others seek to dispense with epistemic bases by different means:

> Wittgenstein and his followers, mainly in Oxford, found a residual philosophic vocation in therapy: in curing philosophers of the delusion that there were epistemological problems [*Ontological Relativity*, p. 82].

This is indeed at the heart of the 'mature' Wittgenstein. Quine would not go so far:

> it may be more useful to say rather that epistemology still goes on [*Ibid.*].

Epistemology becomes, in the words of the title of one of his papers, *naturalised*:

> Epistemology. . .simply falls into place as a chapter of psychology. . .It studies a natural phenomenon, viz., a physical human subject. This. . .subject is accorded a certain experimentally controlled input – certain patterns of irradiation. . .and in the fullness of time delivers as output a description of the three-dimensional external world [*Ibid.*].

Note the determination to use third-person language and the abstention from the old justificatory use of 'epistemology'. He repeatedly notes the charge of circularity against his procedure – the world is assumed in the very account of how (and *that*) we come to know the world. We describe our knowledge as a process *within* the world assumed as known! But he rejects this charge. Or, rather, he thinks that this charge does not matter.

The charge of circularity does not matter on his account if indeed we are, in terms of his favourite quotation from Otto Neurath, on board a seaworthy boat which we can rebuild from its own timbers while remaining afloat. He seems confident that we are indeed on such a boat. To me on the contrary it seems obvious that many societies were or are in *un*seaworthy boats; and that, using Descartes' form of the argument from illusion, we need epistemology to assess the seaworthiness of our own – for we have no reason to assume that ours must be better than some of those which were totally worthless. It seems to me that, by naturalising epistemology, we make it worthless, for it can then no longer provide an answer to the problem which really, historically inspired it. *Naturalising* it means practising it within a given or assumed world. But the problem which inspired it was the problem of choosing between radically different and incommensurate worlds. This problem has arisen on the boundaries between cultures or between epochs. Naturalising the subject means assuming tacitly that *au fond*, there has really only been one world all along. This totally mistaken assumption does underline the whole position, protestations of conceptual relativism notwithstanding.

The enterprise of 'naturalising' epistemology is paradoxical. When naturalised, it can no longer do the job for which it was originally invented – to stand outside and tell us which of the rival, basically divergent worlds we really live in. This task, contrary to Quine's view, does have to be done and cannot be evaded. (Quine appears to think it doesn't really arise because the very general features of the world were always obvious and available. This world is assumed as perennially given, a world in fact roughly similar to that of the empiricists, plus abstract entities when they are essential.) At the same time, such naturalism ascribes to epistemology another job, that of explaining the working of our minds and of our learning capacity. This job, as Chomsky has shown, it is, however, totally unfit to carry out in its empiricist form. So it abandons a job which desperately needs to be done, for another which it is quite incompetent to carry out.

But while repudiating this *use* of empiricism (which to me on the contrary seems mandatory) he *will* use empiricism for the other, genetic purposes. This is where his Skinnerian behaviourism comes in (mitigated curiously by that selective canonicist platonism). He is aware with the usual admirable lucidity of its origin:

> Behaviourism. . .comes of the old empiricism. . .by a
> drastic externalization [*Language and Philosophy*, edited
> by S. Hook, 1969].

Under the impact of N. Chomsky's arguments, he concedes:

> Externalized. . .behaviourism sees nothing uncongenial in
> the appeal to innate dispositions [*Ibid.*].

But, once this is admitted, the burden of explanation should shift to the manner of operation of those dispositions, the structures which sustain or constitute them; these, and not the 'input' of 'irradiations', will explain the output. The sensitivity to irradiations, or to anything else, must itself be explained in this way. In brief, as a schema for genetic models, the externalised empiricism has little merit, and under impact of criticism it generally shifts back again to becoming a covert prior philosophy, a recipe for *testing* theories in general, rather than a scheme for the form of explanations.

The irony is that Quine's pragmatist themes work only at a stratospherically abstract level, concerning the alleged adjustment of total cognitive systems and the history of entire species; while his technicism and his canonicism work at the level of highly specific problems in logic. The excessive ease with which he relates these disparate spheres – the style and rigour of argument at each level is so different as to seem to come from a different world – is itself a piece of happy-go-lucky pragmatism. And this pragmatism does, in our age, risk becoming a kind of technicist opportunism. Take, for instance, his remarks about the possibility of a Pythagorean ontology:

> The Lowenheim–Skolem theorem. . .declares a reduction
> of all acceptable theories to denumerable ontologies. [These
> in turn are] reducible. . .to an ontology. . .of natural
> numbers. . .May we not thus settle for an all-purpose
> Pythagorean ontology outright? [*Ontological Relativity*,
> pp. 58–9].

Apparently not, for quite interesting reasons – which do not, however, seem to include the fact, rather persuasive for other people, that we do not eat numbers, sit on numbers, wear numbers, or shake their hands. Such mundane considerations do not seem relevant.

Technical questions, whether mathematical theories of one form can be mapped onto another, seem to weigh more.

Now the danger here clearly is that pragmatism becomes a kind of technical gimmickry, disconnected from reality by a kind of Pragmatist's Licence – say anything if it works in its technical context, and don't worry. It is nowadays customary to be contemptuous of old Metaphysical Licence, the right to say anything if only Deep Enough, irrespective of its lack of coherence with what we normally believe or act on. But there is a corresponding danger for this technicism. Moreover, this Technician's Licence seems to meld disastrously with the licence accorded by the stratospheric biological pragmatism: because, for instance, in the very very very long run, anything – but simply anything – may need to be changed, therefore we must pretend that, in the time-scale in which we actually live, we shall not distinguish between fact-dependent and conceptually ensured and hence safe propositions. I do not particularly like either of these two (technicist and long-range-pragmatist) forms of licence; but *conflating* them seems to me to lead to a no-language-at-all, to Turko-Magyar.

What claim has such pragmatism on our attention? Does it constitute a plausible account of, as it were, the fundamental principles of the customary law of our intellectual and cognitive practice? As a pragmatist, Quine, of course, cannot believe in any written and definitive constitution of our cognitive life, which might, like another Declaration, begin, 'We hold these truths to be self-evident. . .' There are no such; only such as seem self-evident. Ironically, although the original pragmatism was born in part of an attempt to capture and articulate the American spirit, in its repudiation of Constitution-worship and of self-evident premises it is technically un-American. Happily, however, it escaped the attention of Committees investigating un-American Activities. But, leaving aside these parochial consideratilons, is pragmatism, and this version of it in particular, acceptable as an account of even a customary intellectual constitution?

Certain rather special perils faced pragmatism in mid century, which may have been absent earlier. Pragmatism bids us consider above all the utility of our assertions. The obvious danger inherent in this is a certain opportunism. Anything may do if it works. This danger was not very great *in practice* at the time of classical pragmatism. Those who preached it were profoundly inner-directed men of great intellectual integrity (as also, quite obviously, is Quine):

though they might link truth and utility at a theoretical level, at a concrete level they would hardly sacrifice truth to expedience. More important, the same was true of their audience. Integrity and individualism were so much part of the moral climate that they could be taken for granted, and were in fact built into the assumptions of the old pragmatism. It criticised the abstract olympianism of the Hegelians, and wanted to see it replaced by a recognition of the complex and multiform involvement of thought in life. But spineless opportunism was not a danger which had to be seriously considered.

By the 1950s the situation was quite different. The tradition of inner-directedness had become far less powerful, less pervasive, less automatically self-evident. To preach pliable utility, not to mention a herd instinct, as the main virtue in our beliefs and assertions then acquired a different meaning. There were no self-reliant frontiersmen left, whose earthy practicality might need philosophic ratification against the genteel olympianism of Harvard Anglo-Hegelians – who no longer existed either. Instead, there was a technicist society, a marked diminution of self-reliant individualist inner-directedness, and a sense of bewilderment in the face of both the technicality of knowledge and the size of the corporate units. The universities were not havens for timid studious recluses but important channels of social mobility, by means of certified competence in technical knowledge, some genuine, some bogus, some mixed.

In such a world, to preach that there are no absolute truths, but that all is and ought to be changeable in the interest of avoiding stress and strain within a corporate conceptual system, and that the legitimate unit of knowledge (and presumably anything else) is a large corporate body, acquires quite a different significance.

> [N]o more can be claimed for our whole body of affirmations than that it is a devious but convenient system for relating experience to experiences. . .When. . .predictions of experience turn out wrong, the system has to be changed somehow. . .we retain a wide latitude of choice as to what. . .to preserve and what. . .to revise. . .Our statements. . .face the tribunal. . .not individually but as a corporate body [*Methods of Logic*, xii].
>
> Mathematical and logical laws themselves are not immune to revision if. . .essential simplifications of our. . . scheme will ensue. There have been suggestions, stimulated largely by the quandaries of modern physics, that we

revise the true–false dichotomy of current logic in favour
of some sort of tri- or *n*-chotomy [Ibid., xiv].

There are no absolute standards, but corporate convenience is the
measure of all things. Such a doctrine could have a resonance in the
1950s which was totally different from any meaning likely to attach
to the old pragmatism.

That a doctrine might have a certain application, that it could
logically lend itself to a certain other-directed corporate opportunism, is of course in itself no criticism of that doctrine. As it happens,
the conformism of that age did not use such highbrow and elegant
rationales. And it cannot be stressed too strongly that Quine in person
exemplifies all those virtues of the old pragmatism, and none of the
defects which the new pragmatism could be used to justify. But the
fit between the new philosophy, and the wider social mood of the
time in which it was mainly articulated, is interesting and noteworthy. The difference between the pragmatism of William James
and latter-day Logical Pragmatism, is also in some measure the
difference between two Americas, separated from each other by half
a century.

The new pragmatism operates as stated at two highly disparate
levels. Its biologically inspired epistemological vision is very abstract
– one might say *sub specie aeternitatis*. Ironically, it operates at such
a stratospheric level as to be rather disconnected from here-and-now
earthy concerns and distinctions, which indeed it is liable to violate.
It is also a little perfunctory and metaphorical. When we hear about
the ultimate, long-long-term corrigibility of *any* part of our conceptual scheme, we hear of 'impingement', 'readjustment', 'equi-
librium' and so on. This is, self-confessedly, metaphorical argument
about logic, rather than logic. There is relatively little by way of
serious attempt to work out concretely what it would mean to
change those 'most central and crucial statements of our conceptual
scheme', or to examine concretely just how they come to be 'the
most protected from revision by the force of conservatism'.

By contrast with this very abstract, somewhat perfunctory pragmatism, we get a quite different kind of pragmatism in Quine's own
home territory, logic. Here the voice is not that of a metaphor-
addicted pragmatist and wise-cracking epistemologist, but of a man
who is an effortless virtuoso in his own field. *This* pragmatism is far
more convincing (only diffidence inspired by one's incompetence
prevents one from endorsing it totally.) No doubt, an attitude of

experimental trial-and-error vis-à-vis technical devices in this subject is much sounder than the 'Cartesian' hope of a subject inexorably progressing, without ever retracing any steps, from firm premisses to an ever-growing but never-revised body of consequences. Here Quine records a change in the intellectual climate and in the aspiration of logicians which, so far as an outsider can judge, is entirely salutary.

But one may well worry about the extension of this kind of 'pragmatism', a trial-and-error attitude towards technical devices in a highly technical field, to other areas. The general objection to all forms of pragmatism is not so much its tie-up of truth and utility, but its inherent tendency to assimilate most diverse kinds of utility to each other. Some assertions are useful because true, and some for other reasons, and some may be useful because they are not true. One wants to be able to make such distinctions. Usefulness, like the Absolute, may impose a night in which all cows are the same shade of grey. It is much more *pratique* to be chromatically more discriminating, and pragmatism itself may well fail the pragmatic test. One may feel that he is too pragmatic in spheres which belong to the Absolute – questions such as the primacy of the first person singular in knowledge – and far too absolute in spheres where pragmatic considerations should lead one to make distinctions, such as the difference between the existence of concrete and abstract objects.

In Quine, this indiscriminate, unpragmatic streak of pragmatism is manifested in or reinforced by his canonicism, which of course has an obvious and inherent tendency to reduce everything to one form. The oddities which it generates are then, however, protected by the so-to-speak unworried pragmatist spirit, which does not allow itself to be troubled by oddities, so long as the thing works. One such oddity is the third-person behaviourism married to a first-person platonism; or an ontology in which *subjects* of sentences indicate the existence of the objects covered, whilst *predicates* only indicate the behaviour of speakers and listeners.

The third-person behaviourism in the system is another one of its oddities. Quine refuses to indulge in a first-person epistemology, and wishes to do it in a third-person, 'naturalised' manner. Such an epistemology

> studies a natural phenomenon, viz., a physical human
> subject. This human subject is accorded a certain experi-
> mentally controlled input – certain patterns of irradiation

> in assorted frequencies, for instance – and in the fulness
> of time the subject delivers as output a description of the
> three-dimensional external world and its history. The
> relation between the meager input and the torrential
> output is a relation we are prompted to study [*Ontological
> Relativity*, pp. 82–3].

This input–output relation is what remains of the classical attempt to base theory on data, an aspiration which is firmly disavowed. One may gravely doubt whether such a 'relation' exists at all. The radiations which bombarded Newton or Einstein were not significantly different from those which bombarded their contemporaries.

The implausibility of this whole behaviourist input–output approach to the acquisition of knowledge is one objection. There is no need to rehearse the familiar reasons for it. But there are less familiar and less obvious objections which are, perhaps, *more* fundamental for evaluating Logical Pragmatism. What is presupposed here is the repudiation of that justificatory aspect of epistemology, and of the whole first-person approach (not only because it is first-person, but because it aspires, for justificatory ends, to be *prior* to the three-dimensional world).

Here there is something which Logical Pragmatism shares with its classical pragmatist ancestor. The third-person idiom always came naturally to pragmatism. It feels at home in this world – too much so perhaps – and has a certain aversion to pretending that we do not belong here, that we only stumbled into this universe by mistake, and need a well-authenticated, official guidebook. It does not find the world much of a predicament. As Quine puts it:

> Unlike Descartes, we own and use our beliefs of the
> moment, even in the midst of philosophizing [*Word and
> Object*, pp. 24–5].

It was Descartes' way to hold 'our beliefs of the moment' (in effect, *our world*), in the aseptic pincers of general doubt, and at the same time, let's admit it, to hold his nose with an expression of distaste. The paradox of Quine's general position and style is that whilst he repudiates the very aspiration and possibility of a 'prior philosophy', he unwittingly offers us precisely a specimen of it. His general picture has a simplicity, elegance, generality and what can only be described as a kind of *basic* and in effect stable quality, all traits of a prior philosophy, and not at all characteristic of temporary, expendable, to-be-abandoned adaptive devices. Descartes commended the simplicity and elegance of the designs of a single architect, as against the haphazard, untidy accumulation of ad hoc adjustments of a merely historical development. Quine makes precisely the opposite recommendation, but ironically his practice is in fact Cartesian. The fact that the simple and elegant structure which he offers also has its internal tensions, enhances its interest.

This is the heart of the matter. The most fundamental objection to this kind of pragmatism is that, contrary to its own protestations, it *does* also have its own 'prior philosophy'; and, less important perhaps, it happens to be a false one.

We have seen what its prior philosophy is. The ultimate, entrenched clauses of the system are the evolutionist vision of a continuous, all-in-all sound progression in knowledge, and, presumably, in other spheres, and exemplifying in the end one and the same principle; and, secondly, the guidance of this process, as a kind of guaranteeing pilot-mechanism, by the admittedly hard-to-define 'scientific method', which is not claimed of course to be infallible in each case of its application. With his characteristic and admirable candour, Quine overtly says that this guardian angel possesses no further and more ultimate validation. Hence his authority, such as it may be, is final, or rather, *prior*.

If either of these two entrenched constitutional clauses were ever subjected to serious doubt – and why should they not be? – and found to be wanting, there would be no redress within the system, and there would be dissolution into chaos. This is a good sign of an entrenched clause in the constitutional law of cognition: if it goes, all else dissolves in chaos. This would lead precisely to the kind of pervasive doubt which Descartes experienced and outlined, and which makes the justificatory, non-third-person approach in epistemology mandatory. And not only *may* those clauses be doubted: at least one of them seems to me in fact false.

So the pragmatist crypto-prior-philosophy not merely exists, but it is also in error. The pragmatist picture is of an on-the-whole sound and healthy evolutionary progression. The facts of the case are quite different. Neither life in general, nor mankind or its cognitive history in particular, are on some sound, reliable rails or path. Moreover, those two stories (biology and history) should not be assimilated to each other; the mechanisms of natural selection and evolution, and those of cultural transmission and accumulation, are so different from each other (and no doubt contain enormous differences internally) that no purpose is served by treating them as one plot, even if they were both and all of them sound and trustworthy – which they are not.

The mistake of pragmatism – as of some other philosophies – is to feel too much at home in this world. It knows neither nausea nor vertigo. But in fact stagnations, blind alleys, and dissolutions into chaos, are more characteristic states of the human condition than well-oiled, trustworthy progressions. When crossroads or dissolutions into chaos are encountered, an assessment of alternatives which attempts to stand outside, and places no trust in the flow of things, is the only possible rational approach. There is of course no general proof that a rational approach is a good thing, still less that it will always be attempted or that it will succeed. But it is that, or nothing. Those who (like Quine or Marx) repudiate it, do indeed have one very powerful argument on their side: all those weighty considerations which seem to show that such conceptual extra-territoriality is an illusion. But the idea that we can or do refrain from striving for it, when we think rationally, is an even greater illusion.

12

Pragmatism and the importance of being earnest

There is the oft-quoted remark about the man who tried hard to be a philosopher, but cheerfulness kept breaking through...What is less well known is the end of the story. He found a way out. He became a Pragmatist. Thereafter, he was both a philosopher *and* cheerful.

A certain cheerfulness seems to be of the very essence of Pragmatism, and is in effect one of its defining traits. Moreover, it seems to me a crucial error. It is not my wish to argue that a deep gloom is an absolute precondition of philosophic truth. Rather, a kind of pervasive Angst is a precondition of the correct formulation of the epistemic question. When it is absent, a missing of the point, a begging of the question, if not outright formal error, are the inescapable consequences.

As I hold this to be the central weakness of Pragmatism, I was very pleased to find Quine highlighting the trait, albeit in a deceptively *en passant* manner.[1] Commenting on the difference between the views of the Pragmatist F. C. S. Schiller and those of Sir Karl Popper, Quine suggests that Schiller's 'doctrine of "postulation", which has us believing whatever we wish were true until it proves troublesome' is very much the same as the hypothetico-deductive method commended and described by Popper, *apart from an indefinable element of fun.* (Quine's own words.) Pragmatists are fun people, that much is clear.

Earlier in the same essay, this Joyful Science had already made its appearance, *nur mit ein bisschen anderen Worten.* Discussing the

---

[1] See W. V. O. Quine, 'The Pragmatist's Place in Empiricism', in R. J. Mulvaney and Philip M. Zeltner (eds.), *Pragmatism: Its Sources and Prospects* (Columbia, S.C., 1979).

sources of Pragmatist naturalism – which Quine rightly lists as one of its defining traits – he observes that 'The other...source of naturalism is unregenerate realism, the robust state of mind of the natural scientist who has never felt any qualms beyond the negotiable uncertainties internal to science.'

It is this robust lack of any qualms such as would be discontinuous with the day-to-day ordinary working doubts inside science, which Quine commends, and considers both salutary and inherent in Pragmatism. I entirely accept his diagnosis. We disagree only in its evaluation.

Now if we accept this self-characterisation of Pragmatism, and at the same time hold Pragmatism to be in error, precisely in its addiction to cheerfulness, does this mean that we hold gloom to be philosophically mandatory? Not exactly. Gloom may indeed be a decorous state of mind, and one befitting a man of sense, learning and dignity. Nevertheless, it seems to me philosophically optional, and I for one should strongly oppose making it a necessary condition for senior appointments in philosophy.

Rather, the point is this: the relevant antithesis of cheerfulness is not gloom, but a sense of crisis. Crisis, in turn, must be distinguished from a problem. The distinction is: a problem is a difficulty which may well be serious and the solution of which may call for the utmost exertions, and which may be prolonged and arduous, but which, for all that, does not call for a revaluation of the very criteria of what is to count as a solution, for any overall reassessment of all the criteria of solution themselves. This difference has something in common with the distinction once upon a time propounded by the Existentialist philosopher Gabriel Marcel between a problem and a mystery – where the latter is not simply a more difficult variant of the former, but qualitatively distinct because it involves the very relationship of the self to the object of inquiry. The failure to draw this distinction forcefully enough is also present in Popper's philosophy of science. Popper likes to insist that science consists of the solution of problems (and hence, incidentally, is continuous with evolutionary advances). The stress on solving problems is of course intended to bring out the contrast with the rival and rejected view of science as information-accumulation. But the notion of 'problem' faces two ways: it must be contrasted not merely with data-collection, but also with a crisis in which one no longer knows what is to count as problem and what is to count as a solution. For such situations, the twin injunctions – solve problems, criticise solutions – are no longer adequate. Talk of 'problems' prejudges too much, and does so on the optimistic, complacent side. Equally the difference has some affinity with the recently fashionable distinction between problems in normal science on the one hand, and paradigm shifts on the other. One's ultimate criteria of what is acceptable and what is problematic, are intimately linked to one's very identity.

We can now also refine the concept of cheerfulness. Kant observed that love as a feeling cannot be commanded, and similarly, cheerfulness as a simple affect can hardly be prescribed. To do so would be both illiberal and pointless. If cheerfulness does indeed keep breaking through, why repress it? It is not cheerfulness as a simple affect which concerns us; it is cheerfulness as a strategy or style: that celebrated willingness to try and use any tool that is to hand, inspired by a confident expectation that though any one tool or effort may fail, by and large one's kit contains adequate tools, that all-in-all our criteria are sound. It is this set of assumptions which really constitutes cheerfulness in the relevant cognitive sense. By contrast, it is their suspension which constitutes a crisis.

Thus Pragmatism stands for cheerfulness, as defined, in opposition to a sense of crisis. But it also generally stands for a resolutely third person idiom, as opposed to the first person style characteristic of classical epistemology and of radical empiricism. In fact, it is arguable that what distinguishes Pragmatism from radical empiricism is precisely this trait: that it is a kind of externalisation, objectification of empiricism or sensationalism. Such externalisation certainly is commended to Professor Quine, as he makes plain in a number of contexts. The transition from talking about *ideas* to talking about *words*, which he commends in the essay mentioned, is of course one version of it. A very great deal hinges, of course, on whether one uses a third or a first person idiom. Each of these idioms sums up, embodies, an entire philosophic programme and attitude.

Radical empiricism in effect asserts that all true statements about the world are ultimately stateable in the first person. *Esse est percipi.* To be is to be perceived: to be perceived is to be perceived by *someone*. A fact is an account of someone's perception. Someone has to be able to say, with truth, 'I perceive...' Even if other forms of speech occur and omit this locution, it is always tacitly present if the assertion is true and warranted. This makes the perceiving subject ultimate and distinctive. It is he who examines the data and constructs the world, a world, out of them. In sceptical mood, he may wonder whether the data really and truly add up to a usable world. But the ego comes first, and the world is constructed from the data it has received.

A totally different vision is implied in the use of the third person as fundamental. *I* can stand outside the world; *he* cannot. There are certain irregular expressions. ('I am Oxford; you are Cambridge; he is London School of Economics.') These also occur in philosophy. 'I construct the world, him included', is acceptable. 'He constructs the world, me included', is not. The use of *he* firmly places the cognising person or organism in the context of other things and other centres of consciousness, and deprives him and his cognitive enterprise of any privileged, external, extra-territorial status. The third person is Copernican. If we insist on doing epistemology in the third person, as Quine does, we thereby firmly presuppose a public world within which both the process of cognition and the organism benefiting from it stand alongside other things and other processes, not radically distinct from them, and unable to claim any special status.

The question now arises – which of these two idioms is really fundamental, ultimate, justified?

It would seem that we are in the presence of a stalemate, in as far as each of them appears to possess knock-down arguments for the elimination of its rival.

The argument for the exclusion of the third person viewpoint or terminology is an entirely cogent appeal against *begging of the question*. It runs as follows: if the theory of knowledge is to be discussed at all, its conclusion must not be prejudged, as indeed is mandatory for any other genuine inquiry. If you ask a question at all, if you hold it worth asking, then it must be decided in the light of the evidence adduced, rather than prejudged. It is no use having a debate like the one between the mediaeval King and the Jew about the merits of their respective religions, which had to be carried on on the assumption of the validity of the King's faith. The issue in epistemology is what and *whether* we know; and one possible answer must be that we do *not*. But the whole point of the third person idiom is simply a camouflaged – and not very cunningly camouflaged – assumption that we *do* know the world which we think we know, that it is roughly as we always supposed, and that *within* it, we can find out just how we came to know what we do know anyway. . . This is childishly circular reasoning. Quine endorses it, knowingly and with defiance, and he resolutely spurns the use of camouflage.

There is no doubt in my mind that the charge of childish circularity of reasoning is established. It is of course possible to call it 'robust' or 'fun' – and, no doubt, it qualifies under either heading. But can you really establish a philosophy by stressing that it is held by robust healthy people, when that very philosophy is also allowed to decide what is healthy?

Unfortunately, the rival position is just as vulnerable. The attack against it can be formulated as follows: the first philosophy assumes a self-prior-to-the-world, which chooses whether or not graciously to allow itself to be persuaded of the reality of the world. But every tool – sensory, conceptual, linguistic, physiological – which it employs in its deliberations is part and parcel of that very world which it would judge and 'suspend'! Alternatively, even if this philosophy does not literally believe in a prior-self, it supposes at least that the sceptical cognitive Hamlet can propel himself into a kind of cosmic exile. . .but is this not absurd?

There are various ways of demonstrating the hubris, the absurdity of such a pretension. The way evidently much favoured by Quine, and many others, is from the failure to find a way of characterising 'pure data', which would furnish our Hamlet's mind in his extra-terrestrial exile, and which would avoid being saturated by theories drawn from *within* that world which had supposedly been 'suspended'. . .

There are other ways of attaining the desired conclusion. A recently fashionable one is to insist that any identification or sense of that very 'self' which is to observe its own 'data' is contingent on the practical activity by that self in the world. . .and thus that world is surreptitiously presupposed as soon as we speak of the self at all. I think – therefore *the world* is. Or again, the linguistic philosophers did it through their putative proof that there could be no private language. If so, all languages are necessarily public. Hence, the very speech in which you query the reality of the public world, already presupposes it! We speak, hence the world is. I well remember one such thinker, arguing that solipsism was possible for animals, but not for language-endowed men. Speech guaranteed the world. . .How simple. Or again: the very act of thought presupposes a conceptual and linguistic system of great complexity, whose rules are not even known to the individual operating it, let alone chosen or made by him. These systems can only exist in the world and are sustained by it. They cannot pretend to exist independently – nor can that thought which is only articulated through them.

So be it. I do not wish to dispute the conclusive force of these arguments, which I have sketched out. But if the conclusive force of destructive arguments on each side is conceded, where does this leave us?

The situation is indeed a stalemate. I do not believe that it has any resolution, if we consider the third/first person issue in isolation. But each side of this opposition is intimately and inescapably linked to our initial contrast between cheerfulness and sense of crisis. The third person view is linked to cheerfulness: if the world and its general outlines, and the outlines of what counts as the solution of problems, are all given, then indeed we are only faced with specific problems rather than with an overall crisis. Conversely, a sense of pervasive crisis calls for a radical and *general* reassessment, and this generality can only be genuine if attained without question-begging, and if it proceeds from some independent, external stance.

In other words, the two visions are tied to two alternative possible situations; and hence, by considering our situation within the world (as indeed the third person theorists would have us do anyway), we may, in a way, decide, not so much which of the two visions is correct, but which is mandatory. Thus we are, at least experimentally, playing by third person rules.

We must now look within that given world to see what our situation is really like. Note that, though in one way we are playing the game by third person rules, in another sense the cards are also somewhat stacked against that position. To achieve victory, the first person position does not need to establish that the human situation is permanently and everywhere in a state of crisis. Such a claim would in any case be absurd, and, were it true, our position would presumably be beyond either help or solution. All the first person theorist in fact requires is that *sometimes*, at crucial times, conditions resemble that which we have defined as crisis.

This brings us to the next polarity, which separates pragmatists and their opponents, and which concerns the area from which evidence, and above all the basic image, is drawn. Pragmatism is inspired by two areas: biology (Darwinism, evolutionism), and by nineteenth-century socio-economic and intellectual history.

These two in many ways incomparable and disparate regions, nevertheless have some crucial traits in common. Each of them seems at least to have been a success story. In each case, the success seems to have been unplanned, and attained by uncoordinated or even in the main unconscious individual effort, by repeated trial-and-error, by endeavour which does not spurn the successive utilisation of quite diverse methods or paths, and which receives both its impetus and its checks in the hurly burly of concrete struggle. Marx planned to dedicate one of his works to Darwin, in ironical spirit as Professor S. Avineri has pointed out, as a comment on the manner in which nineteenth-century laissez faire capitalism delighted to find a parable or confirmation in Darwinian nature.

The pragmatists were not necessarily or all of them social Darwinists:

> not all Americans who admired evolutionary thought de-
> rived from it. . .laissez faire conclusions. . .many American
> thinkers dissented from the social doctrines of Sumner and
> Herbert Spencer, for example. . .Dewey's variety of prag-
> matism was probably more distinguished and more lasting
> in its influence than any of the other American movements
> affected by evolutionary doctrine.[2]

Some of them were, of course: the analogy between the alleged improvement of biological species and the improvement of the human stock of ideas, institutions, and indeed of the human stock itself, is too tempting, whether or not it is really defensible. But whether or not progress hinges on *competition*, there are also other links between the two visions. There are many witnesses: 'William James occasionally spoke of his theory of mind as a corollary of Darwinian biology.'[3]

> Pragmatism emphasised not the brute hardness of things
> transparently evident to consciousness, but rather the con-
> trol of an organism's conceptions by its actions and their
> connected consequence in experience. It demanded that
> speculative abstractions be rejected as meaningless unless
> they could be reconstructed as predicting differential
> sensible outcomes of specified operations. It insisted, further,
> that truths acquired their warrant through publicly
> verifiable anticipation of the course of experience, con-
> tingent upon human transformation of the environment.[4]

> In his psychological writings, James consistently presents the
> facts of mental life. . .always in the most intimate relation to

[2] Cf. Morton White, *Pragmatism and the American Mind*, 1973, p. 194.
[3] Morton White, op. cit., p. 96.
[4] Israel Scheffler, *Science and Subjectivity*, 1967, p. 4.

men's biological needs and functions and the constant task of adaptation with which every organism is faced. When he turned from psychology to philosophy. . .he passed to the more exciting. . .thesis that the sole function of thought is to satisfy certain interests of the organism, and that truth consists of such thinking as satisfies these interests.[5]

Various facets of the pragmatic response. . .A dominant theme is the *rejection of Cartesian thought*. . .flowing from this rejection are several pragmatic emphases. . .the *functional view of thought,* relating cognition to the biological, social and purposive life of the organism: the *fallibilistic view of knowledge*. . .*the social and* experimental conception of science. . .and the *representative character of thinking*. . .

The interpretation of *thought as intimately interwoven with action* in a purposive context is stressed by pragmatism as indicating the *continuity of mind and* nature; the mind acquires knowledge through physical interactions within its environment.[6]

Pragmatism [is]: A theory of knowledge, experience and reality maintaining. . .that thought and knowledge are biologically and socially evolved modes of adaptation to and control over experience and reality. . .The ways in which experience is apprehended, systematised, and anticipated may be many. Here pragmatism counsels tolerance and pluralism. But. . .all theorising is subject to the critical objective of maximum usefulness in serving our needs.[7]

The biological vision reinforced the third person view: it could not even be articulated unless an external world were granted as its arena. And there are other connections: the optimistic expectation of long-term improvement, the stress on ordeal by practice rather than by confrontation with some abstract ideal, the expectation and high valuation of concrete diversity, and so forth.

It is possible to attack this Continuity Thesis between biological

[5] W. B. Gallie, *Pierce and Pragmatism*, 1952, p. 25.
[6] Israel Scheffler, *Four Pragmatists*, Routledge & Kegan Paul, London, 1974.
[7] H. S. Thayer, *Meaning and Action. A Critical History of Pragmatism*, 1968, p. 431.

and human history; and, moreover, it is possible to attack it from two quite different sides, each of which is highly relevant, though in different ways.

One argument starts from the fact that both biological evolution and industrial–economic history of the nineteenth century (allowing for a moment that the analogy between them is valid), are most untypical of the rest of human history proper. Each exhibits both instability and growth, albeit in one case this can only be detected at the scale of millions of years, whilst in the other it can be discerned by the participants and so to speak with the naked eye. But in fact the characteristic condition of a very great deal of human history is either stalemate-equilibrium or acute crisis. Sustained growth is alas untypical. Many social forms, notably oriental civilisations, have persisted over long periods and appear to possess mechanisms for avoiding radical change; elsewhere, violent crises have so totally shaken social systems that the criteria of survival themselves have undergone radical transformation.

The examples of cognitive growth favoured by a pragmatist such as Quine seem to be drawn precisely from these two areas – either from biological, organic adaptation, or from within a scientific discipline – where overall criteria are reasonably clear, consensual and established. We have stressed the pragmatist failure to consider crisis and radical discontinuity, and this is indeed the crucial and *decisive* weakness of pragmatism. But in a different way, the blindness to (from our viewpoint) excessive stability, to the self-maintaining rigor mortis of so many social and intellectual systems, is also a very grave weakness, and the complement of the other one. These two blindnesses or insensitivities are correlative. Fundamental crisis characteristically occurs when one of these self-maintaining systems collapses, whether through internal stress or external impact, and then becomes incapable of coping at all.

There is something paradoxical in speaking of biological history and its pattern as 'untypical': within its own terms and area, it must constitute the very norm of typicality. For a variety of reasons, it just happens to be a bad analogy or parable for human history. But the other region in time and space which specially inspired the pragmatists – the economic history of nineteenth-century North America plus those other countries which passably resemble it – is of course highly untypical of human history, and to try and extract a universal philosophy from its underlying spirit is absurd. At some levels, thinkers like William James must have been aware of this,

precisely in as far as they thought they were formulating a distinctively American philosophy, and one based on the American
experience. At the same time, he was clearly willing to see it used
for export. Presumably he believed that though all men are human,
Americans are more so, that the American experience is more paradigmatically human.[8]

But it is not the special temporal narrowness of the evidence alone
which counts against it. One may also question whether the material
has been correctly interpreted. A naïve adherent of laissez faire,
contemplating late nineteenth-century America, might well conclude
that economic competition is, on its own, the secret of economic
growth at any time and in any place. Similarly, an epistemologist
might in analogous circumstances conclude that intellectual competition and pragmatic trial-and-error will automatically lead to
cognitive growth. In fact, in either case, the miracle only works in
the right climate – whether political or intellectual.

It is precisely the once-and-for-all establishment of this climate,
after some stagnant stalemate or general crisis, which is the *real*
secret: but individuals or societies happily born long after the firm
and confident establishment of such a climate, may simply take it
for granted, and be ever inclined to think of it, not as *one* social
climate amongst others, but as the natural and well-nigh inevitable
condition of mankind. (Such a mentality underlies pragmatism.) A
society like that simply does not remember any *ancien régime*. Even
if they know intellectually that things had once been very different,
they may have some difficulty in really feeling it. Traits which elsewhere are anti-traditional, 'radical', are part and parcel of American
tradition itself. As Bernard Crick puts it:[9]

> American politics. . .are almost inescapably 'Lockean'.
> They exhibit. . .a purely utilitarian and contractual view of
> government. . .But all this, while making Lockean whiggery
> still the clearest political sociology of American life, is still a
> Lockeanism that never had to struggle against an *ancien
> régime*. For the 'American Revolution' was never a revo-
> lution at all in the meaning of that term that had dominated
> European politics since 1789. 'The great advantage of the
> American', Hartz quotes De Tocqueville, 'is that he has
> arrived at a state of democracy without having to endure a

[8] Cf. W. James, *Pragmatism*, ch. 1.
[9] 'Liberalism Transplanted', *The Twentieth Century*, June 1957.

> democratic revolution: and that he is born equal without
> having to become so.'

The mistaken supposition that a given environment, which is in fact
historically most specific, is inherent in the very nature of things, *did*
receive much encouragement from a questionable reading of biological history. In brief: the mind of a pragmatist turns easily to
Atlantic economic history of the nineteenth century, or the history
of science *after* the seventeenth century, or to the evolution of the
whole species: but one does not often see it lingering on the ancient
Near East, on the Middle Ages, or on Chinese, Hindu or Muslim
civilisation.[10]

But – to reach the next point – is there in fact any continuity
between biological evolution and cognitive growth? Let us leave
aside the well-known and oft-noted differences between genetic and
social transmission of information, with all that this implies. There
is another highly significant difference. Natural selection selects
through survival by a *multiplicity* of diverse criteria, and at the same
time each of these criteria only operates concretely, in a definite and
well-defined context. They do not, so to speak, extrapolate to hypothetical contexts. Candidates are eliminated only by real, not by
hypothetical ordeals. The animal must be brave enough to repel
attackers who can be repelled, yet sufficiently fleet of foot to flee
from strong ones, and clever enough to distinguish the two, etc. etc.
At the same time, the specific nature of these ordeals ensures that
natural selection only moulds the species for the context in which it
actually finds itself; it does not and cannot as it were train them for
environments which they have not yet encountered. It cannot as it

---

10 In explaining the strong reliance of Pragmatism on the continuity
thesis, I invoke the fact that American culture contains no folk
memory of any *ancien régime*. (The American Revolution was a
defence of the decencies which the continuity thesis underwrites,
and not a defiant act of Reason against Tradition.) This is indeed
so. At the same time it must be admitted that the continuity thesis
is sometimes upheld by thinkers springing from cultures in which
the *ancien régime* is vividly remembered, such as Sir Karl Popper
with his doctrine that the amoeba was a good Popperite. Optimistic
the *ancien régime* is vividly remembered, such as Sir Karl Popper
must of course be carefully distinguished from *static* optimistic
background theories, which evoked, precisely, an idealised *ancien*
régime as the guarantor of our cognitive endeavour, with some
slogan such as that every form of life is valid, by its own lights, and
that there can be no other.

were act at a distance or in anticipation. An ordeal will eliminate those who fail that particular ordeal and that particular ordeal only; it will not prepare an organism for future and different ordeals.

There is an enormous difference between an organ or an organism on the one hand, and a proposition or theory on the other. An organ can in a sense be said to embody an anticipation: the giraffe's neck embodies the assumption of the availability of nourishment some distance above ground and out of the reach of ordinary necks. The consequent survival of animals endowed with long necks constitutes a kind of confirmation of that unspoken anticipation, whilst their elimination might be its falsification – but only with tremendous qualifications. The world is full of creatures with dismally short necks, or even no necks to speak of. More important, animals with unduly long necks might be eliminated not because the tacit anti-cipation of food-at-height is false, but because the anatomical conse-quences of excessive neck lengths are unfavourable. Organs survive not merely because of the truth or falsity of the anticipations which can be said to be tacitly contained in them, but because of their effects on the whole assembly of organs, on the organism. Natural selection is not analogous to scientific selection as it actually is, but as it would be if propositions were never tested directly, but only evaluated through the statistical success of technologies based on them.

By contrast (and *pace* Quine), propositions possess relatively definite and circumscribed meanings or 'anticipations'. They stand or fall by what they *say* rather than by their side-effects. Quine likes to insist on their *esprit de corps*, on how they stand and fall as corporate units, how failure in one place can lead to adjustments elsewhere in the system. But diffuseness of meaning is a matter of degree. The fact that we can often identify the one place in which failure occurred, the fact that we can translate from language to language (though this very consideration leads Quine to be sceptical of translations), shows that propositions have become individualistic to a remarkable degree. I believe that it is relatively isolable mean-ing, *not* facing reality as a corporate body, which is responsible in large measure for the amazing cognitive growth of modern times. There is admittedly in human societies something analogous in the way in which organs stand and fall together, in clusters, and not by the merit of the 'anticipations' seen in isolation: it is found in traditional societies, which have belief systems so intertwined with the status and authority structures of their culture that nothing important can change without imperilling the rest, and hence most parts are systematically protected. The liberation of propositions from this collective responsibility – a liberation which I admit is not total – is I suspect one of the distinctive features of the scientific spirit, which helps to account for its success, and which at the same time precludes the application of the same principle to biological adaptation and to scientific growth. Descartes was no doubt right in including in his principles of method the requirement that all separable questions be in fact separated. This kind of atomisation of issues has at least two effects: it torpedoes traditional ideologies, which depend in part for their compulsiveness and authority on being offered as package deals, on being complex structures so designed that their diverse parts sustain and cover up for each other; but it also has the effect of speeding up selection, by taking candidates one by one, as far as possible, rather than as large and cumbersome teams.

Quine's celebrated holism is moreover in implicit conflict with his evolutionism. Natural selection can only operate on reasonably large species, subjected to a fairly steady environment for some goodly length of time. Human history fulfils none of these conditions: a relatively small number of cultures, so small at the later stages that luck must play a big part in deciding who wins and survives, have competed over a fairly short period of time, in a social environment so unstable in the later period that all conclusions are perilous. (Are the institutions chosen by natural selection in the nineteenth century the ones most fit to serve in the twentieth?) By insisting on holism, on the mutual confrontations of enormous intellectual systems, rather than of isolated statements, Quine in effect makes sure that the number of competing entrants in this selective game is so small that victory ceases to be statistically significant. The collectivism, the sharing of responsibility would lead to the swamping of any advantageous innovations, and to the protection of cognitive lame ducks. The collectives, on the other hand, are so small in number that their 'selection' by history must be strongly affected by accident rather than fitness, whatever fitness may be.

Now consider that mysterious entity we call truth, or whatever it is which so very visibly augments during periods of marked cognitive growth, i.e. in the course of the history of modern science. It does *not* satisfy a wide multiplicity of criteria but, on the contrary, a rather narrow range of them, or perhaps even just a single criterion; and it is also conspicuously extrapolative. To put it in more concrete terms: what distinguishes the scientific thought style from pre-scientific ones is notably the fact that instead of satisfying *many* criteria – including social cohesian, authority-maintenance, morale, etc. – it sheds all but one aim, i.e. explanatory power and congruence with facts.[11] Moreover, far from adapting to one specific environment – which is the only aim that natural selection can serve – it endeavours to cover as wide a range of environments, of situations, as possible, and so to speak to seek them out actively in the process of testing, rather than waiting till *they* test *it*.

In somewhat different words, this point has often been raised against Pragmatism. Pragmatism assimilates truth to that which is useful. Thereby, in effect, it conflates that which is useful because it is true (it is useful to know that there is a precipice ahead, because there is indeed a precipice there), and that which is useful *for other reasons*, independent of or even opposed to truth. It may be useful not to be apprehensive about precipices, because confidence sustains one's endeavours, for instance.

Pragmatism was encouraged in this conflation by various considerations, including the notorious difficulty of defining truth in a non-circular or non-nebulous manner. Usefulness appeared a way out of this difficulty, and one which moreover avoided any need to step outside experience. The conflation has numerous and I suspect insuperable difficulties of its own, such as that of defining the range, i.e. the time-span and the number of individuals, who are to be taken into consideration when 'usefulness' is assessed. But these problems are well known and there is no need to dwell on them once again. What is important here is to stress the pragmatist failure to appreciate the real significance of the contrast between serving *many* ends and serving *one* restricted and clearly specified end.

Old pragmatism was blinded by its conflict with Hegelianism and the Hegelian pursuit of the One, of the great unity (whether in things or in selecting aims), and consequently it simply loved to dwell on the tangled multiplicity of ends in real life. This is indeed so – life is complex – and pragmatists were perhaps closer to 'real life' than Hegelians. But this is *not* the way in which the one–many opposition hits the problem of knowledge.

Knowledge, more even than other forms of production perhaps, hinges in the division of labour and the separation of functions.

[11] Cf. Robin Horton, 'African Traditional Thought and Modern Science', *Africa*, **37**, 1967, pp. 50–71, 155–87.

Scientific thought is distinct from pre-scientific forms of adaptation by being subjected to one, and not to multiple criteria, or at least to a highly delimited set of criteria (compatibility with what is established, elegance and simplicity, extension to new areas). Moreover, it contains an in-built tendency to extrapolate its findings to areas in which 'the environment' is as yet making no impact on the organism or community in question – whereas of course blind, unconscious natural selection can only respond to an environment which is actually making an impact. Science is, so to speak, gratuitously provocative. The nearest thing which may modify this picture is that evolution sometimes also selects for an unspecified general adaptability, as opposed to specific adaptation – in other words for intelligence.

But, in as far as this free-ranging adaptability serves the multiple ends of adaptation, it will still be quite distinct from the relatively single-purpose pursuit of truth. Concretely, the fruits of pre-scientific human intelligence may often have been much richer than those of the relatively austere scientific spirit: the art and culture of some pre-scientific civilisations may well be more exciting than that of scientific ones. 'What James looked for, and indeed found partial proof of. . .was support for his own native conviction that the universe is an infinitely richer, warmer, more varied and indeed more "jumpy" place than nineteenth century materialist doctrines would have us believe.'[12] It is also probably true that such a free-ranging adaptability, which may correspond fairly closely to what is normally termed intelligence, must have been a precondition of the scientific spirit, and also that it may itself have been produced simply by the play of natural selection. But this does not make natural selection and the scientific spirit identical. The turn it has taken when it became science is neither itself dictated by natural selection – how much for humanity's chances of survival now? – nor does it, in the new austere blinkered restriction of its aims, simply exemplify adaptability as such. It is quite distinct.

So Pragmatism has indeed stumbled on an important binary opposition in its interest in the contrast between pluralism and monism of aims, but its tie-up of truth – at any rate of scientific truth – with pluralism is a veritable inversion of the real state of affairs. Natural selection operates by bombarding its candidates from a wide variety of angles and subjecting them to a great variety of

[12] W. B. Gallie, *Pierce and Pragmatism*, Harmondsworth, 1952, p. 24.

tests. It thus selects for a great multiplicity of 'virtues'. Modern cognitive growth, on the other hand, selects only for a very restricted range of qualities. The idea that these qualities make for survival is highly questionable and certainly unproven.

The pluralism which Pragmatism values is intimately connected with another important trait, namely its rejection of discontinuities. Its opponents like to insist on some pretty fundamental, radical ditches in reality: pragmatists on the other hand are sceptical of such dualisms. We have seen that they characteristically insist on what may be called the Continuity Thesis concerning biological evolution and the growth of human knowledge; but they are just as keen on the continuity between commonsensical knowledge and scientific knowledge, between science and philosophy, between cognition and evaluation, between truths of reason and matters of fact, between formal and substantive knowledge. The denial of dichotomies seems to be distinctly habit-forming:

> John Dewey has spent a good part of his life hunting and shooting at dualisms: body–mind, theory–practice, percept–concept, value–science, learning–doing, sensation–thought, external–internal. They are always fair game and Dewey's prose rattles with fire whenever they come into view. At times the philosophical forest seems more like a gambler at a penny arcade, and the dualist dragons move along obligingly and monotonously while Dewey picks them off with deadly accuracy.[13]

There is indeed a kind of affinity, at the very least, between this trait and the pragmatist's other choices in the various binary alternatives we have drawn. For one thing, there is a connection between the pluralism, the insistence on so many diverse ploys and aims, and this feature: many small distinctions as it were drown the big ones which thus disappear. All the small distinctions count, but they do not allow a few of their own number to dominate.

There are also other connections. The Big Divides were characteristically used as the principal means of articulating the Cosmic Exile, of attaining the external, extra-territorial stance from which cognition was to be validated, and in terms of which its Fundamental Constitutional Law of Knowledge was to be drawn up.

[13] Morton White, *Pragmatism and the American Mind*, New York, 1973, p. 121.

Pragmatism denies either the need or the feasibility of such a Prior Philosophy, and is naturally suspicious of the conceptual devices which seem to make it possible. If Big Divides help to formulate a Prior Philosophy, that only reinforces the suspicion in which they are held. William James, in *Pragmatism*, spoke critically of Idealist philosophy as a kind of Shining Temple on a Hill, the simple classical lines of which bore little resemblance to the tangled complexity of real life. In Quine's hands, and perhaps before, Pragmatism itself acquires this quality. The sense of continuity, the eager erosion of those 'dualisms' and radical discontinuities with which other philosophers operated, results in a curious standardisation of everything, a new dusk in which all cows are the same shade of grey, in which all cognitive advances partake in the same status of corrigible adjustments in some big cognitive corporation. Small differences are not denied, of course, but being so small and numerous, like the petty shareholders in a property-owning democracy, they cannot really defy the great organisations, those great 'corporate bodies', which only face experience collectively.

I have now attempted both a characterisation and a criticism of Pragmatism, and the criticism of course hinges on the characterisation. The characterisation is expressed in terms of a whole series of linked binary oppositions, such that the pragmatist is he who thinks in terms of these oppositions, and makes his choice wholly or predominantly from one side of the barrier. The manner of setting out the situation, in fact, owes more to William James himself than to the recent *structuraliste* penchant for binary oppositions. But unlike James' list of tender-minded and tough-minded traits, which of course inspires my approach, this is not meant to be an overall typology of human beings or of styles of thought. On the contrary, I hold this particular series of contrasts, and many of the links between them, to be historically most specific, to arise in a particular social and intellectual situation – but it is precisely in that situation that Pragmatism is born, and Pragmatism is basically a name for that cluster of choices in that series of alternatives. (See p. 258.)

So much for a characterisation, which of course was meant to be as fair and unprejudiced as I could make it, and to bring out the underlying feel and force of both positions. There is an interesting difference between older Pragmatism and Quine's, hinging on the fact that the earlier version was reacting primarily to the Idealists, whereas the modern form is engaged in a debate with other empiricists. The current situation is enshrined in the very form of Quine's paper, which asks, in effect – *within* our wider and shared empiricist faith – is Pragmatism going the right way, or is it heretical?

Pragmatist	*Anti-pragmatist*
Cheerful, in the sense of willing to proceed in a happy-go-lucky spirit, using any tool to hand, trusting own powers	anxiety-imbued sense of crisis, which insists on circumspect and above all methodical inspection of any tools, lest they be contaminated
hence pluralistic in aims and methods	hence monistic or near-monistic
hence inclined to seek continuities between biological and social history, philosophy and science, formal and substantive knowledge, etc.	operates in terms of radical dichotomies
critical of feasibility or need for 'cosmic exile', 'prior philosophy'	suspicious of current trends, hankers after external, independent validation
in this sense 'naturalistic'	extra-natural vantage point sought
favours third person idiom	drawn to ego-redoubt
finds evidence or illustration in successful (or seemingly so) developments – biological evolution, history of science since seventeenth century, modern economic history	sensitive to both the stagnant and cataclysmic periods of human history
favours laissez faire in intellectual sphere	favours at least occasional intervention in name of fundamental principle, when threatened by chaos or stalemate

Now the old Idealists were themselves opposed to dualisms, notably of the Kantian kind. Hence, when they were inebriated by the Great Continuities, more sober men such as the pragmatists would be tempted to stress the idea of sensory evidence against them; hence that occasional inclination to first person sensory language which Quine considers regrettably regressive, rather than to behaviourist talk.

Neo-positivists on the other hand used 'sense data language' (or equivalents) as a tacitly extra-mundane stance from which to establish their position and damn others. Quine is concerned with this internal dispute between brother-empiricists rather than with the earlier one, which helps to explain distinctive traits of his particular version of the pragmatist syndrome. But now for the evaluation.

It seems to me that pragmatism is indefensible, because radical cataclysms do occur. When they do, cheerfulness, in the sense defined – a happy reliance on the existing stock of tools and ideas, without any effort at a prior philosophy – simply is not a workable strategy. The pragmatist illusion that it *is* viable springs from an unacknowledged – and indeed unconscious – reliance on previous and successful efforts by 'prior philosophers' to clear the ground in such crises: and it is unwittingly parasitic on them. Pragmatism is distinctively American not, as is sometimes wrongly suggested, in that it seems to ratify some specific form of economic organisation or ethos, but in that it emerged within a society which takes cognitive growth altogether for granted; and it does this because it only came into being at a time when such growth had indeed become the norm. As Quine himself has it: The naturalistic philosopher 'begins his reasoning within the inherited world theory *as a going concern*' (italics mine). But the inherited human world is generally nothing of the kind. When it *is* a going and growing concern, that is a highly idiosyncratic, miraculous and most fortunate condition. It needs to be understood and explained, rather than invoked as a reason for why no explanation is required at all. But that is what the denial of the need for a 'prior philosophy' really amounts to. A 'prior philosophy' specifies and justifies the general traits or preconditions of cognitive growth *without* invoking an allegedly general, pervasive, natural process as the main explanation. The denial of a 'prior philosophy' hinges on a background theory (which in Quine's case, most laudably, is not tacit but is often avowed) about the overall natural process; and this background theory is false. By contrast, a prior philosophy, rightly treating cognitive health as exceptional, must endeavour to stand outside nature in order to identify and to justify the healthy state. Cheerfulness – the reliance on a happy condition in which, all in all, the tools that are to hand can be trusted – is no substitute at all. It is incapable of identifying and selecting: it loves the lot, or at any rate, much too much of it.[14]

One might sum up all this by saying that it is a refutation of Pragmatism by an argument from Max Weber. What really distinguishes Weber from nineteenth-century evolutionisms, of which Pragmatism is a surviving example, is a strong sense of the discontinuity between the modern outlook and the past: a recognition that, contrary to the feeling of Hegelians, Marxists, Darwinists and others, our outlook is not simply a refinement or perpetuation of what had been going on for a long long time. On the contrary, it was, to speak in these terms, a remarkable mutation which need not really have happened at all and indeed could not have been expected to happen. It needs to be understood not by invoking the same principles as explain everything else, by saying this is just more of the

---

[14] Quine is of course a somewhat idiosyncratic pragmatist. His chief idiosyncratic trait arises from the fact that his vision is produced, so to speak, by the intersection of two distinct, and mutually incommensurate reductionist programmes, the naturalist (third person) one, and nominalism. It is this which gives that vision its singular quality, its so to speak Dali-esque flavour, or the sense of a montage resulting from the completion of two pictures in different dimensions, as it were. But his attitude to these two programmes, and hence their implementation, are also quite different and unsymmetrical, and this adds to the feel of oddity. His implementation of naturalism is enthusiastic and less than fastidious: the transition from promise to execution is facile and less than scrupulous, the hope is easily mistaken for fulfilment, and if admissions are wrung from him about the failure to implement (for instance by Chomsky's points about the innate elements in language learning), one does not feel that the concessions are taken too seriously, or their implications fully appreciated. There seems to be a cheerful confidence that it will be all right on the night, that the programme must be sound, and never mind a few difficulties. By contrast, he is utterly sensitive and severely fastidious with respect to the execution of nominalism, and in fact his standards in this matter are unusually, perhaps uniquely, high. Moreover, his love of mathematics, and hence of the abstract entities which according to him it requires, makes him less than displeased if the nominalist programme fails, as indeed on his view it does. His logical fastidiousness and his ontological preference seem to converge at this point. All the same, one never knows which of the two programmes is put into operation where, or why, or just how far it will be carried out. This gives Quine's world both its unpredictable and its odd flavour.

same, but rather by isolating the specific causes, and traits, of something which historically is so *very* idiosyncratic.

Weber was not specially concerned with the history of epistemology, but it is a field in which his ideas have considerable application. The modern growth of knowledge is as dramatic, unique, and discontinuous with the past, as is the modern productive style and economic organisation. There are many obvious parallels between them. Modern post-Cartesian philosophy is, even or especially when it thinks it is dealing with knowledge in general and at all times, an attempt to understand, delimit and justify this unique cognitive development. Pragmatism is in error precisely because it does not consider it to be unique and consequently tries to explain it by invoking factors relevant at *all* times. This illusion springs from the fact that Pragmatism was born so very much *within* this unique phenomenon that it takes it for granted, believes it to be universal, and really cannot conceive that things could be very different. The protestant work ethic, which appears in Quine as 'scientific method', is taken as self-evident.

The idea that the world is so constructed that this ethic is also, by and large, rewarded, is likewise taken for granted. Quine is painfully caught between his naturalism (which is a kind of protestant egalitarianism – no one is allowed to give himself airs of standing outside nature) and his view of knowledge as man-made. The former leads to a certain realism, the latter to a subjectivism or idealism. The realism is manifested in the insistence that 'posits' such as material objects, forces, or abstract classes, must be seen as full and equal citizens of the realm of being, together with other well-entrenched parts of current science, and *not* treated as ontologically suspect second-class citizens. However, the justification of their full citizenship – 'they expedite our dealings with sense experience' – surreptitiously restores a tacit sovereignty, a prior and fuller, unrestricted citizenship, to sense experiences. It thus constitutes a covert and unwitting recognition of that empiricist prior philosophy which officially he repudiates. I frankly do not understand how he thinks he can square these viewpoints, and the passages in which he claims to do so, such as a remarkable one in his paper, seem to me brilliant displays of literary sleight of hand. At times he also falls back on a coy and playful objectivism-through-ultra-subjectivism – *my* viewpoint is objective for me because obviously *I* cannot have anything else, so there. 'We cannot talk otherwise.' But just as characteristically, and more fundamentally, he falls back on this optimistic evolutionist background theory – the Holy Spirit under the name of Scientific Method is guiding us along the right path, so all's well, and no constitutional law is required for the Republic of learning – and this background theory is mistaken.

Part III
The political predicament

13

Nationalism, or the new confessions of a justified Edinburgh sinner

Nationalism is a problem, for Marxists and others. Tom Nairn's comparative and theoretical study of nationalisms in Britain[1] is a rich, valuable and stimulating contribution to the subject. The book's blurb tells one it is 'the most powerful and original Marxist reflection on the United Kingdom'. For once one has cause (no irony intended) to be grateful to the blurb for a piece of information. The book is indeed powerful and original, but I would have had some difficulty in deciding on internal evidence just what the author's attitude to Marxism is. Whatever it is, it is *nuancé*, complex, not to say tortured. There is no question of some simple unambiguous alignment, such as the flat statement in the blurb might suggest.

Let us begin at the end, with the author's complex and fascinating attitude to Marxism. 'O Lord, help thou my unbelief' is a comic cry that has often been heard. 'O History, restore my faith in thy wisdom', or perhaps, 'reveal thyself at last' seems to be a kind of Marxist equivalent. The Christians have passed through at least three stages: the first, when they really believed what they said, when the actual message and its promise of salvation was what attracted them to it, and when the historic continuity with earlier believers was an irrelevancy; the second, when they had to struggle to retain their faith in the face of increasingly pressing grounds for unbelief, and when many fell by the wayside; and the third, that of modernist theology, when the 'belief' has acquired negligible (or sliding-scale) content, when the claim to continuity with their purely nominal predecessors becomes the only real psychic reward and significance of adherence, and it is doctrine which is played down as

[1] *The Break-Up of Britain. Crisis and Neo-Nationalism*, by Tom Nairn, London, 1977.

an irrelevancy. Marxists seem doomed to pass through the same stages of development. When they reach the third stage (some already have), their views also will be of no intellectual interest. Tom Nairn is still in the second stage, though there are signs of his approaching its terminal period (which is why I have some doubts about that flat statement in the blurb). His struggles with or for faith are still passionate, troubled and sincere, which is what gives the book some of its interest.

In the passages in which he articulates his reasons for doubt, Tom Nairn is devastating. Consider the following observations drawn from the opening of the final, culminating, most theoretical chapter in the book:

> The theory of nationalism represents Marxism's great historical failure. It may have had others as well. . .yet none of these is as important. . .this failure was inevitable. . .but it can now be understood. . .historical materialism can. . . escape from the. . .impasse in which it has been locked on the issue. However, the cost of doing so is probably 'Marxism'. . .It means seeing Marxism itself as a part of history in a quite uncomplimentary sense. . .It means losing for all time that God-like posture which, in the guise of science, Marxism took over from Idealist philosophy (and ultimately from religion) [p. 329].

That would seem to be that, almost. The only thing which does not make this kind of passage a final goodbye to faith is that it is 'Marxism', in single quotes, which is being abandoned, which rather hints at a true, real, quote-less Marxism hidden behind mere 'Marxism' and struggling to get out; and also, that historical materialism is allowed to escape. But if historical materialism is simply the view that the pattern of history is crucially constrained by very earthy factors such as hunger, fear and violence, and not merely by men's concepts or ideas, then historical materialism is indeed a true and admirable doctrine. (Under a variety of forms, Wittgensteinian, *structuraliste*, 'phenomenological' and other, the contrary Idealist phantasy of the *Allmacht des Begriffes* is currently very much in vogue, and even encompasses soi-disant Marxists.)

But, of course, that is not that. This is merely the passage in the saint's autobiography in which he describes the torments of doubt. Precisely by painting so sombre, so harsh a picture of the prospects for faith, tension is built up, and the drama of recovery of a new and purified faith, is all the greater and more glorious. And just what is the phoenix which emerges from the ashes?

It has both philosophical and sociological components. (The two are not to be distinguished sharply in Nairn's view it seems, and I agree with him on this. Nevertheless for purposes of exposition it may be convenient to observe conventional lines of distinction.) It is plain from the last sentence of the book, and from an earlier passage, that Nairn means by philosophy mankind's attempt to understand and orient itself in its predicament, as it reaches that historic stage when at last a measure of understanding, choice and control become possible for us. In the last sentence he makes plain that the failure to decipher the riddle of nationalism is not just *a* failure to deal with *a* problem, but '*the* defeat of Western philosophy' (italics mine). And earlier (p. 350) he also refers, commenting on the excesses of chauvinism, to 'the defeat of Western Philosophy by nationalism' (in marked contrast to the work of Elie Kedourie, who considers nationalism to be the offspring of philosophy). Evidently, philosophy for Nairn, as for Marx, is not one subject amongst others, but is intimately related to the drama of our collective existence, and is the possibly opaque expression of our best aspirations. But it is not unrelated to the concrete conditions of our existence:

> I think it is true that the real basis of philosophical speculation is the complex of issues surrounding economic development [p. 358].

He makes this remark, incidentally, just after rejecting as 'not quite true' my observation that the real subject of modern philosophy is industrialisation. But what I meant by that was virtually equivalent to what he himself says in this passage.

This manner of seeing philosophy does of course in Nairn's case have roots in the Hegelo-Marxian tradition, and thus this is one of the elements which we can discern as surviving from the old faith. He firmly repudiates the view of the 'dialectic' which implies that:

> history is a boxing-match with rules, where we can be secretly sure what kind of 'synthesis' is going to emerge. . .
> On the contrary. . .there has never been any certainty as to who would win. . .the 'antithesis' came near to destroying the 'thesis' altogether [p. 344].

Nevertheless, he does seem to think of history as a conflict in which one can identify goodies and baddies (though without guarantee of happy-end), and in which the goodies are somehow linked to thought, rationality and philosophy. He also indicates approval of the ancient, archetypal opposition of idealism and materialism, aligning himself with the latter, in an unexceptionable sense of the term, by insisting on explanations of nationalism which

> award them a real force and weight in modern historical development. . .by explaining the material reasons for this newly acquired leverage [p. 358].

He also resembles Marx in being a bit ambivalent about 'philosophy' and sliding over into using the term in a pejorative sense, which yet remains related to the other meaning: though philosophy is on the right side, yet it is less than fulfilment or clarity. An intellectual battle 'can never be won or lost' precisely 'because of its "philosophical" character' (p. 358); 'Marxism' is rebuked for its 'inability. . .to escape from the level of philosophy of "dialectical materialism". . .'

So what would be *better*? ' "Real" or historical explanation. . .' And what will this look like?

> 'Marxism' must become for the first time an authentic world-theory. . .a theoretical world-view (the successor of religion and philosophy) which is actually founded upon the social development of the whole world [p. 360].

What would be the internal structure of this theory? It seems to retain something from the older 'Marxism'. In the past

> it was not yet possible to employ the concepts of historical materialism in relation to their proper object, the only object which gives them proper meaning: that is, the world political economy. This is the only genuine, 'structure' which can be held to explain the assorted 'superstructures' of capitalist reality (including nationalism).

In a sense we are (at least intellectually) fortunate to be living at this time, for truth is at last ready to reveal itself. There is something a little suspect about considering one's own time to be the moment chosen by history for its self-revelation, but I suppose it has to reveal itself *some* time:

> the task of framing a 'theory' of nationalism is. . .that of reinterpreting modern history as a whole. . .the puzzle of

Marxism's 'failure' over nationalism is simple: the problem
is so central, so large, and so intimately related to other
issues that it could not be focused on properly before.
History itself is now helping us towards a solution [p. 357].

Qui est donc cette dame? Having mentioned her, Nairn becomes
suitably reverent:

It would be presumptuous and unnecessary to say much
more. . .here [p. 357].

Respectful reverence for *cette dame* is perhaps a mark of the New
Left Books house style. It is found on occasion in the works of Mr
Percy Anderson. It is a pity it inhibits Nairn from saying more, for
what he has to say is of great interest. But the lady (whilst beyond the
reach of reliable prediction which would also comfortably warrant
our future), appears to be nevertheless susceptible to summary in one
unique theory, materialist in kind, and to be the heir of religion,
philosophy and 'Marxism'. So the repudiation of the God-like
posture, inherited from Idealist philosophy and religion, with which
the final chapter begins, seems also to be, at the very least, ambivalent. The idea of a unique truth-summary of global history, even one
which does not predetermine the future, does seem to me somewhat
God-like. This is an observation, not a criticism. This unique world-
theory, founded upon the social development of the whole world,
constitutes the residue saved by the author in his inner struggles: the
need to understand nationalism was the spur, and its decipherment,
even if piously and regrettably left incomplete, leaves us with this
'grain from the husks represented by the defeat of Western Philosophy' (terminal sentence of the book).

So much for the very interesting and clearly inward, un-facile,
philosophic aspect of Nairn's conclusion. But before leaving this for
the more specific, sociological aspects of his theory of nationalism,
one further remark about his relationship to Marxism. His general
position firmly dissociates itself from all Marxist dogmatism and
obscurantism, having been impelled towards this, it appears, by his
struggle with the problem of nationalism and the Marxist failure to
cope with it. But when dealing with specific issues he is not always so
free from it. In one of the two Scottish chapters, Nairn observes:

The Scots know quite well that the North Sea will be
sucked dry mainly to keep this Model-T Leviathan going.
The chances of the new resources being employed effectively

for the long-awaited modernisation of Britain's industrial
economy are absolutely zero. Colossal borrowings have
already been made against the oil revenues. Every single
barrel of North Sea Oil will go on being used to get the
Crown Jewels back from the pawn shop [p. 191].

The passage begins as an account of the Scottish state of mind, but
the author evidently endorses without reserve the pessimistic prediction about the use of oil. I am not qualified to argue with him on
this factual issue. What worries me is the confident tone. Is the
internal British situation really so tightly organised and so transparent as to permit such confident prediction? Is this not the old
Marxist tone, inspired by the assumption that we have the key to
history, an assumption which Nairn repudiates in his general position, where he makes it quite plain that (a) we do not possess the key
and (b) if we do it will not unlock the future?

But now for Nairn's concrete theory of nationalism. This I believe
to be substantially correct, though it is a pity that piety *vis-à-vis*
history seems to have inhibited him from spelling it out in all details.
What puzzles me is why he should think this theory compatible
with Marxism, of *any* kind. The theory in effect stands Marx on his
head. The crucial matter, as Nairn recognises, is the role of the
concept of class. It is best to quote his own words here. The old
Marxist belief was that

class is always far more important in history than the petty
differentiae nationalism seems to deal in. Class struggle was
invariably the motor of historical change, nationality a mere
epiphenomenon of it. Hence, it was literally inconceivable
that the former should be eclipsed by the latter [p. 351].

But in fact

As capitalism spread, and smashed the ancient social
formations surrounding it, they always tended to fall apart
along the fault-lines contained inside them. It is a matter
of elementary truth that these lines were nearly always ones
of nationality (although in certain well-known cases deeply
established religious divisions could perform the same
function). They were never ones of class [p. 353].

One cannot go much further in repudiating the view that history is
the story of class conflict.

But it is important not to misunderstand Nairn's view at this point. He is *not*, most emphatically, replacing the concept of *class* by that of *nation*. That may happen in nationalist ideology, or in some of its variants, but it is not justified by the facts of the case. National-ism is not to be explained by the alleged existence of 'nations'. (It is the other way round.) The crucial fact is that of uneven economic development in a unified world economy and the tensions which this inescapably engenders.

As I believe that my own views on this matter overlap with Nairn's, I shall allow myself to summarise the position in my own words, partly because Nairn tantalisingly circles around the theory and, perhaps from a misguided reverence for history, which has not spoken yet, does not articulate it firmly. There is of course a risk that I may misrepresent him, but if I thereby provoke him into a more definite formulation, we shall all be the gainers.

The position is this: modern industrial economy, unlike earlier social formations, stimulates a certain strong aspiration towards equality. Nairn does not specify the factors which conduce towards this end, but my own list of them (*not* by order of importance) would be something as follows:

1. Occupational mobility, inherent in innovation and economic expansion, which makes it very difficult to make men internalise visions of themselves which contain permanent inferiority. Modern society is not mobile because it is egalitarian; it is egalitarian because it is mobile.

2. An occupational structure which involves constant contact with numerous strangers. Profound inequalities of status would only be tolerable and not lead to friction if the ranking were widely accepted. In a complex and inter-acting mobile society, there is no way of ensuring this; so basic equality becomes the normal presumption.

3. The precondition of employability, dignity, full moral citizen-ship and an acceptable social identity is a certain level of education including literacy. Thus socialisation is standardised and in the hands of a central agency, and not of family, clan or guild. It requires a single cultural/linguistic medium.

4. The separation of working life from private life makes for equality. You cannot be a serf from 10 a.m. to 5 p.m. A real serf has to be full-time. A temporary work-role is not a full identity.

5. Affluence and welfare provisions make men less vulnerable to economic pressure.

6. In the absence of a shared belief system which would sanction inequality and subjection, egalitarianism is a residual legatee, a kind

of moral null-hypothesis. Society needs some moral background assumption if conflicts are to be resolved, simply as a base line for negotiations. Egalitarianism has assumed this role.

7. In the modern complex division of labour, many jobs at least are talent-specific. This makes it harder to use the hereditary principle. This was not so in the past – any fool can be a feudal lord. Not everyone can be a physics professor. (Professors in the social sciences are another matter.)

8. Affluence means that the effective use of wealth is no longer over things, but over symbols and people. In things, we are close to the ceiling of what we can use. But these, in turn, can almost as easily, or more easily, be obtained by occupancy of roles rather than by wealth. This diminishes the role of wealth, and increases the importance of bureaucratic, non-heritable roles or posts. Past quasi-bureaucratic empires had to use priests, foreigners, eunuchs or slaves as bureaucrats. Ordinary subjects were too unreliable, liable to be swayed by their kin links within the society, or to use them to increase their own power. Only slaves who had no ancestry, or priests or eunuchs who had no posterity (avowable or real), offered better prospects of loyal service. The Ottoman Empire went furthest in finding a solution to this problem. In modern society, a *very* large proportion of jobs in fact require bureaucratic virtues. *We are all mamluks now.*

9. Another related factor: the difference between expensive and cheap objects is now mainly status-symbolic. Plonk and good wine differ, but not much. (People are always irritated when told this. They prefer to think they are fastidious rather than snobbish.) But in an increasingly bureaucratic or *mamluk*-ised world, status is obtainable in ways other than by wealth. The sexual revolution, by undermining one important motive for seeking control over people, may strengthen this trend.

10. The pervasiveness of the work ethic diminishes the extent to which people are willing to seek status other than through their occupational role.

11. Power in industrial society is a curious thing. In agrarian society, it consists basically of the means for taking a part of a man's produce from him, and making him work for you. It is persistent and visible. Under the condition of modern division of labour, it consists of the occupancy of a post near a crucial lever, at a moment when that part of the machinery happens to be decisive. Different levers matter at different times, and different individuals are near

them at different times also. So, although in a sense power is highly concentrated, in another sense it is highly elusive and half-invisible.

All this does not mean that modern society is deeply or fundamentally egalitarian. It is not. But the inequality is camouflaged under a similarity of culture and life-style, which in turn arises from the very nature of social organisation; and it attaches statistically to individuals or categories of individuals, and it tends only to erupt into conflict if those categories of individuals possess cultural means for identifying themselves – in other words, if they at least look like a 'nation'. Inequality is moderated, camouflaged and tolerable unless visibly related to the kind of diacritical sign which breeds 'ethnic' conflict and generates self-conscious ethnicity. It then appears as 'nationalism'.

Equality of status and a *continuous, shared culture* (the medium of a society with a centralised socialisation/education process) seems a precondition for the functioning of a complex, occupationally mobile, technically advanced society. Hence it does not easily tolerate cultural fissures within itself, especially if they correlate with inequality which thereby becomes frozen, aggravated, visible and offensive. Thus nationalism, the principle 'one state one culture', *Cuius regio, eius lingua,* is a corollary both of the facts making for equality and of the obstacles they encounter. It is not, as Kedourie says, that nationalism imposes homogeneity; it is the need for homogeneity which generates nationalism.

Above all, the quasi-egalitarianism generated by the new type of division of labour, and the shared kind of culture, which is inherently characteristic of industrial and in some measure of industrialising society, is brutally violated by uneven development. Taking the world as a whole, economic equality is conspicuously absent. Development is uneven.

It is at this point that cultural, 'ethnic' cleavages make their entry. They have a double significance. When they correlate with the statistical distribution of unequal life chances, they provide a means for the less privileged to identify and organise. They also aggravate the inequality: if, let us say, the privileged are blue-skinned and the underprivileged are green-skinned, then this will facilitate discrimination against the green-skinned, by making them identifiable and excluding even those green ones who can make it and hence would otherwise suffer from no disadvantage. (For 'blue' and 'green' you can also substitute any deeply engrained cultural, linguistic or religious trait.) They then provide leadership for their underprivileged green brethren.

So the theory does not replace 'class' by 'nation' as an explanatory notion. It makes the crystallisation of 'nations' a *consequence* of (a) inequality, (b) the situation in which, unlike pre-industrial conditions, inequality can no longer be easily tolerated, and in which (c) the significance of culture ('nationality'), in an economy requiring literate, educated personnel, is very great.

To put the matter in another way: traditional society was compatible with crass inequality, and often found it useful to underscore both differences in status and occupational specialisation by cultural ('ethnic') differentiation, whether real or invented. It was positively useful to have such differentiation *inside* the polity, and there was no need at all to use it to define its *boundaries*. For the various reasons indicated (and perhaps others), modern society is allergic to *conspicuous* inequality, and where cultural differences persist within it which also correlate with inequalities, these are then used as markers for alignment in conflict. The 'classes' that really matter are those which are produced by uneven development; and they attain 'consciousness' through ethnicity. If 'ethnic' differentials are lacking, they fail to reach 'consciousness'.

There are probably differences in stress between Nairn's version and mine. He seems more concerned with collective reaction to backwardness, and less with individual life-chances, than I am. Probably, however, these differences spring mainly from the background beliefs in terms of which the view is articulated. For instance, I do not find his analogy between nationalism and Freud's view of neurosis illuminating (p. 359), nor am I much tempted by the residual element of Marxist optimism which he very cautiously expresses in the same place:

> Socialism over a sufficiently large part of the world *may* represent the necessary condition for a cure one day. But this is a hazardous speculation [p. 359, italics Nairn's].

Having concentrated on what I deem to be his central theoretical concern, I have said little about the bulk of the book dealing with much more specific material. As he says (p. 356):

> In the 1970s there has even reappeared some likelihood of new barriers inside some of the oldest, most stable unified states of western Europe: France, the United Kingdom and Spain.

The bulk of the book deals with the manner of the reappearance of these barriers in the United Kingdom. No doubt the book will be read by many for these parts, as an unusual contribution to the 'condition of Britain' debate. But it is written, above all, from the viewpoint of the author's interest in nationalism.[2]

At least one of the intra-United Kingdom nationalisms presents no problem for the theory outlined. The Ulster conflict is and was one between two groups with rather different life-chances. The deeply internalised religious difference both aggravated the inequality by inhibiting movement from the less-favoured groups, and made it possible to react against it by giving it an easily intelligible symbol. Scotland, on the other hand, presents a difficulty. It was conspicuous by the erstwhile feebleness of its nationalism; and when of late it had become strong, it did not seem to fit the theory. Nairn concentrates on explaining the former fact more than the latter. If nationalism is basically the consequence of uneven development, of suffering the indignities of backwardness in an overall situation which no longer makes inferiority palatable, then it is of course relevant to point out the positive advantages enjoyed in the 'developmental' process by Lowland Scotland. The Highlands were simply crushed after 1745, and that, too, fits the theory perfectly well:

> In 1745 an army from these backwoods had struck to within 120 miles of London...This incredible near-reverse of fortunes decided the outcome. The *Gaeltacht* was to be allowed no further opportunity of disrupting civilised progress. In the subsequent English and Lowland invasion its old social structure was pulverised too completely for any later nationalist response to be possible. This would not have been so easy...if there had been a Gaelic middle class and some Gaelic towns [p. 148].

As for the Lowlands, there is no mystery:

> No new intellectual class at once national in scope and disgruntled at its life-prospects arose, because the Scottish petty bourgeoisie had little reason to be discontented. In the overwhelming rush of the Scottish industrial revolution, even the regions of intermediate social change were quickly sucked in [p. 119].

[2] The book should be read in conjunction with Michael Hechter's *Internal Colonialism. The Celtic Fringe in British National Development, 1536–1966* (Routledge & Kegan Paul, London, 1975).

On the re-emergent, second-round nationalism of our day, Nairn has a less clear-cut answer. Perhaps history has not spoken yet. The phenomenon can hardly be explained in terms of differential life-chances of individual Scots. My own feeble suggestion would be that in an era of economic centralisation, when a large proportion of resources is inevitably controlled by the state, any segment or region of society lucky enough to be endowed with the means for clear self-identification has good cause to constitute itself into a pressure group. Oil provided the Scots with the incentive, and the tartanry, which Nairn despises, with the easily intelligible and accessible symbolic means. Walter Scott may have been anti-nationalist when alive, but he amongst others provided the means for an unforeseen posterity.

It is impossible to discuss all the aspects of this varied yet coherent book, which deals with England and Wales as well, and in connection with most of them I am less than competent to do so. But, purely in the realm of shared values, I'd like to record my pleasure at his castigation of the insularity which leads so many leftists to be hostile to 'Europe'.

> There can be no equivalent of the god-like dynasties which ruled over past multi-national societies here. It is quite difficult to see why radicals should grieve over this. The reality of integration in Western Europe is working for them, as well as against them [p. 328].

14

A social contract in search of an idiom: the demise of the Danegeld state

An extra-terrestrial visitor, equipped with sociological perceptiveness, observing the advanced European countries in the nineteenth century, would have been puzzled by their social organisation. He would have noted a society roughly divided into two classes: the have-nots were a class more numerous, and were exploited by the haves. So far, nothing unusual: social structures in which a minority exploits a majority are extremely common, and they crop up all over the place in the history of mankind. Their presence calls for no comment. It is only their occasional absence which is remarkable.

But in nineteenth-century capitalism, there was nevertheless something quite remarkable: the exploited majority was essential for the system, which needed its labour, but its compliance with the requirements of the system was not enforced by any of the normal and customary methods. Slaves, serfs, members of servile castes, etc., are placed in their subordinate position by legal or ritual constraints, and visible force is present to ensure their submission. Force and ideology conspire in varying proportions to maintain them in subjection. Not so under capitalism...or at least, not so on the surface. On the contrary: it was, as Max Weber put it, formally free wage labour which manned the system. It was legally free to do what it chose, to work or to withhold its labour. Ideologically, the society did not preach submission, but was pervaded by a rampant egalitarianism. The equality before the law, formally enjoyed by the oppressed, was even in due course reinforced by full political rights.

Submission without sanctions
A mysterious situation indeed. No one in his senses would have devised such a system: if you must oppress, then your oppressive

system ought to possess sanctions for bending the wills of those who do not benefit from it. Otherwise it can hardly hope to survive. And, indeed, no one had ever designed this system: it had just happened.

Some thought they knew the secret of the system and of its capacity to survive, despite what it did to so many, and despite its failure to protect itself visibly from their resentment. The relative lack of coercive machinery was but a fraud, a façade. The coercion was, in this case, economic; and downright physical coercion was kept in reserve, to be used only against those who would defy the system of property rights through which the economic sanctions were applied.

Nevertheless, the society *was* inherently unstable and it had its contradictions, even if these were not quite those suggested by its most famous analyst. Why ever should this great majority, formally free, with full civic and eventually political rights, but without a real share in either the physical benefits or the cultural citizenship of the society, tolerate their condition, given the relative paucity of coercion or of ideological justification?

If the extra-terrestrial observer returned about a century later, he would find his puzzlement vindicated: the system was indeed unstable, it could not continue as it was, for these very reasons indicated; and it *had* moved on. It had also spread geographically. But it could move forward in a variety of ways.

The system had worked by employing formally free but economically constrained wage labour, deployed in large masses, switched from one employment to another, or to none at all, according to the convenience of economic rationality. Workers had to adjust to a form of existence in which work and life were distinct and separate, work itself being meaningless, extraneous, arduous and ill-remunerated.

For such a system, there is indeed one way forward which does remove the glaring contradiction between the 'formal freedom', on the one hand, and the great economic inducement to discontent on the other: deprive these helots of their formal freedom! Re-centralise the community, so that, once again, economic and political relations become congruent, as was normal throughout most of history. The economically and the politically powerful then become identical once again, and the economically underprivileged are also deprived of the political power to vent their discontent on the system. The returning observer will note that this solution has prevailed in most of Eastern Europe and is known as socialism.

This solution has the outstanding merit of removing the glaring contradiction of the previous system, in the simplest and most straightforward manner. The solution it offers, apart from its elegant internal coherence and logic, is reinforced by some additional props and advantages: it possesses a validating ideology which justifies the political control over the workers in terms of the workers' alleged own interest, needs and desires. These, admittedly, are not ascertained by any independent method: their endorsement of the system is axiomatic. The ideology possesses a conceptual device for this: 'consciousness' (failure to endorse equals lack of consciousness), a term whose logic is similar to that of 'grace' in Christianity. Anyone not possessed of grace or consciousness is inwardly perverted or unaware of his true interests; the validity of faith is vindicated by the absolute consensus of all those who really do know their own true interests, i.e. those who possess grace or consciousness. Apart from this slightly circular demonstration, the claim that the deprivation of the erstwhile formal freedom is done for the sake of the oppressed themselves has at any rate one piece of genuine factual support: at least the first generation of the new rulers is recruited in large part from the previously exploited class. Furthermore, with time there are also material inducements: labour becomes less arduous, and the material rewards become greater – though in this respect the system compares favourably only with the past, and not so much with other species of industrial society.

The half-integrated labour force

In other parts of the advanced industrial world, however, this system has not been adopted, notwithstanding its great logical elegance. But the great contradictions, noted by the observer in the nineteenth century, have been, if not overcome, markedly attenuated. The economic system continues to be manned by 'formally free wage labour' which does not own the means of production, and which is under some measure of economic constraint. But the constraint is much, much less severe than it was in the nineteenth century. The carrot has largely replaced the stick. The erstwhile proletarians are well organised in bodies protecting their interest. Though not owning the means of production, they are at least half integrated in the culture of the community: they bear little resemblance to that extraneous labour force of the previous era. And yet they are not fully integrated either. Their culture is identifiably other; they still do constitute wage labour, they can be dismissed if they are 'redundant', as the dreadful phrase goes; their work and their identity are distinct, and their productive unit is *not* their community. Work and life are still separated. Work continues to be a means, and not a fulfilment of one's identity.

Here is a paradox indeed. The capitalist state has very often been chary of using political constraint – unbelievably so, when compared with other historic social forms. Now it has gradually also divested itself, or been constrained to divest itself, of the economic stick. Diffused affluence, welfare provisions, defensive organisations, have jointly made the property-less class into something far from passive and defenceless. Yet they are still less well off than other groups. Why do they put up with it? What sustains the social order now?

The extra-terrestrial observer endowed with sociological curiosity might well wonder. Many radicals did indeed also wonder, during those long non-radical post-war years. Often they were puzzled and irritated. The observer will probably conclude that he is dealing with a Danegeld state, especially if he notes a variety of features of the situation: a steady spread of affluence, and the expectation – for the first time in history – of *continuous* improvement, which in due course comes to be seen as a right; a 'Keynesian' style of government, recognising the obligation not to allow much of that unemployment which had previously been the means of social control. The expansion was oiled by a gradual inflation of the currency. The whole mixture is further sugared by, as stated, a diminution of cultural and social distance, egalitarianism in education, and so forth. A regular and expected growth of income, social security and governmental responsibility for employment, constitute a permanent and growing bribe by means of which the system could purchase acquiescence from those who were not its most privileged beneficiaries.

Could such a solution work? For quite a time it did. In some places, and under some conditions, it might perhaps work indefinitely. But in the world's first industrial society, now sadly ageing, it suddenly seemed to break down in the 1970s and produced a frightening crisis. This crisis may be idiosyncratic, or it may be the foretaste of the fate of all Danegeld states; the future alone will tell. But one Danegeld state, at any rate, appears to be tottering on the verge of collapse. Britain stands at the edge of a precipice. But perhaps, under firm leadership, it will now take a step forward!

The Danegeld state

The famous old nineteenth-century analyst of the contradictions of capitalism had said the system needed a reserve army of the unemployed in order to work, and at this point at least, he seems to have been right. The system now had both the will and the means to do away with that reserve army, and on the whole managed to do so. Instead, it meant to purchase compliance in a sweeter way: it paid out its ever-growing Danegeld, and for a time all was well. The Danegeld had two components: full employment (or near enough) and economic growth. Both were produced in a mixed economy, with the help of a mild inflation which did few people much harm and on the contrary generated a gentle euphoria.

As some economists had warned, an inflation is liable to accelerate, and the acceleration combined disastrously with some other factors. Success of development in the third world pushed up world prices and, in conjunction with a new political cohesion, strengthened the bargaining position of the raw materials producers, and reinforced the inflation on the global scale. At home, welfare plus affluence and the general removal of the economic whip enormously strengthened the position of the erstwhile exploited. This occurred at that very moment at which they were threatened with a withdrawal of the newly habitual and as-of-right-expected increment in the Danegeld. The plot is now entirely familiar. The Danegeld state faced its crisis equipped with neither stick nor carrot. It had deliberately deprived itself of the stick, in a naïve expectation of gratitude and loyalty; without means of coercion, with a sudden shortage of carrots, indeed a shrinkage in the supply of carrots, it found it also did not have sufficient moral credit with the half-emancipated to see it through by an appeal to their loyalty.

Once upon a time, it was fashionable for men and societies to have crises of faith. Today we have crises of legitimacy. The mid 1970s are clearly a crisis of legitimacy, and of a specific kind: it is not the legitimacy of power, but the legitimacy of a style of *distribution* which is at stake. This being so, it is necessary to look at the available doctrines concerning the rightful distribution of industrial wealth.

There are at large in the world two major theories of how an industrial society may legitimately distribute the benefits at its disposal: the liberal *laissez-faire* theory, and Marxism. The two theories have close logical and historical links. They share rather more than their upholders suspect. They are, both of them, silly: and what is interesting is that they owe their shared absurdity more to the points which unite them than to those which separate them. Their paths to absurdity, however, are not altogether identical. Economic liberalism has a certain simplicity, which is aesthetically rather pleasing: if its conclusions are preposterous, this is a consequence of the omission of very crucial facts about our situation. Within its limitations, which are considerable, it argues in a neat and intelligible manner. By contrast, Marxism is a baroque structure, a weird combination of elements which might never have fused but for an accident of history.

Distribution according to the market

The *laissez-faire* picture runs roughly as follows: men have needs and desires, and work so as to satisfy these. Their productivity grows immensely through the division of labour and specialisation. This in turn raises the question of the terms on which mutually complementary producers exchange their products. A 'free market' is best: it stimulates further endeavour into production of those goods which 'at the margin' still give most satisfaction. The market price, if not warped by interference, is not merely the one leading to the best utilisation of effort, but also constitutes a fair and legitimate price. Notoriously, this theory is a theodicy: the market, if left alone, justifies the ways of God to man.

Certain objections to this doctrine are familiar and need not be restated: the 'fair' price for products and services, notably labour, need not be expected if those who bargain in the market are of unequal strength or occupy monopolistic positions. But certain other, even more fundamental objections are still not so likely to be perceived.

The ideology of economic liberalism derives its authority and plausibility from a certain background picture. The ideology is all at once normative, descriptive and explanatory. It tells us how the problem of distribution should rightly be solved, but at the same time it also tells us how social life works and how our society, with all the wealth it has available for distribution, arose at all. The normative part is in a loose way a corollary of the other elements. The hold which this vision has over its adherents is generally reinforced by the fact that it is very firmly built into the basic notions of that strange mixture of second-rate mathematics and bad sociology known as economic theory. Within this system, the notions which carry and imply this vision allow no alternatives, and those who have internalised these notions generally simply cannot conceive any alternative to them.

The support it offers for the free market determination of rewards is both positive and negative. The negative element is important, and is particularly often re-invoked in our time. It is an argument from the absence, or the impossibility, indeed the logical and practical absurdity of any alternative to market decisions. The argument is usually put forward in a triumphant tone of voice, implying that the opponent is hopelessly cornered: how – so goes the triumphant argument – how else are you to determine relative rewards and prices? Think of the countless number of commodities and the countless skills and performances. What superman, what supercomputer could conceivably adjudicate between competing claims? Complexity alone would defeat him; and what authority could his verdicts have, anyway? A technical impossibility is compounded by a moral one.

By contrast, the impersonal mechanism of the market, by responding to supply and demand, can, given a little time, adjust all rewards as it possesses an automatic mechanism for correcting its own errors. The market will push up the price of that which is undervalued and pull down that which is overvalued, if only it is not interfered with. This mechanism is both sensitive and impersonal; being impersonal, its verdicts are morally acceptable. By contrast, any human and political decisions are always offensive to at least one party. The argument from the acceptability of the impersonal can even survive the abandonment of the argument from sensitivity.

The negative argument usually comes along with a certain important historic vision, an overall nominalism and empiricism. Superstitious societies of the past supposed that the Nature of Things or a Divine Will decreed the Just Price or Wage. Indeed, the idea of a Just Wage was just the last echo of the theory of a divine allocation of earthly fates, its translation into the idiom of economic life. R. H. Tawney seemed to share such a view when he observed, in connection with the Labour Theory of Value, that Marx was the last of the scholastics. Anyway, the protagonists of *laissez-faire* are proud to be free of such scholastic or animistic superstitions. The universe is, so to speak, axiologically fumigated. Neither commodities nor human performances have any value labels attached to them. They do not enter the world with price tags. God has no Incomes and Wages Policy. Worth or value does not inhere in anything: only Demand and Supply flexibly bestow value on things. Values and prices maketh man. Thus the liberal approach to value, and hence to the problem of distribution (the value and remuneration of effort) is part of an overall Enlightenment, a nominalism which spurns the myth of inherent moral attributes, and shifts the burden of decision to something empirical, testable, observable – namely observable preferences, demand and supply. Thus a theory of distribution is legitimated by a background philosophy, by the de-mystification of the world. It is a philosophy of a rather consciously superior, condescending kind – in the sense that it cannot but be aware of its own radical superiority to its superstitious rivals. (It also depends, less visibly, on a covert, presupposed and most dubious sociology, as we shall see.)

In this argument, the philosophical, practical and political repudiations of an Incomes Policy converge and overlap. You cannot *logically* tie price tags to things or efforts; and you cannot do it politically and practically either, because it is complicated and it offends people, including influential and powerful groups of people; and *because* you cannot do it logically, you cannot do it politically. The lack of logic makes obvious the arbitrariness, the inevitable bias, the political nature, of the attachment of price tags from above.

How much merit in this important argument? It is, alas, vulnerable to a conclusive *tu quoque*. It is true that neither God nor nature has an Incomes Policy; no theology or metaphysics can help us identify the Just Price or the Just Wage. This is true enough. *But the Market does not have one either.* Mankind moved on from the metaphysical illusion of a 'just price' to the equally metaphysical illusion of a market price. In fact, the market only gives its verdict in an institutional and cultural context, which in turn is not given, either by the market or by anything else, but on the contrary is made by man and society. This second illusion of the market as oracle was only camouflaged by the naïve absolutisation of one particular set of market conditions and terms. In reality, these are historically specific and humanly manipulable – which deprives the verdict of the market both of uniqueness and of any extraneous and genuine authority. Successively, mankind passed the buck to the Nature of Things, Divine Will, and the Market – but in the end we have to allow the buck to stay with us, and handle it with the help of the exiguous and inadequate premises at our disposal. Life is hard. We cannot pass the buck for the decision of remuneration to 'market forces' or 'free bargaining' (collective or other). Or rather: we can do so, but this shift of responsibility will be quite fraudulent.

And not only will it be fraudulent, these days it will also be *seen to be fraudulent*. And once the fraud is visible to all, it no longer works; and we are back where we started.

The pleasing idea that the market decides our values for us, in an impartial manner, presupposes that the market is indeed extraneous. It presupposes that it operates in a *given* environment, which is not in its turn manipulated. The vaunted externality of the market is essential if its arbitration is to appear equitable and legitimate. But this is now seen to be an illusion. The truth of the matter is: there is no such given external environment.

Why did anyone ever suppose there was such a thing? The historic circumstances of 'classical' capitalism were in fact rather peculiar and highly specific, and they encouraged this illusion. Our age no longer encourages it.

The separation of the economic activity

The really fundamental trait of classical capitalism is that it is a very special kind of order in that the economic and the political seem to be separated, to a greater degree than in any other historically known social form. (The individualism of capitalism is a corollary of this, and is less fundamental.) In any other social form, productive activities, and those of defence, or order- and cohesion-maintenance, are closely linked. Productive units are social units and social units are political ones – units organised for defence and for the internal maintenance of authority. Under capitalism, this unity disappears; productive units cease to be political and social ones. Economic activities become autonomous and can, for once, be governed by purely 'economic' considerations. The whole conceptual machinery of 'economics' presupposes this separation, which in fact is historically eccentric. An aspect of this is the use of labour 'as a commodity'. In political environments, this would be unthinkable. Normally, labour cannot be a commodity, simply because every labourer is an ally or an enemy, a subject or a threat, or indeed both.

An interesting trait of this system is that it was self-conscious: it was aware of itself. It saw itself as natural; not, indeed, as universal, but as natural: where it did not prevail, this constituted a distortion of the natural order. (Nowadays we hear much of economic 'distortions'.) It had a theory of its own emergence, or of the obviation of those natural-order-disturbing obstacles, and a closely associated theory of the rightful distribution of rewards.

In fact, its own theory of itself is quite wrong. The heart of the matter is this: far from being natural, whatever this might mean, the separation of the economic from other aspects of life, in other words the untrammelled market, is highly eccentric, historically and sociologically speaking. Far from being the natural tendency of human society and endeavour, it can only emerge in very, very special circumstances. Basically, those conditions include the suspension of coercion. The normal human and social condition is that coercion dominates production: the sword is mightier than the plough. The ploughman hands over a big part of his produce to the swordsman. So does the artisan and the trader.

The suspension of coercion arose because there was a state strong enough to prevent private coercion, yet at the same time willing or obliged not to expropriate and exploit the producers itself; and, equally important, the producers themselves, being allowed to accumulate, to become rich and hence powerful, were willing or constrained not to become themselves a new set of sword-endowed exploiters. They were content to remain producers. How could this miracle happen?

Max Weber's famous theory offers one part of the answer: for peculiar ideological reasons, this set of producers continued to be such even when grown rich enough to become powerful and to enjoy the fruits of their previous accumulation. They turned profits neither into swords nor into pleasure nor into ritual display. They had an inner compulsion to carry on, and the modern world was the by-product of their obsessional drive. It is a plausible part of the answer, but clearly not the whole of it. There were other conditions (which Weber, of course, did not deny).

There was the technical opportunity for growth and innovation: the fruits of the application of the scientific revolution were there, ready for the picking. It is doubtful whether this is always so. The capitalist self-image, the picture which it applies to humanity in general, roughly supposes that at all times there is an opportunity for new combinations of 'factors of production' and the creation of wealth. This seems to me most questionable. A given cultural level may easily, it seems to me, exhaust the potential for innovation which it contains. Most of them rapidly do so, I suspect. But here there was, on this one occasion, a great unexhausted potential.

But there is another condition, which is less often appreciated: classical capitalism may presuppose a certain technological level high enough for a sustained flow of innovations, but it *also*, and even more significantly, presupposes that this technological level is fairly *low*, at least by our standards. Classical capitalism presupposed relatively small productive units, sufficiently uncomplex to be set up by single entrepreneurs, and to run on fairly untrained labour; it presupposed, notoriously, a homogeneous labour force – for how else could labour become 'a mere commodity'? One pair of strong arms was much as any other, as far as early capitalism was concerned.

The feebleness of its technology was important and essential in a number of ways: above all, it was feeble enough not to disrupt totally the society in which it emerged, in whose womb it grew. It did not tear that womb apart.

It did not oblige the encompassing state to control and dominate it in sheer self-defence. It did not create a political dilemma in which the new commercial class either had to eat or be eaten by the old power-holders. Marxism teaches that this ought to have happened but, interestingly, it did *not* happen when capitalism was homegrown. So Marxist writers peevishly rebuke history for failing to follow the plan laid down for it. For instance, in a remarkable article, Mr Perry Anderson[1] tells us that the failure of a full-blown bourgeois revolution in England quite confuses and distorts subsequent developments. It really is most naughty of history.

In fact, the non-occurrence of bourgeois revolutions as a consequence of endogenous capitalism seems to me natural and of the nature of things; bourgeois revolutions against *ancien régimes* characteristically occur in those backward societies where the power holders themselves do not pre-empt the drive towards 'development'. Spontaneous development benefits from stability and, cancerous though the new economic order may be for 'tradition' in the long run, during its initial growth what was remarkable was that it did *not* tear apart the surrounding social world. This incidentally made possible the illusion that the economic realm could be autonomous (liberalism) or even dominant (Marxism).

Early observers were of the contrary opinion: they were impressed, favourably or adversely, by how very destructive it was, how brutally it tore apart the social and physical fabric which surrounded it. But this was only because, unlike us, they had rather low standards in these matters. The state tolerated the producers/accumulators partly because it could *afford* to tolerate them, without being itself devoured: they were not so very big or so very

[1] 'Origins of the Present Crisis', *New Left Review*, January–February 1964. That was another 'present crisis'.

destructive. They enjoyed the framework it provided, but they did not smash it or take it over. They rocked the boat a bit – but not so much as to make it unnavigable.

An elephant in a small boat

Not so now. The modern industrial machine is like an elephant in a very small boat. Either the boat is rebuilt around it so as to accommodate it, or it becomes an absurdity.

And it is quite absurd to pretend that nowadays, individuals combine factors of production and then exchange the results. In fact, industrial production presupposes an enormous infra-structure, not merely of political order, but educationally, culturally, in terms of communication and so forth. There is no way of assessing the contribution of this overall cultural and technical atmosphere to the products. Without air you cannot breathe. How could you assess the price of air?

All this was really also true in the days of 'classical' capitalism, but less so, and above all, it was not so conspicuous. But if the main factor of production is the overall cultural atmosphere of industrial civilisation, without which all else fails, and if this can only be sustained by the central state, what happens to the normative distributive model? It loses both its explanatory plausibility *and* its normative authority.

In early capitalism, much of this atmosphere was not state-produced and so it seemed natural, *given*. Hence the verdicts of the market seemed extraneous, and, in that sense, impartial and acceptable. But now we know that the social atmosphere is centrally *made*. It is made both in an overall way, and in considerable detail. So the verdict of the market, its allocation of spoils, is not independent, let alone some subtle measure of the social contribution made by the recipients of the rewards: it is humanly, politically decided. For the 'market mechanism' as an external arbitrator is an illusion *anyway*.

This was much less visibly true in the era of 'classical' capitalism. Both the productive forces *and* the state were curiously feeble, by our standards. The productive processes were feeble enough not to disrupt totally the social and political, or indeed the physical, environment in which they were operating. The state, though of course its operations affected the economic milieu and the outcome of the market operations, was too weak and too new to the game to interfere pervasively, systematically, or with much knowledge of the effects of its own interference. And at the same time it was not obliged to interfere in sheer self-defence.

The independent market an illusion

The present new situation has a number of aspects. For one thing, it destroys the illusion – and ultimately it was *always* an illusion – of the independence of the economic realm, and hence of the moral legitimacy of the market. The market, the play of economic forces, is not an independent Delphic oracle, but is and cannot but be manipulated by us, by our political decisions or those of our rulers. Hence it cannot be the arbiter of just distribution of rewards. *Our* ventriloquist's dummy cannot tell *us* how to distribute the goodies! Not once we know it is our dummy.

And although the autonomy of the economic always was an illusion, yet it is also true that something has changed. Contemporary, post-classical capitalism is much more meretricious than its predecessor, or at any rate it is bound to seem so. In the classical situation, precisely because the state was relatively feeble, it could not generally create opportunities for great and easy profits, or at any rate it was not often seen to be doing so. Once it seemed that the great rewards came for the opening up of objective new opportunities: capitalism was earning its keep. Not so today.

The state is obliged to pervade economic activity, so as to contain all those side effects of industrial production which, if uncontrolled, would tear everything apart. But the consequence is that many of the 'economic' opportunities are in fact fruits of political decisions. In England, land speculation became, no doubt rightly, a symbol of this. A small country must control building if it is to remain habitable; but the control created a scarcity and enormous prices. Where the paradigm of classical capitalism profit was the exploitation of a new resource or a new invention, the paradigm of contemporary profit is the use of something which, far from being the fruit of anyone's inventiveness or daring, is merely the consequence of a tip-off or (at best) of good luck. This picture, of course, deprives the 'market' or 'free enterprise' theory of distribution of its legitimacy. Profit, even inordinate profit, from the exploitation of a new resource or invention, has a kind of rough justice about it. Inordinate profit derived from a perfectly obvious and ever-present resource, rendered scarce and valuable only by political control, is manifestly unacceptable. A free enterprise system which shifts from one of these images to the other, is in trouble.

And the shift is not accidental. Land is merely a conspicuous example. In subtler and less obvious ways, at a time when economic-climate-making is a recognised duty of government, and when governmental operations take up so large a part of economic life, a large portion of the fruits of industry are clearly seen as politically determined. And if *we* qua citizens give out the bonanza, ought we not have a voice in its distribution?

The *laissez-faire* model always was absurd sociologically as well as normatively, as an account of the genesis and the functioning of capitalism, even in its early stages. The key idea underlying it was the autonomy of economics, the existence of an independent sphere of productive life, in which 'economic' considerations could operate in abstraction from social and political ones. Ironically Marxism took over this error; though it supposed that capitalism carried the seeds of its own destruction (it saw the wrong seeds), it nevertheless saw capitalism as *a* social form of some duration, virtually in and on its own terms, and rather exaggerated its viability. Marxism accepted capitalism's own image of itself to a remarkable extent. It turned the autonomous reality into the dominant one; and it created as its ideal a supposed antithesis of the market, which in fact borrowed much from it.

The autonomy of the economic is unthinkable in conditions of really primitive technology, when human groups are far too close to starvation to permit such free play to economic 'enterprise'; economic life is hedged by considerations inspired by the need to safeguard the group as a whole. Similarly, it is unthinkable in days of really powerful technology, such as prevails today, when a free use of such technical means, unhampered by social restraint, would lead to instability and disaster.

It was for a brief and rather special moment between primitive and really advanced technology, that the idea and its application had some superficial plausibility. At most historical stages, there are few 'inventions' to be made; what is conceptually and socially feasible has already been done. But at this stage, there was a whole cornucopia of as yet unexploited technical possibility, and it produced the illusion that the option of 'new combinations' was a kind of perennial part of the human condition (which it is not). By a miraculous combination of circumstances, a state was also available which had neither the inclination nor the need to interfere with the economy. So the miracle occurred – a society in which, for once, but once only, wealth was mightier than the sword. Leftism contains a grotesque ingratitude for this miracle, rooted in a sociological blindness which cannot appreciate that it *is* a miracle. It *was* an eccentricity and a miracle. Marxism generalised it into an overall and crucial stage of social development, and extracted a curious theory of the subservience of power to wealth from this highly untypical situation. *Laissez-faire* had generalised it even more, turning it into a normal or normative human condition.

But it could not and did not last. We are in the process of adjustment to its disappearance and replacement, and do not yet properly understand our new options, whatever they may be.

Unfortunately, the process of adjustment is hampered by the two available ideologies, both inherited from the days when capitalism did look like a social form amongst others, as a long-term if not a permanent option, rather than as a transitional miracle. When conflict about distribution occurs, as it is occurring, these are the ideologies which are invoked. Each of them is grossly inadequate.

The fallacies of Marxism

The most influential recent critique of Marxism is Sir Karl Popper's, and unfortunately it concentrates on the Hegelian elements in Marxism, which are less relevant to the current crisis. The old formula for the genesis of Marxism – French socialism, German metaphysics and British economics – is of course valid: but it is the last of these three ingredients which matters most just now. The Hegelian element – the prostration before a supposed historic Plan, mistakenly treated as a scientific theory – was no doubt present and important, but is not so operative now. It is the vision of the mechanics of industrial society, and of its available options, which is crucial at this stage. The nonsense in Marxism which is really pernicious now is derived from the economics of liberalism.

Marxism's conception of the alternative to the *laissez-faire* model owes far too much to that which it would reject. The night-watchman state theory of liberalism, the state which merely keeps the ring for unfettered economic activity, is, disastrously, taken over. The liberals thought the state should *only* do this. Marxism notes that it *does* indeed do this, and rightly added that holding the ring in this way of course favoured those who were strong in this particular game, i.e. the owners of the means of production. From this it concludes that this was in essence *all* that the state did; hence, when the expropriators are expropriated, no further need for the state.

The Russians and East Europeans are paying dearly for this

dreadful mistake: when politics do not wither away, Marxism and Marxists are deprived of any language in which even to articulate the problem of power. On occasion, this point is even articulated within the Soviet Union. The earlier, crude 'economic' interpretation of social forms can then be rejected:

> In the conditions of struggle, conducted by young Marxist historiography with bourgeois conceptions. . .the main task. . .was the strengthening of the materialist conception. . .Given the insufficient theoretical training of the learned cadres. . .this led to the absolutisation of the economic factor, which in good time became an obstacle in solving serious. . .problems, *notably the problem of socialist and pre-capitalist societies. . .*
>   . . .the dominant form of social relations in primitive society are natural ones of kinship, in pre-capitalist class societies, political ones of domination and subjection. . .
>   . . .discussions reveal with great clarity the inadequacy of the logical apparatus. . .constructed on the basis of the political economy of capitalism. . .the discussions concerning primitive and early class society are connected with contemporary discussions by economists, arising from the need to elaborate a political economy, *serving the practical requirements of socialist society.*[2]

These remarkable passages clearly express an effort to come to grips with the problem of power and politics in contemporary industrial society, by way of the rediscovery of their importance in pre-capitalist social forms.

The Marxist Utopia was modelled on the *laissez-faire* market, in its individualism and liberalism, but goes a stage further – a free market without even a market, just plain free activity without any swapping of products. Where at least the liberals had a theory of why and how free actors would spontaneously harmonise, of how the Hidden Hand worked, Marxism has none. Possessing an absurd single-cause theory of conflict (class antagonism), it absurdly expects

----

[2] (Italics mine). From L. V. Danilova, 'Diskussionnye Problemy Teorii Dokapitalisticheskikh Obshchestv' ('Problems under Discussion in the Theory of Precapitalist Societies'), in *Problemy Istorii Dokapitalisticheskikh Obshchestv (Problems of the History of Precapitalist Societies)*, ed. L. V. Danilova and others (Nauka Publishing House, Moscow, 1968).

the removal of that cause to remove both conflict and the need for institutional controls of it. The Hidden Hand remains.

The two institutions which nineteenth-century Marxists detested were property and the state, and they supposed that the latter only existed to protect the former. It is an interesting and crucial comment on the potentialities of industrial society, and the merit of both liberal and Marxist interpretations of it, that the first of these, property, was fairly easy to abolish, and moreover without, interestingly, any very disastrous consequences, at any rate in the economic sphere. (The economic performance of the Communist states is not brilliant but it is not unbearably bad, and it is not this aspect of them which makes them intolerable.) The state, on the other hand, does not seem so eligible for dismantling. There is no sign of anyone seriously trying, let alone succeeding, or in fact of anyone even remotely looking as if they were moving in that direction.

The crisis of the mixed economy welfare state

These errors of Marxism, sociological and philosophical, are tragically important for one half of the industrial world, and deprive it of the conceptual means for self-analysis and correction; but they are not so directly relevant to the crisis of the mixed-economy welfare society, as exemplified by Britain. British socialism has taken over from Marxism few positive or specific doctrines (not even the façade theory of the state, though Harold Laski notoriously flirted with this idea), but only one negative though important element: the feeling of the ultimate illegitimacy of private enterprise and ownership, and consequently the legitimacy of anything that, given the chance, might be done unto it. When Hugh Gaitskell attacked clause 4, I thought he was in error: clause 4, like foxhunting, maypole dancing or trooping of the colours, was a treasured part of local folklore and ought not to be tampered with.[3] Now I am no longer so sure. When a combination of that allegedly spurious liberal state, of affluence, of social welfare and Keynesianism, offers in a crisis a superb and easy opportunity of doing most disagreeable things to it, the opportunity is seized, by some at least, with alacrity and enthusiasm. Harold Laski, in anticipation of the post-war Labour reformist

---

[3] In *The Governability of Industrial Societies*, Ghita Ionescu argues on the basis of West German evidence that a conviction of the long-term illegitimacy of capitalism by trade unionists is compatible with here-and-now rational restraint. But one suspects there is a divergence between real and nominal belief rather than between two time scales.

programme, warned against the possibility that a civil service and state apparatus, designed for the protection of the bourgeoisie, might sabotage socialist reforms, thereby creating the need for un-constitutional action. In the celebrated court case which followed, his denial of the imputation that he preached revolution hinged on the distinction between social 'analysis' and recommendation. We really now need a Laski case in reverse. It is the Right which feels that the strongest power in the realm, the trade unions, will sabotage any government other than the one they favour, thereby rendering the constitution nugatory. If a libel case does arise, one hopes that one of those colonels or generals, who wish to correct this de facto subversion of the constitution, will have the memory and the sense of humour to invoke Laski's precedent and argument. 'We are merely analysing the implications of a certain course of action...'

The twilight of capitalism

The ironies of the general situation are numerous, hilarious and well known. It is not an increasingly impoverished proletariat, over-concentration of wealth, and deficient demand, but on the contrary an affluent welfare-hedged working class and inflationary *excess* demands which may be killing capitalism, or what is left of it. The Right is moralistically begging for economic central planning of demand and distribution, the Left howling for untrammelled free bargaining. The Keynesian central manipulation of demand, once intended to be the saviour of capitalism, to be its Counter-Reforma-tion, is now an essential element in its self-destruction through inflation. So is the alleged façade state: its welfare provisions and political liberalism ensure that it is not only possible, but positively comfortable to dig the grave of capitalism.

Keynesianism, the intended saviour and reformer of capitalism, proved to be but a new and original path towards its undoing. In effect, it achieved two things. It established a neo-liberal political theory, in which the state became responsible for the maintenance of full employment, making unemployment into a political derelic-tion of duty; the night-watchman assumed responsibility for seeing to it that there was work on the site in daytime. In practice, the 'counter-cyclical' policies used for this end made it plain to all and sundry that the money supply was and could be under political control, and consequently could not be an act of God. Inflation had existed before; now Keynes made an honest woman of her. He made sure that she had a regular medical check-up – but this alas proved not to be very effective. Once upon a time, there were two ways of enforcing social control in an industrial society: unemployment, and Gulags. Keynes seems to have succeeded in adding a third, inflation. But whereas the other two can be used for quite a long time and have an air of durability, inflation is rather unconvincing from that viewpoint.

All this, however, in conjunction with moderate socialism – respectability for trade unions, welfare provisions which diminish economic vulnerability – meant, as Keynes foresaw, powerful inflationary pressure. He left that bridge to be crossed by his successors. It has indeed been reached, but no-one had devised a very convincing way of crossing it. The ideological aspects of this situation are particularly bizarre. A condition has emerged in which private vices and public virtues *alike* become public vices. A society may be like Montesquieu's tyranny, and rest on vice; or, like a republic, it may rest on virtue. But can it go against *both*? Can it, all at once, afford to contradict both its citizens' selfish private interests and their highest ideals (and two rival ideals at that)? The Keynesian mixed-economy social-liberal state has achieved precisely this.

Both ideal conviction *and* private self-interest are now channelled to subvert the system. The ideological equipment of the society comprises two flat-earth theories, inherited from the early period of capitalism. One preaches pursuit of individual advantage within the limits of the law, as a means of advancing the common good. Under the actual conditions of an intricate inter-dependent large-unit technology, with welfare state provisions and given the legitimacy of collective bargaining, this inevitably leads to a totally indeterminate result: quite a number of groups located astride essential nerve centres can, if they really pursue their own interest to the limit (*and* within the law), obtain any reward they choose to name. The proscription of collective bargaining is politically unthinkable and if implemented would lead to the contrary result, envisaged by Marx, of reducing the majority of workers to the subsistence minimum. This in turn is unthinkable sociologically as well as morally, for a modern economy requires a large number of 'workers' who not merely survive, but operate as skilful and responsible men.

The other available ideology says that the system as such is illegitimate, and hence deserves destruction, *ist wert dass es zugrunde geht*. Its destruction is a moral ideal. Never have duty and self-interest converged so perfectly. Ironically, the *laissez-faire* commandment –

pursue your own interest within the law – and the Marxist one – do that which will destroy the system – lead to precisely the same concrete conduct. The combination of trade union power with the existence of a money supply whose political manipulation is permissible, nay obligatory, means that irresistibly strong demands need not *on any one occasion* be restricted. On any one occasion, surrender is the best policy. But the cumulation of individually sound decisions leads to collectively disastrous final inflation. But what arguments could be invoked on the *individual* occasions? Not rational self-interest: for any one group, moderation is about as sensible as restrained conduct by a man in a fire panic in a theatre: he may know that it would be best if *no-one* panicked, but *given* that others are panicking, his own sole hope lies in joining the stampede.[4] And moral principles? Those drawn from current political belief point in another direction. Puritan liberal economists and revolutionary Marxists offer the very same advice to trade unionists. . .

Nevertheless, mysteriously, the system survives. But only at the cost of men doing violence both to their interests *and* their ideals, which is a bit much to ask. They do it from a muddled sense of reality, which they however cannot articulate in terms of their theories. Faced with real decisions, in the end the Marxisants (or most of them) are not quite so ruthlessly revolutionary, and the neoliberal economists are not quite so divorced from reality (at least when making decisions in their own society, as opposed to advising others). But they have no words in which to explain their reservations. The genuine parts of their perceptions are mute. In Britain, only the Labour party can rule. It owes its authority to the fact that, nominally, it repudiates the system and is pledged to dismantle it. Thanks to this *folklorique* commitment, it can persuade the powerful groups to be moderate, and thereby keep the system going. It can, just about, secure the grudging cooperation of those who could destroy the system, and thus, by means of the combination of half-cock self-interest and half-cock repudiation of the very system which is in fact being sustained, keep it all going. It has to complement the fine economic tuning, implicit in Keynesian manipulation of credit, by equally fine political tuning – just enough unemployment to persuade trade unions to moderate their demands and thus to keep inflation in check, but not enough of it to lose elections. Governing under such terms of reference must be a nerve-racking business.

[4] Cf. *The Political Economy of Inflation* (F. Hirsch and J. H. Goldthorpe (eds.), London, 1978, particularly the contributions by Colin Crouch and John Goldthorpe.

The crisis has roots which are of course not ideological but institutional and external. But when the crisis is being met, it suddenly becomes obvious that to face it requires consent and consensus; and at this moment, naturally, the cry for a New Social Contract goes out. But a social contract is a serious matter: it is amongst other things a persuasive principle of the distribution of rewards and obligations, and it can only be persuasive because it flows, in a convincing manner, from an accepted background picture of our shared situation. And at this point, the tragedy is that the only well diffused, widely understood background pictures are those two old running mates, economic liberalism and Marxism – and the pair of them constitute a dreadful misunderstanding of the logic and options of industrial society.

The notion of 'free collective bargaining' is in fact an appalling hybrid of the two of them – the 'free' bit of it deriving its appeal from some residual notion that untrammelled bargaining leads to fair or just results, conflated in a muddled way with the idea that *anything* is fair against an inherently unjust system, whereas of course the 'collective' bit is a survival from the once justified notion that the weak must combine for defence. There is in the air a most curious mélange of Keynes and Marx: from the former, the cornucopia theory of economic growth as of right, hinging on a manipulable total demand, and, from the latter, the idea of the illegitimacy of the ownership of the means of production. The conjunction of these ideas justifies activism when that inherently illegitimate, but remarkably attractive, cornucopia dares to falter, as inevitably it must from time to time, in emitting a growing flow of goodies. At the same time, the complexity of the new technology plus affluence and welfare ensure that the activism is only too effective.

Messianic socialism

For a long time now, socialism has been a doctrine whose inherent destiny was always to be betrayed, whenever it was implemented. Socialism was the negation of nineteenth-century capitalism, of its individualism, its cult of the autonomy of the economic, its acquisitiveness, its economic inequality. So far so good. Unfortunately it also contained messianic expectations that the eradication of these features will somehow lead to an attractive social order. This can be formally spelt out, as in Marxism, with its single-cause theory of evil, or it can be a more diffuse expectation; but either way, alas, it is there. The truth is quite different: in as far as mixed, semi-socialist societies are attractive (*no* fully socialist society is attractive), this is due to the survival of the liberal, constitutional, pluralist state. Far from being a mere fig leaf of capitalism, it is the great and genuine gift of capitalism to mankind and one which happily can survive the economic conditions which had helped bring it about. If by 'social-ism' one means the re-subjection of the economy to political con-siderations, we can confidently expect the victory of socialism anyway; in as far as it means more, we are placing our hope in an empty word. It is not the re-subjection of the economy to politics which brings any social salvation; it is the *kind* of political institu-tion which does the job that matters.

Not much sense can be expected from the Left without a de-sacralisation of 'socialism'. The matter is really simple: there are two overall ways in which a society can distribute material and other benefits. One is some mixture of power-bargaining and of normative considerations. This is known as politics. The other is to break up benefits into negotiable little units and to allow their prices to be determined by the 'market'. This is known as economics. Important decisions about both environment and human culture in fact come in such large packages that they must needs be 'political', if indeed they are consciously made at all. Small items are probably best left to the market, though the terms on which people meet there are determined by decisions or traditions not settled in the market itself, but prior to it. The political method of decision has pre-dominated throughout history and will do so again. This in itself is neither good nor bad; what matters is the *kind* of balance of power and the kind *of norms* that prevail in the political sphere.

The other alternative, the 'market' (strictly speaking: the illusion of the market) can operate over limited areas only. It is probably undesirable to squeeze that method from the detailed determination of rewards, etc., once the overall pattern has been decided politically. In one historical period, however, the illusion arose that 'the market' could and should usefully govern, if not all life, then at least a large part of it, and the larger the better. This delusion then generated an equally illusory antithesis ('socialism'), the weird idea that the abrogation of the market system constituted, in itself, an alternative and a good system. In fact the term must then either cover the entire range of political systems, or express the naïve hope that, within this great range, the *best* options ('true' socialism) will somehow stand out and proclaim their own evident moral authority, like the true messiah. It all somehow generates the fantasy that there could be a system which was neither political nor economic: a *given* moral arbitration, in the image of the extraneous, impartial Hidden Hand, but even better, more humane.

By contrast, we are also faced with a revival of the market idea, in association with 'monetarist' theories of inflation and the present crisis. *Laissez-faire* theories were reasonably subdued during the hegemony of Keynesianism, but have been encouraged to come out again by the present apparent débâcle of Keynesian policies. Keynesianism failed (a) because running an economy in this manner seems like driving a car in which one has to tug at the wheel by a slack rope rather than having one's hands firmly on it; and (b) because it provides a manner of evading painful immediate confrontations at the cost of later inflation, a temptation which democratic governments can hardly be expected to resist.

Inflation and its causation

'Monetarism' sets up to be *a* theory of the cause of inflation, singling out the crucial cause from amongst possible and subsidiary ones. Perhaps those who propound it try to do this and think they are really doing it. The truth of the matter is different, as rapidly becomes obvious if one listens to them. Their position is in fact a language and a theory of distributive justice. It is a language so constructed around a theory of justice, around a certain vision of what is normal and proper in social and economic life, that any cause of inflation other than the 'monetary' one is scarcely perceptible for it. Its coloured lenses are such that any other cause is virtually invisible, or at best subsidiary, whilst the one favoured factor stands out in exaggerated relief. Of course, there can be no inflation without excess of money over goods. But 'root cause' is that part of the total complex of conditions which is most open to manipulation and change. The expansion of the money supply, or institutions or attitudes making it possible, are not that root cause, in this sense. We cannot easily freeze the supply, or pretend that something (e.g. gold) can do it for us. We cannot invent a world in which inflation would be impossible because no-one had the power to expand the money supply. Once it is known that the power exists, it cannot be wished-away by the pretence that it does not exist. Men will not sacrifice very real interests for the sake of maintaining a pretence consistently. But if your language is constructed around a certain norm, which highlights the central creation of credit, then it will seem to you that the 'main cause' of inflation is pretty obvious.

This is an optical or rather conceptual illusion. Given that we cannot think away and abolish the man-made, political nature of the money supply, the real 'cause' of inflation, i.e. the factor we may hope to change, is the social pressures leading to the abuse of that control.

In social contexts, *the* cause of something is that one factor, amongst the whole class of contributory factors, which is most amenable to social manipulation. The language of monetarist economists is not much good at discerning, let alone at assessing the manipulability of other factors. It merely tends to prejudge the issue by its highly selective vision. The monetarists themselves half see this, in a confused way: if they really meant what they say, they would recommend an *immediate* cessation of that inflationary central creation of money. But they do know what the consequences would be (for they speak, however haltingly, languages other than their own). So they only recommend a gradual return to what they consider the self-evident norm. But this is a comic compromise. If their norm is so absolute, so inherent in the only correct way of looking at economic phenomena, why compromise at all? If, on the other hand, it is legitimate in some measure to balance out the cost of resisting the non-monetary pressures, against the cost of inflation, can we not go on weighing these factors, even in the long run? (This is precisely what in fact we shall do.)

Thus by a further irony economic liberalism has now joined socialism as a doctrine ever destined for inevitable betrayal. In association with 'monetarism', *laissez-faire* panaceas, long under a cloud and rather subdued during the period of Keynesian dominance and the memory of the inter-war slump, have now come out again and have their voluble propagandists. But when their proponents are in power, these ideas are also 'betrayed'. As with socialism, betrayal is their destiny. Economic and social realities are too strong; a simple-minded image, however compulsive in the abstract, cannot stand up to the pressures of reality.

Basic elements of industrial society

The basic facts of life in industrial society are the following: the incredibly plentiful cornucopia known as industrial production cannot in any useful or meaningful sense be seen as the product of individual effort or exchange, of men autonomously bringing together 'factors of production' and swapping the results. It is based and dependent on a complex infrastructure, in which cultural, educational, political elements are at least as important as the more obvious physical ones. It is very costly and difficult to sustain, and it is vulnerable. The infrastructure is indeed the fruit of past human achievements, and it is far more important than present economic decisions or contributions by individuals. It is hard or meaningless to give a quantitative estimate of the contribution made by it, but, in any case, the perpetuation of this overall social infrastructure is an absolute condition of the survival of the productive machine; so we must give it what it needs. It must be politically viable; hence, either through consent or constraint (more probably, through a complex mixture of habit, consent and constraint) it must command that minimal compliance which its survival requires.

As stated, it is the negative argument for the market which is proclaimed most shrilly: how else, other than through supply and demand, can the worth of anything be assessed and consensus attained? The enthusiastic proponents of this vision accuse their opponents of a kind of Platonism, an undemocratic eagerness to impose their own values on the public, a desire to rule as philosopher–bureaucrats who know better than the people what the people should want and get. It is thus that Milton Friedman speaks of J. K. Galbraith. But this Platonism, which certainly exists, is not an, eager, but a reluctant and inevitable Platonism, inescapable and inherent in our situation in which the market is spurious and its verdicts circular, feeding back to us decisions which are political anyway – so they might as well be so overtly, after proper, open and rational discussion. The manipulability of social and psychic facts, which had once seemed given, forces us to become Reluctant Platonists, whether or not our background beliefs call for this (they do not). It is the inescapably volatile, manipulable and manipulated nature of human reality which forces this responsibility on us.

This is indeed a difficulty – a universal one, facing mankind at all times, but now aggravated by the complexity and rapid change of modern society. But, basically, this is just the universal human predicament: there are *never* good 'objective', extraneous reasons for *anything* and least of all for principles of distribution. This is the fate of all human societies: to make their members content, they have to invent these reasons, as best they can. Modern secularism, scepticism and so forth make it a bit harder. All the same, we have to do it anyway; there is no hidden hand to do it for us.

The hidden hand will not give us fairness or consensus; but it is also worthless in other ways. To appreciate this, we need to indulge in some elementary reflections on the nature of the wealth of nations – or of individuals. Wealth is control over bits of the physical environment, with a view to adjusting those bits so as to fit in with the needs and wishes of men. Once upon a time, this power was very small, and barely, intermittently sufficed to ensure adequate nourishment and the conditions of survival. Today, this power is enormous and rapidly growing. The market model teaches that this power or its fruits should be divided between the individuals involved in its operation, with only a minimum to be subtracted and bestowed on the central authorities. (If they exceed the economic price of their order-maintaining functions, by means of inflating the currency or otherwise, they are in effect *stealing*. Not property, but inflation is theft, it appears.)

The trouble is of course that the plausibility of the market model belongs to the age of the plough and the hoe, the horse cart and the water mill. It can still be usefully extended from such an economy to the world of the steam engine and the early factory. In such worlds, 'wealth' was indeed constituted by the changes produced in our environment by fairly feeble tools; even those feeble tools could ravage a landscape, but still their effects were relatively tolerable. Very probably the market model also contains the correct recipe for how best to make relatively small, marginal adjustments in the economy – how to draw resources or effort from one field to another. For this kind of operation, 'market forces' are probably much more efficient and less wasteful than direction from above. When it comes to overall questions concerning what kind of human categories and life-styles there are to be in a society, what their relative economic position is to be and so forth, then 'political' decisions are not merely preferable, but inevitable. On these general issues, 'market' arbitration is spurious anyway. The market operates in a context which is not given by the nature of things but by political action. It is that context which determines the verdict of the market. There is a hidden human–political hand behind the Hidden Hand.

Though no doubt an excellent way of carrying out minor adjustments, the 'market' is now useless as an arbitration of the general pattern of distribution, and of making it morally palatable. The only choice which is open is between different kinds of political arbitration. (There was much to be said, perhaps, for political arbitration which pretended to be economic; but this option, whatever its merits, seems no longer open.) In a remarkable article,[5] R. E. Pahl

[5] 'The Coming Corporatism', *New Society*, 10 October 1974.

and J. T. Winkler forcefully spell out the factors making for an overt assumption of political responsibility for the economy. They call this 'corporatism'. The excellence of the analysis is marred by a redundant, verbal condemnation: 'Corporatism is fascism with a human face.' This is in conflict with the authors' own demonstration of the wide range of options available within the general limits of 'corporatism'. Their own examples of the species range from Nkrumah to Scandinavian Social Democracy, which suggests that evaluation will have to be made *within* the species, rather than *of* the species as a whole.

The question is not whether there should be an Incomes Policy. That question does not arise. The only question which does arise is *what kind* of incomes policy is to be imposed and by what means. Of course we can (and must) have a central wages policy, though we may need to call it Free Collective Bargaining. Why not? Its name, principles of operation and imposition, and whether it is to be camouflaged or open – these issues do arise. No doubt, a camouflaged political imposition of distributive principles had its merits, when it was still feasible.

Parameters of the market

'The market' may indeed be the best way of effecting relatively minor changes. But as a means of determining the basic outlines of distribution (and thereby, in complex ways, of rank and power) it is a logical absurdity, a blatant case of circular reasoning. As the overall traits of the social order are in any case determined politically, not given by nature, we cannot seek judgement from a mechanism which is governed by pressures, set up by that very order over which it is to judge...All this is obvious, though not, it appears, to *laissez-faire* economists, whose style of thought is so firmly internalised that it precludes perception of ideas not consonant with it.

But it may be objected that if the market is so good at effecting minor adjustments, what happens when, in given circumstances (which appear to obtain now), a cumulative avalanche of these minor adjustments threatens to carry away the whole structure? Whilst such conditions last, it may be necessary to suspend the sovereignty of the market even in those points of detail where one would otherwise gladly leave it alone. This may be most inconvenient. But the only known alternative seems to be the kind of trauma of total collapse which scares people into moderation; and though such a collapse may well occur, no one will seriously propose it as a deliberately imposed remedy.

So, the overall terms which decide the way the market arbitrates depend on political factors. See how the middle classes complain when a monopolistically placed trade union, protected by the general social climate, behaves in a 'market' manner...though, to their credit, and contrary to Marxist theory, the middle classes do not look for violent means to restore the situation. Instead, they make plaintive and ineffectual moral appeals to the workers' sense of long-term and national interest...alas, the workers seem altogether lacking in 'consciousness'. This used to be a source of deep regret to Left radicals, but times have changed, and now it is the moderate Right which bemoans that very same lack of wider awareness on the part of the labouring masses. They will, damn them, neither make a revolution nor moderate their wage claims.

Perhaps we should learn from Marx after all, and turn labour into something other than a mere commodity. The middle classes remain law-abiding, even when deprived of economic advantage, mainly, as far as I can see, because many of them retain security and relatively meaningful work. So if increased Danegeld has become disastrously inflationary, can one not recover consensus by endowing the non-middle-class segment of the working population with *careers*? The sociologists who contest the 'embourgeoisment' of the workers' thesis do not strike me as convincing; but I am impressed by the fact that one of the most dramatically successful post-war economies, the Japanese, contrary to the erstwhile orthodoxies of both Marxists and economic liberals, does very well indeed with a feudal, paternalistic attitude to labour.[6]

The meaning of wealth

'Wealth' today means the power to effect most drastic changes in our entire environment. If there is a large number of participants in the process of enjoying our mastery of our environment, then to break up this enjoyed 'wealth' into a corresponding number of independently usable packages, simply results in making total nonsense of the environment. Man is no longer wrestling with nature, but with the consequences of his own conquest of nature. The summation of individual choices is collectively disastrous. Collective control of 'resources' is imposed not merely or even primarily by the inevitably great expense of the centrally run infrastructure (let alone

[6] Cf. R. P. Dore, *British Factory–Japanese Factory* (London, 1973).

by tax-greed of governments), but by the very nature of that 'wealth'.

The meaning of wealth has similarly undergone a complete transformation from the viewpoint of the individual, as J. K. Galbraith has shown. In pre-industrial contexts, wealth means two things: access to the minimal preconditions of survival and comfort, which are genuinely precarious and in doubt ('give us this day our daily bread'), plus, when there is some wealth over, power over human services (servants, retainers) with a view to further comfort or, more significantly, prestige and security. But the mechanism of these benefits is radically transformed in post-industrial, 'affluent' contexts. Where affluence is attained, minimal physical sustenance and comforts are no longer in doubt; and, at the same time, a certain pervasive egalitarianism, probably inherent in the basic organisational features of such a society, makes it increasingly difficult and rare for people to possess 'tails' of prestige-enhancing retainers. The precariousness has gone out of the game for mere survival; and the competition for prestige has assumed novel forms. One of the striking points of genuine convergence between rival types of industrial society is the diminution of really conspicuous expenditure by individuals: life-styles vary a great deal less between social strata. Vulgar display has not disappeared, of course, but it is far less conspicuous than, say, during the *bel époque* of Edwardian days. Social stratification can become detached from wealth: one of the most fascinating findings of a thorough study of social stratification under socialism[7] has been that, at even a modest level of affluence of one of the less successful industrial societies, class and status can become detached from income. You no longer need brass to be tops. (Admittedly, newly deprived middle classes may be much irritated by relative financial deprivation; one of the things which the Prague Spring and contemporary Britain have in common is the middle-class annoyance with economic equality.) All in all, industrial society does display a continuing tendency towards the equalisation of conditions, but also, at the same time, towards the concentration of power. It is a very complex, intricate machine whose parts are highly interdependent; and the decisive levers tend to be in definite, delimited places. They are not the same levers at all times and in all circumstances; power *is* concentrated, but its location varies according to the kind of issue. The nature of that power or powers, and their links

[7] Pavel Machonín (a kolektiv), *Československá Společnost* (Bratislava, 1969).

with wealth, are not clear or properly understood; but it is certain they cannot be understood if one relies on the old models of how society works.

But the ideological fantasy of economic liberalism has generated, as its antithesis, a corresponding and opposed nonsense, whose pervasiveness in the intellectual and moral climate makes its contribution to the present crisis. It teaches that the current system is inherently illegitimate (extreme left position), and that its sheer replacement by a radical alternative will lead to a determinate and acceptable (nay, desirable) social order; or (opportunist left) that a collective-action variant within *laissez-faire* is quite in order.

Capitalism's legacy to mankind

In fact, the liberal pluralist state, far from being a façade, is capitalism's unintended and precarious gift to mankind. It was born of economic liberalism but does not necessarily serve it. Economic liberalism is important only in as far as it helps preserve it; otherwise, it is something of instrumental value, absurd in its extreme forms, but in its details to be treated in pragmatic fashion. 'Socialism' is a largely vacuous notion. If it means the re-politicisation of the economy (the application of political criteria to the overall principles of distribution and the general strategy and organisation of production), it is inevitable anyway, though the specific forms it assumes and its self-image are not; but it is vacuous if we seek to extract from it some guidance to the important question, concerning just *how* we re-politicise it.

15
The withering away of the dentistry state

How was sustained money-making viewed before the triumph of capitalism? This is an interesting question in the history of ideas. But Albert Hirschman's study of it[1] is more than an elegant and stimulating footnote to intellectual history. The reflections it inspires relate to our present discontents, and not just to the ancestry of our ideas. This contemporary relevance is only sketched out lightly, not to say tantalisingly, by the author. The main theme of the book is the documentation of one central point: those who argued for capitalism, from a political viewpoint, prior to its full emergence, were not, as you might expect, Sovietologists before the event, but rather predecessors of Sigmund Freud's *Civilisation and its Discontents*. The *problematik* which preoccupied them was not ours, it was not the question whether economic liberalism is a precondition of political and social liberties. (I remember a Czech economist during the run-up to the Prague Spring, to whom a British economist maliciously pointed out that the economic reforms were unlikely to be effective, answering that he didn't care – economic decentralisation was above all a means to social liberalisation.) What they *were* interested in was the control of man's ungovernable passions. If God, Reason, morality, could not control man's violence and lust, perhaps greed could do so. Let our libido be sublimated into cupidity, and we may all live the better for it.

In brief, the merits of acquisitiveness were seen more as a check on the passions within than on the powers outside. There is a double paradox here, if the author is right: it is not only that the merits of

[1] Albert O. Hirschman, *The Passions and the Interests. Political Arguments for Capitalism Before its Triumph* (Princeton, New Jersey, 1977).

capitalism were seen to be quite other than those which are claimed for it now, but what are now said to be its sins were then its virtues. Commenting on 'the contemporary critiques of capitalism', the author observes that 'one of the most attractive and influential' amongst them stresses

> the repressive and alienating features of capitalism. . .
> the way it inhibits the development of the 'full human
> personality.' [But]. . .capitalism was precisely expected and
> supposed to repress certain human drives and proclivities
> and to fashion a less multifaceted, less unpredictable, and
> more 'one-dimensional' human personality. This position,
> which seems so strange today, arose from. . .concern over
> the destructive forces unleashed by the human passions
> with the only exception, so it seemed at the time, of
> 'innocuous' avarice. *In sum, capitalism was supposed to*
> *accomplish exactly what was soon to be denounced as its*
> *worst feature* [p. 132, Hirschman's italics].

In the final passages of the book, Hirschman severely rebukes J. M. Keynes for daring to invoke, once again, almost in the same words, Dr Johnson's justification of money-making as the most innocent of pursuits, one which keeps men out of much worse mischief. Hirschman's indignation with Keynes springs from the consideration that by the twentieth century we ought to know better than that. I find this charge somewhat odd: the work in which Keynes made the observation, the *General Theory*, was meant to propose a Counter-Reformation of capitalism, a reform which would enable capitalism to overcome the *economic* defects displayed in the nineteenth century and in the 1930s, whilst retaining its socio-political merits. The present reviewer, writing in England in the 1970s, is hardly tempted by the supposition that Keynesianism has provided the final answer. But he is puzzled to see Keynes rebuked for the non-originality of his view of the political merits of capitalism, in a work which only claimed originality for the remedies of its recognised *economic* ills. . .

The author makes plain that the book is not meant to be merely a footnote to intellectual history, however interesting, but that it is meant to raise the level of the great debate about the political implications of capitalism. But that debate requires that we distinguish sharply the three distinct charges against capitalism: (1) the marked defects of early capitalism, i.e. uncontrolled economic fluctuations and acute impoverishment of many; (2) the romantic charge, it has made life dull, unidimensional etc.; and (3) that it is responsible for the markedly *un*-pacific conduct of twentieth-century states. It was perfectly consistent of Keynes to consider (2) a virtue, not a vice, as did the thinkers with whom Hirschman is concerned (oh let us live in dull times!); he thought, rightly or otherwise, that he had a remedy for (1); and the nexus between twentieth-century militarism and capitalism is less than clearly established.

Hirschman makes these distinctions, yet his argument does not observe them carefully. The relatively peaceful and un-despotic nature of the post-Napoleonic century is conceded, yet the *ennui* which this generated in the romantics then reappears as a charge with a mention of the usual nomenclature (alienation, anomie, *Entzauberung*); and this romantic complaint, following Marx, is conflated with the impoverishment-of-many charge. They are of course not mutually incompatible, but can one really at one and the same time give a guarded endorsement to the romantic complaint and yet also hint that capitalism may be despotic and bellicose after all? The more *ennui* the better, if that means stability and prosperity. Populations suffering from the genuine miseries of early industrialism crave for such *ennui*; it is only repudiated by the sated *jeunesse dorée* of affluence. Alienation, long forgotten, had to be dug up from Marx's early work for their consumption. Hirschman observes that the Marxists thought that capitalism deserved different evaluations at diverse stages, but he actually praises some of his earlier predecessors for not making such a distinction, but on the contrary pressing these charges simultaneously: 'the earlier formulations are, in a sense, richer, for they demonstrate that economic expansion is *basically and simultaneously* ambivalent in its political effects, whereas Marxist thought imposes a temporal sequence with the positive effects necessarily antedating the negative ones' [p. 124, author's italics]. I find it strange to see a sophisticated specialist in economic growth lumping together the switch from feudalism to commercialism, and modern industrial development, under the single concept of 'economic expansion'.

Part of what Hirschman insists on is that the political worm was in the economic apple from the very start, or at any rate, that some perceptive observers discerned the worms very soon, albeit ambivalently. There are in fact a number of such early worms, and they were noted by Ferguson, Tocqueville and others. They are:

(i) Fear of loss of wealth (downward mobility, relative deprivation of the erstwhile privileged, resentment) leads to conflict, 'reaction'

(ii) Precariousness of a complex economy requires strong protective central guidance

(iii) Preoccupation with acquisition diminishes political vigilance

(iv) Economic preoccupation of the *many* leaves *some* to pursue political passions

It is indeed highly interesting that these possibilities should have been noted so early.

If I am right in supposing that Hirschman's main contention is that the early propagandists of capitalism were preoccupied with the diversionary effect of acquisitiveness on other human passions, and not, as we are, with its politically liberalising influence, then I must say that this case is not fully convincing, even on the internal evidence of the book itself. What is true is that the early panegyrists of commercialism were unlikely to foresee the modern socialist state, which both manages a productive economy *and* dominates society, and hence were unlikely to ask whether it could refrain from doing the latter whilst continuing to do the former. Whatever may or may not have been the case in the 'hydraulic' state, the Western feudal or baroque state was not primarily 'in trade'. But the problem of restraining passions was a *political* problem. For one thing, strong government was provoked or justified by turbulent subjects; if they could become less so, by serving Mammon instead, the state could then also relax. But quite apart from this vicious-circle argument (turbulent subjects provoke tyranny), it is above all the passions of the rulers themselves that are at issue. Hirschman actually spells this out: 'The passions that most need bridling belong to the powerful,' and he then proceeds to quote Montesquieu's account of how commercial mechanisms provide incentives for the ruler to become moderate, in his own interest.

There is a certain irony about these mechanisms, which Hirschman does not underscore: 'All the same one saw commerce emerge out of vexation and despair. Jews, proscribed in turn in each country, found ways of saving their belongings...They invented bills of exchange; and by means of this, trade could elude violence' [translated from *De l'Esprit des Lois*, XXI, 20].

Things have kind of changed. In the modern world, wealth contained in bits of paper is taxable par excellence, and the high price of gold, works of art etc. is due in considerable part to the fact that real things can best elude the fiscal bureaucracy. Montesquieu's observation may be true of some imbecile of a mediaeval monarch, who has to pull out the teeth of his unfortunate subjects so as to persuade them to part with their wealth: 'What happened in England will give an idea of what one did elsewhere. King John imprisoned the Jews to seize their goods...One of them, having had seven teeth extracted, one per day, gave ten thousand marks of silver on the eighth. Henry the Third extracted fourteen thousand marks from Aaron, Jew of York' [translated from *De l'Esprit des Lois*, xii, 20]. I quote at length, because Hirschman's shortened citations from Montesquieu on occasion miss out some of the piquancy and essential character of this distinctive mode of subordinating economic to political considerations.

The modern state does not stoop to dentistry. It has no need for it, and mostly has no time to pursue single objects of wealth such as pieces of jewellery. It simply does not have the resources or inclination to give such personal and intimate attention to its subjects, and indeed this impersonality has often been deplored. The major forms of wealth, of claims over resources, are on bits of paper, which generally speaking are not elusive at all, but need to be registered and are in most cases easily traced. This point is of some importance in relation to the main problem of the book, the relationship of wealth and power.

On the one hand, it seems to me that the thinkers cited by Hirschman *were* in fact concerned with the limitation of political power, and not just with restraint on human passions; and, on the other, that one cannot assimilate the conflict between commercialism and the traditional state with the problem of excessive power in the hands of some or all modern industrial states. The problem posed seems to me *more* continuous than Hirschman allows, and its context *less* so than he seems to imply.

Take the problem of dentistry and extraction of wealth. This business of extracting wealth by torture just about hits off the stature of the mediaeval monarch. Most of his subjects were peasants; it was hard luck on the few Jewish merchants that they also got caught up in his clutches. The state could only live by taking by force from the peasants (and from the few merchants) tangible wealth, i.e. agricultural produce and occasionally valuables such as gold. The ruler was a specialist in applying such force, whether to the subjects or to rivals who would displace him. Naturally, his ethos was military, not productive. With a shift to a more complex economy, which would break down if you habitually extracted the teeth of those who man it, the ruler had to change his methods. Eventually he found that the very methods invented to elude that imbecilic predecessor – claims to resources on paper – in fact greatly facilitated taxation.

In outline, this development is familiar, and the fascinating quotations in Hirschman's book do not really convince me that the taming of human passions rather than of rulers was the real theme. But the question is related to a topic Hirschman brings in towards the end, namely the manner of the emergence of modern economic man, unsusceptible to dentistry methods. Hirschman in effect offers an alternative to the Weberian hypothesis of his emergence:

> the expansion of commerce and industry in the seventeenth and eighteenth centuries has been viewed here as being welcomed and promoted not by some marginal social groups, nor by an insurgent ideology, but by a current of opinion that arose right in the center of the 'power structure' and the 'establishment' of the time...Ever since the end of the Middle Ages, and particularly as a result of the increasing frequency of war in the seventeenth and eighteenth centuries, the search was on for a behavioural equivalent for religious precept...and the expansion of commerce and industry was thought to hold much promise in this regard [p. 129].

Of course, as the author notes, there is no incompatibility between this kind of encouragement outside and from above, and the Protestant Ethic at work within: 'Clearly both claims could be valid at the same time: one relates to the motivations of the aspiring new elites, and the other to those of various gatekeepers' [p. 130].

It seems to me that the two claims are more than compatible: one of them makes the other more plausible. One important factor for the oppressive traditional state was that it could not allow wealth to accumulate in the hands of its subjects, lest they use it to recruit followers and acquire weapons and displace the political authorities. The dentistry was pre-emptive. The reason for allowing commercial activity to pariah groups was precisely that they were less able to do this, and more susceptible to dental treatment. Montesquieu is a bit puzzled by the seeming illogicality of certain anti-Jewish measures:

> In the end a custom introduced itself according to which all the goods of Jews who embraced Christianity were

confiscated. We know about this bizarre custom through
the law which abolishes it. Feeble reasons have been offered
to explain it; allegedly it was done to test the converts, by
way of ensuring that nothing remained of the subjection to
the daemon. But it is obvious that it was a kind of right
of redemption, for the king or the lord, of the taxes levied
on the Jews, of which they were deprived by their conversion to Christianity [translated from *De l'Esprit des Lois*,
XXI, 20].

But of course this made excellent sense. An individual of wealth, no
longer disqualified religiously, could be a great political menace.

The Weberian hypothesis dovetails neatly with what Hirschman
argues, in as far as it provides an explanation of how money-making
came at long last to be innocuous. It explains how economic accumulation could become habit-forming, how riches were no longer
necessarily transformed into prestige, force, power, but willingly
remained politically passive and emasculated. By such voluntary
political restraint, the vicious circle was broken; a ruler was no
longer compelled to take pre-emptive action against the rich, thereby
also freeing them in turn from a corresponding necessity of pre-
emptive self-defence.

But of course the circle was also broken at other points. The feudal
monarchs or seigneurs, whose waning Montesquieu was describing,
were presiding over agrarian societies. Its wealth (the few unfortunate merchants apart) was primarily agricultural produce. Government consisted in the power of extracting the surplus by force, and
protecting what one had extracted from other, rival robber barons.
This force could be applied in a regular and sustained manner, and
came to define a stable, permanent social role – that of a warrior
aristocracy, devoted to war and government.

In a society with a complex division of labour, this is no longer
possible. Hirschman quotes the admirable observations of Montesquieu's follower, Sir James Steuart, on this point:

The statesman looks about with amazement; he who was
wont to consider himself as the first man in the society in
every respect, perceives himself eclipsed by the lustre of
private wealth, *which avoids his grasp when he attempts
to seize it*. This makes his government more complex and
more difficult to be carried on; *he must now avail himself
of art and address* as well as of power and authority.

The power of a modern prince, let it be. . .ever so
absolute, immediately becomes limited as soon as he
establishes the plan of economy which we are endeavouring
to explain. If his authority formerly resembled the solidity
and force of a wedge. . .it will at length come to resemble
the delicacy of the watch. . .which is immediately destroyed,
if. . .touched with any but the gentlest hand [*Inquiry into
the Principles of Political Economy*, 1767, quoted in
Hirschman, italics Hirschman's].

Quite apart from the complexity of the economy and hence also of
the administration supervising it, there is a much simpler consideration on which Hirschman does not dwell: there is no need to use
force to take the modern workman's produce from him. The specialised output of any productive units, unlike that of a peasant, is far
too specialised to be worth retaining (leaving aside exceptional
situations such as, say, diamond mining). It *has to* be exchanged for
other produce. There is of course conflict about the rate at which it
is exchanged, but brute force is not a suitable method for settling
this. Straightforward robbery with violence, which may be the basic
principle of mediaeval government, is of course not unknown in
industrial society, but it is a relatively marginal and above all a
single-shot activity. Protection rackets flourish in the main only in
shady areas, where the questionable legality of the productive enterprise prevents it from seeking the full protection of the law.

What does it all amount to? Hirschman seems to me right in his
general contention that the anticipatory hopes and fears about the
political consequences of economic growth were different from ours.
But I am not sure that the precise nature of the difference emerges
as clearly as it should. The first part of the book concentrates on the
role of money-making as a substitute for moral restraint: a countervailing force was apparently required, not in society, but within the
individual soul. If that is the heart of the matter, then indeed there
is a great difference between *them* and *us*. In the second part of the
book the stress changes, in as far as the political aspects or consequences of the passions come to the forefront.

It is the restraint of the passions of the powerful which matters
most. If we assimilate the greed and violent temper of a baron to
modern totalitarianism – a questionable equation – then we get a
picture of a kind of continuity, a persisting concern with tyranny.

My own inclination would be to accept what seemed to be the

author's first position – namely the doctrine of *dis*continuity between *their* concerns and *ours*.

The author is moving towards something which, though not fully spelt out, at least in this book at any rate, is important, valid, and at least resembles that which he does assert. The simplest way of approaching it is this: in a modern society, it is not the *passions* of rulers (or subjects) which are the causes of tyranny. In the past, the uncontrollable anger of baron, or peasant, may have been the political danger, and restraining either by creating countervailing *interests* may have been an excellent strategy. But it is not some uncontrollable Dostoevskian passion in the hearts of Soviet bureaucrats which inhibits the softening of central rule. In the Brezhnev era, those *aparatchiks* seem sober, not to say dreary men, and rather unpromising material for the *Possessed* or *Brothers Karamazov*. It is useless to suggest that if only they were a bit involved in commerce – provided with a nice little portfolio of equities say – their passions would diminish and they would acquire, in Montesquieu's words, *des moeurs douces*, or, in their own, become more *kulturny*. That is not their trouble. Modern authoritarianism is not primarily rooted in the passions of men. The *problem* is different, and the idiom – rather than the substance – chosen by the ancient discussion does highlight this fact.

The problem of restraining the domination of a baronial class or monarchy is radically different from the issue of the governance of industrial society, and hence it is not clear that there is any justification for treating it all as one continuous debate. What they said was in fact *more* similar to our preoccupation than Hirschman allows, but the problem they faced was *less* so. The case that baronial tyranny (and human passions going with it) can be eroded by a complex division of labour, if it succeeds in establishing itself, is fairly cogent. But this does not tell us too much about the political options facing that complex economy when it is established, and when it faces organisational, not affective problems.

The general relationship of wealth and power, of the means of production and the means of coercion, is of course crucial. There are really two problems: how the miracle of establishing a complex and highly productive economy occurred in the first place, and what is to be done with it when established.

On the first issue, we have at least the elements for constructing a tentative answer. The vicious circle which compels rulers to extract wealth lest they be themselves displaced, was broken, by a number of factors, which include wealth-accumulators who did not aspire to power, an increase in economic complexity which made it preferable for rulers to foster economic activity, and even to take part in the production of wealth. Montesquieu observes: 'It is contrary to the spirit of monarchy that the nobility should indulge in trade. The custom established in England of allowing the nobility to trade has, more than anything else, contributed to the weakening of monarchic government in that country' [translated from *De l'Esprit des Lois*, xx, 21]. But perhaps the most general and pervasive factor was this: productive forces were strong enough to permit the bribing of the rulers, without feeling the cost too much, and yet without disrupting the society and thus obliging the rulers or society to defend themselves. The political restraint of the wealth producers (or the restraint of their passions, in the language of Hirschman's witnesses), perhaps inwardly generated by the psychic mechanisms which preoccupied Weber, were one part of the answer. But another part lies in the sheer physical feebleness of the technology involved. Powerful enough to provide plentiful Danegeld, at the same time it was not so powerful as to disrupt society or its physical environment. The means of coercion could rest, for the means of production did their work, but not in an intolerably disruptive manner. Economy could be separated from polity. The peacefulness of commercial–industrial society can be argued along various lines:

(1) The greater amount of wealth available frees men from the *need* to be aggressive simply to survive.

(2) The form of wealth is such that it cannot easily be seized by sheer governmental robbery.

(3) Governments have more interest in increasing total national wealth than in taking a large proportion of it.

(4) The commercial spirit is itself incompatible with a taste for violence or political ambition.

(5) A complex division of labour discourages aggression between the mutually interdependent sections of society, as it discourages extortion from above.

These factors operated in different proportions at diverse times. They, and perhaps some others, were, however, sufficient to ensure the demise of the teeth-extracting state. Their supreme achievement was the attainment of a conceptual separation of the economy from the polity: it became possible to think about wealth in abstraction from power. The normal human condition had been that you *owned* what you could *defend*: considerations of production could not be separated from considerations of defence. The sheer fact that an independent economics became thinkable illustrates that the famous softening of political *moeurs* had, all in all, been achieved.

I believe this separability and the idea of 'the market' which goes with it to be an illusion, though one which could be sustained during a limited period which was favourable to it – very roughly, the period between the middle ages and the full development of industrialism. Two closely linked ideologies are based on this illusion – economic liberalism and Marxism. The former supposes it makes sense to mini-mise non-economic constraint; Marxism goes further and supposes it makes sense to eliminate *both* forms of constraint. It has been said that Aristotle did not treat of economics because trade was in the hands of resident non-citizens. But he was right, and no explanation is really required. An independent economy is an anomaly.

But of the various factors which helped dismantle the rapacious state, some at least now operate in the other direction. The state is not merely capable of taxing without torture, it is obliged to do so. The modern economy is so complex that the shared infrastructure is more important than the individual productive units, and cannot but be centrally supervised. This incidentally includes the educational/cultural infrastructure: one of the factors which encouraged the 'economistic' illusion was that the shared cultural background was then largely taken for granted, like the air we breathe. Modern technology is so powerful that the collective struggle is less with nature than with the side-effects of our own conquest of nature. For these various reasons, we now see the old vicious circle in opera-tion again, but in a new form. Political considerations must again overrule economic ones, not because rich merchants could hire thugs and replace the baron, but because the side-effects of unrestrained economic conduct would otherwise totally disrupt society and en-vironment.

The idea of an autonomous economy has now lost its plausibility. The question is not *whether*, but *how* the polity is to control the economy. It is now a totally different kind of polity. Productive forces operating autonomously would be far too disastrously disrup-tive, internally and externally. But if the control is to be exercised in a manner which preserves some at least of that *douceur des meours*, it had better retain a good deal of the political culture of the age of the *illusion* of autonomous economics.

16

From *the* Revolution to liberalisation

J.-P. Sartre has written at length on the question of how the myth of the French revolution is possible. The intelligibility, let alone the truth, of his answer need not detain us unduly. But the question is a good one. The past two centuries or so have indeed been the age of the myth of *the* Revolution. As in philosophical logic, the definite article has distinctive and powerful implications and gives rise to very interesting problems. In this case, they are not merely logical, but also, and above all, moral, epistemic and political. The definite article seems to imply existence; and it also seems to imply uniqueness. Even more disturbingly, it seems to suggest, in this case, moral rightness and political authority. *The* Revolution is necessary, unique and inevitable, legitimate and authoritative. But to claim these traits, it must also be identifiable; and it can only be identified, hailed and revered, if it carries some manifest stigmata. But what are they? Can they not be counterfeited? Are there not peddlers of fake stigmata, or, worst still, of false theories concerning what constitutes the stigmata?

If we can speak of *the* Revolution, well then it must exist – at least in the womb of time, waiting for its eventual but inevitable actualisation. There is a thing such that it is a revolution, and that it is the legitimate one; and for any other putative revolution, it must either be identical with the first-specified one or it must be spurious... That, roughly speaking, is the Believing Revolutionary's version of Bertrand Russell's Theory of Descriptions, which was an attempt to give a logical account of the meaning and force of the definite article. This somewhat technical-sounding question, much and earnestly debated in the philosophic trade, but not to my knowledge hitherto applied to political philosophy, has a curious relevance to the problem of *the* Revolution. (Capitalisation reinforces the suggestiveness of the definite article.)

What is the *Revolution?*

The Revolution ushers in the age of legitimacy, of a rightful social order on earth. One cannot altogether say that it will be the Kingdom of Heaven on Earth, for it will generally neither be a kingdom nor, in so many words, divinely authorised or administered; but that's the general idea.

The new order will be legitimate, where the pre-revolutionary old order was conspicuously, even paradigmatically, illegitimate. Hence the change is drastic, fundamental, 'structural'; it is *not* a mere matter of rotation of personnel, like those earlier dynastic conflicts between usurpers and pretenders. But the old order is not merely wrong, it is *méchant – il se defend.* So it cannot be removed by peaceful persuasion or legal methods; its corruption is such that it is blind, or indifferent, to its own illegitimacy. So *the* Revolution must be not merely radical, profound, structural, it must also be violent. Violence is alas imposed on it by the very wickedness of that which it replaces. But the violence is also functional in other ways. It provides the symbolism, the diacritical mark in time, for the new order. A transformation so profound and important needs a worthy herald. Violence is also a kind of purification, a moral fumigation of the corrupt world. A terrible new beauty is born. As Franz Fanon claimed, revolution is the carnival of the oppressed. You cannot have a carnival without fireworks.

The age which subscribed to the belief in *the* Revolution generally took great pride in it. It despised earlier ages, which committed political violence merely for questions of personnel, which thought at best in terms of legitimate and illegitimate monarchs, good or bad kings. Revolutionaries in this age were concerned with the very principles of political (and eventually economic) organisation, not with *nomenklatura* of office holders, the merry-go-round of ins and outs. Thus it felt that its concern was deeper, more moral, and more selfless.

What were the sources of this vision, and its problems?

There is no doubt at all in my mind about the single most important, and 'structural' reason for this way of looking at things. In consequence of industrialisation, or of the drive towards it, virtually all pre-industrial regimes and social orders have become illegitimate or, at best, in need of radical overhaul. They all become, without necessarily changing or becoming worse than they had been in earlier and less troubled days, *Anciens Régimes*. Why so?

Until recently, most of mankind lived in agrarian societies. Most of the members of these societies were peasants. These societies were almost always inegalitarian, displaying a sharp social stratification with a fairly small ruling class (who were, in fact or in conception, warriors and/or priests/clerics). Generally speaking, the inequality was accepted even by those who did not benefit from it, as inherent in the very nature of things. It was, however, further ratified by a written theology, which codified the moral order of the society, and which was in the keeping of literate scribes.

The total transformation of the division of labour which inevitably accompanies industrialisation, or even the movement towards it, made this system unviable in various ways. Above all, the particular *kind* of inequality which is so typical of literate agrarian civilisations becomes simply intolerable. Hereditary privilege, high office, indolence, all combined with hereditary inferiority for others, irrespective of role and achievement, are not unacceptable in themselves and at all times; but they do become unacceptable at a time of rapid mobility and the transformation of the occupational structure of society, when it becomes offensive to those who are now not merely more numerous, but also much more powerful, and above all when the previously segregated social strata rub shoulders in a wide variety of new situations which no longer endorse the old ranking, and often contradict it. Secondly, the old order generally benefited from a written ideology which, once upon a time, gave it powerful support. Now the very content of that ideology is in headlong conflict with that new science and technology, which cannot be ignored because it underlies the new productive and coercive processes. So the old creed not merely fails to offer support, it positively discredits anything damned by its own endorsement. Its stamp of approval now becomes a kiss of death. And the very totality and uncompromising absoluteness of its old claims, which once upon a time powerfully buttressed it, now hamper its efforts at adjustment. They are pre-historic monsters, floundering helplessly in the mud, brought down by their own cumbersome weight.

This is perhaps the main source of the myth of *the* Revolution: most of mankind lived under a variety of such social orders which became manifestly illegitimate, and which were endorsed by belief systems which in turn are now seen to be plainly and conspicuously false.

The fate of the diverse belief systems of agrarian civilisations has not, of course, been the same everywhere. If one considers the four main ones, one finds that their destinies have not been parallel. Christianity, located in the society in which the great change came first, endogenously, and which was consequently allowed the longest time for adjustment, has transformed and redefined itself, and survives in a curious semi-doctrinal and semi-established form, bearing little resemblance either to genuine faith or to whole-hearted secularisation. Confucianism may survive in spirit but is formally repudiated in its homeland. Hinduism survives as a powerful folk tradition, neither endorsed nor denounced by the political élite. Islam seems best equipped to sail through the great Niagara: it was always internally differentiated into a folk and a purer variant, and the latter seems, at least for the time being, to be well suited to serve, all at once, national pride, identification against the outsider, and self-disciplining and the denunciation of folk archaisms. Muslim lands which have taken this turn, or have been led to it by accidents of history, seem to be doing better than the Kemalist-style secularisers.

Nevertheless, by and large, one can say that the myth of *the* Revolution was fed by the blatant moral unacceptability of the old hierarchies, and by the blatant falsehood of the old beliefs. These are negative factors. But there were also positive ones; there was also a certain continuity. *The* Revolution in its way perpetuates *the* Messiah. Some at least of the old faiths contained themes which became specially tempting in the predicament created by the loss of the old legitimacy. The specific previous formulations of those ancient themes might now be beyond recovery; but when restated in a modern idiom, those themes could still be very appealing, or perhaps more appealing than ever. Those themes are *scripturalism* and *messianism*.

Each of these themes is, in its way, a-social or trans-social. Scripturalism teaches that a corpus of writing is the repository of cosmological and moral truth, and that what is said within that corpus is more authoritative than any individual man or group of men, and that it can sit in judgement on institutions, practices and customs. Thus the idea is established that the moral authority over men resides outside their community. Messianism on the other hand teaches that this extraneous authority can intrude into the human and social world suddenly, dramatically and conclusively; indeed, it encourages the hope that it will do so, and the belief that only such an irruption can set things right. Ideological politics were inherent in Christianity, and Islam, and perhaps particularly so in Islam.

The myth of *the* Revolution seems to have its source in this confluence – the perception of the blatant illegitimacy of agrarian civilisation, its hierarchies and its beliefs, with the scriptural–messianic ideas inherent in at least some variants of the literate agrarian belief systems.

The most elaborate and influential form of the theory of *the* Revolution is of course Marxism, which is largely a conflation of three old ideas: the entelechy acorn-to-oak view of human history; a materialist taxonomy of social forms, in which the mode of production is the key to classifying and hence evaluating a social order; and the messianic expectation of some total fulfilment. Not one of these three ideas is valid: there is no unique current of human history, the economic or productive basis of a society does not uniquely determine its political and moral traits, and there is no absolute social consummation available. In the designing of social orders as of other things, some models are much better than others, but rival advantages have to be weighed against each other and no model can incorporate all possible merits...But, apart from being erroneous in isolation, the three ideas are disastrous when combined. They then generate the truly absurd Marxist social eschatology: a perfect fulfilment awaits us at the end of the river; its features need not and cannot be worked out in advance, but will automatically reveal themselves as a consequence of the abolition of the previous exploitative class relations, whose termination is supposed to be both its *causa essendi* and its *causa cognoscendi*. To the earlier stages of human history, there is applied a corresponding mix of sociology and metaphysics. Certain semi-clear notions (e.g. class conflict) apply, but when they do not, are protected by mopping-up metaphysics (e.g. consciousness). Classes which are conscious of themselves plus those which are not conscious of themselves, when added to each other, easily cover all situations in which classes are required by the theory at all. Classes which on the other hand turn up when the theory does not want them, e.g. prior to state formation, are defined away as 'proto-classes'.

The absence of any clear vision of just what this future and glorious, post-revolutionary alternative will be, was so to speak innocent amongst earlier Marxists, being a perfectly natural consequence of a sincere belief in those three conflated ideas. It is by no means so innocent amongst contemporary Marxists, for whom the slogan of 'no blueprints for the future', reinforced by bits of the Hegelian philosophic heritage, is mainly a manner of evading a very awkward question: if the revolution was betrayed before, if indeed it has never yet failed to be betrayed, why exactly do you expect it to be any different next time?

But the revolutionary myth was not without a certain nobility, or at any rate it appealed to what might be called the Protestant conception of heroism. Generally speaking, societies underwrite their values and expectations by a profusion of external reinforcements, by endless ceremonials and rituals and other audio-visual aids of faith. The Protestant by contrast is taught to despise these aids. He knows the truth by inner signs; the external confirmations are, at best, for fools and weaklings, and at worst are simply snares, the self-advertisements of anti-truth. The modern moralistic revolutionary exemplifies this spirit in extreme form, and he applies it particularly to the problem of political legitimacy. All the external cards are stacked in favour of the existing order, but they carry no weight with him. His inner loyalty goes out towards an order which is not yet, and which consequently has no means of externalising and vulgarising itself. If he is also a nationalist, which he frequently is, his love may go out to a nation which has as yet no state to call its own. His political loyalty is given to an order which is not of this political world, which is all the more pure because it can as yet rely on no policeman to enforce its will, and no ritual to advertise it.

This refusal to ratify the Outer and the determination to be guided by the Inner alone has a certain grandeur. We have of late heard a certain amount about the charms of 'expressivism', of the congruence of the personal-inner and of the institutional-outer. It is this congruence that men really covet, we are told. Lack of expressivism, it appears, was the great weakness of the Enlightenment, and its rediscovery was the supreme achievement of Romanticism and in particular of Hegel.[1]

Perhaps so: for my own part, the one trait of the modern revolutionary which induces me to respect him in some measure is precisely his uncompromising anti-expressivism, his conviction, not merely that a cowl does not make a monk, but that institutions or ceremonials do not constitute legitimacy – that it resides elsewhere. But let that pass.

[1] Charles Taylor, *Hegel*, Cambridge University Press, 1975. (Cf. chapter 1 above).

The weakness of the myth

What were the great weaknesses of the myth of *the* Revolution?

The Revolution is generally followed by *the* Terror; and *the* Revolution is invariably betrayed. (Alternative formulation: *the* Revolution turns out not to have been the true one. The revolutionary may well feel like the character in André Gide's *Vatican Caves* who wonders how, when he meets God after his own decease, he will be able to know that it really is the true one. The revolutionary has similar cause for eternal doubt.) The Terror and the Betrayal of the Revolution are sometimes confused, if only because they are liable to be carried out by the same personnel; but they ought to be distinguished. Each is probably inevitable, but they spring from different roots.

The inevitability of *the* Terror springs from a consideration which is old, familiar and obvious, but which the revolutionary myth had somehow succeeded in ignoring, at least in part. In anarchic conditions life is precarious, and there is no good reason to obey anyone. Many will try to rule, from greed or from sheer self-defence, and in the conflict between these numerous would-be rulers, most or all will suffer. Peace can best be established by having *one* and only one sovereign – but how is he to be identified? In logic, all conflicts must escalate to the limit of currently available technology, for the loser always has the incentive to reach deeper into the armoury. A 'society' is a collection of human beings such that it is endowed with devices, not for preventing conflict, but for effectively inhibiting escalation. The simplest device is the *easy identifiability* of escalation-dampers. The more identifiable they are, the less potent they need be. Where one family, principle, institution or whatnot has possessed a monopoly of authority for a long time, the matter is easy. That one centre will then speak with the authority of age and above all of easy and so to speak snowballing identifiability, of being recognised by so many for so long. All those who want peace above everything will rally to it, in the knowledge of similar support from others of a like mind, and this cumulative endorsement will give the sovereign effective authority. Once this is broken, however, by one successful rebellion in the name of an externally validated and new authority, in the name of some ideological Joker card (God, *the* Revolution, etc.), the dam is broken. The point about these Joker cards is that anyone can issue them to himself. Not everyone has the talent or the nerve to play them, it is true, but quite a few take a chance at it. Chaos or at least the prospect of it ensues. The latest ruler must take pre-emptive measures whilst he still has the chance, which of course prompts the next wave of would-be revolutionaries to take their pre-emptive measures in turn, before he does unto them precisely what they want to do unto him. So the thing escalates and soon ceases to be anyone's carnival. Terror is simply compensation for the lack of more humdrum legitimacy. Only fear can replace the authority of custom and familiarity.

The problem of identifying *the* Revolution is of course the myth's inheritance from messianic religion. How do you identify the true Messiah? Pseudo-Messiahs abound. In a Czech humorous-historical film made under Communism, Rudolf II, the last Holy Roman Emperor to use Prague as his capital, is portrayed as sitting amongst some forty-odd copies of the Mona Lisa and musing – if only we knew which is the real one, we could sell all the others! His problem was the same as that of the true believer. It is well known that there is a true Messiah, a true carrier of the real Revolution, somewhere – but the selection procedures for picking Him out are very dicey. The trouble is, each of the candidates claims not merely that he is the True One, but also that, in virtue naturally of being the true one, he possesses the correct criterion for singling out the real one, namely himself. This seems logical enough in religion, which is in effect definable in terms of such logical Narcissism, and of the habit of demanding assent with menaces, but it doesn't help him of little faith who stands outside and who tries to choose. No good arguments being available, *only* Terror can in the end resolve the question and persuade the waverers.

The Betrayal of the Revolution springs from a special source, though the revulsion evoked by the Terror may cause it to seem but an aspect and consequence of the betrayal. The overwhelming and justified sense of the illegitimacy of surviving agro-literate civilisations generates the illusion that there must be some manifest self-evidently valid *other* Order. This is how the old order had portrayed its own standing. The critics simply transplant these claims to a new carrier, conceived as the antithesis of the old Order, but otherwise nebulous. Revolutionary theorists either leave the outlines of this other Order unspecified, or they overdraw its merits. Unspecific, unrealistic, nebulous and glamorous, no real form of solid organisation can conceivably live up to it. No real organisation can both maintain order and refrain from enforcement. Nor can it refrain from using *some* distributive principle, and from favouring those whom it must cajole into conformity and towards the required performance. This pursuit of the absurd, of the over-ambitious or of the utterly un-specific, generally leads to an actual performance much worse than that of polities which have more modest and realistic aspirations. The notion that it was not the basic idea of the Revolution which was wrong, but that it was *betrayed*, is however encouraged by the new wave of would-be revolutionaries, whom it provides with the justification for trying it on once again.

That is *the* Revolution, that was.

It seems to me that the myth of *the* Revolution is on the way out, for various reasons. What are they?

Anciens Régimes, i.e. self-evidently illegitimate traditional agro-literate polities, are getting to be in short supply. (Take Ethiopia; how short a span of years separated the Abyssinian Decembrists from their October!) Those that survive, i.e. those that might be called the CIA-monarchies, are semi-modernised, often possessed of oil money, or are subsidised as part of the cold war, have efficient modern police forces, and are no longer as vulnerable as *Anciens Régimes* once were.

In more developed societies, the balance of military–technological power seems to be tilted against revolution. Barricades are now as archaic as the war horse. Contrary to Lenin's youthful conversion after the execution of his brother, urban guerrillas and terrorism do seem to have some prospects, whereas serious, hard-working, self-respecting, so to speak Protestant-ethic revolutionary activism has much less. In the old days, you could meet a much better class of revolutionary, if you know what I mean. This leaves the intervening zone, the countries whose condition lies between *Anciens Régimes* and those relatively developed countries. In this twilight-zone, *coup*-dictatorships abound to such an extent that they seem to devalue the very idea of *the* Revolution. Those *Dreigroschen* rulers often fail even to be credited with having betrayed the Revolution. They seldom look as if they had ever exemplified it in the first place.

Thus, by and large, the climate seems propitious to the abandon-ment of the revolutionary mystique, which only survives amongst the conventicles of the long-haired young who, in their holes and crannies, perpetuate the mythology, as worthy Noncomformist sects once perpetuated reforming zeal. The invocation of the Revolution, like that of God, devalues the outer order, and upgrades the believer, in at least his own eyes and that of fellow-believers. It sets up a rival hierarchy of merit which actually finds pride and validation in its lack of outward recognition – until The Day. Revolutions are in fact sometimes inevitable or desirable, for there do exist regimes which are wicked and/or disastrous, and which can only be overturned by force. But there is no self-evident and self-authenticating Alternative, and above all there is no force, party, class, leader or whatnot, which can guarantee the legitimacy and soundness of some such alternative, and which would thus provide reliable identification for the true Messiah. This seems obvious enough, but somehow, for well over a century, it was not nearly obvious enough.

Liberalisation

But if the Revolution is dead, a new notion is born: liberalisation. This generic concept was born almost unnoticed: and suddenly it is with us, almost fully grown. The important reality which it covers has received very little systematic generic consideration.

As stated, self-evidently illegitimate, archaic regimes are now fairly scarce. On the other hand, there is a great abundance of regimes which preside over relatively viable societies, economically and culturally, but which are also disagreeably and perhaps unnecessarily authoritarian. They are economically viable in the sense that they seem to be providing at least a reasonable economic prospect for their populations, and likewise a prospect of identification with the dominant culture for very many, usually for the majority, of their citizens. Despite the eco-doomsters, abject poverty and despair are not so very widespread, at least at present.

If this relatively complacent account is at least partly accurate for most of mankind – and it does not claim to be true of all men – certain consequences follow: much of mankind lives in conditions which offer at least a fair amount of positive inducement to identify with the existing social order. Moreover, there is the widely operative negative consideration – the greatly diminished appeal of the revolutionary illusion. It was no accident that the era of the revolutionary mystique was preceded by political theorising, based on the following *Gedanken*-experiment: what would it be like if we restarted society anew? They theorised about a state of nature. We do not. It is the states of culture which provide us with our abstract premises.

For it happens to be of the essence of the human condition that we do not and cannot start anew, that we inherit a constraining situation. The revival of this awareness is the obverse of the demystification of 'Revolution'. (Curiously, there is also a fashion of 'starting anew' political philosophy in American academe, but I suspect that this is a superficial and unimportant phenomenon.)

So the background to liberalisation is different from that which engendered the revolutionary myth. Societies ripe for liberalisation are not totally and blatantly illegitimate. They are offensive but... They cater to numerous vested interests outside the topmost privileged cliques: there is too much to lose for too many. They pander to national pride or identification, at least of some. They are not good; in many respects they are nasty, but they are not so bad as to inspire the feeling that simply *anything* would be preferable. Most important, the ideological climate no longer encourages the illusion that the unspecified 'anything' would be, through some amazing automatism, simply marvellous, or that the identification of the Moses, who would lead one to the Promised Land, is feasible. There is much at risk, and the future alternatives are obscure. This is a time for weighing our options and trying to understand them, not for revolutionary inebriation.

This, roughly, is the mental state of the liberaliser. He is not, of course, necessarily in a state of total sobriety. He may be very excited, or indeed ecstatic. Some may on the other hand be opportunists, wishing to concede just enough and soon enough to preserve the bulk of the benefits accrued to them under the pre-liberal conditions. Others may be heroes and martyrs, who have been pushed to a point at which they are no longer willing to compromise with the existing order, and who then say No without further calculation or personal hope. But the most characteristic liberaliser is perhaps the man with a genuine taste for ideas, in a profession in which intellectual experimentation is of the essence, who finds an intoxication in even partial intellectual liberty. Liberalisation is the carnival of the intellectuals. A demoted university teacher in an authoritarian country observed to me that the one consolation of having to live in his homeland was the thirst and enthusiasm with which students received even half an idea...Such men, when driven into exile in a liberal country, are then liable to be much disappointed by the luke-warmness of personal intellectual relations and activities in free countries. There is nothing like a dictatorship to give flavour to intellectual conversation. The likelihood of being bugged can do marvels for the apparent quality of ideas.

Thus, there does now exist a generic liberaliser, incarnated variously in Left, Right and ambiguous Third-World regimes. The supposition that he is destined to remain with us is based on the plausible assumption that these regimes will not liberalise swiftly and spontaneously, and also on the more debatable assumption that the demand for liberalisation will continue to grow. This, admittedly, is speculative. But the speculation is, however, worth pursuing. One could base it on the idea that there is some universal inherent striving toward liberty in the human heart. Pleasing though it would be to believe this, evidence does not support it. Human beings can accept and internalise extremes both of inequality and oppression, as long as they are stable – and indeed they can identify with them morally. A more promising starting point – from a liberal's viewpoint – seems to me to be the inherent potential of industrial society. Occupational mobility, a high level of fairly rigorous education, urban living, work which invokes the independent use of mental skills, and other factors perhaps, conspire to give at least substantial segments of the population a taste for liberty. At the same time, if my diagnosis is correct, these groups are less prone to the revolutionary illusion, to the supposition that a magical moment of fulfilment may come, that a manifest key to social salvation is in the possession of some identifiable, sacred liberating force. So?

The Liberaliser does not suffer from the illusion that he is standing at the dawn of history. His problem is, rather, that he wishes to remove certain encumbrances without causing an avalanche. He is willing or eager to preserve a great deal of the past, not because he has many illusions about it, but because he is by now strongly imbued with a sense of the perils of loss of legitimacy, of chaos and anarchy. The partial legitimacy which the current system possesses, through its relative age and one or two other supporting factors, is no shining glorious thing, but it is very much better than nothing, better than chaos and the subsequent Terror.

The Liberalisation ideal is also unspecific but in a manner quite different from that of the revolutionary. The lack of specificity does not arise from some nebulous, excessive, messianic and total expectation, but from the very opposite: there is a willingness to perpetuate social features of the political and economic landscape not for their own sake but simply because they are parts of the existing furniture, if that should prove to be the price of liberalisation with stability, as a way of ensuring that liberalisation does not get out of hand and become self-destructive.

A major problem in this endeavour is of course the backlog of political injustice and of ideological rubbish, wedded to each other, and the resentment against them which, once freed, is very difficult to contain.

> In the corrupted currents of this world
> Offence's guilded hand may shove by justice,
> And oft 'tis seen the wicked prize itself
> Buys out the law. . .

Thus mused that rather inefficient authoritarian monarch, Hamlet's uncle. In modern dictatorships, the wicked prize is power. It buys out the law quite easily, and more cheaply, by having at its command a pliable ideology which ensures that any who dare contest the very offence itself are themselves automatically condemned, and that any instrument of justice which fails to turn on them is itself then condemned. Substantive or *Volk* or class justice overrules mere formal or bourgeois justice, and the ideology explains why this must rightly be so, why this cumulative injustice is true justice.

The rules and the skill of the game

Liberalisation must involve the establishment of a more genuine rule of law, and it is hard to restrain the desire to tear down that ideological drivel which had for so long bought out the law, often with brazen intellectual dishonesty, fortified by the confident expectation of being protected by the wicked prize of power itself. So moderation may be no easy matter. It may be small solace to the liberaliser to know that many other erstwhile totalitarian, circular, vicious belief systems have become harmless once they were separated from the wicked prize of power. Those who are free for the first time to call rubbish by its true name, may have some difficulty in doing so in parliamentary language.

The claim which is being made is that *the* Liberalisation is now becoming a generic and indeed a crucial phenomenon, as *the* Revolution had been; that, for good and in the main obvious reasons, it is replacing the earlier myth as a central political preoccupation or category; and that its basic assumptions are not merely more pertinent to our time, but probably also rather sounder by any criterion and at all times. But the phenomenon, and the concept, has received very little comparative investigation, though it seems to cry out for it: liberalisation occurs or is attempted in a variety of dramatically contrasted contexts. Yet it is, in my view, recognisably the same animal; it emerges in the most diverse climates.

The objection might be raised that this animal is not merely common, but so very common as to be a genus rather than a species; and that it is very very broad, and hence analytically useless. There is a perfectly familiar liberal political theory, articulated in various forms but recently most often in Sir Karl Popper's version, which commends 'piecemeal' social reform and stresses the perils of large-scale changes. So what is new? – other than, perhaps, that more people nowadays have cause to be attracted by this doctrine.

This would be a mistaken reaction. *The* Liberalisation is not one moderate socio-political modification amongst others, to be assimilated with all the rest. On the contrary, it is distinctive, perilous and dramatic. This much it has in common with *the* Revolution. It is the transition from a situation in which free discussion of minor reforms and their peaceful implementation is highly problematical, to one in which it becomes institutionalised and a part of normality. Thus it is not one reform amongst others, it is a profound change in political climate, which would make subsequent reforms un-perilous, but which itself is very perilous indeed.

The attitude of liberalisers and of revolutionaries to the problem of violence and the release of uncontrollable forces is of course different. For the revolutionaries, a peaceful transition, should it happen, due to favourable local conditions or traditions, was a kind of bonus, something of a fortunate windfall, but one which one should never count on. The temperamentally more extremist or romantic ones amongst them might even despise it, openly or covertly. If *the* Revolution occurred without cataclism and violence, they felt a bit cheated of their theatre, and they also suspected that it was not too good for people morally to be spared this purification by fear and fire. It was almost cheating, getting it without having suffered for it. By contrast, for liberalisers, the moderation of violence, the containment of discontinuity, is not a bonus, it is of the very essence of the whole operation. If this is not secured, then, in all probability, all else is lost too.

Liberalisation is a curious process which endeavours to modify a political structure profoundly *without* dismantling it altogether, without loss of continuity and with a certain preserved legitimacy, yet without deep respect. There is the story about the newly elected mayor who vowed to follow the narrow path between justice and corruption. Liberalisers face similar predicaments: the path seems narrow and precarious, requiring enormous delicacy of touch, patience, sensitivity; it is unlikely that key strategies or ploys can be worked out in advance or mechanically applied. I remember a Czech Communist (and one who loyally remained such) deploring the failure of Dubček. He commented, borrowing the terminology of soccer – *nedoved' to prokličkovat.* He did not know how to dribble through with the ball, to sell dummies right and left and get past the defenders. It is evidently a game which requires the utmost skill and nimbleness. As yet, we have seen no great masters of the art, no George Best of Liberalisation.

Two manifest perils surround this operation. It may go too far; or it may revert to the initial condition. From contemporary Spain we must borrow the notion of the *Bunker* describing those constrained by their situation and/or conviction to uphold the old order with a *verkrampt* and dangerous rigidity. The Bunker too must become a generic concept. Every East European country has its Bunker. Every authoritarian regime also has a backlog of injustice and resentment and carries a varying load of ideological rubbish. Once some injustices are acknowledged, remedied or compensated, what rational principle could serve to draw the line beyond which one should not go, in the interests of stability? No such principle is conceivable. The addicts of *the* Revolution faced no such problem, at least in theory. The emotive charge of their activism was precisely that Justice was coming at last, and there was no need to dole justice and truth out in careful rations. The more complete, the better. Not so for the liberalisers. Again, once you can criticise and highlight the errors of the erstwhile official ideology, how can you stop short of pointing out its total silliness, or restrain those who wish to say this? Over and above the inherent momentum of all this, due to the impossibility of rationing justice, or truth, there is the enthusiasm of our surviving revolutionaries-by-temperament, who may wish to practise liberalisation with the same totality as revolution had once been preached.

The impulsion to go too far of course generates or reinforces the contrary impulsion to go nowhere at all, or even to retreat. If you cannot arrest or restrain the forces you unleash, why take these dreadful risks at all? The politics of liberalisation, or of a pre-liberalisation period, exhibit a very characteristic spectrum of attitudes. Some inertia or linguistic poverty has made us take over the language of 'Left' and 'Right' for this range, but this is probably unfortunate and misleading. In the current and inadequate and incoherently applied language, the 'Left' generally stands for the goodies, who want lots of liberalisation, and the 'Right' for the baddies who oppose it. In as far as *this* spectrum however is quite independent of the older meanings of these terminologies, the usage tends to end in chaos.

At either end of the spectrum are those who are not real liberalisers at all – those who genuinely believe in the system or at any rate
unambiguously wish to preserve it, and those at the other end who
value its destruction above all else. But in between, there are all the
nuances of liberalisation. In the characteristic political game accompanying or preceding liberalisation, one marked trait is the mutual
interdependence of the positions. They actually *need* each other, not
just as allies, but simply to *give sense* to their positions. They are
logically parasitic on each other. Every moderate – and there are
gradations of restraint – appeals to the very existence of more extreme,
or more reactionary, positions, to explain why his own slow tactic
makes sense. If you go too far and too fast, you will inevitably
provoke the backlash and we shall lose everything! And equally: if
we do not go far enough soon enough, we shall drive the moderates
into the arms of extremists who will then destroy everything. . .The
logical paradox of these positions is that they would cease to be true,
if those who articulate them really succeeded in persuading their
listeners. The very position presupposes that there *are* others who
will lash back, and that there are others still who will get out of
hand. . .

The game has now been played a number of times, and a number
of polities seem on the verge of playing it. It is high time we tried to
explore the rules of the game. The actual course of various games is
bound to vary greatly. All we can do as yet is to list the themes which
will need to be explored. Is there a generic difference between Left
and Right Liberalisation? How much difference does economic
centralisation make to the process? Or the existence of a large and
indispensable class of technical, or literary, intelligentsia? Or the
existence of a precise and codified ideology, with fairly unambiguous
sources of scriptural authority, as opposed to loose or even plural
ideologies? Or the presence of regional nationalism, available as
allies? Or the intrusion of international politics, given that, curiously, the precise degree of internal freedom can serve as a badge of
block-adherence and loyalty? Is Liberalisation favoured by economic
success or by failure? Do the groups which crystallised out in a
previously centralised state bear any resemblance to the traditional
categories of 'class' etc.? The questions are here. No doubt there are
others. But these and similar problems are the ones which could guide
a comparative interest in both the South and the East European
liberalisations which we can now observe.

17

Plaidoyer pour une libéralisation manquée

It is a great honour to provoke not one, but two sustained reactions from Raymond Aron,[1] and I can only hope that his prediction of the initiation of a *vaste debat* concerning this issue will indeed be fulfilled. For my own part, I have few if any serious disagreements with what he says in his article, notwithstanding the fact that it has the form of a critical examination of my own position. The differences are matters of stress, interpretation, and perhaps temperament, rather than genuine disagreements of fact or argument.

Some years ago, the joke circulated about the difference between an optimist and a pessimist: the former teaches his daughter Russian, the latter teaches her Chinese. By this touchstone, evidently my daughter should be immersed in Pushkin whilst Aron's should be well advanced in Confucian studies. But this difference will not lead to a headlong confrontation between us. Neither his pessimism nor my optimism are dogmatic. We present general considerations which support one view or the other, fully aware that these considerations do not uniquely determine the course of future events.

Aron's disagreements, if I understand them properly, can be summed up as follows:

(1) He challenges my theory of *the* Revolution, or to be more precise, of how the myth of *the* Revolution arose, where Revolution means, basically, a radical discontinuity in the political and social organisation of society, such that, *after* it, mankind attains a total moral consummation, which luminously and evidently justifies *the* Event which initiated it, whilst an era of moral/political darkness, an Age of Ignorance, prevailed prior to *the* Day.

---

[1] Cf. Raymond Aron, *Plaidoyer pour l'Europe décadente*, Paris, 1977, p. 459 et seq., and *Government & Opposition*, 1st issue, 1979.

On Aron's view, Revolutions are Libéralisations *manquées*. So on this view liberalisation is not, as I suggested, a later and superior preoccupation, in which moral idealism is tempered by a realistic or cynical awareness of the price of discontinuity and political intoxication, but, on the contrary, *preceded* the revolutionary mystique, which only emerged from frustrated liberalisations. Such a view calls not merely for a re-interpretation of certain past, supposedly paradigmatic Revolutions, but also, significantly and ominously, is full of weighty implications for the future of those societies (notably East European ones) which on Aron's account are bound to inhibit their own liberalisations. Aron doesn't say that they are thereby doomed to undergo a revolution: the pressure generated by a frustrated liberalisation obviously is not sufficient to ensure the effective coming of a revolution. There has to be an opportunity, as well as a weakening at the top, and Aron predicts nothing of the kind. But a part of his pessimism – perhaps the most significant part – is that the logic of the situation allows but two alternatives to Eastern Europe as it now is: either a suppressed striving for liberty, or a revolution.

(2) He criticises me for failing to account for the great differences in the hold which the myth of *the* Revolution has over various countries and cultures.

(3) Apart from insisting (rightly I think) on a differential theory of the diverse degree of susceptibility to revolutionary Romanticism, he also queries the homogeneity of the phenomena which were meant to be covered by my notion of Liberalisation. Here too, we must *distinguish*, he insists. He ends by doubting or denying whether Eastern European developments warrant the honorific title of Liberalisation. This, of course, is another way of referring to his pessimism.

At a formal level, I could reply to this point by saying that a concept is not undermined if it be shown that there are things to which it fails to apply. On the contrary. A possible conclusion which one could reach in this field would run as follows: Right totalitarianisms allow liberalisations (at least under conditions which are quite probable), whereas Left ones do not. In fact, Aron's position would seem to be some kind of refinement of this idea. But one can only articulate this kind of generalisation with the help of a generic notion of liberalisation – whose usefulness is thereby demonstrated.

But I am not eager to stress this formal point unduly, and prefer to discuss on substantive grounds whether or not the pessimistic view is warranted.

The view that Revolutions occur because, or when, Liberalisations fail, is supported by Aron by an appeal to the actual course of the French Revolution. But even if the (relatively speaking) micro-history of the Revolution supports this, can it be supported by the more general ideological situation of the eighteenth century? Was not the most important strand in the thought of the Enlightenment one which insisted that both the organisational principles, and the ideological premisses, of the *ancien régime* were *fundamentally* unsound and illegitimate? This does not, of course, prevent those who wish to change it, from proceeding in a gentle and soft manner, if the old system will but co-operate; but if it does not do so, as is to be expected – both in fact, and from the premisses of the reformers/ liberalisers – then have they any choice, either morally or politically, but to proceed further and have a Revolution proper? Even the greatest avalanche must needs begin with a slow movement of snow: this does not preclude the possibility that the weight and position of the dislodged man are such that, once moving, nothing can arrest it and prevent its dreadful acceleration.

I can only fall back on the very general and abstract premisses which seem to me to make this cogent. Most of mankind until recently lived in agrarian societies. Agrarian societies generally, though not universally, have the following traits:

(1) They are severely inegalitarian.
(2) Most of their members have small or negligible prospects of social mobility.
(3) Their systems are sustained by transcendental premisses held in an absolutist, illiberal manner.

Agrarian societies are universally being replaced by industrial ones, because the material and military superiority of the latter makes this inevitable. But industrial societies

(1) are relatively egalitarian, or at any rate, incompatible with the agrarian forms of inequality;
(2) presuppose, either during their formative period, or possibly, forever, a fairly high level of occupational and other mobility, at any rate sufficient to make them incompatible with the rigidities of most agrarian societies; and
(3) they employ a technology and science which is (or whose

plausible philosophical accompaniments are) logically incompatible with the earlier transcendent beliefs and their authority, and which are thus undermined, and actually *weaken* the institution which they underwrite. Their blessing becomes a curse.

In brief, the inevitable changes inherent in the transition from agrarian to industrial society are incompatible with the preservation of the forms and beliefs of the former, and cannot be justified in terms of its beliefs and pieties. It would seem to follow that a radical discontinuity ('revolution') is overwhelmingly probable, and can only be avoided in exceptional cases.

Only such an approach, it seems to me, can help explain one of the most striking facts of our time, namely that students and intellectuals of the Third World countries speak Marxism as automatically and self-evidently as they speak prose. They do so because it is the most easily available, optimally orchestrated theory which accounts for the visible, luminous illegitimacy of the old order. Moreover, it simultaneously explains both the necessity and the immorality of the impact of more advanced countries.[2] Only this can explain the amazingly well-diffused and deep Manichaeanism: the conviction that the actual social world is profoundly evil and illegitimate and that true legitimacy can only be located in some other, more ultimate, order which is yet to be.

So I continue to uphold the view that the myth of *the* Revolution was inherent in our situation. This is not in conflict with the point stressed by Aron, namely, that the first efforts at transformation may be carried out by men who wish also to proceed gently, avoid a bloodbath, etc. It is also not incompatible with the fact that both the myth and the reality of revolution will impinge on diverse societies in a very different manner. For instance, the first society to modernise maintained political continuity during the Industrial Revolution proper (though not in the seventeenth century). There were cases of effective pre-emptive modernisation-from-above (Prussia, Japan), in the interests of strengthening the state in the face of other states.

Not all *ancien régimes* are alike. The country which gave us this term and the notion was one in which the Reformation had failed, whilst the baroque centralising monarchy had succeeded, and in which political and ideological unification and absolutisation were particularly developed. The revolutionary ideal of strangling the last

[2] Cf. Donald Macrae, *Ideology and Society*, 1961, ch. XVI, 'The Bolshevik Ideology'.

King with the entrails of the last priest (or was it the other way round?) is specially seductive in a land where Kings and priests were both prominent and powerful. Possibly such lands are specially revolution-prone, and perhaps this is one of the roots of Aron's pessimism.

But nothing in my approach committed me to any kind of unilineal and single-track theory of the Great Transition. I hold no such theory and, on the contrary, welcome exploration of the differences such as Aron initiates. At the same time, the pervasiveness (albeit in unequal intensity and in diverse form) of the myth of the Revolution seems to me obvious enough to require explanation. As yet, I see no reason to retract the explanation which I offered.

But Aron's pessimism is not oriented only to the past. Its possibly most significant aspect looks to the future, and concerns the difficulty of liberalisation in 'ideocratic' states. He is saying, in effect, that they either will not liberalise, and continue to be oppressive, or will blow up in revolutions which follow on abortive liberalisations, in which case we presumably cannot hope for much from them either.

If I could refute this prognosis I should be happy, and Aron himself no doubt would feel the same. Of course I cannot *refute* it. But it is possible to show that its conclusion itself is also not demonstrated, and that some good reasons at least allow one to hope that it may be false.

There are, as far as I can see, two main theories about the developed ideocratic societies. One of them is prominent in Aron's article and runs as follows: the ideological and organisational monopoly of one doctrine and party means that any relaxation, any freedom of expression and association, inevitably deprives a privileged minority of its position, and endangers it so much – not only its privileges, but its very physical survival are at stake – that it cannot tolerate rivals. (The oldest official faith in the West has in fact learnt to do so, and contains a variety of accommodation-devices for doing so notwithstanding the logical totalitarianism of its position.) Some of the right-wing authoritarian régimes which are capable of liberalisation were also ideocratic: but the ideologies they upheld, though logically total, had lost their capacity to inspire serious belief in a sufficient proportion of the population. The argument from the totalitarian implications of the ideology is, admittedly, not its most important part (though it is supported by obvious features of Marxism, notably the lack of room it allows for legitimate conflict in post-revolutionary society, etc.), but it is often invoked.

The central part of the argument, however, invokes the self-interest of the *ruling* stratum itself.[3] But there may be many paths to organisational and institutional pluralism, through the emergence of tolerated special interests within the ruling stratum, to the emergence of cross-cutting links across it and the rest of the population.[4] Perhaps one day someone will have cause to mutter – of course we may have a liberal society, provided we do not too blatantly call it such, at least at first.

The counter-argument to Aron's pessimism seems to me to run as follows: an advanced industrial society requires a large scientific, technical, administrative, educational stratum, with genuine competence based on prolonged training. In other words, it cannot rely on rigid ideologues and servile classes alone. It is reasonable to assume that this kind of educated middle class, owing its position to technical competence rather than to subservience, and inherently, so to speak professionally, capable of distinguishing reality and thought from verbiage and incantation, will develop or has developed the kind of tastes we associate with its life-style – a need for security, a recognition of competence rather than subservience, a regard for efficiency and integrity rather than patronage and loyalty in professional life, a recognition of the fact that errors in good faith are not morally culpable but part of the normal healthy working of institutions and call for no witch-hunts, a measure of freedom in leisure activities. At the same time, this class is large enough and indispensable enough not to be lightly or pointlessly thwarted. It can exercise a sustained, quiet, pervasive pressure. It may infiltrate high places. Overt dissidents are its miniscule, heroic, probably indispensable, yet expendable advance guards; but the real battle may be won by the incomparably larger, cautious, compromising but pervasive and persistent main body, which advances like an insidious sand dune, rather than by dramatic self-immolation. This class is large, and it cannot be penalised effectively without a cost to the economy which may no longer be acceptable. The main body may sacrifice or even disavow its own 'dissident' advance guard, whilst benefiting from its courage, though it may perhaps secure some

---

[3] A witty exiled dissident, Valentin Turchin, has described this as the 'bolshevik' position within the dissident movement. Cf. *Inertsiya Strakha (The Inertia of Fear)*, Kronika Press, New York, 1977, to be published in English by Columbia University Press. See also my review of it in *Times Literary Supplement*, 25 November 1977.

[4] Cf. Ghita Ionescu, *The Politics of East European Communist States*, Weidenfeld and Nicolson, 1967.

moderation at least in the price exacted for that courage by the old authorities.

Furthermore, relative economic success, national pride, and the legitimacy conferred on any regime by sheer longevity, may make it easier – because less risky – for the rulers to make concessions to this class. As material resources become more plentiful, competition for them may become less acute. Affluence, if not classlessness, may at least reduce antagonisms and thus, for good Marxist reasons, diminish, though it cannot eliminate, the need for a repressive state. The end of ideology, erroneously predicted in the West, may yet get its second chance in the East. Could it not perish from sheer boredom? So, as the system gains in authority through stability, it may afford to relax without putting itself intolerably at risk.

It is arguable that in some small measure, all this has already happened. The complaints that things have worsened in the USSR since 1965 or 1968 may reflect, not so much any objective deterioration, but a very great rise in the level of liberal expectations (both inside and outside the country).

I have not the least desire to pretend that the optimistic argument is demonstrably valid. That would be both complacent and irresponsible, or callous. The argument that concessions only feed the appetite they nourish, and thus stimulate cumulating demands which in the end must be unacceptable to the power-holders, and consequently that all concessions are always both inadequate and excessive, and hence that the very logic of the situation will prevent any sane authorities from making them – this argument is also very persuasive. But it has not *always* applied. A mixture of complicity, interpenetration, Danegeld, weariness, new elements in the situation, cooling of ideological ardour, shared concern with interests which would be put in peril by confrontation – such factors may at least on occasion make it possible for political–ideological monopolists to acquiesce without violent resistance, if without joy, in the gradual erosion of their own position. The monopolists surrendered in Prague in 1967/8, and, but for external intervention, would not have dared raise an arm in defence of their own erstwhile position. There are of course no guarantees whatsoever that such hopes will prove justified. But we are not obliged to abandon hope either. The hope is at least not demonstrably absurd, and the issue between pessimism and optimism remains an open one.

18
Gone and gone forever

It is impossible to resist the temptation to read the entrails of Czechoslovakia in pursuit of signs and omens of the political destiny of industrial society. Tantalisingly, for anyone seeking (certainly in vain) an unambiguous interpretation of the evidence, Czechoslovakia, more even perhaps than other societies, is at once both idiosyncratic and symptomatic. All its reactions can be seen in two ways – as generic manifestations of advanced industrial organisation, or on the contrary as expressions of the local spirit and tradition.

Available prognoses for industrial society range along the entire spectrum from outright optimism to outright pessimism. The softening impact of affluence on social conflict, the shift from the predatory spirit to the productive one, the individualism and the interdependence engendered by a complex technical division of labour, the roots of industrialism in individualist commercialism and Protestant inner-directedness, all these and no doubt other factors can be invoked in support of expecting industrial society to be liberal. On the other hand, the mammoth size of late industrial productive units, the increased effectiveness of military and police technologies and their inevitable concentration at the political centre, the fact that most industrial societies now have authoritarian traditions (because most of mankind has them), which can only be reinforced by the travail of imitative industrialisation, the feasibility of cultural centralism in an age of mass media – all this and more can at least as convincingly be invoked in support of the contrary expectation. Which is it to be?

What does the Czech experience prove? Czechoslovakia (at least as far as the Czech lands are concerned, and my argument will ignore the Slovaks) is one of the early and successful industrial societies, and it is today under a dictatorship. Clearly, the second fact cannot simply be explained by the first. It also has something to do with the Red Army. Nevertheless, the two facts must be brought into some kind of relation with each other.

The Czechs are not a nation doomed to dictatorship by their own character: they are neither so turbulent as to make any other form of government unworkable, nor so reverent as to require government to embody and impose absolute verities and the good life. In fact, they are markedly lacking in both turbulence and reverence. There can be few nations whose soldiers could sing an ironical song about their own failure to fight:

> Už je to všecko pryč,
> A nevratí se víc,
> Kanóny, pušky, náboje,
> Vzali nám Němci bez boje

> [It is all gone
> And gone forever
> Guns, rifles, ammo
> The Germans took
> And we did not fight]

Nor are they one of those cultures amongst whom orderly work habits can only be imposed with threats and menaces. On the contrary, a deeply engrained and endorsed work ethic, virtually part of Czech identity, has been severely hampered by Communist organisation, by handing industrial leadership to over-zealous loyal hacks. The Czech Communist Party resembles English public schools at least in this, that it produces an economically inept élite. The manifest disproportion between economic potential and performance greatly aided liberalisation, by making it appear economically imperative. Nor are there any irresoluble internal conflicts within the nation: on the contrary, Czech politics are remarkably consensual. Though not resolute, in face of adversity they combine rather than split. (This consensual trait, however, does not prevent the texture of daily life from being abrasive and irritable.) Egalitarian, pragmatic, consensual, lacking in romantic or moral ardour, given to both the work ethic and to comfort, dictatorship amongst them would seem redundant and to correspond to neither psychic nor social need. It may be natural in Bucharest, but in Prague it is puzzling.

However, the manner in which dictatorship was nonetheless imposed is not central to Professor Skilling's monumental book,[1] but it is a highly relevant, perhaps the most relevant, background issue. Professor Skilling offers only a summary description, rather than an explanation, of this phenomenon – largely in terms of the policy chosen at the time by Gottwald:

> Gottwald seemed obsessed with an almost suicidal drive
> to extirpate not only national traditions but also those of
> the party itself. . .[and] embarked on a slavish adoption of
> Soviet practice in every sphere.

Towards the end of the book, the author confesses himself baffled:

> It is difficult to explain why Stalinism took such extreme
> forms in a country whose strong democratic traditions made
> this Soviet system particularly inappropriate.

Is that not part of the explanation? The more it goes against the grain, the more firmly it may need to be imposed.

Some idea, even speculative, concerning why and how this came about, would have helped to illuminate the theme which *is* central to the book – namely, the manner in which liberty was re-born. The book is, in the main, about the liberal revolution within Czechoslovak Communist dictatorship: notwithstanding its title, it only deals to a much lesser extent with the manner in which that revolution was *interrupted*. It seems to me, for reasons to be indicated, that a proper theoretical treatment of this subject will need to deal with all three topics at once: why the revolution was necessary in the first place, how it happened, and how it was aborted.

Professor Skilling's theory of why it happened at all is of the release-of-pent-up-tendencies form. In his conclusion, he unfortunately spends too much time discussing the question whether the Prague Spring should or should not be called a 'revolution' – to my mind, a somewhat scholastic question, and perhaps a residue or echo of the metaphysic of revolution (which requires one to identify a 'true' one). More significant is the question concerning whether the impetus of this transformation, call it what you will, could have been arrested somewhere short of the point at which it threatened the outside power-holders so much that it forced them to act violently. This issue is of course immensely important, for on it hinges the possibility of a peaceful thaw under Communism in general, or one

[1] H. Gordon Skilling: *Czechoslovakia's Interrupted Revolution*, Princeton University Press, 1976.

without external intervention in the case of a satellite. (Is a peaceful transition from Communism possible?) As far as the internal factors in the situation are concerned, Professor Skilling believes that an optimistic answer is probably correct. He even seems to endorse the liberalising Communists' own way of viewing th ... ation:

> What the Czechs and Slovaks sought to do was. . .not. . .a negation of socialism as such, but. . .the replacement of an obsolete and unsuited Soviet model of socialism with a new one. . .this would have made socialism in Czechoslovakia more viable and would have enhanced its appeal to the people of Western Europe.

No doubt, this is the kind of language which radicals within the Communist Party would have chosen or did choose. Švejk would indeed beam, this time Moscow-ward, looking as if butter could not melt in his mouth, and utter something of this kind. But what does it mean? If 'socialism' means refraining from restoring the full legal trappings of private ownership of the means of production, it is probably true that socialism was in no danger. But if socialism is given its realistic meaning, i.e. the centralised organisation of an industrial economy, it is not at all clear whether liberalisation was indeed compatible with the maintenance of the existing power structure, even in softer form. Skilling thinks it was possible, indeed likely:

> Other factors in the situation suggested a greater likelihood of the victory of the cause of fundamental change, but with the Communist Party retaining its commanding position.

The reasons? The party had no immediate challengers, and gained popularity

> as the inspirer of the movement of reform and as the defender of national independence.

But these factors were short-term ones. Nevertheless, Skilling thinks that

> barring outside interventions, the process of change would have been accelerated. . .and would eventually have produced a thoroughly revised socialism, democratic in form, and national in content.

Still, I am inclined to agree with him: not because I am willing to admit that this language, which conveys the possibly woolly inside vision of optimistic participants, is very meaningful, but because I think that the Czechs, left to themselves, would indeed have found an internal accommodation and compromise. The alien power holders would have had neither the need nor the opportunity to take extreme measures. I am not clear whether an internal liberalisation in the previous Communist dictatorship, without violence, terror and other self-defeating features, is possible *in general*; but I do believe it to be well within the capacity of the Czechs. If all the world were Czech and submerged in a Communist Dark Ages, one could at least be sure that a Renaissance is politically *possible*, and perhaps even likely.

But the most important and difficult question concerns not the possibility of peaceful liberalisation, but of its peaceful suppression or suffocation. That it *can* be done has been demonstrated. The question remains – how long, under what conditions, over what range of societies? Unfortunately, only a small terminal part of Professor Skillings' admirably researched book deals with this question. What are the mechanics of imposing a totally unwelcome political solution on the great majority of a country, with relatively little actual violence (as distinct from the threat and possibility of it)?

Professor Skilling does not theorise about this. It seems to me imperative that we try to do this, however tentatively. Impression-istically, post-Stalinist Soviet Communism seems to me to possess a very distinct style of social control, which is also much mirrored in the satellites. Ironically, this style satisfies T. G. Masaryk's definition of democracy, *democracie je diskuse*, the essence of democracy is debate. It does not proceed by barking out orders, it endorses no *Führerprinzip*, it has no cult of brisk obedience, either as a condition of efficiency or as a form of aesthetic satisfaction. In so far as this is dictatorship, it is dictatorship without the theatre and ritual of dictatorship. This has profound implications for the whole style of politics, and hence it would be a great mistake to discount it as simple façade, or hypocrisy only.

Discussion, prolonged, tedious and exhausting discussion, is I think characteristic. But to understand how it works, one must begin by the distinction between proceduralism and substantivism. Western liberalism is proceduralist, in the sense of starting from the sceptical assumption that the correct answer cannot ever be identified with confidence, but that we are less likely to go against it if at least we follow due process. This corresponds to the belief in science that final truth is not to be had, but we know what violates canons of method. By contrast, Marxism is deeply substantivist: the proceduralism of others is discounted as mere deception. And one's own? Its status is not clear. Ideally, and in the end, it should be redundant. And in the meantime...its status is ambiguous. It is important, but not so important as to overrule real, substantive and ultimate considerations. (And what are *they*? There can in the nature of things be no *procedural* rules for identifying them.) This kind of substantivism, many observers suggest, fits in well with Russian traditions: if the ruler is good, procedures are quite redundant, and indeed offensive; if he is evil, they will not save you.

This spirit engenders a certain way of conducting affairs, which is not demonstratively authoritarian but in which long and tedious discussions, the normal pattern of office or political intrigue and infighting, is nevertheless very sensitive to the ultimate realities of power, of the force which could be invoked if substantive right were in dire peril. But it is not invoked easily or often. Of course, substantive right is not really identifiable, whether you think it is or not, so in practice its stigmata are tied to the real power situation. In the discussion, procedural propriety is by no means ignored. It is just, shall we say, not quite ultimate, it provides no safety. It has a sliding-scale, power-sensitive quality. But he who has power does not brandish it, he prefers to proceed by discussion, and within the rules. He will just go on a bit longer and more persistently than anyone else. It is just that he has the advantage of knowing that the rules may (but preferably will not) be abrogated in his favour now and then. Thus the power balance does not often need to irrupt brutally into a political life, and it does not do it either gratuitously or in flagrant symbolism. It is not the object of any fetishism, as is the case in other kinds of dictatorship. Force irrupted during the Soviet invasion of Czechoslovakia, indeed; but the interesting thing is that it did not need to do so again or repeatedly.

The deeply consensual nature of Czech politics then reasserted itself, as it did during the early years of the last world war, when the collaborationist government in Prague, and the Beneš government in exile, were in communication with each other and exercised pressure on each other, as if they were separate branches of one political machine, which indeed they were. Skilling's book, and particularly its final parts, should be read together with Vojtěch Mastný's *The Czechs under Nazi Rule. The Failure of National Resistance 1939– 1942*.[2] The pattern is astonishingly similar.

2 Vojtěch Mastný: *The Czechs under Nazi Rule. The Failure of National Resistance 1939–1942*, Columbia University Press, 1971.

But if the Russians are natural substantivists, then the Czechs are natural victims of substantivism. It would be unfair to speak of salami tactics, for it was not a question of slicing them up and destroying one part or another. Quite the reverse. Paradoxically, if some significant part of the nation were really willing, if the need arose, to take a brutal stand against the rest, then the nation as a whole might also be capable of a more determined outward stand. National resistance movements generally kill more deviants from within their own nation, than they kill of the enemy – as indeed their denigrators like to stress. For better or for worse – and who is to judge – the Czechs have not been inclined to do this. No collaborator has fallen at the hands of a patriot–assassin: indeed, the very notion of collaborator, in the full pejorative sense, seems inappropriate to apply to men who see themselves, and are seen, simply as pursuing the national interest by other means. It was precisely because, on the whole, they loyally hung together, that it was possible to preserve legitimacy, to exercise pressure and more pressure, until by a series of compromises and transitions, the desired end-state was reached without ever a radical or violent break. A new balance of power in the end crystallises a new substantive verity. At first it is not perceived as true, and is even vehemently repudiated. But discussion goes on, and on and on. Little by little, as one side is obliged to pull its punches and show 'realism', the other relentlessly pushes on, and the right vision becomes manifest at last. Substantive truth makes itself felt through the balance of power, though power is, preferably, not used. It all takes patience, but the Russians seem to have that. This political culture does not encourage bravado or *machismo*. In Russian, *adventurist* is a term of abuse. So in the end, though, contrary to the Czech national motto ('*Pravda Vítězí*'), truth does not prevail, substantive truth *does* prevail.

When substantive truth has revealed itself (i.e. when the underlying power balance has been effectively translated into visible intellectual terms), the defeated minority cannot in this system take refuge in the fact that, though in error, they had behaved in a procedurally correct manner and in good faith. Procedural propriety and subjective good faith cut no ice, when substantive rightness is paramount, and when it is well known that substantive error is fiendishly cunning and positively delights in using specious formalistic arguments, and when the very notion of good faith on behalf of error is inadmissible. So the rest is silence. But the days seem gone when this defeated minority simply disappears. What now disappears are the institutes, organisations or whatnot which were the base from which they argued and fought. Their jobs disappear from under them. But the liquidation of institutions rather than of people certainly constitutes progress.

All the same, there is a problem. Procedural propriety may not be ultimate, but it is now pervasive and important; you simply cannot run a large, anonymous, complex, industrial and bureaucratic society without rules. Moreover, though procedural propriety will not save you from the consequences of substantive error, procedural *impro*priety will greatly aggravate your substantive error, should you be found to be in error (and who is to predict the gyrations of substantive truth? – you'd better play it safe, and that goes for the law-enforcers as well nowadays); and, moreover, procedural error will count against you even if you are substantively neutral or sound, so to speak. Socialist legality is no longer a mere empty phrase. So better be careful and not push your power advantage too much, lest it be temporary. Substantive considerations will overrule mere legality in grave and crucial matters, no doubt, but not in day-to-day life. In a wide variety of petty and pervasive ways, the Soviet Union for instance now seems to be a *Rechtstaat*: even harassment of dissidents is carried out to a large extent by the law book. There is evidently a large and indispensable technical and administrative intelligentsia which can only operate in a procedural-propriety recognising context, in which at least the minor substantive issues are recognised to be open to discussion, doubt and dispute. The real question is: what will prevail? Will the tendency towards respect for rules, reinforced by the taste and interest of a large and indispensable social stratum, crystallise in the end in some kind of recognition that substantive truth is *not* available in any definitive edition and hence must not overrule procedural propriety, or will the official substantivist epistemology prevail? (In other words: is the tendency towards *thaw* inherent and endemic?)

Of course it is not just a matter of two rival ideals, proceduralism and substantivism. What counts is whether power is concentrated at one centre. But the two issues are interdependent. Pluralism favours proceduralism; and proceduralism favours pluralism. But proceduralism is *also* favoured by the needs of modern social and economic organisation; and thus pluralism may benefit. My own guess is that, for quite some time at least, the two tendencies will co-exist uneasily.

The questions remain. Professor Skilling sometimes discusses them, and occasionally hazards a tentative answer. The discussion will go on amongst us, for the time being at least, with procedural propriety and without any need for us to look over our shoulder at substantive truth. Truth (either kind) does not seem to be established about the general issues, either in this book or anywhere else, so we do not know whether indeed it does prevail.

19

The Kathmandu option

Kathmandu, like Timbuctoo, has become a code-word of ordinary speech. Timbuctoo stands for a city located on the border between fiction and inaccessibility; in reality it happens to be a fascinating centre of scholarship, today as in the past, only mildly cut off by marshes to the South and, in conformity with image, by the desert to the North. The Tuareg still walk through it, veiled and with sword and hand-in-hand, but today they are more likely to be raided by the central government than vice versa. Such is progress. Kathmandu, on the other hand, is known to stand at the end of a viable road, literally and morally. It stands for an option, or rather an opting-out. Europeans no longer inquire of each other, are you Catholic or Protestant? – are you monarchist or republican? – but rather, are you for Economic Growth, or for Kathmandu?

This, if they ever think about it, must be somewhat offensive and irritating for the citizens of Kathmandu and adjoining areas, who after all possess an intrinsic reality which is quite independent of, if not contrary to, whatever symbolic meaning their habitation may have for others. The Kathmandu option, if taken literally, would contain some surprises for those who flirt with it. Here is a distinctive, fascinating, half-explored and quarter-understood society – the last great patrimonial state or oriental despotism; the one pure bit of India unconquered by Muslim or British; the only state in the world in which Hinduism is the established religion, where astrology (under the title 'Predictive Aspects of Culture') discreetly figures on the university curriculum; the only surviving princely state of British India, from whose citizens the sad news of Queen Victoria's death has been tactfully withheld; where government is referred to as HMG; where Indian money can still be called the *Company* rupee; an amazing

Himalayan patchwork of diverse cultures and faiths with a merely nominal unity; an experiment in something called Panchayat Democracy.

Systematic scholarship, as opposed to mere by-products of restricted diplomatic, military or commercial dealing, has only been possible for outsiders since 1951. Till then, if this was, as many would hold, a patrimonial society, it was an uncommonly well insulated one.

The fashionable notion of the patrimonial state owes a great deal to Max Weber. The starting point is the idea of a state which is like a household, and is run for the benefit of its master:

> In the patrimonial state the most fundamental obligation
> of the subjects is the material maintenance of the ruler, just
> as is the case in a patrimonial household. . .the difference
> is only one of degree.[1]

Yet, as in the household, the authority, though not legally circumscribed, is not wholly tyrannical:

> As a rule. . .the political patrimonial ruler is linked with
> the ruled through a consensual community which also exists
> apart from his independent military force and which is
> rooted in the belief that the ruler's powers are legitimate
> in so far as they are *traditional* [Ibid., p. 1020].

Though possessing this consensual element, yet

> The continuous struggle of the central power with the
> various centrifugal local powers creates a specific problem
> for patrimonialism when the patrimonial ruler. . .confronts
> not a mere mass of subjects. . .but when he stands as one
> landlord above other landlords, who. . .wield an autono-
> mous authority of their own. . .Some Roman emperors,
> Nero, for example, went far in wiping out private large
> landowners, especially in Africa. However, if the ruler
> intends to eliminate the autonomous *honoratiores*, he must
> have an administrative organisation of his own [Ibid.,
> p. 1055].

[1] *Economy and Society*, trans. G. Roth and C. Wittich, New Jersey, 1968, vol. 3, p. 1014.

All these observations find echoes in the history of Nepal as it was until very recently, with perhaps one qualification:

> Even under purely bureaucratic patrimonialism no administrative technique could prevent that, as a rule, the individual parts of the realm evaded the ruler's influence the more, the farther away they were from his residence...This is also a consequence of the need...for rapid decision-making by the officials in the case of enemy attacks on these marches [Ibid., p. 1051].

This last trait does not ring so true of Nepal in, say, the second half of the nineteenth century. No enemy seemed very threatening for any distant province, notwithstanding some trouble with Tibet and China, and hence its administrators had correspondingly less opportunity to attain autonomy. And, of course, there was a good reason for this exceptional state of affairs: *this* patrimonial state, if such it was, did not have fuzzy boundaries. It was embedded, on three sides, in an impeccably, indeed paradigmatically, bureaucratic state, namely British India. This was a territorially circumscribed, underwritten, guaranteed patrimonialism, with frontiers secure from aggression or secession. This unusual, strong and secure context is one element which defined the character of Nepal.

The Himalayas are an ethnic and religious patchwork, where Mongoloid and Indo-European populations and tribal groups meet and mingle with even older autochthonous strains, and where two great religions compete, be it for souls or for social allegiance, with previous shamanistic beliefs and practices. (The theoretical applicability of the very term 'shaman' has been challenged by a notable Nepalologist, Professor Alexander Macdonald; but it may do as shorthand.) This is where Hinduism, which hardly possesses the conceptual tools for proselytising, nevertheless absorbs tribal groups and operates a social alchemy, by which erstwhile clans are transmuted into new castes. Anthropologists such as Dor Bahadur Bista, Alexander Macdonald, Ch. von Fürer-Heimendorf, Lionel and Patricia Caplan, Alan Macfarlane, Nicholas Allen, Naresh Gurung, Michael Allen, Stephen Greenwold, Barbara Aziz, Anca Stahl, Don Messerschmidt, Doss Mabe, Harvey Blaustein, Nancy Levine, Bernard Pignède and others have now shown us something of this process. This is also where it meets and competes with that Hinduism-for-export, Buddhism, returning with the prestige of another,

Tibetan civilisation. But there is also an intervening cultural buffer zone. As an American anthropologist, Gerald Berreman, observes:

> Throughout most of Nepal...there is a broad belt on which Tibetan culture does not directly meet Indian culture.

It is these cultural and religious marchlands which provided the seedbed in which this fascinating polity emerged. Perhaps, as the great French scholar L. Lévi speculated at the beginning of the century, Nepal is India in the making – though we shall probably never know just how India was made.

The modern Nepalese state has its origins in the meeting of Hindu refugees from the Muslim conquerors of India with the local Mongoloid tribes. In some ways, the Gurkha kingdom, as it was initially known, is to Hinduism as the Ottoman Turks were to Islam – it is the sword arm of a religion.

There is a difference. The Turkic tribes emerged from central Asia and came to Islam, embraced it for the legitimacy or prestige it conferred on their rulers, or for the convenience it provided for their administrations. In the Himalayas, it was the other way round: Hinduism came to the mountains rather than vice versa, in the form of migrating Hindu populations and ideas. Hindu brain and tribal brawn led to the emergence of a whole set of hill kingdoms, religiously legitimated and supported by a sturdy peasantry, just as there was a whole group of Turkish principalities in Anatolia. From their rivalry, the Gurkha state emerged victorious, as the Osmanli sultanate had done in Anatolia. And the brain/brawn, legitimacy/military base formula worked well, in both cases.

Father L. F. Stiller, S.J., opens his *The Rise of the House of Gorkha*[2] with the words

> The rise of the House of Gorkha is undoubtedly the most significant event – the critical turning point – in the history of modern Nepal. It marks the transition in the hill regions of Nepal from the era of Himalayan valley-centred petty states to the period of true national growth.

And later he goes on to confirm the presence of the first, and, for Karl Marx, the distinctive trait of the Asiatic mode of production

[2] *The Rise of the House of Gorkha*. By Ludwig F. Stiller, S.J. Manjusri Publishing House, New Delhi, 1973.

(or what an inspired typing error once described as 'the Asiatic Motor Production'):

> All land was understood to be the property of the state.

There were some interesting exceptions to this. Some tribes submitted to the Gurkha conquerors only on condition that their traditional land-tenure system was respected. This has been well explored by the anthropologist Lionel Caplan. The characteristically patrimonial arrangements had some local traits, most suitable for a land which straddles glaciers and tropical jungle:

> Instead of obliging each village to supply a portion of the expenses of the royal table and for the salaries of the royal servants [the ruler] set apart special villages for the support of particular departments of the Rajah's service. . . A line of villages. . .was set apart for supplying the royal table with snow.

Taking over the term 'sanskritization' from the Indian anthropologist Srinivas to refer to Hindu cultural diffusion, Stiller goes on to observe, speaking of the pre-Gurkha period of political fragmentation:

> the ruling class of most of the hill states had been subjected to a process of sanskritization, as a result of which the ruling class throughout most of Greater Nepal was Hindu. . . in such a society it was not only the king's right to rule, to enforce law, and to punish transgression, it was his religious duty to do so.

And to underscore the circle which connected legitimacy and economy:

> To put the political aspect of land control in the clearest possible focus, the land was life; the land was security; the land was wealth and prestige. And the land was the rajah's; the rajah, therefore, controlled life; he controlled security; he controlled wealth and prestige. And therefore he controlled his people.
> Ultimate ownership of the land was vested in the crown. This ownership did not. . .extend to those who farmed the land. The peasant was not a serf bound to any particular locality, but remained free to migrate. . .However, if the

> peasant opted to till the soil – and. . .this option was the
> obvious one – his rights to the land. . .were limited to
> tenancy rights. . .the rajah was under no obligation to keep
> him on the land.

The noble was no less vulnerable to the royal will.

The power base with which the Gurkha kingdom entered history
was not large: 12,000 households, at most 15–20,000 men, of whom
a third were exempt from military service in virtue of being
Brahmins. . .Nevertheless, the thing was achieved. The key step in
the establishment of the Nepalese kingdom was the conquest of
Kathmandu valley.

A certain misconception needs to be corrected. The phrase 'Kathmandu valley' conjures up, to those who have not visited it, the
image of a kind of Alpine valley writ large, at a Himalayan scale – a
long valley cut off by rock ridges from other similar valleys, with,
presumably, a glacier at its head. In fact, Kathmandu valley is
nothing of the kind. It is roughly circular in shape, surrounded by
low hills, with nothing remotely resembling a glacier near it. Both
legends and geology say it was once a lake, and its soil is correspondingly rich.

Above all, its inhabitants are no kind of crude, simple mountain
peasants. Quite the reverse. If the Gurkhalis were the Anatolian
Turks of this empire, then Kathmandu valley was its Constantinople.
Its final capture was preceded by prolonged encirclement and much
fighting, but

> the conquest [of the three cities of the valley] was something
> of an anti-climax. After so many years of struggle and. . .
> so many. . .battles, the Gorkhalis literally walked into
> Kathmandu. The attack was planned for late September
> 1768, during the festivities of Indra Jatra. The Gorkhali
> lines were pushed right up to the walls of the city. . .
> [The inhabitants], together with their king, celebrated the
> Indra Jatra festival as usual. The festival seems to have
> gone on with very little concern about the Gorkhalis
> camped outside.

Who were these inhabitants, who accepted their conquerors with
such passivity and devotion to ritual?

Calculation as well as resignation and ritualism may have contributed to their supine attitude. The man who is the most productive and perhaps the most brilliant of Nepalese historians, Mahesh C. Regmi, thinks so:

> The Gorkhali conquest was. . .welcomed by the mercantile community of Kathmandu valley, particularly the Newars. [The conqueror] served their interests additionally by expelling Indian traders from the area. Within a few years after the conquest of the Kathmandu valley, we find Newar merchants trading even in the interior Western regions, as physical and political obstructions to trade were eliminated as a result of political unification. Moreover, a centralised administration enabled Newar merchants and financiers to diversify their operations.[3]

If the Gurkhas were the Ottomans of this empire, then the Newars were its Greeks. The Newars are the original inhabitants of Kathmandu valley, still accounting for over half its population. Fanciful theories about their origin apart (*cf.* Gopal Singh Nepali, *The Newars*, Bombay, 1965), they share physical and linguistic traits with other Himalayan tribes. But there the resemblance ends. Where the mountain tribesmen stand for simplicity, the Newars possess one of the most sophisticated cultures of the world, and indeed a traditionally urban one, though Mahesh Regmi observes that in the eighteenth century 'Kathmandu, Bhadgaon and Patan were probably the only settlements which could be described as towns'. Nevertheless, theirs is clearly an *urban* culture. Three towns in a not very large valley would in any case indicate this. Moreover, even their other compact settlements, with their superb courtyards and proliferation of shrines, look far more like agro-towns than like villages. They possess one of the finest folk architectures in the world, less dramatic perhaps but more quietly elegant than that of the Atlas or southern Arabia. There is a restfulness about the proportions of a Newar house or courtyard which makes it the Asiatic's Georgian.

The anthropologist Michael Allen goes as far as to say that they 'have been, for at least 2000 years, an essentially urban people'. Some are Buddhist and some Hindu, and their Buddhism is unusual in managing without monks. Michael Allen considers ('Buddhism without Monks', *South Asia*, vol. 2, 1973)

[3] *A Study in Nepali Economic History*, 1768–1846, Mahesh Chandra Regmi, New Delhi, 1971.

the necessity for Buddhism without the patronage of the
powerful to move from élitist monasticism to popular folk
religion. . .the Newars have done so in part by maintaining
their *vihara*s as temples for public worship, in part by
offering their priestly services to pure castes, and in part
by espousing an ideology that places high value on women,
meat, drink and other good things of the sensory world.

The majority of Newars are Buddhists, but they have replaced
Buddhist monasticism by Hindu principles of heredity. Stephen
Greenwold, another modern student of the Newars, notes (in 'King-
ship and Caste' and 'Buddhist Brahmins', *European Journal of
Sociology*, 1974 and 1975) that

No other institution of Newar society has aroused the scorn
and condemnation of Western scholars more than that of
the hereditary caste of priests. . .who have come to replace
Buddhist monks. . .

Although Newar Buddhism rejects ascetic renunciation,
the rituals and symbols of renunciation are still employed. . .
Even though [the priestly élite] in point of fact return to
the world of the social, they are said to continue to embody
the values of the ascetic. . .

Perhaps this is mere mystification propagated by
obscurantist priests as Rosser would have us believe. . .
but. . .one cannot overlook the very important factor that
this ideology is accepted by the Newars themselves.

Whether victims of false consciousness or living contradictions, using
an ascetic idiom for a sybaritic existence, the Newars are intriguing
and unique.

Three Newar traits strike the visitor: artistic genius, commercial
flair, and addiction to ritual. The Gurkha conquerors arrived
in the middle of a festival: one's impression is that a more tactful
conqueror would still have had some difficulty in timing his arrival
so as not to intrude on a carnival. Weberian sociologists may well
speculate how such addiction to religion and its audio-visual aids
(or perhaps to the aids for their own sake) can go together with
outstanding commercial success. In fact they do. Kathmandu has a
certain resemblance to Venice, in that it seems arranged to be a
setting for carnivals, in its alternation of exuberance and elegance,

and in the proportion and size of the older palaces. The striking thing about the artistic richness is its quantity as much as its quality: it is the shrine in each obscure courtyard, not just the celebrated one, which is impressive. Goethe observed on his first Italian journey that he realised life had only at that point begun for him: one may well feel the same when strolling through a Newari town. To appreciate it fully, alas, it is better now to choose some town other than Kathmandu. Newar towns proper are, thanks to their brick, a delightful light red: in Kathmandu, the dirty *feldgrau* of modern concrete is beginning to predominate.

Hindu rulers, Mongoloid peasant-warriors under their leadership, and the talented Newar traders and craftsmen: these are some, but not all the elements which go into the mix. This Hindu version of the Ottoman empire had not only its Anatolia and its Istanbul, but also its Egypt: the Terai. Mahesh Regmi quotes the conqueror writing to one of his generals that the Terai is 'superior and revenue-yielding territory', and adding 'We should not relinquish territory in the Terai...even if there is war.' The Terai is the long strip of tropical lowland which belongs to Nepal, even though its geographic and ethnic affinities are more with the Indian Gangetic plain. If it was revenue-yielding then, it has become all the more valuable now. Where Egypt was made more exploitable by cotton, the Terai was made so by the modern ability to cope with malaria. Today, when the trading activity of the uplands is being asphyxiated by the partial closure of the Nepalese–Tibetan border, the hillmen are swarming into the newly habitable Terai. But even in the days when only those who were habituated to it could survive there all the year round, semi-absentee land-grantees could do well out of it. The Nepalese anthropologist Dor Bahadur Bista investigated a typical village in the Terai: the tenant settlers had come from India, but the tax-exempt semi-absentee beneficiaries of land grants came from the Nepalese élite. In their early wars with Nepal, the British could overrun the relatively accessible Terai, even if they could not achieve much higher up; but sensibly they eventually handed it back. They noted that this state needed some region to exploit, and there was no point in depriving it of this economic base. Better to lop off some bits at the Eastern and Western ends, to prevent a possible Burmese–Nepalese–Sikh alignment.

The conquest of the Valley and the unification of Nepal were not a mere crude grab for taxable peasants and grantable land; that might apply in some places, but the overall economics of this expansion was far more sophisticated. Mahesh Regmi tells us that:

> The primary objective was to take advantage of the strategic position [of Kathmandu valley] in the Indo-Tibetan trade.

But there was more still in this patchwork, over and above the hills, the Valley, and the exploitable Terai. The political boundary between Nepal and Tibet follows, on the whole, the highest watershed in the world; but the cultural boundary is not congruent with this. South of the high Himalayas, there is a long strip of territory which is neither Hindu nor tribal, but Tibetan in culture and Buddhist in religion.

In the nineteenth century, two crucial and connected developments happened to this amalgam-empire; the rise of the Ranas (hereditary prime ministers with *de facto* complete control of the state) and the British alliance. The Ranas emerged after a period of palace strife in 1846. They did not deprive the previous ruling house, the Shahs, of formal status – only of effective power. The problem facing a patrimonial state, as Weber noted – how to control the powerful dependants striving for local or central power – was solved with economy and elegance by the founder of the new *de facto* dynasty, Jang Bahadur Rana. Two American specialists, Leo Rose and Margaret Fisher, sum up the situation in *The Politics of Nepal* (1970):

> This remarkable man was able to smash all rival political factions in an efficiently conducted massacre in the royal palace courtyard. . .after which he stripped the king of power and centralised absolute power in the hands of his own family.[4]

In an Introductory Sketch to his *History of Nepal*, published in 1877, Daniel Wright, late Surgeon-Major in HM's Indian Medical Service and Residency Surgeon in Kathmandu, writes:

> in 1846, the massacre took place of almost all the leading men of the country.

D. R. Regmi gives the figure of 134 victims for the initial massacre (not bad for a technically backward country) and this does not

---

[4] *The Politics of Nepal: Persistence and Change in an Asian Monarchy*, Leo Rose and Margaret Fisher, Ithaca, 1970.

include the subsequent follow-up. But this is clearly much cheaper than entertaining a potentially dissident aristocracy interminably at some oriental Versailles. And the period of super-patrimonialism, underwritten from outside, was soon to begin. Caste rigidity inside, insulation and the British connection outside, fortified by aid to the Company during the Mutiny and the recruitment of Gurkha troops, became the formula. The new ruler was, in due course, knighted, and also made a voyage to England, the first of the Indian princes to do so. A Nepalese historian of strong nationalist sentiments, D. R. Regmi (not to be confused with Mahesh Regmi), writes with contempt (*A Century of Family Autocracy*, 1950, 1958):

> By making a sea voyage with the single purpose of person-
> ally paying homage to the British throne, Jung Bahadur
> had also betrayed his weakness to over-zealously act the part
> of British protected princeling. . .his remiss conduct in
> breaking caste rigidity involved in sea voyage which was
> a taboo at that time, and for which no other prince was
> prepared. . .When a man. . .in his country behaves the
> cruelest task master in respect of enforcing caste rigidity.

Why should a ruler, whose internal authority hinges on the prestige of Hinduism, violate a caste prohibition and cross the sea? – and indeed be the first of his class to do so?

This question of motive is not uninteresting. The official reason was

> to see and bring back intelligence respecting the greatness
> and prosperity of the country. . .the perfection to which
> social conditions have been raised there and arts and
> sciences have been made available to the comforts and
> conveniences of life.

This makes the Rana ruler sound like a new Peter the Great. If so, these aspirations left few marks. But he had other motives, emanating more directly from the condition of his realm:

> Jang had concentrated all political authority in his hands
> by the end of 1847. He now sought to establish his
> monopolistic control over the finances. . .As a first step he
> sought maximisation of the revenues from the Terai which
> was the largest single source of revenue. . .This created the
> problem of absconsion of the collectors of revenue to the

British territory. . .the prevalance of 'awal' [local disease considered fatal for people from the hills] prevented the permanent residence of persons from the valley or the hilly regions for purposes of revenue collection. This right had, therefore, to be farmed out to the local inhabitants who could escape into the British territory. Hence his problem came to be: How should the revenue collectors be prevented from escaping? [M. S. Jain, *The Emergence of a New Aristocracy in Nepal*, Agra, 1972]

The British authorities in India had been handing over people who were *prima facie* guilty of dacoity or thuggee, but not those accused of cattle-lifting or misappropriation. M. S. Jain argues, convincingly, that the real motive of the trip was to by-pass Delhi and stop this dreadful leak on patrimonial resources. Though apparently not immediately successful, in the long run a reasonably well-sealed frontier does seem to have been achieved.

During the Rana period, caste rules were indeed enforceable by law, even if they did not prevent the ruler's trip to London. The British recruited Gurkha troops from the 'Hindu Kingdom of Nepal', as the agreement described it, and indeed the troops had Brahmins as their padres – notwithstanding the fact that, in reality, they were recruited from tribal groups whose hinduisation was far from complete.

Not all the hill tribes were available for recruitment. For instance, the Tamangs, who live in the hills surrounding the Valley, and who presumably have the same aptitudes and rustic simplicity and toughness as the Magars, Gurungs, Rais or Limbus who did provide recruits, were not available. So close to the patrimonial centre, the rulers did not wish expectations or standards to be raised, even relatively, in a servant and concubine catchment area. In fact, in the hills the Nepalese state is a kind of machine for turning tribes and clans into castes and sub-castes. Though in pure Hindu theory, caste status is beyond the reach of political power, in fact it is ratification by the central state which confirms or creates caste ranking. Keeping up with the *jats* becomes both a preoccupation and a political necessity. Status is expressed by what one refrains from eating, and a complex vertical and horizontal pattern of differential abstinence, from alcohol and one kind of flesh and another, articulates social structure. Inverting the famous German pun, man is what he does *not* eat.

A fragmented pluralism, religious legitimation, and some degree of religious limitation on power; pious foundations, here as in Islam, proliferated and offered some protection from confiscation (religion is not only the opium, but also the tenancy protection of the people); and that external boundary-maintenance by the orderly British régime in India which eliminated, from this patrimonialism, that endemic weakness of nebulous frontiers of authority which Weber noted. This was the formula; and it seemed to provide stability at least. (It was clear enough what the British received in turn; a large chunk of the Himalayas administered without trouble or expense, a catchment area for superb troops, and a convenient, trouble-free buffer state to the North.) The Gurkha soldier served the Raj faithfully for a couple of decades, thereby earning a gratitude which benefited above all his own local ruler in Kathmandu. But during his decades of service, he also arduously saved up most of his pay, and on his return, these savings sufficed to buy just enough jungle land at the uncleared upper part of a valley to start a farm. The money went to the village headman, who was given authority to allocate such land, and it was, in effect, his salary. Thus this self-financing and economical system obviated the need for local officials to be paid from the centre. The soldier sustained the system many times over: he first helped secure the good will of the overlords of the subcontinent; then he paid the local civil service; and in return, he was graciously allowed to clear land, which the Kingdom was only free to allocate precisely thanks to a situation brought about by the soldier's service...

There seemed no reason why the system should not last: patrimonialism embedded in and symbiotic with an efficient external bureaucracy, but almost hermetically sealed off, seemed as good a recipe for indefinite survival as one could find. But it was not to last. One weakness arose through a fission in the élite, given to fissiparousness despite its kin bonds and the amazing advantages which collectively it stood or stands to lose; and partly through a kind of independent effect of the religious ideology. After a disastrous earthquake in 1934, the then Rana ruler drew proper conclusions from this act of God and deprived a certain class of kinsmen, originating from miscegenation in violation of caste rules, of some of their privileges. The Ranas had evidently always been spread-eagled between the use of Hinduism as legitimation, and the evasion of its rules for their own advantage. This time, this heeding of the wrath of heaven turned out to be misguided, for it created a disaffected group, well placed to combine with others against the régime.

But the decisive factor was no doubt the new independence of India. A free India was less interested, or not interested at all, in maintaining a buffer patrimonialism in the Himalayas. When the revolution came in 1950, it had, as M. S. Jain noted, the outward form of a Meiji restoration: the rebels used the prestige of the *roi fainéant* against the all-powerful court stewards. Above all, they also had a base in India from which to operate.

The result of the conflict was a compromise. The *rois fainéants* became the true rulers; the all-powerful chamberlains stepped down, but remained economically powerful. (One of them, an able Oxford-trained economist, Pashupati Rana, was rumoured a year or so ago to be the next – legal – prime minister; which would be a Rana restoration, of a kind.) Patrimonialism is dead, long live patrimonialism – the critics might have said. The Ranas were stripped of their power but not of their wealth; at least one of their palaces, with its somewhat *L'Année dernière à Marienbad* elegance, peeling stucco and all, was turned into a hotel. Power shifted back to the Shah family.

The formal mechanics of the coup might have been that of the Meiji restoration, but there the resemblance ends. The revolution did not trigger off a dynamic drive towards modernisation. The 1950s were a decade of parliamentary politics and the party game, ending in a royal coup in 1960. A local and locally published comment on the abandoned parliamentary experiment is worth quoting:

> Nearly all [the] leaders had spent most of their life
> outside the country and were strongly influenced by the
> examples and experiences of other countries. They failed to
> realise that Nepal had neither a network of transport. . .
> nor the long hard years of campaigning against a colonial
> power that might have laid an infra-structure of political
> education. . .Nor was there a middle class with an indepen-
> dent source of income. . .And, perhaps most importantly,
> there was not that fundamental consensus about the ends of
> the society. . .politicking went on in the Kathmandu Valley.
> The rest of Nepal, cut off from the capital, was ignored.

This characterisation comes from the pen of Dr M. Mohsin, in his contribution to *Nepal: A Profile*, published in 1970 by the Nepal

Council of Applied Economic Research and printed at His Majesty's Government Press, Kathmandu. So what is the alternative? *Panchayat Democracy*, which would seem to be Hinduism's answer to democratic centralism. In practice, it consists of a hierarchy of councils, hierarchical in the sense that the local ones elect regional ones and so on upward, though all are equal in that none of them has much power. Dr Mohsin tells us of the aims of the system:

> The cardinal points that underlie the. . .Panchayat are
> basically three. Firstly, the. . .system is committed to end
> all kinds of exploitation. . .Secondly, it aims at realising
> [this]. . .not through. . .class struggle, but through class-
> co-ordination. And thirdly, it does not regard the existence
> of political parties a *sine qua non* for democracy.

The background assumptions are interesting:

> Although strongly committed to build up a communitarian
> exploitation-free society, the Panchayat System, never-
> theless, does not ignore the socio-economic realities. . .
> Hence it rules out the possibility of a classless society. . .
> purely a utopian concept. . .the Panchayat System strives
> to build up an elastically organised, mobile and dynamic
> social and functional hierarchy.

Constitutionally Nepal is a Hindu state, and Hinduism is normally held to require caste and hence inequality. But clearly there seems some intention to limit the extent of this. All men are born unequal but some will now be less unequal, perhaps. The actual fate of caste is well described by Dr Prachandra Pradhan in *Nepal in Perspective*:[5]

> the century-old legal codes were remodelled in 1964 in. . .
> the spirit of equality before the law. The new legal code
> abolished caste discrimination and social disabilities.
> However, [a]. . .conference for the protection of religion. . .
> vehemently opposed the new legal code on the ground
> that its provisions were contrary to Hindu tradition.
> Acknowledging the opposition, the. . .Royal Secretariat
> announced that the new legal code had not abolished

[5] *Nepal in Perspective*, Pashupati Shumshere, J. B. Rana and Kamal P. Malla (eds.), Centre for Economic Development and Administration, Kathmandu, 1973.

the caste system. . .The announcement added that those
who indulged in actions prejudicial to the customs and
traditions of others would be punished.

Caste is not legally enforceable, but conduct offensive to custom is
sanctionable. But caste *is* custom. So? Dr Pradhan also comments
on the political system:

Out of the legitimation of authority. . .by tradition and
custom, the King has drawn incomparable political
authority. . .The King occupies the most vital role. . .there
is no institutionalized opposition. . .His authority cannot
be questioned in any law court. He is supreme in all fields
of political life. . .While the bureaucracy is weak in relation
to the King, in comparison with other political institutions,
it is strong. In effect, the National Panchayat has only
advisory functions: by and large it performs the ritual
function of legitimization.

Dr Pradhan also gives some fascinating statistics on the ethnic origin
of ministers. Of a total of 75 office-holders between 1960 and 1972,
49 were drawn from Chetris and Brahmins, i.e. upper levels of the
Hindu population proper. Of the remaining 26, 10 were drawn
from the talented, geographically central and traditionally urban
and educated Newars.

What the less articulate outsiders think, one can only speculate.
But there is criticism from the inside. In the same volume, in a
passionate article on 'The Intellectual in Nepalese Society', one of
the two editors, Kamal P. Malla, writes:

The most primary prerequisite for the emergence of a truly
independent intellectual class is. . .a sufficient degree of
economic independence. . .In Nepal, except for a few self-
supporting intellectuals like Mr Mahesh Chandra Regmi. . .
or erstwhile politicians. . .or 'affluent aristocrats'. . .nearly
every one of the established names in the creative and
influential fields are in the full time service of the establishment. One plain, but primary reason for the poverty of
intellect in Nepal is the poverty of the intellectual.
    The rise of Panchayat ideology has given, in a sense,
unsought-for opportunities to the writers who have a gift
for phrasing.

This almost suffocating milieu is vitiated by a great deal of inbreeding among the Nepalese intelligentsia. . .on either extreme end of the spectrum there are two parallel and mutually inaccessible cultures: 1. The traditional, sanskritized, Hinduistic, spiritualistic, didactic, introvert, and aggressively nostalgic and nationalistic intellectual culture of the pundits, and 2. The Westernized, a modern jargon-ridden, empirical, critical, at times sophisticated, extrovert intellectual culture of the neo-Brahmins. . .

. . .it will be fruitless to hunt for Russells, Sartres, Gramscis. . .we have none, except decent, and respectable cogs. . .persistently striving towards the beatitude of an exploitationless state.

This kind of cri-de-coeur once provoked a spirited reply from Dr Harka Gurung, an Edinburgh-trained geographer who has attained very high office in the bureaucracy and who comes from one of the mountain tribes – the Gurungs – who previously supplied soldiers rather than clerics to the state:

In the Nepalese situation where purveyors of ideas receive minimal popular patronage, the intellectuals are inevitably drawn to the economic security of the patron-government bureaucracy. The government has not only been the largest client for intellectual concerns and skills but the chief agent in creating educated personnel as well. The increasing incorporation of intellectuals into organised institutions is indeed a contributory factor to the deflating of tensions between intellectuals and the powers.

My main contention is that Nepalese intellectuals have little relevance to the larger society they presume to address. If the traditionally educated, who continue to dominate the realm of the mind by *ascription*, confine themselves to the ivory tower of past heritage, most modern intellectuals derive their inspiration from alien concepts. . .There is also the dichotomy of two Nepals owing to the inbreeding of urban intellectuals.

A classic example of how Nepalese intellectuals confound rather than illuminate fundamental issues is the prevailing lop-sided banal emphasis on Sanskritic and Indian aspects of the national culture. . .Most intellectuals continue to subscribe to the erroneous notion of Mongoloid tribes being

mere castes with the Aryan hegemony. . .One of the
important tasks that beckon intellectuals in Nepal is the
formulation of a nation out of tribes and communities
[*Vasudha*, Kathmandu, July–August 1970 vol. xiii, No. 8].

It would be both impertinent and pointless for a foreigner to offer
advice. But an outsider may be fascinated and eager to know more
of this distinctively Hindu way towards a Nirvana of a unified – but
stratified – exploitationlessness.

Sources

The author and editors thank the editors and copyright holders who have given permission for these pieces to be reprinted. As follows: Chapter 1, 'The Absolute in Braces', appeared under the title 'Hegel's Last Secrets' in *Encounter*, volume 46, April 1976, pp. 33–49; Chapter 2, 'The Re-Enchantment Industry, or the Californian Way of Subjectivity', *Philosophy of the Social Sciences*, volume 5, number 4, December 1975, pp. 431–50; Chapter 3, 'A Wittgensteinian Philosophy of (or Against) the Social Sciences', *Philosophy of the Social Sciences*, volume 5, number 2, June 1975, pp. 173–99; Chapter 4, 'Period Piece', appeared in shortened form in *The Spectator*, vol. 237, 23 Ocober, 1975, pp. 23–4; Chapter 5, 'Chomsky', *Philosophy of the Social Sciences*, volume 7, number 4, December 1977, pp. 421–4; Chapter 6, 'Notes Towards a Theory of Ideology', in *L'Homme* (July–December 1978, xviii (3–4), pp. 69–82; Chapter 7, 'Options of Belief', appeared as a pamphlet published by the South Place Ethical Society, 1974; Chapter 8, 'The Pure Enquirer', appeared in shortened form in *The New Statesman* 26 May 1978, p. 708 under the title 'The Slopes of Certainty'; Chapter 9, 'An Ethic of Cognition', R. S. Cohen, P. K. Feyerabend and M. W. Wartofsky (eds.), *Essays in Memory of Imre Lakatos*, Dordrecht: Reidel, 1976, pp. 161–77; Chapter 10, 'Beyond Truth and Falsehood', *British Journal for the Philosophy of Science*, volume 26, number 4, December 1975, pp. 331–42; Chapter 11, 'The Last Pragmatist or the Behaviourist Platonist', *The Times Literary Supplement*, number 3828, July 25 1975, pp. 843–53; Chapter 12, 'Pragmatism and the Importance of Being Earnest', in R. J. Mulvaney and Philip M. Zeltner, editors, *Pragmatism: Its Sources and Prospects*, University of South Carolina Press, 1979. Chapter 13, 'Nationalism, or the New Confessions of a Justified Edinburgh Sinner', in *The Political Quarterly*, volume 49, number 1, January–March 1978, pp. 103–11; Chapter 14, 'A Social Contract in Search of an Idiom, the Demise of the Danegeld State?', *The Political Quarterly*, volume 46, number 2, April–

June 1975, pp. 127–52; Chapter 15, 'The Withering Away of the Dentistry State',) *Review*, 1979; Chapter 16, 'From the Revolution to Liberalization', *Government and Opposition*, volume 11, number 3, Summer 1976, pp. 257–72; Chapter 17, 'Gone and Gone Forever', *Government and Opposition*, volume 12, number 13, Summer 1977, pp. 371–8; Chapter 18, 'The Kathmandu Option', *Encounter*, volume 45, October 1975, pp. 56–68.

Bibliography of Ernest Gellner (II)

Compiled by I. C. Jarvie

The first part of this bibliography appears at the end of Ernest Gellner, *The Devil in Modern Philosophy*, London, 1974, pp. 235–45. In order to incorporate corrections and additions, this supplement starts after item 1972 (*i*).

Those items which have been republished in the volumes of selected papers are marked as follows:

      * *Cause and Meaning in the Social Sciences*
    ** *Contemporary Thought and Politics*
  *** *The Devil in Modern Philosophy*
**** *Spectacles and Predicaments*

1972

(*j*) Review of Peter Laslett, W. G. Runciman and Quentin Skinner, eds., *Philosophy, Politics and Society*, 4th Series, in *The Times Literary Supplement*, no. 3694, 22 December, p. 1552.

(*k*) Review of Magali Morsy, *Les Ahansala*, in *L'Annuaire de l'Afrique du Nord*, vol. xi, pp. 960–2, Aix en Provence.

1973

(*a*) 'Post-traditional forms in Islam: the turf and the trade, and votes and peanuts', *Daedalus*, **102**, no. 1, Winter, 191–206.

(*b*) Ed. with Charles Micaud, *Arabs and Berbers*, London, Duckworth. Contains an Introduction, pp. 11–21, and reprints of 1962(*e*), pp. 361–74, and 1964(*e*), pp. 59–66.

(*c*) Preface to the English translation of Robert Montagne, *The Berbers*, London, Frank Cass, vii–ix.

(*d*) 'Thought and time, or the reluctant relativist' (review of Michael Krausz, ed., *Critical Essays on the Philosophy of Collingwood*), *The Times Literary Supplement*, no. 3708, 30 March, 337–9. ***

(*e*) 'Scale and Nation', *Philosophy of the Social Sciences*, **3**, no. 1, March, 1–17. **

(*f*) 'Reflections on Philosophy, especially in America', *Worldview*, **16**, no. 6, June, 49–53. ***

(g) *Cause and Meaning in the Social Sciences*, I. C. Jarvie and Joseph Agassi, eds., London, Routledge and Kegan Paul.

(h) Introduction to Cynthia Nelson, ed., *The Desert and the Sown, Nomads in Wider Society*, Research Series no. 21, Institute of International Studies, University of California, Berkeley, pp. 1–9.

(i) *Populismo, Suo Significago y Caracertisticas Nacionales* [Spanish trans. of 1969 (a)], Buenos Aires, Amorortu Editores.

(j) Review of Yu. V. Maretin and D. A. Olderogge, eds., *Stranyi i Narody Vostoka* (Countries and Peoples of the East), in *Man*, n.s., **8**, no. 3, September, 505.

(k) Review of G. V. Osipov, ed., *Town, Country and People*, in *Man*, n.s., **8**, no. 3, September, 506–8.

(l) 'Primitive Communism' (review article on *Ochotniki, Sobirateli, Rybolovi* (*Hunters, Gatherers, Fishermen*), *Man*, n.s., **8**, no. 4, December, 536–42.

(m) Review of John H. Barnsley, *The Social Reality of Ethics, Man*, n.s., **8**, no. 4, December, 645–6.

1974

(a) *Contemporary Thought and Politics*, I. C. Jarvie and Joseph Agassi, eds., London, Routledge and Kegan Paul.

(b) 'Prof. Imre Lakatos', *The Times*, 8 February, p. 18.

(c) 'Options of Belief', 56th Conway Memorial Lecture, London, South Place Ethical Society. ****

(d) Review of E. Daumas, *The Wages of the Desert, Middle Eastern Studies*, **10**, no. 1, January, 99–100.

(e) Review of Michael Gilsenan, *Saint and Sufi in Modern Egypt*, in *Religious Studies*, **10**, no. 2, June, 243–5.

(f) 'The Phoney Revolution', review of P. F. Strawson, *Freedom and Resentment and Other Essays*, in *The Spectator*, **231**, 8 June, 708–9.

(g) *The Devil in Modern Philosophy*, I. C. Jarvie and Joseph Agassi, eds., London, Routledge and Kegan Paul.

(h) 'The Unknown Apollo of Biskra', *Government and Opposition*, 9, no. 3, Summer, 277–310.

(i) Translation of Yu. I. Semenov, 'Theoretical Problems of "Economic Anthropology"', *Philosophy of the Social Sciences*, 4, no. 3, September, 201–31.

(j) 'The Soviet and the Savage', *The Times Literary Supplement*, no. 3789, 18 October, 1166–8; reprinted in *Current Anthropology*, **16**, no. 4. December, 595–601. [Cf. 1975(n).]

(k) Contribution to an item on influential books read in childhood, *The Times Literary Supplement*, no. 3796, 6 December 1370.

1975

(a) *Legitimation of Belief*, London: Cambridge University Press.

(b) 'Cohesion and Identity: The Maghreb From Ibn Khaldun to Emil Durkheim', *Government and Opposition*, **10**, no. 2, Spring, 203–18.

(c) Review of Bryan S. Turner, *Weber and Islam*, *Population Studies*, **29**, March, 168–9.

(d) 'A Social Contract in Search of an Idiom', *Political Quarterly*, **46**, no. 2, April–June, 127–52. ****

(e) 'A Wittgensteinian Philosophy of (or Against) the Social Sciences', *Philosophy of the Social Sciences*, **5**, no. 2, June, 173–99. ****

(f) Review of Donal Cruise O'Brien, *Saints and Politicians*, in *Times Higher Education Supplement*, no. 191, 13 June 16.

(g) 'Théorie du Nationalisme', in *Identité Culturelle et Conscience Nationale en Tunisie, Cahiers du C.E.R.E.S.*, Série Sociologique II, June 1975.

(h) 'The Last Pragmatist or the Behaviourist Platonist', *The Times Literary Supplement*, no. 3828, 25 July, 843–53. ***

(i) Review of Jaroslav Hašek, *The Good Soldier Švejk*, in *Political Quarterly*, **46**, no. 3, July–August, 358–9.

(j) Review of Vincent Crapanzano, *The Hamadsha: A Study in Moroccan Ethnopsychiatry*, in *Africa*, **45**, no. 3, 336–8.

(k) Review of Vanessa Maher, *Women and Property in Morocco*, in *African Affairs*, **74**, no. 297, October, p. 497.

(l) 'The Kathmandu Option', *Encounter*, **45**, October, 55–68. ****

(m) 'Period Piece', review of J.-P. Sartre, *Critique of Dialectical Reason*, in *The Spectator*, **237**, 23 October, pp. 23–4. ****

(n) 'Reply to CA* Comment, *Current Anthropology*, **16**, no. 4, December, 614–16.

(o) 'Beyond Truth and Falsehood', review-essay on P. K. Feyerabend, *Against Method*, in *British Journal for the Philosophy of Sciences*, **26**, no. 4, December, 331–42. ****

(p) 'The Re-Enchantment Industry or the Californian Way of Subjectivity', *Philosophy of the Social Sciences*, **5**, no. 4, December, 431–50. ****

(q) 'Epistola de Ayer a los Russos', in *Filosofia y Ciencia*, Rafael Beneyto, ed., Valencia, Universidad de Valencia. [Spanish translation of 1963 (h).]

1976

(a) 'Comment Devenir Marabout', in *Bulletin Economique et Social du Maroc*, Numero double 128/129, Rabat, n.d., pp. 1–43. 'Ce texte constitue le deuxième chapitre du livre de cet auteur sur "Zaouia Ahansal" publié sous le titre *Saints of the Atlas* [1969 (j)],' trans. Paul C. Coatalen.

(b) 'The Sociology of Robert Montagne (1893–1954)', *Daedalus*, **105**, no. 1, Winter, pp. 137–50.

(c) 'Saints and their Descendants' (review of Paul Rabinow, *Symbolic Domination*, and A. R. Vinogradov, *The Ait Ndhir of*

Morocco), *Times Literary Supplement*, no. 3857, 13 February,
p. 164.

(d) Co-translator (with Diana Ferguson) of F. Stambouli and A.
Zghal, 'Urban Life in Pre-Colonial North Africa', *British
Journal of Sociology*, **27**, March, pp. 1–20.

(e) 'Hegel's Last Secrets' (review of several recent books on Hegel),
Encounter, April, **46**, pp. 33–49. ****

(f) Preface to Akbar Ahmed, *Millennium and Charisma Among
Pathans*, London, Routledge and Kegan Paul, 1976, pp. ix–xii.

(g) 'From the Revolution to Liberalization', *Government and
Opposition*, **11**, no. 3, Summer, pp. 257–72. ****

(h) 'An Ethic of Cognition', in R. S. Cohen, P. K. Feyerabend and
M. W. Wartofsky, eds., *Essays in Memory of Imre Lakatos*,
Dordrecht, Reidel, pp. 161–77. ****

(i) 'Languaje Ideal y Estructura de Parentesco', in L. Dumont, ed.,
Introduction a dos Teorias de la Andropologia Social,
Barcelona [Spanish translation of 1957 (g)].

1977

(a) Review of Robert Nisbet, *Twilight of Authority*, in *Partisan
Review*, **44**, no. 1, pp. 139–43.

(b) 'Patterns of Dissidence', review of Walter Laqueur, *Guerilla*, in
Millennium, **6**, no. 1, Spring, pp. 73–9.

(c) 'High and Low in the Himalayas', review of Alan Macfarlane,
Resources and Population, and Donald A. Messerschmidt,
Gurungs of Nepal, *Times Literary Supplement*, 13 May, no. 3922,
p. 594.

(d) 'Gone and Gone Forever', review of H. Gordon Skilling,
Czechoslovakia's Interrupted Revolution in *Government and
Opposition*, **12**, no. 3, Summer, pp. 371–8. ****

(e) Comment on Dr Pershitz' Paper, *Current Anthropology*, **18**,
no. 3, September, p. 414.

(f) 'The Marabouts in the Market Place', review of Dale P.
Eickelman, *Moroccan Islam*, and Kenneth L. Brown, *People of
Salé*, in *Times Literary Supplement*, 19 August, no. 3936, p. 1011.

(g) Edited with John Waterbury, *Patrons and Clients*, Duckworth,
London, pp. xii + 348, Introduction, pp. 1–6.

(h) 'Premisses for Dissidence', review of Valentin Turchin, *Inertsia
Strakha* (The Inertia of Fear), in *Times Literary Supplement*,
25 November, no. 3948, p. 1369.

(i) Review of Noam Chomsky, *Reflections on Language*, *Philosophy
of the Social Sciences*, **7**, no. 4, December, pp. 421–4. ****

(j) Review of John Waterbury, *North for the Trade. The Life and
Times of a Berber Merchant*, *Middle Eastern Studies*, **13**,
no. 3, October, pp. 401–2.

(*k*) Review of Abdallah Laroui, *Crisis of the Arab Intellectual*, *Journal of the Middle East Association of North America*, vol. 11, no. 3, 1 October, pp. 52–3.

(*l*) Review of Eugene Kamenka, ed., *Nationalism: The Nature and Evolution of an Idea* and Anthony D. Smith, ed., *Nationalist Movements*, British *Journal of Sociology*, **28**, no. 4, December, pp. 513–14.

(*m*) 'Ethnicity and Anthropology in the Soviet Union', *European Journal of Sociology*, Tome XVIII, no. 2, pp. 201–20.

(*n*) 'State Before Class, the Soviet Treatment of African Feudalism', *European Journal of Sociology*, Tome XVIII, no. 2, pp. 299–322.

1978

(*a*) 'Trousers in Tunisia', review of L. Carl Brown, *The Tunisia of Ahmed Bey*, *Middle Eastern Studies*, **14**, no. 1, January, pp. 127–30.

(*b*) 'Myth and Reality in Nepal', review of Frederich H. Gaige, *Regionalism and National Unity in Nepal*, *Government and Opposition*, **13**, no. 1, Winter, pp. 127–9.

(*c*) 'Nationalism, or the New Confessions of a Justified Edinburgh Sinner', review of Tom Nairn, *The Break Up of Britain*, *Political Quarterly*, **49**, no. 1, January–March, pp. 103–11. ****

(*d*) Review of Louis Dumont, *From Mandeville to Marx*, *Times Literary Supplement*, 10 March, no. 3963, p. 275.

(*e*) Review of David Montgomery Hart, *The Aith Waryaghar of the Moroccan Rif*, in *Man*, vol. 13, no. 1, March, pp. 151–2.

(*f*) 'Ernest Gellner on Sandcastles and the Search for Identity', interview with Bryan Magee, *The Listener*, vol. 99, no. 2558, 4 May, pp. 567–70. Also as 'Philosophy – The Social Contract' in Bryan Magee, ed., *Men of Ideas*, London, 1978.

(*g*) 'The Slopes of Certainty', review of Bernard Williams, *Descartes: The Project of Pure Enquiry*, in *New Statesman*, 26 May, pp. 708–9. ****

(*h*) Review of Harvey E. Goldberg, *Cave Dwellers and Citrus Growers*, in *Middle Eastern Studies*, vol. 14, no. 2, May, pp. 251–2.

(*i*) 'The Other Half', review of Isaiah Berlin, *Concepts and Categories. Philosophical Essays*, *New Statesman*, **96**, no. 2485, 3 November, pp. 588–9.

(*j*) 'Getting Along in Czechoslovakia', *New York Review of Books*, vol. XXV, no. 17, 9 November, pp. 30, 35–8.

(*k*) Review of Leo R. Rose, *The Politics of Bhutan*, *Political Studies*, vol. XXVI, no. 4, December, p. 536.

(*l*) Review of Paul Pascon, *Le Haouz de Marrakesh*, in *Man* (n.s.) vol. 13, no. 4, December, pp. 690–2.

Name index

Subject index